Folded, Spindled, and Mutilated

MIT Press Series on the Regulation of Economic Activity

General Editor
Richard Schmalensee, MIT Sloan School of Management

Folded, Spindled, and Mutilated
Economic Analysis and *U.S.* v. *IBM*

Franklin M. Fisher,
John J. McGowan,
and Joen E. Greenwood

A Charles River Associates Study

The MIT Press
Cambridge, Massachusetts
London, England

Charles River Associates, a Boston-based firm founded in 1965, provides consulting support to private businesses and law firms as well as to decision makers at all levels of government on economic, technological, and management issues. The firm's professional staff includes economists, transportation experts, financial experts, operations research specialists, engineers, and computer scientists. CRA's work covers a wide spectrum, including antitrust policy; communications; economic/engineering feasibility studies for new ventures; fuel industries, electric power, and energy economics; industry regulation; international trade; market forecasting for metals, minerals, and other commodities; market research for products and services; science and technology policy; strategic planning for a broad range of industries; and transportation planning.

© 1983 by
The Massachusetts Institute of Technology

This book was set in Times Roman
by The MIT Press Computergraphics Department
and printed and bound by Halliday Lithograph
in the United States of America.

Library of Congress Cataloging in Publication Data

Fisher, Franklin M.
  Folded, spindled, and mutilated.

  (MIT Press series on the regulation of economic activity; 7)
  Includes bibliographical references and index.
  1. United States. 2. IBM. 3. Antitrust law—United States. 4. Computer industry—Law and legislation—United States. 5. Antitrust law—Economic aspects—United States. 6. Computer industry—Law and legislation—Economic aspects—United States. I. McGowan, John J. II. Greenwood, Joen E. III. Title. IV. Series.
  KF224.U54F57 1983   343.73′072   83–935
  ISBN 0–262–06086–8   347.30372

In memory of John J. McGowan, 1936–1982

Folded, Spindled, and Mutilated offers us the fruits of Franklin Fisher's massive, detailed examination of the computer industry—or better, their distilled essence. Together with the late John J. McGowan, Joen E. Greenwood, and other staff members of Charles River Associates, he made this study over the last dozen years, as an economic consultant to IBM in the government's antitrust case and the related private suits against IBM. The government's case was initiated in the beginning of 1969 and finally resolved by withdrawal of its complaint thirteen years later. The private suits by a variety of plaintiffs started later; all were resolved much earlier.

Close examination of the workings of a particular industry is an old genre in applied economics. It had its origins in the study of economic history, with a focus on the growth of output, changing supplies of inputs and locations of production, and the development of technology. From these origins, the industry study has developed in two different directions. The first could be termed business history and is oriented toward the examination of the management strategies of particular firms and their consequent fortunes. The second, usually called industrial or market organization, involves the examination of the working of an industry in terms of analytical models of competition and monopoly in order to compare actual outcomes in the market with those expected on theoretical grounds.

In the United States, studies of the second kind have naturally developed in relation to the enforcement of the antitrust laws. Over the last half-century, such studies have particularly flourished under the leadership of Edward S. Mason of the Harvard Economics Department and his students and successors. Antitrust proceedings in the courts or before the Federal Trade Commission typically provide a wealth of detailed information on products, prices, costs, profits, technical developments, investment and marketing strategies, and other aspects of the behavior of firms constituting an industry that together make a thorough industry study possible. So also, on occasion, do investigations by committees of the Congress, often those concerned with overseeing antitrust enforcement. In the absence of such by-products of the legal and political process, regularly available published information from government and industry sources—Census, I.R.S. and S.E.C. materials, corporations' annual reports, trade journals and other trade association publications—frequently lack specific information required for a satisfactory industry study; there are, nonetheless, a few examples of successful studies based only on such materials.

Most scholarly studies based on antitrust materials are made after the event, using the court records available to the public after legal proceedings are concluded. Only a few have been made by participants in the process. The F.T.C. has made and published industry studies both as a prelude to formal proceedings and after they have been concluded, since, unlike the Justice Department, it functions as a provider of information to the Congress and the public as well as in the capacity of litigant. In 1950–1952 I served as "law clerk" to Judge Charles E. Wyzanski, Jr., in the trial before him of *U.S.* v. *United Shoe Machinery Corp.*, and subsequently published the economic analysis of the case I had made for his use. This unprecedented arrangement has not been repeated.

Fisher participated in the IBM cases in two ways. First, he supervised the elaboration of an overall scheme of economic analysis that IBM used as the basis for organizing and presenting its defense. Second, as an expert economic witness, he prepared and presented testimony in the cases. This activity in behalf of IBM, and his reliance in this book on the analytical framework and study of evidentiary materials prepared in the course of it, may raise doubt as to the objectivity and scholarly quality of the study. There need be none.

Before agreeing to appear as a witness, Fisher, together with Charles River Associates, undertook his own analysis of the issues independently of the lawyers representing IBM. It convinced him that the government had no case. The government's argument was based on erroneous conceptions of competition and a grossly inadequate understanding of the facts, particularly in respect to the nature and definition of the market in which IBM operated, the experience of other firms in that market, and the significance of IBM's introduction and pricing of new products in the context of market developments.

I participated briefly in this preliminary analysis. Much later, toward the end of the government case, I reviewed the evidence and arguments, also on behalf of IBM, and my conclusions were the same as Fisher's. The government's analysis of the market for electronic data processing machines and its arguments in support of its contention that IBM was a monopolist acting in violation of Section 2 of the Sherman Act paralleled in many ways my own analysis of the shoe machinery market made twenty years earlier, on the basis of which the Court found United Shoe Machinery Corp. in violation of Section 2. How influential the analogy was in persuading the Antitrust Division to initiate the case against IBM, I do not, of course, know. But I am certain that the analogy is totally inappropriate.

The factual situations in the two markets differ at every significant point. USMC was a firm with a constant large share over a period of nearly thirty years in a nearly static market that showed only modest technical progress. During this time only one small rival, producing one of the many varieties of major shoe machines, successfully entered and grew. United's representative customer was a small firm with little command of United's technical skills and dependent on United in a variety of ways. IBM's market share declined fairly steadily beginning shortly after the time the industry was born and had fallen to about half its original level by the end of the case. It operated in a rapidly growing market in which superior new technologies succeeded each other with breathtaking speed. IBM's most important customers were giant firms and agencies of the U.S. government in command of expertise on the characteristics and use of computers equal to IBM's, well capable of seeking out or even creating alternative suppliers if not satisfied with IBM's offerings. USMC and IBM engaged in certain practices that were superficially alike; but they differed from each other in every important detail. The different market contexts in which the two firms acted meant that even the superficial analogies were irrelevant to an understanding of the respective economic meanings of the practices in the two cases.

Moreover, as Fisher and his coauthors point out, the private suits that followed the government's complaint rested on the same allegations of market dominance and monopolizing behavior that formed the heart of the government's case and relied on the same framework of argument and selection of evidence. Thirteen out of the fourteen judges on trial and appeal courts reaching decisions in these cases found against the plaintiffs and for IBM. The single judge finding against IBM was on a trial court, and was reversed on appeal. Thus Assistant Attorney General Baxter, who withdrew the government's case as "without merit" after making his own review, was not alone with Fisher and me in that conclusion.

Finally, and most important, is Fisher's reputation for analytical ability and intellectual honesty. As he himself points out in his last chapter, the most important asset that any professional has, his reputation among his peers, far outweighs in value whatever he might gain in access to knowledge or in money by his work in the case.

A further word is in order as to the value of a record produced by antitrust litigation as the source for a scholarly study. As I noted earlier, most of the best academic studies of market organization rest on this kind of source. Litigation produces more detailed information on a wider range of important questions than any regularly available public source; the relevant corporate archives are otherwise not usually open to scholars. Because of its enormous scale, the broad scope of the government's requests for IBM documents that the Court granted, the large number of customers, technical experts, and executives of rival firms called as witnesses by both sides, and the coverage of statistical inquiries ordered by the Court, the IBM case produced an unusually rich record. Since all the evidence was subject to the scrutiny of vigorous cross-examination, much that the documents themselves might leave unknown or unclear is brought out. All in all, it is hard to hope for more or better evidence.

This study is noteworthy for reasons of deeper intellectual importance than the circumstances of its genesis. The computer industry is itself of particular interest as the carrier of one of the most rapidly advancing and broadly significant technologies in today's economy. The dynamic interaction of technical progress and market competition is of great theoretical and practical interest to economists and framers of economic policy, but it is one about which the received theory of markets has so far been able to offer less coherent and compelling accounts than that theory can offer on other matters. Therefore a full and careful analysis is of more than ordinary value as an industry study.

Further, the views of Fisher et al. on the bearing of this case on the rationale and application of Section 2 of the Sherman Act also merit particular attention. *IBM* is one of the few cases that turns on the issue of the apparently dominant firm—a firm whose role as by far the largest seller in the market raises the twin questions whether the firm is a "monopolist" in the legal sense and what constraints, if any, the law should place on its behavior. It differs from *Alcoa* and *United Shoe* in its outcome and from *Cellophane* both in the circumstances of the market and, more important, the erroneous analysis on which in that case the Court based its conclusion. From the perspective of those who apply economic analysis to the interpretation and enforcement of the antitrust laws, this study (chapters 2 and 9) is of unusual interest.

Finally, in their examination of the relation of profits as shown by conventional accounting measures to the economic concept of monopoly profits (chapter 7), the authors offer a radical and convincing critique of accepted ideas. They reject the usefulness as indicia of monopoly of a variety of profit measures that have been widely relied on in the literature of industrial organization. Their criticism rests on a theoretical analysis of a set of models that show the wide variations in book profits that can arise from a corresponding variety of dynamic disequilibrium situations in competitive markets. These are contrasted with the comparative static concept of monopoly power. Recognition of bad theory is a first indispensable step toward constructing good theories; this chapter makes that step in an important area of industrial organization.

The rest of this study displays the application of the instruments of economic analysis to the typical issues in an industry study: the purpose and practice of market definition; the measurement of market share and its relation to conclusions about market power; barriers to entry and the record of entry; the significance of IBM's marketing and pricing practices as evidence of "intent." While these offer no far-reaching theoretical novelties, each is an incisive examination of the issues in the specific market context. The whole forms a model of its kind.

Carl Kaysen

January 1983

Acknowledgments

This book is based on Franklin M. Fisher's testimony in *U.S.* v. *IBM* and reflects work lasting for more than twelve years. In the course of that work, we received assistance from a very large number of people. It is impossible to thank all of them in detail, and unfortunately the work continued over so long a time that we cannot recall every name. We apologize for omissions in what follows and, of course, accept full responsibility for error and for the opinions expressed.

Typing of drafts of the underlying testimony was done by Maguy S. Brown and Margery Davis, among others, and Elaine Douglass typed the book itself. Patricia Lockhart assisted with much of the proofreading. Gordon Brumm did the index. Ruth Pelizzon's and Scott Williamson's work on the footnotes is particularly to be commended in view of the size and complexity of the job involved.

Ellen P. Fisher read the manuscript and made helpful stylistic suggestions. Abraham, Abigail, and Naomi Fisher (who was born a few days after our involvement in *U.S.* v. *IBM* began) provided proofreading and other assistance. In a project that seemed for a while as though it would literally go on for generations, familial support and understanding are particularly important. In this regard, we know that John McGowan would have wished us to thank his family.

The research here reported is based directly on the trial record of *U.S.* v. *IBM*, but background preparation was important and extensive. Among those within IBM who assisted us were John F. Akers, Charles J. Bashe, George B. Beitzel, Richard M. Bennett, Jack Bertram, Erich Bloch, Manson Drummond, Richard M. DuBois, Nicholas deB. Katzenbach, Warren Lynde, Thomas F. Mierswa, Earl Orchard, Paul F. Rizzo, Michael deV. Roberts, Nathan Rochester, Francis G. Rodgers, L. I. Spector, Gene J. Takahashi, and Ace W. Vanderwinckel.

Others in the industry or involved with computers who spoke with us included H. Dean Brown (Zilog), Fred C. Buelow (Microtechnology), James Burkhard (Ball Computer Products), Lou Geiger (Lockheed), Ed Gelbach (Intel), Cuthbert C. Hurd (Cuthbert C. Hurd Associates), Scotty Maxwell (Rockwell), Thomas J. Perkins (Tandem), Neil Peterman (Systems Enhancement Associates), Mel Shader (TRW), Bud Sprague (Applied Magnetics), Paul Teicholz (Guy F. Atkinson), William Terry (Hewlett-Packard), and Leland H. Williams (Triangle Universities

Chapter 1

IBM and the Sherman Act: An Overview

In some ways, *U.S.*v. *IBM* was one of the great single-firm monopoly cases of all time.[1] Certainly this was true in terms of the time and resources expended on it. Brought in January 1969 in the waning hours of the Johnson Administration, it went to trial in 1975. The trial on liability lasted for more than six years (with the case on relief, if any, still to be tried). The trial transcript contained over 104,400 pages, and thousands of documents were placed in the record. In addition, there were several large private suits that prompted changes in the case, not to mention investigations and actions in the European Economic Community. The computer industry was perhaps the most technologically progressive industry in the U.S. economy; certainly it was one of the fastest-growing industries and of central economic importance. IBM was the best known and obviously the largest company in the industry; its computers were widely used.

It may thus have appeared a shocking anticlimax when William F. Baxter, the assistant attorney general in charge of the Antitrust Division in the Reagan Administration, agreed in January 1982 to a complete dismissal of the case, stipulating that it was "without merit." (The stipulation is given in the appendix.) How could this happen? Was it "political"? What had been happening all those years? Were the antitrust laws, as at least one commentator suggested, simply obsolete—ill-equipped to deal with the economics of modern industry?[2]

This book, which is derived from Franklin M. Fisher's testimony as an expert witness for IBM, considers the IBM case from the point of view of economic analysis and provides answers to these questions from that point of view. We take the position that, at least as far as single-firm monopoly cases are concerned, the antitrust laws are not obsolete; judicial interpretations of them are consonant with sound economic analysis of competition and monopoly. The disaster of the IBM case came about in part because the government's economic analysis was not sound. We believe that when the assistant attorney general stipulated that the government's case was "without merit," he did so for a very simple reason: it was.

Section 2 and the Legacy of *Alcoa*

It is now nearly a century since Section 2 of the Sherman Act made monopolization or attempted monopolization an antitrust offense.[3] In that time a series of great but relatively infrequent Section 2 cases have seen a change of focus of judicial interpretation. The early cases, the first *Standard Oil* and *American Tobacco* cases,[4] centered mainly on practices seen in themselves as anticompetitive; the post-World War II cases of *Alcoa* and *United Shoe Machinery*, however, centered on the possession of monopoly power acquired or maintained by means not illegal in themselves but adopted through choice rather than necessity.[5] Firms could be found to be in violation of Section 2 if they had monopoly power and had deliberately acted to attain it through means "honestly industrial" but "not economically inevitable."[6]

Such a shift in emphasis inevitably involves the use of economic analysis. What is monopoly power? How can its presence be demonstrated? What acts are those compelled by competition, and how do these differ from acts of monopolization? These are all questions of economics. Nevertheless, although the judiciary has phrased its answers to these questions differently from economists, we believe that judicial interpretation of Section 2 is not at odds with the economic analysis of competition and monopoly when that analysis is properly performed.

To be sure, there are differences and there have been difficulties. To the noneconomist, as in some elementary treatments of the subject within economics, the hallmark of monopoly is size, especially the possession of a large market share. In his *Alcoa* opinion in 1945 Judge Learned Hand recognized this, laying down the dictum, which has been cited regularly ever since, that over 90 percent "is enough to constitute a monopoly; it is doubtful whether 60 or 64 percent would be enough; and certainly 33 percent is not."[7]

In that same opinion, however, Hand faced the fact that a large market share could have come from more than one cause; in particular, such a share can be due to the very kinds of behavior that competition and a procompetitive policy encourage—"superior skill, foresight, and industry" and the passing of the attendant benefits along to customers in order to attract business. To make a large market share per se illegal would be to condemn such activities, hindering the very benefits that competition was to promote.

This was not a new problem in the interpretation of Section 2. In the *U.S. Steel* case of 1920, the Supreme Court had recognized that "the law does not make mere size an offense."[8] However, the possibility after *Alcoa* that the act could be violated by a course of actions not wrongful in themselves but designed to gain monopoly power made it particularly important to distinguish such actions from the ordinary behavior of an aggressive and efficient competitor. Judge Hand himself was very conscious of this, stating that "the successful competitor having been urged to compete must not be turned upon when he wins"[9] and making "superior skill, foresight, and industry" a defense.

In fact, as we shall see in later chapters, the apparent dilemma of the *Alcoa* standard is not, in principle, a dilemma at all. When a large market share is maintained solely through "superior skill, foresight, and industry," monopoly power is not truly present regardless of how large such a share happens to be. Monopoly power is the ability to maintain a large share while *not* being superior in such ways; that is, the ability to keep prices high or products inferior while excluding competitors. It is the identification of monopoly power with the very crude indicator of market share that leads to the problem.

This is not to say that Hand's treatment was substantively wrong. It ought to make no difference in principle whether one treats cases of large share acquired by superior skill, foresight, and industry as cases in which monopoly power is absent or as cases of legal monopoly power. In practice, however, there are likely to be important consequences in terms of how Section 2 antitrust cases are brought, fought, and possibly decided.

The first such consequence concerns the close relation thought to exist between market share and monopoly. Since Hand's dictum, plaintiffs and defendants have struggled over the size of the market share held by the latter. Since market share depends on how the market is defined, and since, contrary to simplistic views, the proper market definition is not always, or even usually, obvious, concentration on share has often meant a struggle over the definition of the market, particularly since the landmark *Cellophane* case of 1956.[10] Such struggles can be a great hindrance to proper analysis, substituting word play and the binary decision on whether something is "in" or "out" of the market for an examination of the real forces constraining monopoly power. Yet the interplay of these forces is what matters, and such forces are independent of the definition with which one chooses to categorize them.

Second, concentration on market share together with the fact that a firm can violate Section 2 through a deliberate course of action without ever committing a single act illegal in itself has meant that any or all of the acts of a large, successful firm can come under attack. Since any firm seeking to compete successfully necessarily acts so as to take business from its competitors, and since its competitors are injured if it succeeds, there is a tendency to regard such injury to competitors as injury to the competitive process even where it is a natural outcome of that process itself. Moreover, since the successful firm generally knows what it is doing, the process of pretrial discovery will often turn up documents describing an intent to succeed, and there will be a tendency to interpret these as showing an "intent to monopolize."

These are not simple matters to resolve; how to draw the line between monopoly and competition in such circumstances can be a difficult question whose answer depends on both a grasp of the facts of the case and a full understanding of the economic analysis of competition and monopoly. Only the proper application of such an analysis to the actual facts is likely to produce a correct answer; superficiality in either analysis or factual investigation is likely to prove disastrous.

Some Objectives of the Book

This book presents an economic analysis of competition in the computer industry and of the question of IBM's monopoly power. Beyond the analysis of the particular case at issue, *U.S.* v. *IBM*, we show how a proper analysis of Section 2 cases should proceed. We also consider how such an analysis should not proceed, for, as already indicated, the economic theories advanced by the Antitrust Division and its economists were not very sensible. This is not simply a matter of disagreement between opposing experts over the facts or the application of economics to close questions. As we shall see, the government's economic case often lacked coherence; some of the propositions could not have been true or relevant under *any* reasonable interpretation of the facts.

This is a matter of considerable importance. The IBM case involved the expenditure of much time and vast resources. Further, it carried in its train a great deal of additional litigation. Had the government won, the future of a major American industry might have been profoundly affected and the example brought home to other firms and industries as well. It is no light matter for such a suit to be brought or pursued; too much is at stake for such litigation to involve poor economic analysis.

The Computer Industry and System/360: A Sketch

A full understanding of the economics of competition and monopoly is only one of the crucial requirements for analysis of a Section 2 case; a good grasp of the facts is the other. This book discusses the important facts of the computer industry. In particular, a good deal of historical material is provided in chapter 3 (Market Definition) and chapter 8 (IBM's Actions). Nevertheless, the book is not a full economic history of the industry, the approach being analytic rather than chronological.[1.1] To put the analytic issues of *U.S.* v. *IBM* in some perspective, however, requires a thumbnail sketch of the history of the industry, particularly of the development and consequences of the IBM System/360 family of computers. That sketch barely touches even the high points; it is intended only to set the stage. Such a sketch, however, can let us see the *Alcoa*-induced problems that the government encountered.

IBM was not the first (or nearly the biggest) firm to enter the computer field; indeed in the early 1950s, all computers were known popularly as "Univacs."[1.2] IBM was close behind, however, bringing its earlier experience in punched-card office equipment to bear in the new field.

That field grew rapidly. While early projections forecast that only a very limited number of computers would ever be placed in the United States, the development of technology and of more and more uses for computers resulted in a very rapid growth in demand—an unexpected experience repeated over and over during the life of the industry. This occurred even during the "first generation" of vacuum-tube-based machines. In particular, IBM's 650, announced in early 1953 and delivered in 1954 as a small scientific machine, quickly found wide acceptance among business as well as scientific customers.[11]

1.1. A much more complete historical discussion is given in the trial record as part of the testimony (for IBM) of Franklin M. Fisher, Richard B. Mancke, and James W. McKie. It is referred to very frequently in the present volume as the "Historical Narrative" (Defendant's Exhibit 14971). A revised version is being published as Franklin M. Fisher, Richard B. Mancke, and James W. McKie, *IBM and the U.S. Data Processing Industry: An Economic History* (New York: Praeger, 1983).

1.2. Because the identity of the parent company making Univac computers changed through acquisition and merger, we also use "Univac" to refer to that company, which, after 1955, was the Sperry Rand Corporation.

At the end of the 1950s, such vacuum-tube-based machines were superseded by the faster, more compact, and more reliable "second generation" of computers based on transistors, and, of course, there were other improvements. During this period, while it did well with large scientific machines such as the 7094, IBM became particularly successful with its 1400 series of small, supposedly business-oriented computers. The 1400 series, partly because of the very high quality of the 1403 printer, proved extremely popular, with placements outstripping those of any ☌previous machines.[12]

System/360
Despite this success, however, IBM was already planning a family of computers that would make the 1400 series (and IBM's other existing computer systems) obsolete, for it realized that if it stood still, others would seize the opportunity. On April 7, 1964, it announced the System/360 family and changed the face of the industry. This event was crucial both for the history of IBM and the industry and for the litigation.

System/360 was an immense project into which IBM put all its resources. It involved substantial improvements over existing computer systems and correspondingly substantial risks. Its widespread popularity largely accounted for IBM's success and industry position. The following were some of the principal features and risks of System/360.

1. In terms of speed, reliability, and pure hardware performance per dollar ("price/performance"), System/360 was a major step forward from existing systems. Such improved performance was due in large part to the replacement of pure transistor-based technology with Solid Logic Technology (SLT), which combined transistors and partially integrated circuits. In making the decision to use SLT and investing in the plants required to manufacture SLT components, IBM ran the risk that transistor improvements together with better design of transistor-based machines (a path followed by Control Data Corporation) would yield comparable or better hardware performance per dollar. Further, there was the risk that SLT was not a big enough step and that the time was ripe for a move to a large-scale integration of circuitry. But SLT was successful, and as had been foreseen within IBM, the SLT experience provided much of the tools and know-how for the later move to fully integrated circuits.[13]

2. Earlier families of machines had offered a very limited range of performance within which machines were compatible. Users with li-

braries of application programs[1.3] written for one machine typically had to convert those programs in some manner if they acquired a different system even from the same manufacturer. System/360 in its original announcement offered five processors with a considerable performance range so that programs written for any one processor in the line would run on any other (if appropriate peripheral equipment and memory capacity were available). This provided users with substantial flexibility.

In attempting to provide such compatibility, IBM ran certain risks—apart from the complex technical question of whether such compatibility was feasible at all. First, there was the danger that the performance of the large, high-speed processors would have to be downgraded to achieve compatibility, leaving IBM open to attack at the high end of the line from specialized competitors not so constrained. Second, at the low end of the line, there was the danger that the provision of compatibility would involve sufficient expense to make the prices of the small machines too high relative to those of competitors.

3. The compatibility and other features of the System/360 were achieved through a new systems architecture—the overall design of the way the system worked. The new architecture was designed to carry over into future systems for a very long time. (It was, in fact, carried over into System/370, introduced in 1970, and many later machines.) It was, however, a definite departure from the architecture of IBM's existing lines. Indeed, the existing computers, including the highly successful 1400 series, were not compatible with the System/360. This left IBM open to attack by competitors facilitating the transition of users of IBM second-generation equipment to their own lines, a strategy followed by both Honeywell and General Electric.[14]

4. As indicated, earlier machines had been oriented either toward "business" or "scientific" uses, although users generally found ways to use one machine for both sets of applications. System/360 was intended to be equally useful for all sorts of applications. In attempting this, IBM ran the risk that System/360 would not be optimal for any specific class of applications and that IBM would lose in competition with machines that continued to be relatively specialized such as those of Control Data Corporation (CDC).[15]

5. To take full advantage of both the processor-compatibility of System/360 and its ability to handle different sorts of applications required

1.3. An application program (software) is a set of instructions that, when acted on by the hardware, leads to the performance of a particular task or set of tasks.

a flexible use of peripherals. This would not be possible if, as in earlier systems, specific peripherals (particular models of printers, tape drives, disk drives, etc., used to perform tasks such as input, output, or auxiliary storage) required the use of specific processors. Instead, System/360 provided a standardized "interface" between peripherals and processors, so that the same peripheral (or, more precisely, its control unit) would attach to any of the processors—generally by attaching to a "channel," a box with some control capability that provided a means of buffering data between relatively low-speed peripherals and relatively high-speed processors.

By providing a standard channel-to-peripheral interface, IBM provided the user with considerable flexibility in peripheral use. It made System/360 modular, permitting users to upgrade or change their systems by changing individual boxes rather than entire systems. In addition, such interchangeability permitted savings in design, testing, and production costs. With x peripherals to work with y processors, there were xy combinations, but the standard interface permitted the design and production of only $x + y$ rather than xy pieces of equipment. This reduced design costs and lengthened production runs.

The standard interface brought risks with it, however. Similar to the case of compatibility in the processors, there was the risk that peripherals produced to operate with all the processors would be either too high cost for small systems or too low in performance for large ones. In addition, the very modularity of the system that the standard interface was designed to achieve brought with it an additional risk. This was the possibility of competition in peripherals on a box-for-box basis. Precisely because a given peripheral could be used with many different system configurations, the demand for a particular peripheral model would be high. Since much business was done on a lease basis, that high demand would make replacement of a particular peripheral by a copy "plug-compatible" with the rest of the system an attractive opportunity for other manufacturers. By designing their products to attach to the standard IBM interface, such plug-compatible manufacturers (PCMs) could themselves take advantage of the economies of design and long production runs that interface afforded. This possibility, extending also to central processor unit (CPU) replacement, was foreseen by IBM and later occurred.[16]

6. Peripherals were quite important to the success of System/360. Of particular importance were disk drives, a form of auxiliary storage that IBM pioneered and in which it has remained a technological leader.

In the early 1960s, other ways of accomplishing the same function (drums, data cells, the RCA RACE and NCR CRAM files) were being utilized by others, and it was not at all plain, as it later became, that disk drives would prove superior. Yet System/360 was designed to be disk-based—first with the 2311 Disk Drive and later with its successor, the 2314—and the design presumed that users would in fact accept disks. This was a risky choice in 1961–1964.[17]

7. The developments so far described involved mostly hardware, but new, greatly improved software was also to be offered. This took the form of operating systems, of which more than one was to be made available. Such operating systems took over from the programmer and operator much of the management of the internal resources of the system, allowing more efficient use and reducing human error. The development of the most sophisticated of these operating systems proved a massive task whose magnitude was greatly underestimated by IBM— an experience also encountered by many others in the industry.

Competition and the Aftermath of System/360
System/360 proved extremely popular; demand for it considerably exceeded IBM's expectations. Competitors responded with new product introductions of their own and with price cuts. However, certain of the foreseen possibilities that made System/360 a risky undertaking did in fact come to fruition.

System/360 provided a large range of capabilities for many users. Further, IBM followed its traditional successful approach of regarding itself as in the business of producing solutions to users' data-processing needs rather than simply providing hardware capability. It included with System/360 an array of software and support services at no separately stated charge, a practice known as "bundling" and widely followed in the industry. Certain users, however, particularly scientific ones, themselves sophisticated in the use of computers, wanted more hardware power and less of the other facilities that 360 provided. This proved an opportunity for other manufacturers, particularly CDC and Scientific Data Systems (SDS—later Xerox Data Systems, XDS), to take business away from IBM by providing systems more closely specialized to the needs of such users. This in turn caused IBM to respond with its own more specialized machines.

System/360 in its original form also failed to provide what many leading-edge users considered appropriate capability for time-sharing— a mode of operation in which many users simultaneously use the same system. This opened an opportunity for others, particularly General Electric (GE), in turn causing IBM to respond.

System/360 tended to centralize the data processing task in a single system. As time went on, however, the developing technology gave new smaller processors—so-called minicomputers—the capabilities of large processors of a few years before. Many users turned to such processors, manufactured by Digital Equipment Corporation (DEC), Data General, Hewlett-Packard, and others, first for specialized individual uses, then to off-load work from a larger system, and finally, by the 1970s, for use in networks of processors or collections of stand-alone systems, alternatives to the IBM approach as manifested in System/360.[18]

Other forms of competition developed as well. As foreseen, plug-compatible manufacturers, especially of tape drives, disk drives, and add-on memories came into being; firms such as Telex, Memorex, Ampex, and Storage Technology Corporation (STC) began offering replacements for IBM boxes. By the mid-1970s, such competition extended to central processing units (CPUs), where it was led by the Amdahl Corporation (whose founder had figured importantly in 360 development) and included such firms as National Semiconductor, Hitachi, and Fujitsu as well as Control Data, which also made plug-compatible peripherals. Starting in 1970 (after the original complaint in *U.S.* v. *IBM*), IBM responded to the plug-compatible competition with a series of price and product actions.[19]

In addition to all of this, the modularity and compatibility of System/360 and its long-lived architecture, together with the desire of many users to lease rather than purchase, made many companies regard it as profitable to purchase System/360 equipment from IBM and then to lease that equipment to end users at reduced rates. Those doing so banked in part on an easy availability of capital and a slower rate of obsolescence than turned out to be the case. Many of these leasing companies took losses in 1970 when the economy turned down and IBM introduced the successor to System/360—System/370—but they continued to compete, successfully offering the older equipment at reduced prices and acquiring System/370 and other equipment. For, of course, technology did not stop in April 1964. IBM and many other companies went on improving their products and offering new ones, and by the 1970s, System/360 was largely obsolete.

That rapid advance was and is the most important characteristic of the industry. Firms that failed to improve quickly enough sold out or merged their computer activities with others. In particular, this happened to General Electric in 1970 (*after* the complaint), to RCA in 1971, and to Xerox in 1975.[20] Other firms, such as Data General, Amdahl, Tandem, and Prime, which offered new ideas or improved products, entered the industry and grew.

The Litigation and Its History

System/360 had another major consequence, which may or may not have been foreseen within IBM but was certainly not wanted; its success and the events that followed spawned *U.S.* v. *IBM* and a plethora of private antitrust suits.

U.S. v. *IBM*

The Antitrust Division began its investigation of IBM in 1967, having noted that IBM's market share as reported in the industry's trade press was around 70 percent.[21] In so doing, it apparently did not deeply consider the meaning of that market share statistic, which was not IBM's share of current computer placements, but its share of "installed base," the stock of all computers ever shipped and still in use valued at original prices (at best). As we discuss in chapter 4, this is not a measure calculated to reveal much about IBM's power.

As we have seen a large market share—even when equated with monopoly power—is not enough to violate Section 2 under the *Alcoa* standard, so the investigation naturally looked at IBM's conduct, spurred on by complaints from competitors, particularly Control Data, which itself sued IBM in December 1968.

It cannot be said that this was a very careful investigation. The decision to proceed with the complaint was made on the basis of a memorandum from Acting Assistant Attorney General Edward Zimmerman. In discussing IBM's policy of making no separate charge for its software, that memorandum implied that IBM refused to price its hardware boxes separately and would only offer an entire system at a single price.[22]

This was flatly false. It is true that IBM, like others in the industry, "bundled" its software and support services (and its maintenance on leased machines), charging for them in the price of the hardware. However (aside from the fact that IBM announced an end to that practice in December 1968), a glance at any IBM price list or a discussion with any IBM customer[1.4] would have shown that hardware was offered on a box-by-box basis. Indeed, there was not and never had been a "systems price" as such; the "price" of a system was simply the sum of the prices of the boxes included in it. Thus, the decision to bring this major antitrust suit began with a mistake.

Curiously, while Zimmerman's mistake as to hardware pricing did not persist into the trial itself, the misconception that a computer system is somehow a single product did, becoming a basis for the government's market definition. This is, in its way, ironic, for if a computer system were in fact a single product as required for the government's market definition arguments, there would be nothing wrong in pricing it as such—the suggested "act" that played a prominent role in bringing the lawsuit in the first place.

In any event, the complaint was issued in January 1969, and the litigation began. In a sense it is hard to say precisely what the issues were, for even when the case on liability ended in 1981, there was still no agreed upon statement of triable issues. The *Alcoa* decision made it possible to attack an entire course of conduct, and the Justice Department did just that until nearly every act of IBM was seen as anticompetitive—not excluding the introduction of System/360 itself.

Moreover, the time period in which monopolization was said to have taken place did not remain fixed. When the Telex Corporation sued IBM and won an initial victory at the district court level in 1973, the government amended its complaint to include the *Telex* issues (and did not remove those issues when the *Telex* decision was reversed in early 1975). (The original and amended complaints are given in the appendix.) Those issues related to IBM's responses to plug-compatible competition in 1970–1972 (after the original complaint). Throughout the trial of *U.S.* v. *IBM*, the government insisted on extending the time period forward, requesting and obtaining midway through the trial a reopening of discovery as to IBM's actions and future plans in the late 1970s.[23]

1.4. Listening to customers does not appear to have been the Antitrust Division's long suit, however. While it called industry and economic experts and many, many competitors as witnesses at the trial, it did not call a single commercial customer, and the scientific customers it called early in the trial were asked about history or called for their industry expertise.

The Private Litigation
The government case did not, however, proceed quickly to trial, and long before it did in 1975, there had been significant developments in other litigation, much of which had been prompted by the government suit. These developments, as in the case of *Telex* v. *IBM*,[24] interacted with the government suit, with private and government plaintiffs cooperating and each using material developed by the other.

Control Data, as already mentioned, sued IBM in December 1968, just before the government, on issues similar to those raised in the government's original complaint. That case was settled in early 1973 before trial.[25]

Before that settlement, however, the first of the major private suits had been tried. *Greyhound* v. *IBM*[26] was tried in federal district court in Phoenix, Arizona, in the late spring and early summer of 1972. Greyhound, which had two leasing company subsidiaries, alleged that IBM had monopolized a "market" consisting only of leased computers (purchased computers were not included) and done so, in part, through manipulation of the relationship between its lease and purchase prices. District Court Judge Walter Craig entered a directed verdict at the close of the plaintiff's case and did not require IBM to put in a defense. That decision was reversed much later by the Court of Appeals for the Ninth Circuit, which ruled in August 1977 that the jury could have found there to be a market for leased machines and remanded the case for retrial. The case was settled in early 1981 before the retrial took place.

Telex v. *IBM* was tried in federal district court in Tulsa, Oklahoma, in the spring of 1973 and was the only private suit tried without a jury. Telex, a manufacturer and vendor of IBM plug-compatible equipment, alleged that IBM had monopolized three "markets," tape drives, disk drives, and add-on memories plug-compatible with IBM systems. District Court Judge A. Sherman Christensen found for Telex and awarded very substantial damages, also finding on a counterclaim that Telex had stolen IBM trade secrets. The *Telex* verdict on the antitrust claims (but not the trade secret counterclaim) was reversed by the Court of Appeals for the Tenth Circuit in January 1975. Telex petitioned to the Supreme Court for a writ of *certiorari* but agreed to withdraw that petition in exchange for an agreement by IBM not to pursue or enforce its verdict for $18 million on the trade secret claim.

IBM's initial loss in *Telex* (its only loss in the entire series of cases) had serious further consequences. The government added the *Telex* claims (including the *Telex* "markets") to its case. An investigation of IBM by the Commission of the European Economic Communities was begun, which resulted in a formal statement of objections in late 1980. Not surprisingly, some additional private litigants sued IBM on the same *Telex* grounds. None of these developments vanished when *Telex* was reversed, although the private litigants then found it important to differentiate their cases from *Telex* instead of claiming that they were the same.

The first of the additional suits to reach trial was brought by California Computer (CalComp), another PCM.[27] That suit was tried in federal district court in Los Angeles in the winter of 1976–1977, by which time *U.S.* v. *IBM* had been in trial for about a year. As did later plaintiffs, CalComp read evidence from *U.S.* v. *IBM* into the record. District Court Judge Ray McNichols, as had the judge in *Greyhound*, entered a directed verdict for IBM at the close of the plaintiff's case. This time the directed verdict was upheld by the Ninth Circuit and CalComp did not proceed further.

The second *Telex*-induced suit was brought by the Memorex Corporation, a PCM, and its subsidiaries. (Memorex was also active in the government suit and in the EEC commission's investigation.) The *Memorex* case[28] was tried in federal district court in San Francisco beginning on January 16, 1978. For the first time, the case went to the jury, which was unable to decide it. District Judge Samuel Conti then took the case from the hung jury and entered a directed verdict for IBM, stating that the case was inherently unsuited for jury trial. That verdict was upheld by the Ninth Circuit, and *certiorari* was refused by the Supreme Court.

The last of the major private suits was brought by Transamerica Corporation. Transamerica (through a subsidiary) had acted as a leasing company and been particularly active in financing Telex machines through assignment of leases. The testimony in this suit against IBM[29] was presented in federal district court in San Francisco from December 4, 1978, through July 19, 1979. As in *Memorex*, the trial ended in a hung jury and (by previous agreement of the parties) was then decided by District Judge Robert H. Schnacke. Judge Schnacke found for IBM. The appeal to the Ninth Circuit has not yet been decided.

Lessons for *U.S.* v. *IBM*

A few major facts relevant to consideration of *U.S.* v. *IBM* stand out from this history.

First, the private suits involved many of the same issues as did the government case. Indeed, the government amended its complaint to include the post-1969 PCM-related issues of the *Telex* case and the *Telex* market definitions; a good deal of time in *U.S.* v. *IBM* was spent on such matters, aided by witnesses employed by Memorex and by document production in the private suits and incorporating a good deal of the *Telex* record into the case. On the other side, the *CalComp, Memorex,* and *Transamerica* plaintiffs all read large amounts of testimony from the ongoing government case into their respective records. Thus many of the issues in the government case were tried over and over in the private litigation and with an unambiguous result. With the single, reversed exception of the district court judge in *Telex*, every court and every judge who decided one of these cases on the merits[1.5] found for IBM, in two cases without requiring IBM to put in a defense. (Counting both district and appeals court judges, this is thirteen out of fourteen judges.) In considering Assistant Attorney General Baxter's stipulation that the government's case was "without merit," it is well to bear this in mind.

Second, each of these trials, large though they were, was tried in about six months. Three of them, brought more than four years after the complaint in *U.S.* v. *IBM*, went to trial while the government was still putting in its direct case and were decided (and in two cases through the appeals process) by the time the taking of evidence on liability in *U.S.* v. *IBM* ended in 1981.

For *U.S.* v. *IBM*, which took six years from complaint to trial, also took six years to try, about twelve times as long as any one of the private suits—a record, we believe, for antitrust litigation (or perhaps any litigation since *Jarndyce* v. *Jarndyce*).[30]

As either its absolute length or comparison with the private suits suggests, *U.S.* v. *IBM* was a juggernaut out of control. Many of the manifestations of that lack of control involved procedural matters. For example, the trial judge, David N. Edelstein, had depositions read aloud to an empty bench, a process that went on for 70 trial days.[1.6] The Antitrust Division staff trying the case underwent complete changes, and, as we have seen, the government's case itself kept changing to

1.5. The Ninth Circuit, in considering the *Greyhound* case on appeal did not decide on its merits; it considered only the question of whether the case should have been allowed to proceed.
1.6. A deposition consists of sworn testimony taken outside of the presence of the judge.

include new issues and massive further discovery, with no agreed upon statement of triable issues ever in existence.[1.7]

Purely procedural matters were not the only ones that led to loss of control or hampered an organized, coherent trial. The changing nature of the government's case reflected a deeper and more substantive problem which is the subject of this book. The positions advanced by the government were not a consistent whole based on a proper understanding of the economics of competition and monopoly. Because the *Alcoa* case made it possible to prove a violation of Section 2 through deliberate acts not themselves wrongful, this lack of a sound grasp of economic analysis led the government to adduce evidence on a great variety of subjects and place in the record any IBM document that seemed to state an intention to take business from others. The length and relatively uncontrolled nature of the proceedings were thus no accident in this respect.

The Role of the Authors

The support for our criticism of the government's use of economics is developed in the course of this book. While this book should be evaluated on its own merit, it is important to understand our own involvement in the IBM case. That involvement began in May 1970 (a little more than a year after the complaint) when Fisher and Charles River Associates were retained by IBM counsel to provide consulting services in economics. An independent investigation was to be made, and if that investigation came out as IBM's counsel thought it would, expert testimony was ultimately to result.

Our involvement continued throughout the case. In particular, Fisher was prepared to testify as an expert witness in the *Greyhound* case (but never testified since the judge found for IBM before IBM's defense) and did actually testify in *Telex*. In *U.S.* v. *IBM* itself, he gave three depositions and testified in both IBM's direct and surrebuttal cases. That testimony was in written (narrative statement) form. It consisted of a 1,527-page history of IBM and the computer industry (the "Historical Narrative") written by Fisher, Richard B. Mancke, and James W. McKie and of approximately 1,150 pages of analytic testimony, the

---

1.7. A full account of the conduct of the trial is beyond the scope of this book. A revealing description is given in Steven Brill, "What to Tell Your Friends about *IBM*," *The American Lawyer*, April 1982, pp. 1, 11–14, 16–17.

testimony on which this book is based. Charles River Associates' involvement, particularly that of McGowan and Greenwood, was also substantial, including research and support for Fisher's testimony and that of IBM's other economic witnesses.

Such involvement is not the way in which economists typically do research, and the question of how objective the results can be naturally arises. We discuss in chapter 9 some of the problems and pitfalls this presents and the ways in which objectivity can be retained. But in the end, this book must speak for itself.

Chapter 2

The Analysis of Competition and Monopoly

The economic analysis of competition, especially perfect competition (numerous small sellers of a single homogeneous product), is a familiar one. Unfortunately, such familiarity can lead to misuse in the analysis of antitrust cases. A relatively superficial understanding of the competitive model—and, by contrast, its monopoly opposite—can lead to a number of errors when considering real situations. Such errors include the belief that a large market share must be due to monopoly and the consequent belief that the definition of the "market" is crucial; the view that anything that makes it expensive or time-consuming to enter constitutes a "barrier to entry"; the interpretation that all or most profits are due to monopoly; and the view that the "invisible hand" works anonymously so that price cutting by incumbent firms, particularly large ones, is likely to be predatory.

To a large extent, all these errors stem from a common source, a focus on the long-run equilibrium of the competitive model to the neglect of the process that brings that equilibrium about. Because disequilibrium is transient (and perhaps because of the beauty of the analysis of equilibrium), there is sometimes a tendency to view disequilibrium as necessarily very short-lived. This in turn gives rise to a tendency to analyze real markets as though they were always in long-run equilibrium and, indeed, sometimes to forget the precise nature of the definitions (profits, costs, entry barriers) that make the beautiful equilibrium propositions true.

Such a focus on long-run equilibrium can be a major error in the analysis of a real industry. This is particularly so in an industry like the computer industry in which the driving force has been technological change and which has again and again experienced a totally unexpected explosion of demand as new users of and new uses for computers came into being.[1] In such an industry, the competitive process—including the special role of innovation—is what matters. That process cannot be understood and monopoly power cannot be evaluated by assuming, in effect, that all innovations have long since been made, that all demand has been anticipated, and that the industry has settled down to a comfortable steady state.

Competition and Monopoly in Different Types of Markets

Most real markets fall in between pure competition and pure monopoly. Thus, virtually all firms possess some "market power" in that they are not constrained at every moment of time to follow a single set of decisions on outputs, prices, product quality, investments, and so forth. A firm has monopoly power when it is sufficiently insulated from competitive pressures to be able to raise its prices or withhold the introduction of new technology, either in product innovations or in process (cost-reducing) innovations, without concern about the actions of its competitors and with relative impunity because its customers lack reasonable alternatives to which to turn. Monopoly power is the ability to *raise* prices above competitive levels or to market inferior products while excluding competition. This is the economist's version of the law's definition of monopoly as the "power to control prices or exclude competitors."[2] The ability to gain business through lower, remunerative prices or through better products is not monopoly power but the manifestation of "superior skill, foresight, and industry."[3]

Homogeneous Products and Many Firms
It is relatively easy to analyze competition in a market in which there are many small, equally efficient sellers of a single homogeneous product for which there are (by assumption) no close substitutes. In particular, such a case presents no problem of market definition. There are few, if any, markets such as this in the real world, however; hence the usefulness of such an analysis is as a theoretical polar case with which to start.

In such a market, price differences among sellers cannot persist forever. A supplier who offers the homogeneous product at a higher price than do other suppliers will lose business as soon as his customers detect the differences and shift to cheaper sources of supply. How long that takes will depend in part on how informed customers are about price offerings. The more information customers have about the prices that the various suppliers are charging, the faster they will shift their purchases from high-priced to low-priced suppliers and the faster price differences will be eliminated.

Moreover, in such a market when customers have good information about prices, prices will tend toward costs. When the general price level in the market is well above costs, some firms will reason correctly that they can attract business from their competitors and earn increased profits by shading the price somewhat while leaving it enough above cost to earn a profit. The firms losing customers will be forced to follow suit and lower their prices too or see their customers and profits dwindle away. The lower prices will therefore inevitably spread to all sellers. This process will tend to drive prices to a level that just covers costs, which are here defined to include "normal profits"—the return necessary to keep the firms in this business (as opposed to some other) with neither investment nor disinvestment taking place.[2.1]

Thus, in such a classically competitive market, prices tend toward equality among suppliers, and the common value of price tends toward costs. Moreover, the same competitive process will force all the firms in the market to adopt the most efficient means of production available so that all firms will produce at the lowest possible cost. As soon as any firm realizes that it can adopt a more efficient mode of production (a process innovation), it will do so, and if a firm continues to sell at the preexisting price (equal to the costs of the inefficient firms), it will earn higher than "normal profits" as a reward. Indeed, such a firm will make even greater profits by lowering its price below the costs of its inefficient competitors and bidding away their business. As the efficient firm does this, the remaining firms will either have to follow suit by adopting the most efficient means of production or lose business. Costs will be driven down as far as possible, and prices will come to reflect these minimum costs.

Note that this says nothing about how fast such adjustments will occur. If the innovative firm can adopt the new method of production and expand its production very substantially and rapidly, then the process will occur rather quickly, especially if other firms can promptly copy the innovation. In real life, however, such changes take time, and firms face practical constraints on their ability to expand. Thus, the innovative firm may earn "economic profits" (above normal profits) for some period, and prices will gradually, not immediately, reach the new cost level.

2.1. There are other differences between accounting definitions of costs and profits and those used in economic analysis. These important matters are discussed in chapter 7.

Familiar as this model is, there are several lessons to be drawn from it about competitive markets that will be helpful in considering more complicated cases. These include the question of who benefits from competition; the role of profits and losses; competition and "predatory pricing"; and indicia of competition: constraints on behavior.

Who Benefits from Competition?   The ultimate beneficiary of the competitive process is the customer. Suppliers are driven to adopt efficient means of production by the reward of positive economic profits if they are among the first to do so and the threat of losses if they lag behind other firms in this regard. Prices are driven down as competitors vie with each other to keep their own customers, take customers away from others, and win the business of new customers. Customers are able to obtain efficiently produced goods at prices that are continually pushed downward toward the level of the costs necessary to amass the resources required for production and distribution.

Those firms quickest to perceive that more efficient methods of production are possible, and therefore earning extra profits before the less efficient firms copy them, are also beneficiaries, but only in the short run. The efficient firms are unable to continue earning high profits, since their new methods are adopted by others, prices are lowered, and the extra profits are competed away. Only if further efficiencies become possible, can a new cycle of temporary extra profits arise. As we shall see in considering technological change and innovative competition, continual improvements and continued new technical opportunities can lead to repeated "temporary" and hence long-lasting profits.

There are also victims of the competitive process. Those firms slow to adopt the most efficient methods suffer losses as customers turn from them to more efficient firms charging lower prices. If they are slow enough in responding, such inefficient firms will go out of business. Losses and the failure of some firms are inevitable results of competition, particularly when new technical opportunities exist.

The Role of Profits and Losses   The foregoing description of the competitive process underlines the important role that profits and losses play in it. Profits and losses are, respectively, the carrot and the stick of the marketplace. The hope of higher profits draws firms into the use of more efficient productive methods. The inevitability of losses, if they do not adopt such methods once discovered, prods sluggards to follow suit or drives them out if they remain sluggish. Profits are both the reward and the incentive for efficiency in serving customer needs. Losses are the penalty for not doing so.

Profits and losses also provide the incentives and punishments that lead a competitive economy to produce goods that customers desire. Thus, when customer needs change, with customers desiring more of good A and less of good B—so that, at given prices, the demand for good A rises and the demand for good B falls—the price of good A will increase, creating an opportunity for economic profits for firms offering good A. That profit opportunity will lead existing suppliers of good A to expand their production and, possibly, lead new firms into the production of good A. Firms quick to expand or enter will earn profits. As the supply of good A expands, its price will fall (although generally not back to the original level) until the profit opportunities disappear.

Similarly, the decline in demand for good B will produce a lower price. If price originally just covered cost, it will now not do so, losses will be incurred, and firms will find it to their advantage to cut back on their production of good B. Some firms, the least efficient ones, may find that they have to leave the production of good B altogether. Firms that are sluggish in responding to such signals will suffer the greatest losses. The reduction in supply of good B will cause its price to increase (although generally not back to the original level) until it is once again just profitable to produce. The net result of all this will be a transfer of resources from the production of good B to the production of good A, matching the changed needs of customers. These roles played by profits and losses remain essentially the same in more complex market situations.

Competition and "Predatory Pricing"   In the simple case we have been discussing, competitive price formation is the mechanism that forces firms to adopt efficient means of production and forces prices down to costs. Customers seek lower prices, and more efficient firms increase their profits by lowering prices and bidding away business from less efficient ones. Firms set prices above their own costs but below those of less efficient firms. Pricing below costs of inefficient rivals is the natural and desirable result of the competitive process and is not "predatory pricing" even though inefficient firms are driven from the market. Were firms unable (for legal reasons, for example) to cut prices below other firms' costs (while still making a profit themselves), competition could not force inefficient firms to adopt more efficient modes of production, and prices might never fall below the level of the *least* efficient firm's cost. Efficiency would be somewhat rewarded (since the efficient firms would make higher profits), but inefficiency would not be discouraged. Most important, the inefficient firms would survive at the expense of customers who would be paying excessive prices to keep them in business. Price cutting by some firms and losses by others are not only natural but essential to the workings of competition. The competitive process favors the customer and not the competitor.

Indicia of Competition: Constraints on Behavior   The most important lesson of the simple competitive model is the way in which each firm's behavior is constrained and compelled by external market forces. Firms in a competitive market cannot choose to use inefficient methods of production and hope to survive. If they attempt to follow that course, the competitive pressure of lower-cost, lower-priced rival offerings will threaten their survival. They also cannot choose to charge unduly high prices, for if they do, they will lose business and ultimately fail. The requirements of efficient production and consumer demand determine the price of the product and the quantity sold, even though they do not determine the identity of the firms that survive in the market.

To be sure, it generally will take time for customers to switch from a high-price firm to a low-price firm, and it will take time for new means of production to be adopted. Thus, even firms in a competitive market can avoid the external compulsion of the marketplace to be efficient and to set prices that just cover costs (including a return to capital)—but only for a time. In all real markets, firms have power to avoid competitive constraints on prices and costs to some degree. The hallmark of monopoly is the power to avoid such constraints to a great degree and for an extended period of time. The inability to avoid such constraints to any great degree or for more than a short period of time is the hallmark of competition.

There are two basic features of competitive markets that provide constraints on the firms participating in them. First is the existence of alternative sources of supply. Second is the presence of customers who are knowledgeable about the prices charged by alternative suppliers.

When there are alternative sources of supply, customers are not forced to deal with any specific firm; rather, they can choose from a variety of suppliers bidding for their business and seeking to meet their needs. In the model sketched earlier, we assumed that there are numerous firms in the market, none of them having a large share of it. All are actively bidding for the customer's business. Competition could be equally effective and could work in the same way if there were only a few firms in the market and one or more of them had large shares, provided either that entry into the market were easy or that smaller firms could readily expand.

If entry is easy, an attempt by the incumbent firms to exploit their positions by charging higher prices would prompt the entry of more firms, lured by the profits to be made by bidding away the business of the incumbents. New firms would charge lower prices than those charged by the incumbent firms, since the profits earned by selling at lower prices would be enough to induce their entry. Incumbent firms would lose business if they did not lower their prices, exactly as if they had been faced with all of those competitors initially. Thus, when entry is easy, competition is effective and monopoly power is absent. Moreover, this is true whether or not entry does in fact occur. If incumbent firms are forced to lower their prices to avoid losing business to new entrants or to potential new entrants, competition is effective. Lower prices are the result it produces.

Furthermore, even without easy entry by new firms, competition will be equally effective if existing firms can readily expand. Thus, even if entry is difficult, the question of whether a particular firm has monopoly power does not directly depend on its current share of the market but on what would happen to its share if it attempted to charge high prices. This, in turn, depends on the ability of existing competitors to expand, which has the same effect as entry.

To illustrate this point, consider two cases in which entry is difficult. Suppose there is a single firm with a very high share, say over 70 percent of current sales, and a collection of competitors that both individually and in the aggregate have a small share. In one case, the small competitors are, for some reason, unable to expand their output. The large firm in that position is referred to in economic theory as a "dominant firm." It can set prices, calculating the demand it will face at any given price as the total industry demand minus the necessarily limited supply that its competitors will be able to offer at that price. It faces a demand curve consisting of the industry demand curve less the limited supply curves of the other firms. When that supply is limited and small relative to the total market, the large firm has a great deal of market power and may have monopoly power. When a full monopolist (one who faces a situation in which its competitors can, by definition, only supply zero because they never exist) can raise prices without losing any share, the large firm in this case can raise prices without losing very much share.

The dominant firm model, however, is very misleading when competitors can expand their supply. If competitors can easily increase their supply, then a sustained attempt by the firm with a large share to depart from competitive behavior by raising prices or offering inferior products will lead to an expansion by competitors, who will bid away its business. Its share will drop rapidly as a result of such an attempt. The same result occurs when new entrants appear and bid away the business of the large firm. When either new or existing competitors can readily expand, the firm is not "dominant" and does not have monopoly power even though it has a much larger share than those of its rivals. In such a situation, the firm in question can only keep that share by keeping prices low, by being more efficient than the others in the market, and by passing the benefits of that efficiency along to consumers in the form of lower prices. Thus, it is never the case that monopoly power can be inferred from a high market share. Only in the presence of blockaded conditions of entry and the inability of competitors to expand their outputs will a large market share provide evidence of monopoly power.

There is some apparent tension here between this formulation in terms of economic analysis and judicial interpretation of Section 2 of the Sherman Act. As discussed in chapter 1, such interpretations have long recognized that "superior skill, foresight, and industry" is a defense to a monopolization charge.[4] A defendant who is deemed to have attained and kept monopoly power solely by such means is not to be found in violation of the antitrust laws. The formulation given here has the same practical effect but expresses the matter differently. A defendant who maintains a large share solely through superior skill, foresight, and industry has no monopoly power at all. In this view, the necessity for the superior skill, foresight, and industry defense comes from falsely equating large share with monopoly power.

The second basic feature of the simple model that constrains sellers' behavior is the information possessed by customers. Where customers know about the range of price offerings in the market, high-price firms are forced to lower their prices. This point is obvious in the context of the simple market with a single homogeneous product, but it has an important corollary for more complex situations involving technological change and innovation: when customers are sophisticated and informed about both the prices and the product offerings of suppliers, suppliers will be forced to meet the real needs of customers in terms of the value of the products that they offer or suffer losses and eventually go out of business.

In short, then, it is the presence of alternative sources of supply (either actual or potential but readily available) together with sophisticated and informed customers that creates the essential constraints that characterize competition. In the absence of high barriers to entry and competitive expansion, when customers have alternatives and are informed about them, monopoly power cannot exist.

Many Firms with Differentiated Products

The second kind of market setting to be examined is somewhat more complex than the first. Each firm in this type of market offers a product that differs from the products offered by other firms. The differences among products may be physical differences or they may be differences perceived by customers but perhaps not readily apparent to uninformed outside observers. The markets for furniture or clothing illustrate the former case; preference for brands of beer or cigarettes exemplify the latter.

Product and Quality Competition   The significant distinction between the present market and one for a homogeneous product lies in the area of product competition. In a market for a homogeneous product, firms are distinguished in the eyes of the customer only by the prices they charge. Customers, given good information, automatically find it advantageous to buy from the firm with the lowest price. In a market with differentiated products, firms are distinguished not only by the prices they set but by the products they offer. A large number of additional dimensions are thus added to the user's evaluation and choice and thus to the firm's competitive efforts. Importantly, customers will not necessarily buy from the firm that offers its products at the lowest price. Those products must also meet the customers' needs reasonably well, and their deficiencies relative to other product offerings may more than offset any price advantage.

Indeed, when products are differentiated, simple price comparisons are meaningless, since the prices charged by different firms relate to different products. Customers who pay an apparently higher price and receive a product better suited to their needs may in a real sense be paying less than those who pay a lower price for a product less suited to their needs. If it is possible to construct a measure of product quality as perceived by customers, then nominal prices can be converted to prices per unit of quality, and comparisons among such quality adjusted prices will be meaningful. Such adjustments, however, are always difficult and often impossible for an outside observer to make. The customers themselves are the best judges of how much they get for their money, at least provided that they are informed and sophisticated in their understanding of the alternatives that different suppliers offer to them. And, the customers' judgments are demonstrated by their actions in the market.

If the choice among product varieties is important and involves expending large amounts of money, customers will undoubtedly find that it pays to become sophisticated if they are not so already. When, in particular, customers are businesses themselves, they will tend not to make procurement decisions without appropriate information, for they run the risk of unnecessarily increasing their own costs. Indeed, if the customers themselves operate in competitive environments, they will be compelled to make rational, economic choices. If they are large, they may find it profitable to acquire the necessary expertise within their own organizations. However, even small customers can often achieve sophistication in their important purchasing decisions, for when there are numerous small customers, it will be profitable for consultants to offer the necessary expertise.[2.2]

When products differ in complex ways, price comparisons will be similarly complex because there is unlikely to be a readily constructed unidimensional measure of quality. Discussions of "price/performance" in the computer business, for example, represent attempts to correct price for rather rough measures of technical attributes of computer equipment. In general, such attempts cannot adequately account for all such attributes. Moreover, such discussions do not and cannot take into account equipment reliability, responsiveness of the supplier's service organization, the supplier's reputation for supplying reliable equipment suitable to customer needs, or the functions offered by the supplier's software. Yet these are important parts of product quality, however difficult they are to measure. Different customers will generally differ in the weight they give each such attribute, just as different customers will generally differ in the weights they give the various more tangible attributes.

2.2. Large sophisticated customers are common in the computer business (Union Carbide is an example well brought out at the trial). Consultants are also common (Mancke Testimony, pp. 921–929; Historical Narrative, pp. 1412–1426).

This discussion provides the major points for an understanding of how competition works in a market with differentiated products. Customers are presented with an array of products with attributes more or less suitable for them; associated with each product of the array is a price. Customers who are sophisticated and informed enough to understand the alternatives facing them, or who hire sophisticated consultants to advise them, choose that product from the array that gives them the best value, taking into account their particular needs, the characteristics of the product, and its price. Firms that do well in serving customers' desires per dollar of price will do well in sales. Firms offering unnecessarily expensive items or, similarly, products less suited to customer needs at the same prices as their rivals will lose business.

Competition in a market with differentiated products will take the form of product innovation as well as price and cost reduction. As discussed later, a successful product innovation by a firm in an industry characterized by competition and product differentiation will stimulate imitation of the innovation by others. Firms that are initially less successful will be forced either to lower their prices or to change their products so that they meet customer demands as well as their more successful rivals do.

As in the homogeneous product case, prices in theory ultimately will reflect costs. A firm pricing its products above cost will eventually find business bid away by imitators offering essentially the same product at lower prices. Firms unusually successful in meeting customers' needs will initially make extra profits, but those profits will be eroded over time unless the firms continue to offer successive products that customers find exceptionally desirable. Those profits (as in the homogeneous case) are the rewards that spur the firm to meet customers' needs well in the first place. Unfortunately for the successful firm they are also the lure that draws imitators to produce similar or even more attractive products and compete away the business. The speed of successful imitation or new product introduction will determine the duration of high profits. Only if the first firm continues to meet customer needs consistently better than its rivals can it continue to make extra profits over the long run.

As in the homogeneous product case, costs will tend to be driven down to the lowest level allowed by the state of the technology at any moment of time. Inefficient firms will find that they cannot afford to continue to be inefficient; their more efficient rivals will produce the same product at lower cost or a better one at the same cost, offer equivalent quality for lower prices or higher quality for the same price, and thus bid away their business. In addition with differentiated products, there may often be different production techniques or technologies in use by different firms, and it may not be immediately clear which technology is in fact the most efficient one for a particular quantity and quality of product. Therefore, differences in economic profits, resulting from differences in cost levels and prices, may persist longer than would theoretically be expected in the case of the homogeneous product. It may take quite some time for one firm's choice of technology and production processes to be proven inferior in the competitive struggle, and it may be difficult for that firm to shift direction and catch up when it becomes apparent that it is going the wrong way.

As in the homogeneous product case, there will be both winners and losers in the competitive race. The winners will be those firms that are technically efficient, that have the lowest costs and are thus able to offer given products at a low price, that are most adept at meeting customer needs, that offer products preferred by at least some customers over the alternative products available, or that combine these attributes. The losers will be firms that use technically inefficient means of production or that are unable to offer products well-suited to customers' desires, and for either or both reasons cannot supply satisfactory products at acceptable prices while covering their costs.

But here, as in all competitive markets, the ultimate winners are the customers. They are offered a variety of products from which they choose those best suited to their needs and desires, given their budgets, and they spend only those amounts of money technically necessary to get those products. The rewards that the efficient and well-performing firms earn are not earned at customers' expense but are the result of serving their customers better than do alternative suppliers.

Again, it is noteworthy that good performance (low prices, efficiency in production, and a variety of products well-suited to customers' desires) is not a matter of choice for the firms offering it if imitation is rapid. Rather, the competitive constraints of the market enforce good performance. Only well-performing firms survive. Their less competent rivals are penalized by the market process to the benefit of their customers. As before, the presence of responsive alternative suppliers and informed customers cognizant of alternatives compels the results, at least in the absence of substantial barriers to entry and expansion. Given these two ingredients, competition must emerge (absent collusion and regulatory impediments).

The Role of Market Definition   In this analysis, we have deliberately begged the question of how the "market" is defined, a question that all too often becomes central in antitrust cases. In the simple case of a single homogeneous product, that question is settled by assumption and does not arise, but it is hard to avoid in more complex cases. When there is a range of differentiated products, each substituting for the others to some extent, but not perfectly, should one group these products in a single market, consider each of them as constituting a single market, or group clusters of them in one market and other clusters in other markets? Moreover, how should one draw the boundary between the spectrum of products to be considered and other products in the economy?

To understand how a market or group of markets should be delineated, one must keep in mind the purpose to which market definition is to be put. For antitrust purposes, the goal of market definition is to facilitate the analysis of the way in which competition works or, alternatively, the assessment of whether a particular firm possesses monopoly power with respect to a particular group of its products and services.

Market definition is a convenient and useful tool for these purposes, but it is not an end in itself. Further, it must not be a tool that determines the outcome of the analysis. The underlying facts of the market situation are what they are no matter how the products bought and sold have been categorized into "markets" for the purpose of analysis. The way competition works in a particular market cannot and does not depend on how an observer organizes or classifies the products traded in it. Thus, in examining whether a particular firm possesses monopoly power, the behavior of the firm either is or is not constrained by market forces to a greater or lesser degree. The presence or absence of such constraints does not depend on how one looks at them. The basic facts cannot be changed by choosing to describe the products of a particular firm (which in the differentiated product case are to some extent unlike those of any other firm) as constituting a separate market by themselves or choosing to include them in a market with similar products of other sellers.

Thus, consider the analysis just given of competition with differentiated products. Suppose that the market is defined somewhat more narrowly, leaving out the products and firms placing the least constraints on the alleged monopolist. Competition among the firms within the more narrowly defined market would operate in exactly the same way as described earlier in terms of a broader market definition. Customers would choose those products best suited to their desires in terms of both the quality and the price of the products. However, the effects of the substitute products now placed outside the market and of entry into the market as defined must also be considered when the somewhat narrower definition of the market is used. Customers may find that they can better satisfy their needs for the same price (or satisfy them as well at lower prices) by dealing with firms and buying products now excluded from the more narrowly defined market. Further, if the firms inside the market are the ones who are receiving the rewards of adeptly satisfying customer needs (that is, economic profits), then the kind of imitation of success discussed earlier will appear as entry into the narrowly defined market by firms previously outside it.

If the question is whether a particular firm is so insulated from the compulsions of competition as to warrant the attribution of monopoly power to it, it does not matter which market definition is used, so long as it is used consistently. In the first case, with all the relevant firms included in the market, however, mistakes of omission are less likely to occur than in the second case of the narrowly defined market, since it will be immediately apparent in the former case that there are many alternative suppliers constraining the behavior of the firm or firms in the market. If the slightly narrower market definition is used, a large market share of the firm or firms in question might appear itself to warrant an inference about monopoly power. Such a conclusion, however, drawn without considering the facts of entry and potential entry would be plainly wrong. To assess market power, the constraints on the alleged monopolist's behavior from substitute products outside the market and from entry and potential entry into it must be taken into account as well as those arising from the offering of firms inside the more narrowly defined market.

The fact that the precise location of the boundary does not matter does not make market definition a matter of no consequence, however. It is one thing to consider placing firms or products near the boundary outside rather than inside the market, bearing in mind the way in which they compete; it is quite another to do this with much of the market, arbitrarily deciding on a narrow definition that excludes much of the real competition constraining the behavior of the included firms. To do so while attempting to bear in mind the way in which the excluded firms and products compete is to defeat the purpose of market definition by adopting a course designed to confuse rather than to aid analysis. Similarly, it is true that defining a market so broadly as to include many things that do not much constrain the power of the alleged monopolist is to misuse market definition.

As this suggests, what matters are the constraints themselves, not the way in which they are classified. A market with heterogeneous products will include some that constrain the alleged monopolist less than do others. Analysis and understanding of these different effects is what is important, and this can be done without deciding on a definition of the market.

Despite this, market definition tends to play a major role in antitrust cases and certainly in Section 2 cases. This is largely due to the mistaken belief that a large market share (generally according to the guidelines laid down by Judge Hand in *Alcoa*[5]) can prove monopoly and that a large share can be proven by definitional arguments about the "market." While we believe such emphasis to be totally misplaced, the importance of the issue in practice requires an extended discussion (both in general and in terms of the IBM case), and we give that discussion in the next chapter.

Technological Change and Innovative Competition

Technological change has not been present as a major factor in the market models considered so far. Yet the most apparent and distinctive characteristic of the computer business is dramatic technological change.

The groundwork for an analysis of the case of "innovative competition" has already been laid in the consideration of markets with a number of competitors and differentiated products. What happens when the prospects of the continual introduction of new, improved or innovative products or new, improved production techniques are added to the model?

Under competition, firms that cannot meet customer needs as well as their rivals will lose business. When innovation is possible, the threat that others will produce better or cheaper products puts pressure on firms to find new and better ways of meeting customer needs. Under that pressure, firms will continually introduce new products that serve customers' needs better than existing products. The first firm successfully to market a superior new product[2.3] is rewarded for the risks it took in

---

2.3. It is the bringing of an invention to commercial practicability—the successful marketing of a superior product—and not the invention itself that characterizes an innovating firm in the only sense relevant for economic analysis.

developing that new product by acquiring the ability to attract customers preferring the improved product or the ability to charge a premium price reflecting the improvement. Thus, in the period immediately after it introduces a new product, an innovating firm earns higher profits than firms in the market that do not make such an innovation. Those profits are both the incentive for innovation and the reward for success in producing it. They are also an incentive for other firms to equal or better the innovation.

This is only the first step of the competitive process, however. Other firms are induced to imitate or improve on the innovation to defend their existing business and to attempt to reap similar high profits. Gradually, as other firms learn how to make the same or similar products, the innovative firm's capacity to attract additional customers or charge higher prices for its special products is diminished. The period in which business is competed away from firms with existing products by an innovator who has created a new one is followed by a period in which the profits of the innovator are competed away by the price competition of imitators. Ultimately, the innovative firm will be on a par with everyone else, unless it is able to respond to the competitive pressure by making further innovations. Of course, a given innovation is followed not only by direct imitators and price competition but by further innovation by others and by the original innovator. These, in turn, tend to make the first innovation obsolete. Under technological change, both price competition and product competition are present. The latter, in terms of both imitative development and leapfrogging innovations, plays a particularly significant role in the competitive process.

As in all competitive markets, the presence of alternatives to which customers can turn and their knowledge of those alternatives provide both the incentive and the threat causing firms to seek to discover better ways of meeting customers' demands more effectively and more cheaply. In a market with technological change, absolute prices may rise. However, that rise is illusory. While the innovative firm may well be able to charge a higher price for its new products than other firms charge for their old ones, it can do so only because the new product offers more value for the money. On a properly measured basis (taking product characteristics into account), the innovator has actually cut prices. That is why it attracts customers. Further, even such a "higher" price will fall as imitation or further innovation occurs and forces prices down. The cycle is then repeated—in innovative competition, time and the time sequence of events are of critical importance.

The Benefits of Innovation

In the process of innovative competition, as always in competitive markets in general, customers are the ultimate beneficiaries. They receive a succession of better products and lower prices. There are, however, other beneficiaries in the short run; and there are also losers.

The innovative firms, the risk takers, benefit from the competitive process. They run the risk that the potential innovation will not be technically feasible, that it will not be accepted by customers, and that other simultaneous or closely following innovations will make it obsolete as it is born. If such risk taking is successful, innovative firms will reap rewards. By succeeding in serving customer needs better, they achieve a profit. But in the face of continuing technological competition and price competition from imitators, their ability to earn high profits from any single innovation is transitory, although such "transitory" effects may last for several years. Innovating firms can continue to earn profits only if they continue to innovate. It is true, however, that a firm having forged ahead in the race may be in a better position than others to remain ahead, provided it keeps running.

The profits earned by the innovative firm in these circumstances are in no helpful sense "monopoly profits." One important difference between these profits and monopoly profits is that the firms must keep on serving customer needs better in order to continue to earn high profits. If they slow down, become less innovative, or incorrectly predict the movement of customer preferences or technology, their profits will not last. The monopolist, by contrast, can continue to earn high profits simply by virtue of its monopoly position. It does so by restricting output and by not offering product improvements while retaining customers who have nowhere else to turn.

Other firms may also earn profits in markets where technological change is occurring. Successful imitators who are quick to see what makes a particular innovation successful and who quickly follow the lead of the innovator may also make profits. However, imitators of new products are likely to earn smaller profits than do successful innovators because their products will be on the market for a shorter period of time before they are made obsolete by further innovations. In addition, the first imitator is likely to be followed soon by others so that the profits in that type of product will soon be competed away. Thus, successive imitators are likely to earn diminishing profits in comparison with those of the first imitator.

In a market with rapid technological change, some firms also suffer losses. Those who invest in new products that turn out not to be particularly well suited to customer needs will lose money. Those who are slow to perceive that new ways of doing things have arisen and that the old ways are no longer favored by customers will also lose. The process of innovative competition is like a race in which it is necessary to run and run well to endure and to prosper, but the race is more like a marathon than a sprint.

Other Forms of Innovation

Beyond product innovation—the development and marketing of a new product—other kinds of innovation exist that may be less visible but of equal importance. The first of these has already appeared in part: innovation in the techniques of production, sometimes called "process innovation." Such innovation involves an invention that makes production techniques more efficient. This may be a technological innovation or a reorganization of the way in which production is structured or both. Firms successful at process innovation will make profits because they will reduce their costs. Such profits, which are the rewards of efficiency, will last until other firms become equally or more efficient by imitating the innovation or surpassing it.

How long that will be depends on the kind of innovation involved. Unlike a product innovation, which is produced and can be seen and possibly copied by competitors, a process innovation may remain relatively invisible to the outside world. Thus, as opposed to product innovation, the competitive process here is more likely to proceed by other firms innovating and discovering alternative ways of reducing costs than by imitating a particular process. This will be particularly so where the firm making the innovation does so using only its own personnel and resources and has no particular incentive to publicize it.

When the innovation is patentable, however, the innovating firm may be induced to reveal it. If patents are relatively freely available, then so will be the innovation (perhaps with a share of revenues going to the innovator). Further, process innovations may be prompted by inventions from wholly outside the market, where they are available to all firms. In such cases, process innovations are likely to be imitated fairly quickly. In an intermediate case, the innovating firm, if it has to design or use special manufacturing equipment, may cooperate with outside vendors in its design or procurement. In time, the equipment so designed may become available to other firms competing with the innovator.[2.4] In any event, as with product innovation, process innovation will result in an advantage for the innovating firm, leading to profits.

Other forms of innovation may not be technological at all. One form of process innovation can involve reorganizing the way production is structured. Another form of innovation is the creation of a management system that keeps the decisionmakers in touch with the marketplace and links that awareness with the design and manufacturing activities. In competitive markets with differentiated products and product innovation, firms that best serve customers' needs and desires are the ones that survive and prosper. This, in turn, requires knowing what customer needs and desires are, and firms that create effective methods for discerning them will be able to take better advantage of innovative opportunities. Moreover, firms with good market information systems are more likely to perceive when better products are being offered by others, imitate them, and enter successful areas quickly. Customers benefit when firms have the information to respond quickly to changes in their needs and market situations. A firm that develops better ways of gaining and using such information and organizes itself in a manner that helps to ensure that the products it develops and manufactures are responsive to customers' needs and desires will be rewarded in the competitive process.

Another important related form of innovation is the perception of new uses for existing products, or new versions of them, and the expansion of business through the education of potential customers. This form of innovation may be especially important when combined with new product development to make product lines more suitable for use by those new customers.

Finally, to succeed in a market with shifting customer demands and rapid technological change, a firm must be able to make informed, intelligent decisions quickly. In addition, the firm cannot be paralyzed by disputes; they must be resolved quickly and effectively. Thus, the internal organization of management is of considerable importance to the results of the firm over time. Superior management can bring profits; ineffective management can bring losses.

2.4. The Gardner-Denver wire wrapping machines, for example, originally designed by IBM in cooperation with the manufacturer, became generally available throughout the computer industry.

The Importance of Time

An obvious but important lesson from this analysis of the process of competition in a market with rapid technological change is that in assessing whether a firm in such a market has monopoly power, one must be sure to examine the market over a sufficiently long period of time to be able to observe the process of innovative competition at work. A snapshot taken at a single moment in time can be entirely misleading. It might, for example, show one firm (the innovator) well ahead of its rivals and with a substantial share of even a reasonably well-defined market. But since the snapshot could not reveal either the competitive process whereby the firm attained its position or the competitive response of rival firms, it could not form a reliable basis for making inferences about the presence or absence of monopoly power.

Similarly, a short period analysis might be misleading in other ways. If one observes the process of innovative competition in the period after a successful innovation has been made and when imitators begin to enter, one will see the innovator with a large share and high profits. As others follow that lead, prices, as we have seen, will be bid down as part of the competitive process. The "invisible hand" is not literally invisible, however. Such price adjustment comes about through the actions of imitators (who may not have had the same research and development costs as the original imitator) offering similar products at a price lower than that originally set by the innovator. As those products prove reliable, customers will turn away from the innovator to take advantage of such prices. Then the original innovator *must* lower prices or lose share. That is the essence of competition. If the innovator were able to retain its share without lowering its prices or improving its product, one might infer that it had monopoly power. If, looking at the process during this period, one sees the original innovator lowering prices in an attempt to ward off competitors, it would be a complete mistake to regard such lowering of prices as the action of a monopolist determined to drive out competition. Rather, that lowering is the result that competition inevitably brings about and that benefits the consumer.

Consideration of the entire process is important in the analysis of all kinds of competitive markets, not merely those characterized by innovative competition. In the real world, in which things take time, competitive markets will often not be at equilibrium with prices equal to marginal costs equal to average costs and no economic profits being made. When demand or cost conditions change and, especially, when new opportunities appear, competitive markets will be thrown into disequilibrium, and the process of adjustment will begin. That adjustment may not be complete before the next change occurs. Under innovative competition, this is particularly important. Only in a world in which new opportunities do not arise and old ones disappear as competitors take advantage of them can one be sure that the competitive process will even approach equilibrium.[6] When new opportunities continually arise, one will see under competition a continuing process of change that carries with it continual opportunities for profit and growth. One cannot hope to understand the competitive nature of such a process by examining it in the terms of static competitive equilibrium. Such an examination will tend to lead to the false conclusion that the market is not competitive when in fact competition is operating fiercely.

A snapshot taken at a moment in time might show one firm ahead. It would give only a very incomplete picture, however, for it would fail to show that what is going on is a continuing race. What matters is not the snapshot but the movie. Even though a firm initially ahead may well be in a better position to stay ahead than firms that are initially behind, what matters is whether it can do so only by continuing to compete and whether the race is fair.

Structure, Conduct, and Performance: Indicia of Competition or Monopoly

Our discussion of the several market models presents a description of the competitive process and competitive activity as distinguished from the presence of monopoly power. Often an examination of the actual activity of firms in the market and the results of their interaction can reveal whether the market is effectively competitive. Economists, however, have traditionally undertaken the analysis of the competitiveness of a market by an examination of indicia of competition and monopoly categorized under the headings of market structure, market conduct, and market performance.

Market structure consists of the environment within which a given firm does business. It comprises such things as the number and strength of competitors, the technological opportunities, and the underlying conditions of entry. Other relevant factors are the pattern and rate of growth of the market, the sophistication and nature of the customers, and the availability of product and price information to the participants in the market. In the language used earlier, analysis of market structure is an examination of the more or less fixed constraints within which a firm does business, viewed in the perspective of several years rather than a month or a year.

In some situations, analysis of market structure alone answers the questions of interest. In markets with several suppliers, with customers sophisticated about the alternatives presented, and in which either no one supplier has a particularly large market share or entry and expansion are easy, the market structure constraints compel competition. Little more need be discussed. In other situations, however, the relationship between market structure and the outcome (performance) or behavior (conduct) in that market is not so clear. In particular, a situation in which there are several supplying firms but one has a much larger market share than any others and the conditions of entry and expansion are not favorable may be either competitive or monopolistic. For example, assuming that the large share is not simply a product of an inappropriately narrow market definition, that share may reflect a firm that has been successful in innovative competition in a particularly risky and rapidly changing market. Alternatively, it may mean that customers are limited in their capacity to find alternatives to the offerings of the firm with the large share, even if that firm does not offer good value. In such situations, further analysis is necessary.

Consideration of the case in which a large market share is the product of success in innovative competition reveals the fact that there are circumstances in which some aspects of market structure, at least, cannot be treated as exogenous—taken as given for the analysis of competition. Particularly when technological change is important, certain aspects of market structure will be endogenous—themselves produced by the workings of the competitive (or noncompetitive) process. In innovative competition, one cannot understand the significance of a large market share without understanding how that share came to be and how it is maintained. Similarly, in such circumstances, the number and identity of firms in the market are not immutably given but are determined by the competitive process itself. One must understand that process as a dynamic whole rather than as a static situation.

Market conduct consists of the ways in which firms interact with each other and the ways in which individual firms decide to do business. Conduct encompasses the actual competitive activity: pricing practices, terms and conditions, marketing policies, product offerings, and the like, whether such activity reflects vigorous rivalry, predatory behavior, or an inability or unwillingness to compete aggressively. An examination of market conduct can help to decide whether the market position of the alleged monopoly is due to conduct constituting an exercise of monopoly power that frees it from competitive constraints or from the threat of such constraints, or is due to successful risk taking, superior products or services, excellent business management, or a particular skill in meeting customer demands.

Market performance consists of the results of the working of the market in terms of the major economic variables of prices, costs, product quality, variety of customer alternatives, responsiveness of the suppliers to the demands of the customers, and the interrelations among these variables. An examination of market performance may determine whether the workings of the given market structure and market conduct result in the kind of outcome that competition is designed to produce: efficient production, technological improvement (with the implementation of technological advances in the products and services offered to customers), ample and expanding customer alternatives, responsiveness to customer demands, and prices tending to fall toward costs. If the outcome differs significantly from that which a competitive market is expected to produce, then the market is not competitive. If the performance is what is expected from a competitive market, then one should suspect that the market is competitive. As a matter of theory, it is possible that, even though the market is not competitive, firms with freedom of action and monopoly power may choose to act in such a way as to duplicate the workings of the competitive market, but this theoretical possibility is not likely to be realized in observable market situations. A judgment that observed performance is compatible with competition supports, as a practical matter, a judgment that the market is in fact competitive. This judgment will be inevitable if the analysis of the market shows behavior on the part of all firms that can only be interpreted as being responses to market constraints. When one can observe that the competitive process is at work and that vigorous rivalry among independent firms is creating strong pressure to push market performance toward the desired results, monopoly power cannot exist.

Chapter 3

Market Definition in the Computer Industry

We have seen that market definition is, in a sense, unnecessary for the analysis of competition or monopoly. The constraints on the power of the alleged monopolist are the same regardless of how the market is defined, and, properly handled, different market definitions can only succeed in describing the same phenomena—the constraints—in different but equivalent ways.

Why then discuss market definition at all? Aside from its customary role in antitrust cases, market definition can be a convenience. If handled in a sensible way, with the object of analysis—the assessment of monopoly power—firmly kept in mind, market definition can be a useful analytic expository device. It can define the universe of discourse— those products and firms that must be studied together to understand the nonnegligible constraints on the behavior of the firm.

It follows that, to be a useful concept, the market should include all products and firms that in fact do or easily could offer reasonable alternatives to customers if the alleged monopolist were to charge high prices or offer inferior products. The appropriate boundaries of the market can never be decided precisely, but this will not matter if it is remembered that entry from outside can provide constraints and that not all products and firms included provide equal constraints. What matters are the constraints themselves, not the way in which one chooses to summarize them.

The fact that the exact position of the boundary does not matter is not, however, a license for arbitrary market definition. If market definition is to serve any useful purpose, it must include those items that constrain the monopolist. Thus, while it is possible to err in either direction, errors of overly broad market definitions are not likely to prove as serious as errors of overly narrow market definitions. Where the market is defined broadly to include some items that do not constrain the alleged monopolist as much as others, those items at least remain in the arena being discussed and their relative lack of constraining power can then be further analyzed. An arbitrarily narrow market definition, on the other hand, is likely simply to exclude from any but the most cursory further examination items that do in fact provide substantial constraints.

Unfortunately, either way it is all too easy to lose sight of the purpose of market definition and to substitute an arbitrary decision on "in" or "out" for a proper analysis of constraints. Consider, for example, the leading case on market definition, the *Cellophane* case.[1] Here the issue turned on whether other flexible wrapping papers were in the same market as cellophane. Faced with evidence of substitution, the Supreme Court said that they were in and concluded that DuPont was not a monopoly. As several commentators have pointed out, however, such a conclusion overlooked the fact that other flexible wrapping papers were produced with different technologies and at higher costs than those of cellophane.[2] Substitution between other wrapping papers and cellophane may only have occurred because cellophane prices were set high enough that other flexible wrapping papers could profitably compete as some users turned to these otherwise inferior substitutes. In this view, such substitution merely reflected monopoly pricing in cellophane; it did not prevent it. Hence those other products should not have been considered in the same market.

This is the proper analysis, but, in a real sense, the wrong conclusion. What matters in this situation is the extent to which substitution of other flexible wrapping papers put constraints on the pricing of cellophane. It is indeed crucial in assessing monopoly power in cellophane to know whether the costs of producing those other wrapping papers would have made them nonviable substitutes at lower cellophane prices. But once one has analyzed this, there is nothing further to be gained by deciding that such flexible papers are "out" of the market. Such a decision, like the decision that they are "in," substitutes a binary choice for what is a continuous phenomenon. It conceals, rather than preserves, information. While such concealment need not prevent the correct conclusions from being reached, it cannot be of help in itself.

Indeed, when used by less careful practitioners, such a procedure invites the dismissal of evidence about substitution on the unsupported supposition that such evidence merely reflects the appearance of inferior substitutes at the monopoly price. This occurred to some extent in the *IBM* case, despite the fact that there is no evidence that the products and services excluded by the government from its "market" were inferior substitutes only able to compete at a supposed monopoly price.[3] On the contrary, unlike the situation in *Cellophane*, the excluded products are generally produced with the same technology as the included ones; in fact, they are sometimes the identical products offered by different vendors (leasing companies). In other cases (plug-compatible replacements for IBM products), they are closer substitutes for the products of the alleged monopolist than are other products that were included. Even when this is not the case (so-called "minicomputers," for example), the evidence shows increasing substitution as the price of computing comes down, with the strong possibility that the supposed "inferior" substitute may be the wave of the future.[4]

Unfortunately, as in the *Cellophane* case, discussion of market definition tends to become central in antitrust cases, with intelligent analysis of the constraints obscured by a binary decision on "in" or "out." Worse, the argument can degenerate, with semantic debate replacing any analysis of the underlying facts in an artificial attempt to raise or lower the defendant's market share. When this occurs, not only is there a misunderstanding of the role of market share, but market definition has become a major hindrance rather than an aid to analysis. One need know little of the facts of Nestlé's acquisition of Stouffer, for example, to see that analysis has been left behind when the issue appears to be whether there is a "market" consisting of frozen, high-priced, nonethnic entrées.[3.1] Unfortunately, as we shall see, examples just as peculiar occurred in the *IBM* case.

To summarize, market definition forces an arbitrary choice. Both choosing too broad and choosing too narrow a market are wrong—if the choice then leads one to forget the facts. In practice, too narrow a market definition is more likely to prove harmful. The definition of the market provides the universe of discourse for the analysis of the problem. Products left outside are likely to be given only cursory treatment, if they are treated at all. Products inside the market, on the other hand, at least become the subject for further investigation of how they do or do not constrain the power of the alleged monopolist.

It follows that the sensible way to handle market definition when there are differentiated products is to draw the market boundaries sufficiently broadly to encompass all the products and firms whose competition with the firm under study constitutes substantial constraints on its behavior. Any lesser constraints provided by distant substitutes

3.1. It may or may not be a coincidence that after the acquisition was challenged by the FTC, Stouffer's began a series of television commercials that featured someone tasting a Stouffer's product and saying something like "What is it? It tastes like lasagna, but it isn't lasagna."

should also be taken into account in terms of entry. Analysis can then proceed to consider the differing ways and strengths with which different constraints operate. However, to define a "market" that excludes those firms and products with which the firm in question obviously competes is to ignore the real economics of competition and to risk finding monopoly simply on the basis of a definitionally high market share in an arbitrarily narrowly defined market.

Demand and Supply Substitutability

A number of practical consequences flow from this view of market definition. The use of the term "market" by firms or in the everyday language of businessmen or even industry reporters is not a reliable guide to market definition. Such usage does not match the proper use of "market" as a term of art in the analysis of competition or monopoly. That is not to say that such usage provides no guide; it is wise to include the firms and products with which the alleged monopolist sees itself competing. But it is wrong to rely on a categorization of how the firm does business, even if it is couched in terms of "markets," as if it were a substitute for the analytic task of summarizing constraints. That task is not held firmly in mind by all lawyers and economists, let alone businessmen or reporters, who are generally not concerned with it at all.

Similarly, since the object of market definition in a monopoly case is to assist in organizing the facts to assess the constraints on the alleged monopolist, what matters is the competition that the latter faces. The fact that particular competitors may view the market differently because they choose to compete in particular ways is irrelevant. In private antitrust suits, this means that one must pay attention to the constraints on the defendant, not to the market perceived by the plaintiff. Naturally, plaintiffs may not take this view. In the series of private suits accompanying (and, in part, spawned by) *U.S.* v. *IBM*, the market in which IBM operates was variously defined by different plaintiffs as the market for leased machines (Greyhound, a leasing company); the market for peripherals that are plug-compatible replacements for IBM peripherals (Telex and other plug-compatible manufacturers); and even the market for certain specific forms of software usable on IBM processors (Symbolic Control, an unsuccessful vendor of such software). Yet, however relevant such market definitions may have been for the competition felt by the various plaintiffs, they were each much too narrow to reveal the constraints on IBM, which (along with others) competed with all of them.

To define a market properly then, one must proceed directly to analyze the constraints on power, which are themselves the ultimate object of study. This means considering what actions customers and competitors can and do take that limit the power of a firm to raise prices above costs or to offer inferior products. Dividing the investigation into analyses of demand substitutability and supply substitutability is often useful. The first reflects the constraint imposed by customers' ability and willingness to turn to other products and services as alternatives to the products and services of the alleged monopolist; the second reflects the constraint imposed by other suppliers' ability and willingness to direct their production toward offering new products and services that are alternatives to those of the alleged monopolist.

Demand Substitutability
Products and services are substitutes in demand when they are reasonable economic alternatives satisfying a particular set of customer demands. Demand-substitutable products and services constitute the first alternatives to which customers can turn to satisfy their demands if the alleged monopolist fails to perform well in terms of prices or product quality. Thus, such demand substitutes constrain a firm's behavior and are part of the same economic market containing the products and services over which the firm supposedly has monopoly power.

For products and services to be included in the same market they need not be direct, one-for-one replacements for one another. For example, if, as an alternative to using a firm's product, customers can reasonably satisfy their demand by using two or more products or services from other suppliers in combination, then that combination will constrain the firm's price and product performance. The products and services making up such a demand-substitutable combination must therefore be considered in the same market as the alleged monopolist's product. This conclusion is the same whether the alternative combination consists of more than one of a particular product or a variety of different products and services. Similarly, if customers can reasonably use a product or service as an alternative to the use of an additional (or a larger or more expensive version of a) product of the firm under study, the existence of that alternative will constrain that firm's price and product performance. Again, those products or services constituting the alternatives must be considered in the same market as the alleged monopolist's product.

The best indicator of demand substitutability is the fact that customers regularly consider and choose between two or more products as alternatives for the same purpose. The perceptions of users, the selection processes they employ, and the actual choices that they make provide the most conclusive evidence of demand substitutability.

Supply Substitutability

The market being examined for the presence of monopoly power must also include those firms that could readily supply products or services that would be reasonable economic alternatives for an alleged monopolist's customers. When such firms exist, a failure by the alleged monopolist to perform well in terms of prices and product quality will lead those firms (lured by the opportunity to make economic profits) to begin to produce demand-substitutable products or services in an attempt to bid away the alleged monopolist's customers. Such supply substitutability constrains the alleged monopolist in its price and product performance. The greater the ability of potential suppliers to respond to market opportunities, the tighter the constraints.

Assume that certain firms make size 9 men's shoes and that other firms make sizes 8 and 10, among others. Are all of those shoes of different sizes in the same market? Generally, the size 8 or size 10 shoes would not be effective substitutes on the demand side for the man who had size 9 feet. In addition, it would probably not be economical to attempt to alter existing size 8 or size 10 shoes to fit the size 9 feet. Nevertheless, if the size 9 shoes were priced much above the comparable quality shoes in sizes 8 and 10, almost certainly the manufacturers of those sizes would begin to make size 9 shoes. Thus, the various sizes of men's shoes belong in the same market, and the suggestion that a firm has monopoly power over the supply of size 9 but not size 8 or size 10 shoes is implausible.

Other examples may exhibit elements of both demand and supply substitutability. For example, assume that there is only one manufacturer of red carpet but many of green carpet. Though customers carpeting a room previously decorated for the color red reasonably can use only red carpet, the manufacturers of red carpet and of green carpet ought to be included in the same market. That is so not only because customers carpeting newly decorated rooms can and do choose between red and green carpet but because any attempt on the part of the red carpet manufacturer to raise the price of red carpet above the price of green carpet (by more than any difference attributable to different costs of production, for example, the costs of the dyes) and thereby exploit those customers temporarily "locked" into red will lead the green carpet manufacturers to substitute production of red carpet for some of their production of green carpet. The first possibility corresponds to demand substitutability; the second, to supply substitutability. For either reason or both, the two colors of carpet are in the same market.

As we saw in chapter 2, supply substitutability and new entry are closely related. Consider an artificially narrow market definition, with firms outside the market arranged in order of ease and quickness of their entry into it given appropriate incentives. The firms whose entry would be relatively substantial and relatively easy should be included in the market; firms farther out should be classified as potential entrants. The precise location of the line is not important so long as the constraints provided by firms outside the line are taken into account; the prospect of easy entry from outside the market is a substantial constraint on an alleged monopolist's performance. Nevertheless, if market definition is to serve any useful purpose, it is critical to include within the market at least those firms using a production technology essentially the same as the alleged monopolist's and possessing in addition the requisite know-how in both production and marketing to move readily into its area. To fail to include such firms is to exclude from the market the real constraints on the behavior of the alleged monopolist. That defeats the entire purpose of market definition.

To identify those firms that should be included in the market on the basis of supply substitutability, the history of actual entry by other firms provides the best evidence. Firms situated in positions similar to the positions of actual entrants prior to their entry are very likely potential entrants and could presumably duplicate the actions of their predecessors with similar ease and success.

The Electronic Data Processing (EDP) Market: An Overview

Computer systems are collections of individual hardware products, software, and related maintenance and services. These collections enable users to manipulate data to satisfy their needs for information processing, storage, and transference by electronic means. This concept has meaning only in the context of the users' applications and the combination of products and services working together to perform those applications.

Computer systems perform a combination of functions broadly grouped under five categories: input, processing, storage, control, and output. Each of these functions can be accomplished in a variety of ways, and this fact is important in understanding the substitution possibilities in the EDP market.[5]

Virtually no two computer systems in use are identical. Systems differ across manufacturers, and even systems from the same manufacturer, with the same central processing unit (CPU), will differ in their con-figurations of peripheral equipment, hardware options, and software. Further, CPUs produced by the same manufacturer may differ in internal logic or memory circuitry and even in the technology employed. Hard-ware and software approaches to the organization and performance of the five computer functions vary. This is reflected in variations in system architecture and software; differing capabilities of the individual hardware boxes and software options; variations in the number, type, and variety of boxes offered to users; and differing degrees of flexibility with which systems can be configured from the component parts. Nevertheless, all computer systems perform the same five functions, and the similarities and common features outweigh the differences.[6]

In the early computers (before, say, the late 1950s), the variety of computer systems was quite limited. In those computers, produced by Univac, IBM, and others, input generally involved punched cards (or sometimes tapes) that had to be carefully prepared in appropriate form by the user. Those cards, often sorted externally, were read into the central computer by means of a card reader. Processing of data took place inside a central processing unit with memory first on mercury tubes and then on magnetic cores. Auxiliary storage, as well as main memory storage, was extremely limited. Intermediate results that could not be contained in the main memory had to be punched out on cards or, sometimes, written on tapes. Those cards (or tapes) would then be reread into the machine at a later stage. The chief form of output was again punched cards, which were then printed on an off-line printer. Consequently, a limited number of configurations of computer systems were available to users. Each CPU could be used to form a few different configurations with the choices of peripherals available.[7]

In some ways the most important limitation came from the relatively rudimentary methods of control, which were largely entrusted to the user. It took a great deal of manual intervention to move from one part of a program to another. Operators played a fairly substantial role in the operation of the system, particularly in the management of the system's resources. It was the users who transferred cards (or tapes) by hand from one part of the system to another and who started the next job when the previous one was complete.[8]

The users also did most of the programming, which was no small matter. Early programs had to be written in cumbersome machine language. After the advent of FORTRAN and other high-level languages, programmers could write their programs in a language that was closer to English, but they still had to keep careful track of the memory used by the program at various stages (although they no longer had to keep track of the exact address of each bit of data).[9]

From the days of such early systems onward, however, the EDP industry has been characterized by rapid, often interrelated, change and improvements.[10] First, hardware efficiency increased phenomenally. In broad outline, electronic technology evolved first from vacuum tubes to transistors, then from transistors to integrated circuits and semiconductors, with continuous improvements within each technology as well as between them. As circuits became smaller, faster, and less expensive, internal speeds rose dramatically, and circuits became more reliable. Similarly, improvements in hardware permitted storage of ever-increasing amounts of information in a given space, either on disks or tapes or main memory, and made storage and retrieval even faster.[11]

Second, devices proliferated to accomplish the five computer functions. Today, for example, disks, data cells, and automated tape libraries and mass storage systems provide alternative methods of storage. On-line printers, computer output microfilm devices, and terminals provide various ways of obtaining output. Terminals, point-of-sale devices, optical character readers, and key-to-disk devices, as well as other CPUs and auxiliary storage devices themselves, provide alternative ways of submitting input. Processing and control, once nearly exclusive functions of the CPU, are decentralized through channels, control units, communication devices, front-end processors, and intelligent terminals.[12]

Third, executive software or operating systems developed, enabling the computer system to manage its own resources—to perform control functions previously done by applications programming and operators. This reduced the risk of human error and permitted the efficient management of a complex system comprised of a variety of expensive hardware components. The operating system analyzes the sequence of tasks and assigns work to different hardware devices to make the best use of the computer system's available resources. Similarly, the development of operating systems and virtual memory increasingly liberated the programmer from concerns about limited main memory capacity and the interactions of different hardware devices.[13]

The development of disks and virtual memory provides a good example of the interrelated nature of these developments and of some of the ways in which different combinations of hardware and software substitute for each other. As the industry progressed, main memory—first in the form of ferrite cores and later in the form of semiconductors—increased tremendously in speed and capacity but remained relatively expensive. The relatively cheap tape drives, on the other hand, while also greatly improved, remained far slower than main memory. Further, the usefulness of tapes for many purposes was severely limited by the fact that access to data on them was only available in a serial fashion. It was as though one had to read through all the names in the telephone directory in alphabetical order until a desired name appeared.

The gap between tape drives and main memory devices, both in cost and in speed, was filled to a large extent by the invention of and tremendous improvements in disk drives, starting in the mid-1950s. Such drives—a technology largely pioneered and led by IBM—can be thought of as stacks of records in a juke-box. Data are stored as magnetized spots on both sides of each record in the stack. The entire stack spins very rapidly, and data are read or written by means of magnetic heads that literally fly above (or below) the disk surface at very small fractions of an inch. Because data are stored in this way, information can be retrieved relatively directly; to read an entry in the telephone book, one need only go to the disk and track on which the name appears and wait for rotation to bring it around. Disk storage has been of great importance in computer development and usage.

Despite such improvements, the speed with which information can be recovered from or written on a disk is far slower than the speed with which modern logic circuitry operates in performing the processing function. This means that high-speed main memory remains indispensable. Thus, because of its cost, the size of the main memory was for many years an important constraint on users, always present in the minds of programmers writing complex software. That constraint was largely lifted by the introduction of virtual storage, or virtual memory, developed by IBM and others.

In virtual storage, the applications program does not reside totally in the main memory at any one time. Instead, much of it and much of the data are located on disk. As computing progresses, the operating system uses an algorithm to forecast which parts of the program and which data will be needed soon, and the necessary information is transferred from disk to main memory in time for use. (In some systems data are also moved from mass storage to disk.) This is accomplished by means of a combination of software and hardware that, at least within IBM, was earlier developed to allow time-sharing. This hardware-software combination, together with the disk drives, substitutes for a larger main memory, making it appear to the user as though such a larger memory is in fact at his disposal.

Virtual memory and disks are but two of the developments that have made computer systems increasingly flexible and more readily useful in a wide range of applications. In the 1950s, because of their cumbersome operation, relative slowness, and expense per computation, particular computers were often designed to perform particular kinds of applications. While given operations could be performed much faster using hard-wired instructions than using software, the expense of hardware circuits limited the number of instructions that it made sense to hard-wire. It was most efficient to hard-wire only frequently used instructions and hence to tailor the instructions hard-wired into each machine to its expected applications. Thus, for example, it was expensive to provide both ordinary decimal and floating point arithmetic in the same machine, and computers were offered as optimized either for "business" or "scientific" applications. While the theoretical work of Turing implied that any stored program computer could, in principle, be made to do what any other stored program computer could, that idea was not yet practical in the 1950s.[14]

As technology advanced, however, specialization was no longer clearly the efficient choice. Moreover, although "business" applications were done on "scientific" computers and "scientific" applications on "business" computers, an increasing number of customers with a variety of applications were faced with the need to use two or more computers. The use of a single system for all their applications was an attractive prospect. As computers became faster, circuits less expensive, and software more flexible, it became easier for manufacturers to meet such customer needs by designing computers useful for many different kinds of applications. With System/360, announced on April 7, 1964, IBM virtually erased the distinction between so-called "business" and "scientific" computers. (Indeed, the name "360" indicated the intention to cover every point of the compass.) Other manufacturers also introduced equipment intended to be used for a wide variety of applications, including both scientific and business. Similarly, as processors became increasingly powerful, the dedication of computers to single process control applications became less efficient, and the same machine was used both for other types of applications and for process control.[3.2] Because of the evolution to more flexible computer systems, users could choose among processors and peripherals, allowing configurations of systems on a continuum between those "optimized" for a relatively narrow range of applications and those of more generalized capability. By the late 1970s, most systems configurations could do most applications, although the relative costs might vary from system to system.[15]

All these technological developments were accompanied by industry changes that greatly expanded user alternatives. Thus, in the early days, sources of software were limited. During a period when users were largely unfamiliar with computers and the industry was in its infancy, the manufacturer was best suited to develop and provide software. Users, however, rapidly wrote and exchanged applications programs and user groups developed to promote such exchange. Independent software houses also entered the market, offering both systems and applications software. The range of software available to customers expanded. Users could acquire software from the manufacturer or from software houses or they could write it themselves (an option that has been and continues to be the one chosen by users for the great bulk of their software).[16]

At the same time, growth in the number of vendors substantially increased the choices of hardware boxes available to users, and the choice among vendors took several forms. An increasing number of vendors offered entire systems, with many, such as Digital Equipment Corporation (DEC) or Data General, offering as time went on small and medium-size systems with capabilities roughly equivalent to the larger systems of some years before. Where more computing power was needed, the user could often employ several small systems instead of a single big one or a combination of a large and a small system in place of a single, even larger one.

Further, users could acquire different parts of their systems from different vendors, such as Telex, Ampex, Storage Technology Corporation (STC), AT&T, or Beehive. Thus, they could acquire memory, disks, tapes, terminals, and other peripherals made by manufacturers other than the manufacturer of their central processing units. Depending

3.2. A process control application generally uses the computer to regulate an industrial process as in control of machine tools, temperature, or chemical inputs.

on the manufacturer, such devices could be acquired either directly or through a marketing intermediary.

Finally, users could acquire given equipment from more than one vendor and under a variety of arrangements. They could purchase or lease from the manufacturer. They could also purchase used equipment or lease from a leasing company, such as Decimus or Greyhound—alternatives that became increasingly important toward the end of the 1960s. If they needed less than full-time use of a computer or an additional computer, they could rent time from a time-sharing facility or, along with other services, from a service bureau such as Automatic Data Processing (ADP). Whatever combinations users selected from among all these alternatives, however, each user acquired the services of the same basic product, a computer system doing input, output, storage, processing, control, and output.[17]

A partial list of vendors of EDP products and services (in addition to IBM) as of 1980 is given in table 3.1.[18]

Systems, Boxes, and Modularity

Users demand the use of a computer system for the performance of their data processing. That does not mean, however, that users buy "computer systems," that suppliers sell "computer systems," or that there is a market for "computer systems" in the sense of a composite product. Consumers demand the set of functions—input, storage, processing, control, and output—that computer systems perform. They obtain these functions in many different ways, using a variety of equipment and services. It is important to recognize that the individual boxes offered by IBM and other systems suppliers as parts of systems are priced separately and that the "system" price is simply the sum of the prices of the individual boxes and software selected by the customer to be configured as the customer's system. The price of a box is the same whether it is bought alone or with other boxes. Hence IBM and other systems suppliers have a direct concern with the effect of the prices of individual boxes, software, and services on total system price and demand as well as a direct concern arising from the effect of individual box prices on the demand for the individual boxes themselves.[19]

In the 1950s, it was relatively common for suppliers to market and for users to acquire entire systems in a single transaction. When users wanted to increase their computing capacity or change their applications, their installed equipment offered few options for easy modification or upgrading. Users who needed more capacity were virtually required to

Table 3.1

A. B. Dick

Alanthus

Action Communications

Amdahl

American Telephone & Telegraph

Ampex

Anderson Jacobson

Ann Arbor Terminals

Applied Digital Data Systems

Automatic Data Processing

Applied Data Research

BASF Systems

Bank of America (including Decimus)

Beehive International

Bell & Howell

Boeing

Boothe Financial

Bradford National

Braegen

Bunker Ramo

Burroughs

California Computer

Cambridge Memories

Centronics Data Computer

Cincom Systems

Citicorp

Comdisco

Computer Automation

Computer Sciences

The Computer Software Company

Computer Systems of America

Computervision

Comshare

Comserv

Continental Information Systems

Control Data Corporation (including Comma)

Cray Research

Cullinane

Data General

Table 3.1 (continued)

Datapoint

Dataproducts

Decision Data Computer

Digital Equipment Corporation

DPF

Documentation

Electronic Associates

Electronic Data Systems

Electronic Memories & Magnetics

Evans & Sutherland

Exxon

Ford Motor Credit

Formation

Four-Phase Systems

Foxboro

Fujitsu

General Automation

General Electric

General Instrument

General Telephone and Electronics

Gould

Greyhound Computer

Harris

Hazeltine

Hewlett-Packard

Hitachi

Honeywell

ICL

Informatics

Intel

International Telephone & Telegraph

Intersil

Lear Siegler

Litton Industries

Lockheed Aircraft

Magnuson Computer Systems

Management Assistance

Management Science America

Martin Marietta

Table 3.1 (continued)

McDonnell Douglas

Memorex

Mitsubishi Electric

Modular Computer Systems

Mohawk Data Sciences

Nanodata

National CSS

National Semiconductor

NCR

Nippon Electric

Nippon Peripherals

Nixdorf Computer

Northern Telecom Systems

Okidata

Olivetti

OPM Leasing Services

Optimum Systems

Paradyne

Perkin-Elmer

Philips

Prime Computer

Qantel

Randolph Computer

Raytheon

Recognition Equipment

Reliance Group

Reynolds & Reynolds

Rockwell International (including Collins)

Rockwood Computer

Sanders Associates

Shared Medical Systems

Siemens

Software AG of North America

Sperry Rand (including Varian Data Machines and Information Storage Systems)

Storage Technology Corporation

System Development Corp.

Systems Engineering Laboratories

Tandem Computers

Table 3.1 (continued)

Tektronix

Telex

Texas Instruments

Tiger Leasing Group

Toshiba America

TRW

Two Pi

Tymshare

United Telecommunications

Wang Laboratories

Wyly

Xerox

change systems. However, during the 1960s, a major change in acquisition patterns occurred. The product offerings of the systems manufacturers, led by IBM with System/360, became increasingly modular. Individual boxes could be replaced, added, or removed so that an installed computer system would often be in an almost continuous state of evolution or transformation. Thus, an upgrade of a particular CPU type could be accomplished by the addition of main memory; a CPU upgrade to a new type could be achieved by the replacement of only one box (the CPU); or the system could grow and its capacity increase by the addition of peripherals, by the replacement of peripherals with models of greater speed or capacity, or even by increasing the number of one peripheral type and decreasing the number of another. Thus, every box in the initial system could be replaced by a new one, but there would be no single point when one could say that one system replaced another.[20]

As a result, acquisition decisions were increasingly made on a box-by-box or modular basis. More and more of users' acquisitions represented the selection of replacement or add-on boxes. More and more of the systems manufacturers' sales were of boxes for replacement or additions. Thus, RCA's Edwin S. McCollister estimated that perhaps 25 to 30 percent of RCA's EDP revenues in the 1960s came from sales of parts of systems rather than systems themselves; NCR's John J. Hangen estimated that by 1975, 20 to 40 percent of NCR's revenues came from "add-on" sales; and IBM's John Akers estimated that by 1979, 75 percent or more of IBM's data processing division revenues were from "nonsystem" sales. (See the appendix for a list identifying witnesses mentioned in this book.)[21]

These modular combinations of boxes configured by or for users according to their data processing plans often consist of products from several manufacturers. Such mixed systems became common and accepted in the 1970s, although they existed earlier. In particular, numerous firms have engaged successfully since the late 1960s in manufacturing and marketing boxes (first tapes, then disks and other peripherals, and, in the mid-1970s, CPUs) as direct, one-for-one, plug-compatible replacements for IBM boxes in "IBM computer systems." The evolving computer system in the user's installation most often consists of products and services from numerous and constantly changing suppliers.[22]

Defining the "Market"

One cannot understand events in the computer industry or properly evaluate the constraints on IBM's behavior by adopting a market definition that fails to reflect the full richness of context just described. The many ways in which users can and do satisfy their data processing needs and the many ways in which different systems or parts of systems substitute for each other make it unwise to segment the overall market. To understand this, it is useful to consider in more detail the ways in which the government proposed to define the market.

The Government's Market Claims
The government contended that the product market that is the "foundation of the electronic data processing industry" is the market for "computer system[s]" and "[t]he most significant class of computer systems, as well as the . . . 'heart' of the computer industry, is the general purpose electronic digital computer system." This was identified as the market in which IBM allegedly has monopoly power.[23] The only "products" that compete in the market were said to be computer systems that constitute "an identifiable product" in the industry. Such systems were described as "composite product[s] . . . composed of four basic elements: hardware, software, maintenance and services." However, no firm was viewed as competing in the "systems market" without offering "all four elements of this composite product. . . ." Suppliers of some but not all of the parts of a system were excluded.[24]

Further, not all computer systems were included in this "market." Systems also had to be "general purpose" by the government's definition of that term. At the beginning of the trial, this meant that such systems must be members of "a class of systems comprising hardware, software, maintenance and service which are manufactured and marketed primarily to perform a broad range of commercial or business applications." These "general purpose" computer systems were distinguished from computer systems said to be in some sense "special purpose," including "minicomputers," "super computers," "scientific" computers, and computers "manufactured and marketed" "primarily" for applications such as "process control," "communications processing," "typesetting," "seismography," "data entry," and "military." All such products (and their suppliers) were thus excluded from the government's market. And, as we shall see, the requirements for inclusion as "general purpose" became even more stringent as the trial progressed until, by 1977, of all the firms listed in table 3.1, only Univac, Honeywell, and Burroughs were said to be "in the market" in addition to IBM.[25]

An additional requirement for inclusion related to the supplier rather than the product. A firm had to be a "manufacturer" to be a competitor in the government's market. It is not completely clear what this meant, since how much must be manufactured was not specified and many firms buy boxes from others for inclusion in their own offerings. In any event, leasing companies—which admittedly market products that are in the market and which the government called "primary competition" for the included IBM products—were not competitors in the market. Similarly excluded were brokers, dealers, and systems integrators as well as service bureaus and time-sharing companies offering data processing services as a partial or complete alternative to an in-house computer system.[26]

The government, following the initial success of Telex at the district court level, also identified three "submarkets" in addition to the "general purpose systems market." Those submarkets consisted of tape drives and their associated controllers that are plug-compatible with IBM "general purpose" computer systems; disk drives and their associated controllers that are plug-compatible with IBM "general purpose" computer systems; and memory devices that are plug-compatible with IBM "general purpose" computer systems.[3.3] These claims were not withdrawn after the *Telex* verdict was overturned.[27]

All these "markets" were restricted to the United States.[28]

The IBM Computer Systems Included

Although its market definition varied from document to document and even from witness to witness, the government generally included in its "general purpose market" the preponderance of the IBM processors introduced from the late 1950s on. These included, as of 1977, the 305, 650, 702, and 705; the 1401, 1410, 1440, 1460, 7010, 7040, 7070 series, 7080, and 7090 series; all of System/360, except the Models 44, 67, 90 series, and 195; all of System/370; and the System/3 Models 6 and 10. Systems announced later, such as the 3000 series and 4300 series, doubtlessly would also have been included. In addition, the market presumably included all the IBM computer products and services (except terminals) that were available as part of any of the systems that included these CPUs. However, the only products and services included were those actually installed as a part of such systems. Thus, in principle, all peripherals used on systems with excluded CPUs, such as the 360/44 or 360/67, were outside the market while the identical peripherals were in the market when attached, for example, to the 360/50. (This did not, however, prevent the counting of those excluded peripherals in IBM's market share.)[29]

Analyzing the Government's Market Claims

The government's position on market definition, as it ultimately evolved, was based on testimony by its industry expert, Frederic Withington, who testified in the summer of 1977 as to a "rigorous definition" of "general purpose." According to that definition, a "general purpose" computer system must offer "multimodal operation"; that is, it must operate efficiently in transaction processing, batch processing, and time-sharing modes apparently simultaneously while utilizing an integrated data base through a functional data base management system. As described later, the government's chief economic witness, Alan K.

3.3. Additional submarkets for plug-compatible printers and terminals were also alleged to exist, but these claims were never pursued (Plaintiff's Pretrial Brief, p. 88).

McAdams,[3.4] who testified in the fall of 1977, took that definition, added some requirements of his own on how such systems had to be offered, and came up with a "market" that included only Burroughs, Honeywell, and Univac in addition to IBM.

A market definition based on such considerations is not based on the analytic principles set forth earlier and does not reflect the realities of the computer industry.[3.5] A clear picture of the inapplicability of this and all the other government market contentions to the crucial question of the constraints on IBM can be obtained by considering later testimony by Withington himself directed to that question. Returning to the stand in 1980, Withington was asked to "put himself in the position of IBM and identify the primary competitive concerns he would have in establishing the price" for IBM's new 4300 systems announced in early 1979. Such "concerns" are what market definition is all about.

From my knowledge of what products were being offered at the time, and what their degrees of compatibility were with IBM products, embracing an IBM machine, I would surely have considered first and foremost the plug compatible product offerings already being offered to customers in that price range. I would also perhaps next in order of importance have considered the products with the greatest price/performance in that price range which would represent the larger models of the small system vendors, such as, for example, Digital Equipment's largest PDP-11, the Model VAX, or some other machines from Hewlett-Packard or Data General. Since they represented the best price/performance in the price class although not general purpose in nature, though some of them were, as I testified before.

. . . .

. . . Having accounted first for the plug compatible competition which I would certainly regard as most severe, I would then probably look next at the leading edge product of the time in terms of price/performance. These leading edge products of the time were the largest and latest models of small systems offered by the major vendors of small systems, some of those products being of general purpose capability.

3.4. The government called four economists to testify at the trial. The testimony of three of them, Alan K. McAdams, Lee E. Preston, and Leonard W. Weiss, is discussed in detail throughout the book. The fourth, Frederick M. Scherer, testified early in the trial on general principles of economic analysis and industrial organization and did not return to testify about the application of those principles to the computer industry. The government also listed Hendrik S. Houthakker as a witness. He gave a deposition but withdrew before appearing at the trial.

3.5. Withington first formulated his "rigorous definition" during his deposition in *U.S. v. IBM* in May 1977, about one month before he testified at the trial (Withington, Tr. 58168–70 and 58175–80). He did not use this definition in his publications.

I would also then consider comparable models of independent vendors, meaning those offering full lines of general purpose products, I mean companies such as Burroughs, Honeywell and Univac. And I suppose I would also look at potential foreign competitors not now offering machines in the United States. All of those would be actual or potential forces serving to make up my mind as to what I felt the price level should be for these new products.

. . . .

Q . . . Would you also have considered plug compatible manufacturers of disk drives or tape drives?

A All that I have said so far applies to the central processing units, the 4300 series themselves. Insofar as I was planning to offer new peripheral equipment with the central processors at the same time, I would consider competitors in the peripheral equipment business. These would include, first and foremost, those offering plug compatible models and beyond that I suppose I should generalize and say the state of the price/performance level of the manufacturers of these kinds of peripheral equipment offering them on an OEM [original equipment manufacturer] basis to my system competitors.

Q How about the tape drives and disk drives manufactured by Univac, for example?

A Yes, I would consider those. I attempted to generalize my answer slightly by saying I would identify the OEM state of the art in price/performance as that which I must meet because Univac probably does not do any better than that. Nevertheless, I would undoubtedly look over all of the significant competitive models before deciding on a final price.

Q You mean by OEM in that answer both the people who manufacture disk drives and tape drives, for example, and market them to systems vendors as well as the systems vendors themselves who manufacture their own tape drives and disk drives, for example; is that correct?

A I did not include them, that is, the vendors of alternative general purpose systems who also manufacture and market their own peripheral equipment. I should have said so. I would certainly include them as well.[30]

This testimony should be held firmly in mind while we analyze the government's specific contentions.

The Exclusion of Parts of Systems

In defining the market as one for computer systems, the government excluded computer products and services marketed by suppliers not offering complete systems. In particular, it excluded the products of the plug-compatible manufacturers (PCMs), whom Withington would have considered "first and foremost" had he been setting IBM's prices.

PCM products were excluded whether those products were marketed as part of an original computer system installation, as replacements for boxes in existing systems, or as add-on boxes to existing systems.[3.6]

Such an exclusion ignores a basic fact about competition and pricing. As we have seen, the IBM "system" price is simply the sum of the prices of the IBM products in the user's configuration. Thus, prices of systems can be raised only by raising the prices of at least some of the boxes in them. In considering the consequences of such a rise, IBM can ignore neither the competition from suppliers of plug-compatible boxes nor that from the manufacturers of complete systems. Yet the fundamental question is that of the constraints on price.

Such constraints played no role in the government's market definition analysis. McAdams acknowledged that the products of a number of plug-compatible peripheral suppliers, including CalComp, CDC, Electronic Memories and Magnetics, Lockheed, Memorex, and STC, compete directly with IBM products both when the IBM products are marketed as parts of "general purpose computer systems" and when they are marketed as "add-on" products to such systems. Nevertheless, he excluded those suppliers from the market.[31]

That exclusion stemmed not from considerations of demand and supply substitutability but from a supposedly clear distinction between the original systems placement and the plug-compatible box acquisition. As we have seen, that is not the way the market works. Plug-compatible products are often acquired with a "system," for example, when a leasing company markets an IBM CPU with plug-compatible peripherals or when a user selects a system by configuring boxes from various sources. Users are able and willing to configure their own systems from the alternative boxes available. Withington testified that by 1970, "many acquisitions decisions were already being made in a modular fashion. They are much more so today."

Q Is it true that users today are more likely to make their decisions to acquire individual modular processors, peripherals, communications devices, printers, document readers, and other types of devices normally associated with the general purpose computer system in a modular fashion as opposed to changing entire computer systems at one time?

A Most users typically do so, though as I testified before there are examples of entire system changes occasionally.[32]

3.6. The government also totally excluded terminals regardless of who manufactured them. That exclusion raises issues related to but slightly different from those considered in this section and is discussed in the appendix to this chapter.

Thus, many actual transactions in the market cannot be distinguished as being system acquisitions or box acquisitions—"add-ons". Box-by-box replacements may over time result in a complete "system" change with no economic activity occurring in the "systems market". (Indeed, the box-by-box replacements could even result in the replacement of an "IBM computer system" all at once by a computer system consisting totally of non-IBM manufactured boxes from plug-compatible suppliers—none of whom are in the government's market—utilizing only software from IBM.) To further complicate matters, IBM, as well as the other systems manufacturers, often develops and announces new products on a box basis, rather than as a new system, including new CPUs such as various additional models of System/360 and System/370 as well as the 3000 series. Thus, given the spectrum spanned by actual transactions, no line can be drawn separating two distinct types of activity in which users engage.[33]

A similar problem exists if one attempts to justify the government's exclusion of PCMs on the grounds that they are only manufacturers of parts of systems. Almost all of the traditional "systems manufacturers" did not, at least for certain important periods, manufacture all the boxes marketed as part of their systems. Instead, they acquired peripherals and in some cases CPUs from other manufacturers. As of 1980, that was still true of several of the most recent entrants into the computer systems market, such as Tandem. Thus, the definition of a "systems manufacturer" is not clear, and it is not clear how one is to distinguish such cases from those of leasing companies or systems integrators (discussed further below) that combine parts of systems manufactured by others and, in some cases, add software they provide themselves.[34]

Further, there are also numerous manufacturers of IBM-compatible CPUs, such as Amdahl, Magnuson, or Fujitsu. The government excluded them from its market because a CPU is not a system. But what additions must be made to the offerings of CPUs before those suppliers constitute systems manufacturers? Apparently it is not enough also to offer a full line of peripherals. Control Data Corporation (CDC) markets both IBM-compatible CPUs and plug-compatible peripherals but apparently is not a full systems supplier when doing so (as opposed to when it markets non-IBM-compatible systems) because these compatible systems run on IBM software. Yet the CDC-produced IBM-compatible equipment competes directly with the IBM equipment included in the market. Indeed, those offerings provide more direct substitutes for that equipment than does CDC's non-IBM-compatible equipment, which requires a change in software to replace IBM equipment; they also are more direct substitutes than the Univac, Honeywell, and Burroughs equipment included in the market. Similarly, Withington described Fujitsu and Hitachi in 1980 as moving from IBM-compatible toward "general purpose" systems because they had begun to differentiate their systems software. When less direct substitutes are included and more direct ones excluded, the purpose and principles of market definition are being ignored.[3.7, 35]

These difficulties with the government's "market" arise because that concept was indeed arrived at as a *definition* rather than as the *result* of analysis of the demand and supply substitutability relationships that constrain IBM's market power. We can approach this matter directly.

As we have seen, systems manufacturers, including IBM, price on a box basis and compete for box business as an important part of their overall business. In pricing individual boxes, they are constrained by the offerings and prices of those vendors offering similar and sometimes almost identical boxes. Yet the price of a system is the sum of the prices of the parts that make it up, so power over "systems price" is also constrained by the same vendors, and such constraints extend, for IBM, to every part of the system.

Moreover, even if IBM did not face such constraints on every box, constraints on individual boxes (such as the disk drives, tape drives, and memories of the government's "submarkets") would still provide substantial constraints on the system price. It is not true that the different parts of systems are used in fixed proportions so that their relationship is solely one of complementarity. As we saw in the case of different types of storage and virtual memory, different parts of the system substitute for each other, and the configuration of systems is affected by relative prices. Hence, were IBM to attempt to raise its systems price by raising prices on boxes that (under the current hypothesis) did not face plug-compatible competition, it would find customers configuring

---

3.7. Leonard Weiss had some difficulty on cross-examination with the exclusion of combinations of IBM-compatible CPUs and plug-compatible peripherals (Weiss, Tr. 70367–68, 70274–75, 70384–85, 70388–92, 70394–95). Weiss later concluded that since plug-compatible "peripherals are virtually perfect substitutes for those supplied by systems producers, it seems incorrect to exclude them from the market." He would, however, still include the value of the IBM plug-compatible peripherals in IBM's share (Leonard W. Weiss, "The Structure-Conduct-Performance Paradigm and Antitrust," *University of Pennsylvania Law Review*, vol. 127, no. 4, 1979, pp. 1104–1140; reprinted in Oliver E. Williamson, ed., *Antitrust Law and Economics*, (Houston, Texas: Dome, 1980) pp. 260–261, 264).

or reconfiguring their systems to substitute for such boxes, turning to other boxes whose prices had remained constant. The incentives involved would be substantial; by the early 1970s, peripheral equipment accounted for roughly 50-70 percent of the value of the average system. Further, such substitution need not require total reconfiguration; for many customers the addition of more or better peripherals substitutes for the acquisition of a new replacement system, an additional system, or a CPU upgrade. Moreover, in addition to such demand considerations, there is a considerable common element to the technology of different parts of the system, making supply substitutability also a constraint on the behavior in question. Suppliers of boxes whose prices have not been raised can move to offer alternatives to boxes on which monopoly profits are attempted.[36]

From the late 1960s on, IBM was faced with continual competition from plug-compatible manufacturers. Many of its pricing and product activities affecting systems prices and performance were in response to such pressure. To leave such suppliers out of the market is to try to understand a play in which the principal actors never appear and much of the action occurs off-stage.[37]

The Government's Plug-Compatible Submarkets   It would be more precise to say that much of the action in the computer industry takes place off the main stage of the government's market, since, following the initial *Telex* decision, the government defined three "submarkets" in which IBM was said to have monopoly power: submarkets for plug-compatible tape drives (and controllers), plug-compatible disk drives (and controllers), and add-on plug-compatible memory products.

Except as a way of categorizing information, there is no meaning to the term "submarket." We saw earlier that market definition is a way of defining the universe of discourse, of summarizing the constraints that must be analyzed. If that has been done properly, submarkets can play no special role other than as markets in their own right.

There is, moreover, one fundamental logical property that a submarket must possess if the term is to mean anything at all, even for the purpose of organizing information. A submarket must be a subset of a larger market. This property is not possessed by the government's submarkets for IBM plug-compatible products, since, as we have seen, the government *excluded* such plug-compatible products made by IBM's competitors from its systems market but included them in its supposed submarkets. (The IBM products with which such plug-compatible products compete were included in both, however.) Thus, where the analysis already given was concerned with the reasons that PCM products could not be excluded when considering IBM's competition, we must now turn about and examine the reasons that those products are not the *only* ones to be included.

The fact that systems prices are the sums of box prices means that just as box competition constrains systems pricing, so systems competition constrains box pricing; IBM can "control" box prices only if it "controls" systems prices, so that there are not separate "markets" for systems and boxes. There are, however, further reasons for rejecting the suggestion that the competition IBM faces for its tape, disk, and memory products comes *only* from plug-compatible suppliers.

The plug-compatible boxes in question are direct replacements for the IBM boxes. However, the IBM boxes face competition as parts of IBM systems from the boxes of other systems suppliers marketed as parts of their systems. Similarly, all other boxes that are compatible with those competitive systems and can be marketed for or used as parts of those systems compete with IBM boxes in the IBM systems with which those systems compete. Thus, all of these peripheral devices, whether IBM plug-compatible or not, are demand substitutes for the IBM devices and cannot be put into different markets.

Substantial supply substitutability leads to the same conclusion. Many of the manufacturers of IBM plug-compatible peripherals also manufacture peripherals compatible with other systems (usually, but by no means always, sold to the manufacturers of those systems rather than directly to end users). Indeed, with the exception of the interfaces, these are generally the same peripherals. Such firms can readily switch capacity from the manufacture of non-IBM-compatible peripherals to IBM-compatible peripherals. Even when the peripherals differ in various features or designs, the experience and technology involved are similar, the marketing force is in place, and the production of the IBM-compatible devices could be easily expanded at the expense of other devices. Thus, all peripheral devices manufactured by the plug-compatible suppliers would belong in the same market on supply grounds alone.[38]

In addition, Neil Peterman, an engineer who had done such work commercially, performed different peripheral attachments at the request of IBM's counsel, and did so at relatively minor cost, attaching non-IBM-plug-compatible peripherals to IBM CPUs. As this suggests, interface development has not been a significant cost for many of the firms that developed IBM-compatible peripherals. There is even evidence that some users have undertaken interface changes themselves.[39] What matters for supply substitutability, however, is whether a *manufacturer* of non-plug-compatible peripherals could readily produce a new interface (or, if cheaper, modify an old one) if IBM's price or product performance created an incentive for that supplier to offer customers a more attractive offering than IBM's. The history of the market makes it clear that the answer is yes.[40]

In general, the suggestion that there is a market (or a submarket) for IBM plug-compatible peripherals takes an extremely narrow view of substitution. It makes IBM a "monopolist" of each new product that it introduces until plug-compatible suppliers appear for that product.[3.8] The true substitution possibilities are large. Once a system is in place, if IBM raises the price of a particular disk drive, for example, the user can most easily substitute a plug-compatible disk drive. The user with a system installed can also reconfigure that system to substitute CPU capacity for peripherals or, at the extreme, replace the IBM system with that of another manufacturer. Users planning to change systems or acquire a new system are likely to make such substitutions even more readily than a user not planning a major system change.[41]

Moreover, if the price of the IBM disk drives increases or performance improvements lag, other manufacturers will have an incentive to shift their capacity toward increased production of IBM-compatible drives. Interfaces to make noncompatible peripherals compatible with IBM will be readily designed if it is profitable to do so. Only in the *very* short run could user choices be restricted to plug-compatible peripherals. All these substitution possibilities constrain IBM's alleged power over the price and performance of peripherals and must therefore be reflected in a proper definition of the market.

The Exclusion of Particular Computer Systems

Not all (or even most) complete computer systems were included in the government's "market." Instead, systems were excluded based on the applications they performed, their size, or their capability in terms of multimodal operations, as in Withington's "rigorous definition" and further restrictions imposed by McAdams.

3.8. Or perhaps, as McAdams suggested, a monopolist only *if* plug-compatible competition appears (McAdams, Tr. 64599–601).

Exclusions Based on Applications   The government alleged that a variety of computer systems that are recognized in the industry as "general purpose" are not in the market in which IBM's "general purpose" computer systems compete because they are manufactured and marketed "primarily" for certain sets of applications. Such excluded systems include those that the government categorized as "scientific," "military," "process control," "communications processing," "typesetting," "seismography," "data entry," and "special purpose."

Certain facts are common to all these excluded systems. First, they are stored program computer systems recognized in the industry to be "general purpose" computer systems.[3.9] Second, the applications for which the excluded computer systems are supposedly manufactured and marketed are applications for which IBM intended its "general purpose" systems to be used and for which they, in fact, are used. Third, the excluded computers are all capable of efficient performance of applications other than their "intended" or "primary" application; in fact, they are so used.[42]

System/360 was designed and intended by IBM to cover the entire spectrum of uses. As GE's John Weil stated in his contemporaneous evaluation of its April 1964 announcement: ". . . System/360 integrates into a single set of equipment the capability for business data processing, scientific calculation, data communications, and process control. It seems clear that all of these are now but facets of the basic information handling and processing system."[43]

Since IBM intended to market System/360 for all applications, other firms' supposedly more "specialized" computers marketed for particular sets of applications represented a significant part of the competition the System/360 was to confront. Thus, those product offerings constrained IBM's pricing and product planning for the System/360 line. In pricing System/360, IBM had to take into account the existence of competitive equipment supposedly specialized for applications such as scientific or process control, since IBM hoped to offer the users of such equipment a reasonable economic alternative for the performance of such applications. IBM was successful, and many System/360 computer systems were actually used for such applications. When customers with particular needs selected System/360 equipment, they were substituting

3.9. Most witnesses who were asked (including many called by the government) testified that "general purpose" simply described a stored program computer, if it meant anything precise at all. (Mancke Testimony, pp. 126–137).

that equipment for the more specialized equipment that could economically perform the same tasks. When potential customers consider both the more and less generalized equipment for their applications, the fact that some select the less generalized equipment does not mean that such equipment is outside the market including the more generalized equipment.

Substitution need not be between identical products or on a one-for-one basis for products to be included in the same market. Substitution opportunities, when products are heterogeneous and complex, are not restricted to simple replacement of one piece of equipment by a functionally identical piece of equipment. Customers who can meet their data processing needs by using a single, expensive, large computer system may choose, instead, to use two or more smaller, less expensive machines; to use a middle-size one and have the extra work done by a service bureau; or to increase a smaller computer's capacity by adding peripherals and memory.

Customers rarely acquire a computer for a single application. They generally perform a mix of different applications. Thus, even assuming the correctness of the characterization that certain computers are marketed "primarily" for a set of applications, customers can choose between a "general purpose" computer system and a combination of a "scientific computer" and a "small business computer." They can take either their business or their scientific applications or both to a service bureau and satisfy their remaining needs with relatively specialized (excluded) computers. They can use small computers, excluded from the government's market on grounds of size, to off-load work from computers included in that market, thereby gaining more total capacity. Customers using one or more computers that the government excluded from the market may be able to install computers that the government included, replacing the existing equipment and enabling them to automate applications previously done by nonelectronic means or not at all. Finally, customers may simply be able to replace more generalized computers included in the government's market with two or more less generalized computers. All of these substitution possibilities are relevant to market definition and constrain the pricing of the included computers.[44]

The case of "scientific" computers offers a leading example. Despite the previous considerations, McAdams argued that exclusion of "scientific" computers was appropriate because competition between "general purpose" computers, as he defined them, and more specialized "scientific" computers was "one-way" only: "The fact that IBM offers the same hardware, which is effective in the general purpose market and the market for scientific computing, where it is less effective and where it meets more effective systems offered by other manufacturers does not make the systems of those other manufacturers offered in the scientific market effective in the commercial market. It is one-way competition."[45]

In fact, applications cannot be easily divided into the categories "scientific" and "commercial," and most users require a variety of applications. Thus, the real life issue would not normally be whether a user with all "scientific" applications would choose a "general purpose" computer or whether a user with all "commercial" applications would choose a "scientific" computer but whether users with different mixes of applications would consider and choose between "scientific" computers and "general purpose" computers, as defined by the government, as real economic alternatives. The same conditions apply to the other types of distinctions that the government attempted to draw to create its "general purpose market." Thus, the factual predicate for the so-called "one-way" competition does not generally occur. Instead, users select among computer systems to be used alone or in combination to perform various mixes of applications; and all of the computer systems capable of economically performing some or all of the applications, given each user's situation, compete with one another for that range of applications.

For example, the 1971 ADPE (Automatic Data Processing Equipment) Acquisition Plan of the NASA Manned Spacecraft Center recommended that the center's management data processing and scientific and data reduction computing be merged and run on a single UNIVAC 1110, stating, "There no longer exists a clear distinction between management and scientific computer applications nor is there a clear distinction between the techniques, software or hardware employed." Such cases are not exceptional. Withington testified that "somewhere between one-third and one-half" of users of general purpose computer systems have both business and scientific applications and other witnesses stated that there is no clear way to divide scientific and business applications from each other, with a large area being hard to characterize.[46]

Because of the inherent flexibility of modern stored program computers, most computer systems are marketed for, and used for, a variety of different applications (including various "commercial" applications), and no rigid boundaries separate the design or use of those machines. Computer users know this. So do manufacturers, whose product and pricing actions must take the competition from all such computers into account. A definition of a market based on the "primary" application for which a product is intended simply ignores the effect of demand substitutability in other uses on the pricing of any product, especially of computers. If IBM attempted to raise the prices of its peripherals and CPUs, users—including those whose applications are in large part scientific—would substitute away from IBM's equipment toward competitive equipment that would now be more desirable. The extent to which such substitution would involve heavier use of "scientific" computers initially depends on the extent to which IBM computers are now used for scientific applications, since it is the users (and prospective users) of those computers who are most likely to switch.[47]

Let us assume there are users who prefer to use "scientific" computers and assume further that IBM has been less successful in selling or leasing to these users than to others. That preference does not put those computers in a separate market. In any market with heterogeneous products, some users will prefer some products to others. In such markets, all firms generally face downward-sloping demand curves, but differences in customer preferences do not imply that the products are in different markets for purposes of assessing monopoly power. If this were not so, manufacturers succeeding in differentiating their products to any degree, even by their brand names, would become, by definition, monopolies in the markets consisting of their respective products.

To exclude "scientific" or other "specialized" computers from the market simply because the users who selected them have preferred them to IBM's computers is to exclude those particular application areas in which IBM is less successful and where constraints on IBM's power are most visibly effective. To eliminate IBM's losses while counting its wins guarantees a distortion in at least the market share evidence.

In sum, IBM had and has a single set of prices for boxes that make up its computer systems. Not only is there a single set of prices regardless of application, but, since computers can be resold and, indeed, since computers can be bought from IBM and then leased to others, IBM is compelled by the market to charge the same prices to all users. IBM's ability to control price or to withhold technology, therefore, is constrained by the existence of alternative computer systems. If IBM were to raise its prices, it would have to raise prices to all of its customers, whatever their particular applications. Because many of these customers, confronted with higher prices for IBM equipment, could and would choose competitive computers emphasized for particular applications, such competitive computers must be included in the market encompassing IBM equipment.

It is interesting to note in this regard that McAdams conceded that IBM "general purpose" computers, particularly System/370, compete with "scientific" computers and that IBM's prices are constrained by that competition, stating "[T]he identical IBM computer system does compete with the scientific system, but the fact that the scientific system constrains the price of that IBM system is not an indicator to me that the scientific system is in the general purpose market."[48] When the analysis is to determine if monopoly power exists, the fact of constraint is *the* crucial issue for market definition.

Even apart from demand substitutability, supply substitutability between "scientific" and "general purpose" computers implies that they should be considered in the same market. The technology is essentially identical. Manufacturers have in fact moved over the spectrum of users, giving computers broader and broader functions. The mere possibility of "optimizing" systems for one use rather than another by making choices between available designs suggests supply substitutability. The fact that some manufacturers have chosen to emphasize approaches to one sort of user rather than another does not put their computers in a separate market.

There are no sharp distinctions between business and scientific systems; separate design and manufacturing facilities are not required; and it is not necessary that systems be optimized for one type of application or another. There are, instead, a variety of design choices, which have diminished in importance over time, by which a manufacturer can make certain of his system configurations somewhat better suited for certain applications than for others. Most manufacturers seek to achieve a balance so that the range of their systems are capable of performing all applications efficiently and are "optimized" for a particular *mix*, not for one extreme or the other. To the extent that systems tend to be optimized one way or the other, the same manufacturers often offer different systems with different optimized mixes of applications and do so as part of the same product line with the same marketing force and from the same design and manufacturing facilities. In fact, the optimization often consists primarily of differences in software and peripherals.

The testimony of a number of government witnesses—some from firms the government regarded as making specialized computers—supports these propositions. Thus, Scientific Data Systems' Harvey Cohen testified that the Sigma 6, advertised as "our business computer," had a CPU "virtually identical" to that used in the Sigma 7 and differed from the Sigma 7 principally in "configuration details." He also testified that considering only CPU, input/output processors, and main memory (but not the array of peripherals and software available with System/ 360), the Sigma 7 itself could do everything that the 360/50 could do, a claim matched by his company's advertising as SDS expanded into applications for business and industry. Max Palevsky, the founder of SDS, testified that "the distinctions between business and scientific processing became blurred because of changes in the technology" by the period 1966–1968, and "[m]ore and more customers started using a single computer for both types of computation." Control Data's William Norris testified that "[t]he applications of computers have broadened out, so it is much more difficult now to distinguish what you might call a business application and what you might call a scientific application," and that hardware had reached the stage of development where it was quite adequate for most applications. RCA's Arthur Beard testified that the RCA 601 architecture was "equally efficient for massive business data processing and complex scientific computations"; that the RCA 3301 could perform business, scientific, real time and communications applications; and that the Spectra line above the 70/15 and 25 could perform that same list of applications. He acknowledged that technology had made it possible to design product lines to provide "a reasonably well-balanced capability in both data processing type applications and scientific applications." He provided as examples of such product lines System/360 and the RCA Spectra.[49]

Revealingly, Withington, on whose classifications the government largely relied, testified that "[b]asically the equipment does not differ very much from one class to another [general purpose, scientific, small business and special purpose]. The differentiation among these classes is most clearly found in the systems programs which in every case must accompany the equipment before it can usably process the customer's application programs." He stated, "In fact, I depend on systems programs as my primary means of differentiating classes of computer systems."[50]

Thus, firms supplying systems called "scientific" can and do become suppliers of "business" or "general purpose" computer systems. Examples of that transformation include DEC and Hewlett-Packard, which, by 1980, met even Withington's "rigorous" definition of "general purpose."[51]

This supply substitutability means that no distinction can properly be made between such systems for market definition.

Exclusions Based on Size   Many of the same issues are involved in considering segmentation of the market by size. So-called "minicomputers" came originally, at least, with fewer supporting services than did bigger machines. They were used in process control applications, sometimes even being incorporated physically into other machines. To the extent that these smaller computer systems offered fewer functions or less capability, the preceding anaysis of exclusion based on application directly applies. "Minicomputers" are in the market if "minicomputer" manufacturers constrain IBM's price and product performance. This is a question of demand and supply substitutability, not of nomenclature.

Even at the level of nomenclature, however, there is no clear agreement on what a "minicomputer" is or how to draw a line separating it from other computers. For example, Clarence Spangle of Honeywell, which manufactures "minicomputers," described a "minicomputer" as "a small general purpose computer, and small is a relative term, smaller than other computers." And J. Presper Eckert of Sperry Rand testified in 1975 that "I have recently read about a minicomputer that has a memory that is expandable up to a million bytes of memory, which is a fairly expensive machine and a fairly fast machine. My thoughts wouldn't have considered such a machine a minicomputer . . . I personally think of a minicomputer more in terms of how much it costs. A minicomputer in my thinking probably costs $20,000 or less."[52]

In general, a "minicomputer" is considered to be a small computer that sells for a price below some arbitrary line. By that distinction, however, it is clear that many so-called "minicomputer" manufacturers offer machines that far exceed any "minicomputer" price range. The products of Prime Computer, DEC, Data General, and many others cover a wide range of machine sizes and prices. Tandem, for example, makes computers designed to be used in groups of 2 up to 16 processors, which, linked up, can operate as a large system. Moreover, distinctions based on price have been blurred by technological change and the appearance of present-day minicomputers that are more powerful than the large computers of earlier years. Winston Hindle of DEC agreed that "because of the improvement in price performance in the computer business over time . . . computers or computer systems today that would fit within [his] definition of a minicomputer might have the performance of computer systems which ten or fifteen years ago would have cost many hundreds of thousands of dollars." Richard Bloch of General Electric similarly testified that "[t]here is now a distinct move toward utilizing these smaller processors, which are smaller physically, they are smaller dollarwise, but they certainly aren't smaller in terms of power when contrasted to the earlier days." Such earlier computers, made by IBM, were included in almost all versions of the government's market and were *always* included in IBM's share.[53]

There are numerous examples of even the small minicomputers competing with larger machines. This competition takes the form of several minicomputers being substituted for a single large machine and of even more complicated substitutions. Substitution can occur in several ways. Users often have a choice between centralized and distributed or decentralized computing. In a centralized system, there is a large central computer, access to which can be by remote terminals. The terminals can have varying degrees of intelligence, but at one extreme, they have none and all computing is done in the central installation. Alternatively, users may choose to accomplish the same work with a decentralized system in which, instead of dumb terminals, stand-alone computers, perhaps linked to a centralized location, are used at the remote locations. Often such stand-alone computers are minicomputers. The debate about the relative merits of centralization and distribution of the processing function has gone on for some time, and, depending on the needs of users and the available technology, each mode has at times appeared preferable to the other.[54]

Moreover, the substitution choice is not limited to a choice between centralization and decentralization. Users faced with a rise in the price of large computers can substitute away from those computers by off-loading some of their work to a minicomputer and reducing the size of the larger computer. Alternatively, they can add a minicomputer instead of upgrading to a larger size computer or instead of adding peripherals. The minicomputer in such a situation is a substitute for the additional computer power that would otherwise be required.

Differences in size represent a continuum or chain from small computers to large computers. There are no gaps in that chain, no lines that can be drawn so that one can say that the computers on one side are so distinctive from the standpoint of use or ability from the computers on the other side that manufacturers or users on either side of the line could ignore the alternatives on the other side. When temporary gaps have appeared, firms have seized the opportunity to fill the gaps with new products. Thus, no sound line can be drawn to separate one size from another for purposes of market definition.[55]

Minicomputers must be included in the market for reasons of supply substitutability as well, for the same continuum exists on the supply side. Every firm can quite easily offer products somewhat larger and somewhat smaller than its existing products. DEC, Data General, and Hewlett-Packard began by providing minicomputers marketed for a limited number of applications. They went on to provide near "general purpose" capability, even by Withington's "rigorous" definition in 1977, and then to become "general purpose" computer systems manufacturers by that definition in 1980. A similar path has been followed by Prime, Wang, Datapoint, and many others.[56]

Similarly, manufacturers of "general purpose" systems have expanded their product lines to include minicomputers. Honeywell, for example, reported in 1973 that "[o]ur minicomputer orders showed substantial improvement this year. . . . This activity emphasizes our continuing commitment to the minicomputer business as part of our general purpose systems operations."[57]

Hardware technology is no bar to such expansion either way. To the extent that support services and marketing are required for competition with manufacturers of larger systems, the manufacturers of minicomputers can and do develop marketing and maintenance organizations and can, if they choose, subcontract for the performance of such activities. Independent sales organizations exist that perform such functions. Further, many systems integrators exist that purchase computers, add software (and sometimes peripherals), and market them to end users.[58]

Minicomputer manufacturers, however, in some cases also provide fewer services than do other computer manufacturers as a way of profitably serving those users who are willing to accept fewer services for lower prices. Some choose to conserve capital by a sales only policy. McAdams gave these as reasons for excluding such firms from the market. A market, however, can only be segmented by looking at business practices such as service and support pricing or selling rather than leasing if such practices result in sharp differentiation in conditions of demand and supply. They do not do so here. To the extent that the offerings of IBM and other manufacturers did not exactly meet the demands of certain users, an opportunity for and an inducement to entry was created (to be discussed further in sections on bundling and leasing in chapter 6). To define away that entry by placing it in another market by reason of the innovation or differences in offerings that accounted for its success is a grave mistake. To define the market by including only those firms with every product, service, capability, or term of sale of IBM is equally mistaken. The results are predictable; the analyst will arrive at an analytically useless market definition and reach distorted conclusions.[59]

The Simultaneous Multimodal Requirement and McAdams's Additions   The narrowest version of the government's market emerged for the first time during McAdams's testimony in 1977. As we have seen, the government excluded a large number of computer systems from its market because of their failure to meet Withington's "rigorous definition" of "general purpose" by offering "multimodal operation." To meet that definition, systems had to operate efficiently in transaction processing, batch processing, and time-sharing modes apparently simultaneously while utilizing an integrated data base through a functional data base management system. This technical multifunction requirement is at best analytically similar to market definition criteria based on applications and size, and the analysis rejecting those exclusions also compels the rejection of the exclusion based on a multimodal requirement. The multimodal requirement makes even less sense than the business/scientific computer distinction, however. The business/scientific computer distinction might possibly be viewed as an anachronism left over from the 1950s, but at no time in the history of the market, past or present, has the simultaneous multimodal requirement for market definition borne any relationship to economic reality.[60]

The requirement that a system be capable of simultaneous operation in batch, time-sharing, and transaction processing modes to be in the market does not reflect the desires of or substitution possibilities available to users. Customers can and regularly do choose between computers that do not have all of those properties and the relatively few, if any, computers that do. Actual choices made by customers are relevant to an economist's market definition, but an arbitrary delineation of a machine's functions or a machine's design is not.[61]

The excessive narrowness of a market definition based on this "simultaneous multimodal" definition of "general purpose" is revealed by the fact that Withington himself testified that the number of companies supplying systems meeting that technical definition increased from four in the mid-1970s, with three more "approximating" the definition by 1977, to eleven (or possibly fourteen) in 1980, with a large number (sixty or seventy) of well-placed potential entrants.[62]

Nevertheless, McAdams based his market definition on the technical "multimodal" requirement. Indeed, he went even further in the direction of narrowing the market than simply accepting Withington's "rigorous definition" of a "general purpose" computer system.[3.10] He imposed a variety of *additional* requirements that a company must meet to be included in the "general purpose computer systems market." Those requirements included that the product be offered for sale and lease, be "optimized" for commercial applications, be in "new build" as opposed to being supplied out of an existing inventory, and be part of a compatible family, the largest members of which either meet certain capabilities or have such capabilities promised or expected.[63]

These additional "requirements" imposed by McAdams are irrelevant to the proper definition of an economic market and were associated with a misunderstanding (in fact, a definitional exclusion) of an important phenomenon, called by McAdams "niche entry." McAdams testified that "the possibilities of entry [in the 1960s] were more likely for firms which had established a niche, could create a base and an organization and then gradually expand from that base" while success was less likely for firms attempting "a frontal assault" on IBM. Yet, it was the full ramifications of the latter approach—replication of IBM's entire line of offerings—that McAdams turned into the minimum requirements for inclusion in his market. He stated that "[t]he firm had to have the capability to provide the full system, hardware, software, maintenance, and services. . . . There are multiple opportunities to fail when *all* these capabilities *must be* assembled by a *single* organization *all under one roof*, all at one time, and . . . that became magnified by the *need* to have a *family of systems* offered simultaneously, magnified further by the *need* to have a *compatible product line* of follow-on at the time. . . ."[64] On this basis, together with the multimodal requirement, only IBM, Univac, Honeywell, and Burroughs were said to be in the market in 1977.

The purpose of market definition in the *IBM* case should have been to summarize the constraints on IBM in order to assess whether IBM has monopoly power. To accomplish that purpose, one must look at

---

3.10. McAdams's reliance on Withington was selective. He testified, "In general, I tend to rely on Mr. Withington except in those instances where my own investigation suggests that the criteria which he has used are different from the criteria which I have used and, therefore, I would not come to the same judgment" (McAdams, Tr. 63678–79).

what products and services users consider and select as reasonable economic alternatives to satisfy their demands. The question is not which firms are the best copies of IBM.[3.11]

"Niche entry" has a two-fold economic significance. First, as we shall discuss further in chapter 6, it *is* entry and is a substantial competitive constraint that intensifies with expansion. Second, the history of entry demonstrates the existence of supply substitutability among the activities of supplying various systems and parts of systems. Virtually every firm that has entered the business, including IBM, has followed a "niche" strategy as McAdams defined it. Of course, virtually every one of them was defined not to be in the "market" at all.

The irrelevance of imposing all these requirements as a basis for market definition can be seen by considering Withington's testimony on the firms IBM should have taken into account in pricing its 4300 series. The three firms included by McAdams (Univac, Honeywell, and Burroughs) appear only some way down the list, with *excluded* firms rated as most important. Most of the listed firms do not make computer systems fitting Withington's "rigorous definition" of "general purpose" and for that reason would not be in McAdams's "market." Indeed, Withington included Fujitsu and Hitachi as firms meeting his "rigorous definition" only because they had altered their operating systems programs resulting in small differences from IBM. Had they been more exact copies of IBM, he would apparently have excluded them. Obviously, demand substitutability played no role in Withington's categorizations, as it must in any analytically useful market definition.[65]

Neither did supply substitutability. Even in a "market" based on Withington's "rigorous definition," between seven and eleven firms entered from 1977, when Withington and McAdams testified, to 1980, when Withington testified again, and by that time sixty or seventy additional firms were well placed to do so. If one credits such a market definition, one must conclude that entry into that market is extremely easy and that no monopoly power can exist therein. This is, indeed, a correct conclusion. However, such fantastically rapid entry—largely by firms that were already participating in the EDP market—should more properly be regarded as evidence of such substantial supply substitutability that the entering firms *and all like them* should have been con-

---

3.11. Curiously, as we have seen, the government *excluded* those firms that make the best copies of IBM *products* included in its market—the makers of IBM-compatible CPUs and plug-compatible peripherals.

sidered in the market in the first place. This also shows no monopoly power.[66]

The Exclusion of Nonmanufacturers

The government excluded from the market suppliers of complete general purpose computer systems, or the services thereof, that do not manufacture some or all of the systems themselves. Such suppliers include leasing companies, service bureaus, brokers and dealers, and system integrators. All of these entities make computer systems, including IBM computer systems, available to users on a variety of bases ranging from a rental of time on the system (the service bureau or time-sharing company) to purchase from a broker or dealer.

Leasing Companies   Demand substitutability between IBM's products and services and those of leasing companies is very high. In fact, the government referred to leasing companies as "primary competition" to IBM's general purpose computer systems. This demand substitutability is most striking where IBM and leasing companies are offering the very same hardware to end users. The trial record is filled with testimony and examples of customers considering leasing companies as alternatives to the direct acquisition of both IBM and other manufacturers' equipment. Leasing companies advertise their wares as substitutes for IBM-offered equipment and emphasize the replacement of IBM-offered equipment in their marketing. From the late 1960s to date, IBM has regarded the leasing companies as competitors, particularly when the leasing companies were remarketing equipment to second users. Hence, in terms of demand substitutability, leasing companies belong in the market.

Because they do not manufacture equipment, however, the role of leasing companies requires closer examination. We consider two types of situations: first, when the leasing company offers only IBM equipment; second, when the leasing company functions essentially as a systems integrator and markets products and systems consisting at least in part of plug-compatible equipment. Of course, leasing companies also market products from other systems manufacturers.[67]

Leasing companies constrain IBM's pricing in three ways. First, leasing companies arbitrage the spread between purchase prices and lease prices. If IBM raises its lease prices relative to its purchase prices, as it did in 1966, IBM's sales will increase relative to its leases because some customers will find purchase more attractive at the new prices and because leasing companies will purchase IBM equipment at the new, lower purchase price and lease it by undercutting IBM's new, higher lease price. That market force will tend to cause lease prices to fall relative to purchase prices. As a result, IBM cannot materially alter the relationship between its purchase and lease prices in this direction, since competition from the leasing companies will tend to reestablish that relationship at a level consistent with market forces. That constraint, together with the traditional importance of leasing in the EDP market, means that any analysis of IBM's alleged monopoly power in the computer systems market must include leasing companies.[3.12]

Second, leasing companies constrain IBM's selection of terms and conditions and the alternative bases on which it markets its products. For example, if IBM fails to offer leases of a type or length or with terms and conditions that customers demand or at prices that do not reflect their values as perceived by users, then leasing companies (and other suppliers) will take advantage of those weaknesses in IBM's offerings and fill the customer demands. IBM will be compelled to respond with improved offerings in order to compete effectively for that business. For example, IBM's 1971 announcement of its Fixed Term Plan was, in part, a response to the lease terms offered by leasing companies.[68]

Third, leasing companies constrain IBM's pricing of its new computer systems by marketing existing computer systems that they own. Since computers are extremely durable goods that do not wear out physically and since in many cases older computer systems offered at the right prices are competitive with new computer systems offering better performance, the stock of existing computers, especially those in the inventories of leasing companies, brokers, and dealers, constrains IBM and other computer manufacturers in the pricing of new ones.[69]

Consequently, all existing computers must be considered as being in the market until they disappear from use.[3.13] Manufacturers, when setting prices, must consider that one of the alternatives of some of their customers is to continue with their old computers instead of replacing

3.12. The tempting analogy with automobile manufacturers and car rental companies is very misleading. Automobile manufacturers principally sell rather than lease their products. Further, car rental companies provide a convenience service that (in the case of short-term rentals) is not a substitute for car ownership. By contrast, leasing is a major part of the business of computer manufacturers, and leasing companies provide a complete alternative to acquisition from the manufacturer. In addition, computers, unlike cars, do not wear out.
3.13. We consider the problems this creates for market share measurement in the next chapter.

them with new ones. This alternative is enhanced by dealers in used computers. If there were no such dealers, purchasers of new equipment might have to allow old equipment to stay idle or underutilized. First-time users would have to acquire new equipment. Where there is active marketing of existing computers for sale, exchange, or lease, however, a computer manufacturer, especially IBM, pricing its new computers must consider the possibility not only that particular existing computer users will go on using their old equipment, but also that they will acquire additional old equipment as an alternative to the new products being offered by the manufacturer and that potential new users will do likewise. By reducing transaction costs, leasing companies make the stock of used computers a substantial constraint on the price of new ones.

Consequently, new product announcements generally must offer a substantial price/performance advantage over the manufacturer's existing products in order to attract users. Further, older equipment can be enhanced. Thus, leasing companies successfully enhanced System/360 equipment by the addition of plug-compatible peripherals and software, making it competitive for many users with System/370. As long as computers do not wear out, leasing companies with their portfolios of old equipment constrain the prices of new computers.[70]

Leasing companies also constrain IBM's pricing and product performance by marketing plug-compatible equipment. As the government put it, "[t]hey acted as brokers who would assemble parts of systems from several different suppliers, peripherals from PCMs and services from independent service companies. The leasing companies were in effect breaking that large and expensive package into manageable portions to be supplied by different companies."[71] Thus, leasing companies act as suppliers of additional alternative systems for users and provide marketing services that facilitate the entry and growth of firms offering products and services that constitute parts of systems. By marketing "systems" consisting of products and services from more than one manufacturer, leasing companies, brokers and dealers, and systems integrators act as additional systems suppliers to users of new systems configurations and provide a direct vehicle for the marketing of products and services as systems by manufacturers that do not produce entire systems themselves. Thus, these suppliers belong in the computer systems market, both because their products are highly demand substitutable for the IBM computer systems in the market and because they provide a high degree of supply substitutability by their ability to configure readily a wide variety of mixed-vendor computer systems.[72]

Service Bureaus and Time-Sharing Companies   Service bureaus and time-sharing companies, like leasing companies, compete with manufacturers of computers, enabling users to make more efficient use of the existing stock of computer systems. A time-sharing company (or other lessor of computer time) leases time to users. This computer time is a close substitute for the computer time available to users when they lease computers from manufacturers, and it can be leased in smaller and more convenient amounts. Moreover, a service bureau often provides, together with raw computer time, its own services and software. Many users find the use of service bureaus and time-sharing companies a convenient and cost-effective way of utilizing computers. The government admitted that the Atomic Energy Commission (AEC), for example, "attempted to meet its [ADP] automatic data processing requirements by considering all reasonable alternatives with a view toward obtaining the most cost effective solution." Such alternatives included utilization of excess equipment; sharing of existing equipment within the AEC or with other government agencies; purchase or lease; and use of commercial ADP services.[73]

Service bureaus and time-sharing companies advertise their services as alternatives to the acquisition of computers, and they are so employed by users and so regarded by manufacturers. The alternatives offered need not be one-for-one complete substitutes for the acquisition of computers in order to be included in the market on the basis of demand substitutability. Users considering the acquisition of a larger computer system may instead choose to off-load extra work to a service bureau. When they do so, they substitute service bureau time for the acquisition of additional computer capacity. Service bureaus may also substitute for peripherals, since users can contract out to service bureaus those applications that require intensive use of peripherals instead of acquiring additional peripherals that would be used only in those particular applications.

Such substitution is emphasized by service bureaus themselves. A series of radio advertisements in the Boston area advertised the ADP Corporation as the "computing company" to whom one talked instead of the "computer company" and featured a series of (presumably fictional) interviews with customers who had gone to ADP instead of acquiring additional computer capacity or, indeed, any computer at all. The emphasis was on the need for services rather than for equipment. After all, it is the desire for computer services that leads to the decision to acquire a computer.[74]

Several witnesses discussed these substitution possibilities. Thus, Norris of CDC testified that CDC's data services business is an alternative to users for their own computer systems or additional computer system equipment. Large and small companies, as well as the government, use data services and data centers as alternatives to owning or leasing data processing systems. Companies that already have computers use data services or centers instead of acquiring additional EDP systems or equipment. CDC tries to convince users to use their data services instead of taking the computer hardware of other companies such as IBM. CDC also expects that the use of data services as an alternative to owning or leasing commercial business computer systems is going to continue to grow.[75]

Similarly, F. Rigdon Currie of Xerox testified that Xerox Computer Services (XCS), particularly the interactive accounting service, has replaced small business computer systems and that users often view these two options as alternatives. Such services are an effective competitive alternative to a computer system, since users can have their data processing applications done on their own hardware or by a company like XCS. Senior management of data processing equipment users view the use of their own internal hardware and the use of service bureaus as alternative ways of solving their data processing problems.[76]

According to Withington, a service bureau is a complete alternative for a user who has a small number of business data processing applications and a limited requirement for "functionality"; that is, it is an alternative to a small business system. Moreover, according to Withington, a "scientific computer system use[r]" with administrative and accounting needs "has several options." These include a larger general purpose system or a smaller general purpose system plus, possibly, a service bureau. Finally, a user with both business and scientific applications will often perform business data processing applications on a general purpose computer system or a small business computer system and scientific applications at a service bureau. The use of a service bureau can also obviate the need for some immediate adjustment in CPU hardware and postpone acquisition of a larger CPU when computing needs increase.[77]

Computer manufacturers recognize such competition. R. W. Macdonald of Burroughs testified that service bureaus compete "rather extensively" with Burroughs, offering "an alternative means of solving the problem for the medium-sized and smaller customers." Reginald Jones of General Electric testified that "we have always understood that the service bureau, in effect, competes with the manufacturer, because you attempt to sell the customer service rather than have him go out and buy his own machine. We say, 'We'll put a terminal in your place and you can use our system.' " Internal reports in IBM reflected competition for the System/360 Models 25 and 30 coming from time-sharing companies and service bureaus. Service bureaus were also reported as a source of expected competition for System/370.[78]

. The existence of such companies constrains IBM's pricing. They offer services that are demand substitutable with IBM's products and services. Also, like leasing companies, service bureaus allow users to make more efficient use of the existing stock of computers. If users could not lease time and services in small and adjustable amounts, computer manufacturers would have more freedom in their product and pricing actions. Service bureaus, time-sharing companies, and leasing companies must be included in the computer system market if one is to understand how that market operates.

The Government's Reasons for Excluding Nonmanufacturers   The government's economic witnesses Alan McAdams, Lee Preston, and Leonard Weiss advanced essentially two reasons for the exclusion of these competitors despite the evidence of substitutability.[79] The first reason was that those firms are not manufacturers and thus do not add to the amount of computer products produced. Such a statement is at best relevant to the calculation of market share. It says nothing about the constraints just analyzed, which such firms place on manufacturers. Moreover, it ignores the value-added created by leasing companies in the form of software and services.

The second reason for exclusion was the claim that IBM controls the costs of such competitors and, therefore, ultimately their prices because IBM controls the supply of computer systems they utilize or market.[3.14] In fact, service bureaus and leasing companies also market the services or use of non-IBM computer products, over which IBM does not have "control." More important than this is the fact that the useful life of computer systems is relatively long and new products are constantly appearing. Leasing companies and service bureaus can and do continue to compete with IBM's new products and services by using

3.14. A similar reason was the basis for Judge Hand's treatment of secondary aluminum ingot in *Alcoa*. See *U.S.* v. *Aluminum Co. of America*, 148 F. 2d 416 (1945), at 424–426.

products acquired perhaps even ten years or more ago. In a market unlike that for aluminum, characterized by such rapid technological change and product innovation, ten years is a very long time. IBM cannot control the costs of those firms; they have too many different ways of providing their services. Even assuming that IBM might be able to control the costs that such firms incur today in order to be able to compete with IBM some five to ten years from now in the unknown and unpredictable future of this market, that does not materially diminish the competitive impact of those firms today, and it is unlikely to diminish their impact then. IBM charges the same price to all customers. Efforts to alter the costs of these particular competitors in anticipation of some unpredictable situation in the distant future would affect the competitiveness of IBM's offerings to the whole range of its actual and potential current customers.

Indeed, the entire view that when an alleged monopolist can foresee and take account of the reappearance of his products on the market, those products can be excluded (or counted in the alleged monopolist's share) is mistaken. Even when such constraints are foreseen and taken into account, they remain constraints, forcing the alleged monopolist to a lower level of monopoly profits than would otherwise be the case. In some circumstances, as may have been true in *Alcoa*, those constraints may turn out to be weak because secondary products will eventually become unimportant, but this cannot justify excluding such products as a matter of market definition so that the constraints are never evaluated.[80]

In the EDP industry, the ability to take such constraints into account years before they materialize is severely limited. Further, the exclusion of such companies by the government, combined with the exclusion of suppliers of only parts of systems, resulted in a particularly sharp understatement of IBM's competition: parts of systems were excluded because they were not offered by full systems suppliers; yet when those parts were combined and offered as systems (either for lease by a leasing company or for use by a service bureau), they were excluded because they were not offered by the manufacturer.

The Limitation to the United States

The government limited the market that it defined to the United States, excluding the EDP products and services marketed abroad by both U.S. and foreign suppliers. There can be no question that even if the United States constituted a market separate from other geographical areas, any supplier of computer systems or services or parts of computer systems to the United States should be included in the market no matter where that supplier happens to be based. In particular, companies such as ICL (England), Nixdorf (Germany), Philips (the Netherlands), Siemens (Germany), and the Japanese companies that ship computer products into the United States necessarily constrain the pricing behavior of U.S. manufacturers. Further, even foreign EDP suppliers that do not at the moment market in the United States are potential entrants that must be taken into consideration by U.S. manufacturers in their pricing and product decisions. Such firms were all excluded by the government.[81]

Turning to the geographical issue itself, the relevant question to ask to determine whether the United States can be considered a separate market in which to assess IBM's alleged monopoly power is, Do computer products and services marketed abroad constrain IBM's price and product performance in the United States? If so, an analysis of IBM's alleged monopoly power must include those products and services, and a market limited to the United States is too narrow for the analysis.

IBM develops, manufactures, and markets the EDP products included in the government's market on a worldwide basis. The same products are marketed outside the United States and domestically. Many other U.S. EDP companies market their products on a worldwide basis, and foreign sales have been a significant source of revenues to these firms and to IBM. Since IBM markets the same products outside the United States as it does domestically, IBM's pricing and product decisions must take into account the price and performance of products with which the IBM products compete anywhere in the world regardless of whether those products are marketed in the United States. An attempt by IBM to raise its prices or offer poor performance would (among other things) cause it to lose the business of foreign customers both to American firms and to foreign firms competing for that business. This is demand substitutability.[82]

Even if this is ignored and only customers in the United States are considered, foreign firms must be included because of supply substitutability. The important test here is whether one would expect relatively poor price or product performance in the United States to attract competition from abroad. Is there something that shelters suppliers in the United States from competitive pressures from outside? So-called geographical markets are usually determined by transportation costs and tariffs and other government-imposed restrictions. If transportation costs and tariffs are high in relation to the value of the product or there are governmental restrictions on the shipments of products into or out of countries, then suppliers within certain countries may be protected from competition from outside. However, if transportation costs are a small percentage of the value of the product and no governmental regulations impede competition, then opportunities for profits in one country can be expected to result in products being shipped there from other countries.

The latter situation characterizes the U.S. EDP industry. Fujitsu, Hitachi, Mitsubishi, Toshiba, Nippon Electric, Sharp, NPL, and Okidata manufacture EDP products and systems in Japan and ship them to the United States. Siemens and ICL manufacture computer products in Europe and ship them to the United States.[83] U.S. companies such as Honeywell and DEC manufacture computer products in the United States and ship them abroad.[84] And IBM itself manufactures its computer products and their parts all over the world and ships those products worldwide, including shipments from the United States to other countries and vice versa.[85]

With low transportation costs, EDP suppliers can offer their products and services wherever the profit opportunities are greatest. That ability to respond to the profit incentive provides constraints on the pricing and product decisions of particular firms within particular geographical areas. Thus, suppose that IBM lags in the price and product performance of its offerings in the United States. What are the products and services that could be readily offered to supply users' demands in the United States? First, all of the EDP products and services marketed worldwide by the U.S. manufacturers could be readily supplied here. Next, all of the EDP products and services marketed worldwide by the foreign manufacturers that also market in the United States could be readily supplied. Finally, all of the EDP products and services marketed worldwide by foreign manufacturers who do not already market in the United States could be readily supplied in the United States.

Therefore, even if only customers in the United States are considered relevant, the relevant market for assessing IBM's alleged monopoly power in the United States must include the EDP products and services marketed anywhere in the world. Even if EDP firms not currently marketing in the United States are not included in the market, they must be recognized as constraints on the power of IBM because of the substantial potential competition that they represent.

Consequently, consideration of either demand substitutability or supply substitutability or both leads to the same conclusion: the appropriate market is worldwide.[3.15]

Conclusion

Another way of seeing the artificial narrowness of the government's collection of exclusions and proposed "markets" is provided by a listing of "significant wins and losses" as reported to IBM management for the period January 1, 1974, through October 31, 1979. That listing treats as significant all bidding situations reported by IBM sales representatives where the gross point value (dollars of monthly rental)[3.16] involved was judged to be more than $20,000. Such transactions are only a small percentage of the total number of competitive situations reported—less than 5 percent—and IBM's system of field reporting is itself incomplete. Nevertheless, there is some utility in examining these "win/loss" reports at least to see what companies IBM was encountering and competing with in some of its largest potential transactions.[86]

1. One hundred forty different suppliers are shown as competing against IBM's computer product lines in the years 1974-1979. Of those, the only three that McAdams included in the market—Univac, Burroughs, and Honeywell—account for only about 13 percent of the total number of competitive situations with less than 15 percent of the total points at stake.

2. The single competitor that by a wide margin appears most often in these reports, in numbers of wins and losses and in amount of gross points involved, is a company excluded from the government's market: Amdahl, the first manufacturer of IBM-compatible processors. During 1974–1979, IBM encountered Amdahl in about one-third of the reported significant wins and losses that involved 370 processors, a fact all the more remarkable since Amdahl did not ship its first processor until 1975 and did not begin quantity shipment until 1976.[87] Other vendors of plug-compatible processors also began to show up in these reports, including Itel, CDC (with its Omega line), National Semiconductor and Magnuson. These plug-compatible CPU competitors (excluding Itel) won situations worth almost $15,000,000 of monthly rental and ac-

3.15. With the possible exception of Eastern-bloc countries, which involve special restrictions.
3.16. Gross points differ from net points in that no subtraction is made for returns of existing equipment.

counted for more than 40 percent of the value of the listed IBM losses in the years 1976–1979. All these competitors were wholly excluded from the "market" said by the government to be relevant for assessing whether IBM possesses monopoly power.

3. IBM is identified in the reports as bidding peripheral and memory equipment (separately from other systems equipment) in competition with over fifty companies, among them such familiar names as Ampex, CalComp, CDC, DEC, Hewlett-Packard, Memorex, STC, Teletype, and Telex, as well as Burroughs, Honeywell, and Univac.

Of the fifty companies, only the last three were said to be relevant to an assessment of IBM's power—and none of the peripheral products that *any* of these companies separately marketed against IBM's peripherals were in the government's market.

4. As a group, leasing companies appear as competitors in these win/loss reports much more often than any single manufacturer except Amdahl. In all, leasing companies are shown as winning in over 140 situations, worth about $7,500,000 of monthly rental and accounting for more than 20 percent of the value of IBM's listed losses in the years 1976–1979. Well into the 1970s, they appear in these reports bidding System/360 equipment against IBM System/370 and later equipment. They also appear frequently bidding their 370 equipment against IBM-owned 370 equipment as well as against IBM-owned 3030 and 4300 series equipment.[88]

These win/loss reports provide no support for the government's contention that IBM's competitors "in the general purpose systems market were a small, identifiable group of vendors" or that IBM "perceived themselves [sic] to be competing in the market for total computer systems as distinguished from a market for separately marketed systems components."[89]

There is a wealth of evidence—in addition to the fragments reflected in these win/loss reports—about the competition IBM has faced in its computer lines and about the alternatives computer users have available to them now and have had over the past fifteen or more years. If we consider these alternatives and the constraints they impose on IBM in an effort to assess whether IBM possesses or possessed monopoly power, there can be no justification for confining the market relevant for that assessment to one encompassing only a handful of products from three competitors together with IBM's entire System/360 and System/370 lines (with insignificant exceptions).

Let us review briefly the various alternatives in the marketplace from the user's perspective at the end of the 1970s. For the broad range of users, with a variety of applications ranging from routine accounting tasks to sophisticated on-line inventory jobs or advanced modeling applications or any of a host of others, the alternatives available would certainly include one or more IBM System/370 computer systems or one of IBM's new 4300 systems. They could also include an IBM System/38 or System/34, extremely capable and sophisticated systems introduced in the second half of the 1970s but excluded from the government's market.[90]

A user considering such alternatives could also obtain a complete computer system from another systems manufacturer, and many manufacturers offered systems just as capable as IBM's System/370 or 4300 series—not just the three manufacturers ultimately included in the government's market. Such manufacturers included CDC, DEC, NCR, Data General, Hewlett-Packard, Wang, Prime, Tandem, Harris, and Perkin-Elmer, among many others.[91]

In addition, users could also choose to acquire one or more IBM 370 computer systems but elect to acquire only some equipment and services for that system from IBM and acquire the remainder from any of a number of plug-compatible equipment manufacturers (Amdahl, National Semiconductor, STC, Memorex, Telex, Data 100, or others) and from software companies;[92] elect to have some or all of their data processing performed by service bureaus or time-sharing companies, such as ADP, GE, Xerox, or McAuto;[93] acquire some or all of the equipment or services for a system from a systems integrator or leasing company, such as Alanthus, Comdisco, Comserv, or others.[94]

These alternatives are facts of life in the real world market in which users make their choices. No users are compelled to make their selection solely from the multimodal offerings of four manufacturers.

Moreover, the alternatives noted here are only a few of the even larger number of alternatives available to users in the market. As John Jones, the head of data processing at Southern Railway, put it: "The problem is not to find alternatives; the problem is to get the alternatives down to a reasonable number which can be evaluated."[95]

The nature of electronic digital computing technologies has increasingly permitted users to configure their computer systems, acquiring systems and services from a multitude of vendors in attempting to meet their varied data processing needs. There need not be only one "central" processor as there generally was in the early 1950s; there can be networks of processors, with or without a "host" computer or with a host computer much smaller than would be necessary in the absence of the newer, distributed computing capabilities available to users everywhere. Users need not—and do not—depend on a single vendor to supply their storage, input/output, central processor, or other equipment; users routinely choose from a variety of PCM competitors and systems manufacturers. The extensive testimony at the trial from users at Chemical Bank, Union Carbide, Southern Railway, American Airlines, and General Motors Research, as well as other evidence, amply demonstrates many of these alternatives and how they are selected and combined in the real world computer market.[3.17, 96]

In the market for general purpose computer capability, the question users generally ask is not "what computer system manufacturer should I go to?" or "what system should I get?", although certainly those questions are sometimes asked. The question is more often "how shall I implement a particular application?", such as the production control application at Union Carbide's Battery Products Division, the funds transfer application at Chemical Bank, or the waybilling and car inventory tasks at Southern Railway. In seeking solutions to such questions, users have a wide range of choices among system and equipment configurations and among alternative suppliers, including leasing companies and time-sharing services.[97]

If the concept of an economic market of buyers and sellers in the computer industry is to be useful at all in organizing analysis of the alternatives available to users and hence the competitive constraints on IBM, the market so defined must include the alternatives that are available to users generally for their electronic data processing tasks. Those alternatives, and the relevant economic market here, must certainly include: all stored program electronic digital computer systems; all of the parts of computer systems; and computer equipment and services marketed by nonmanufacturing suppliers, including leasing companies, systems integrators, brokers and dealers, service bureaus, and time-sharing suppliers.

We shall call this market for computer products and services the computer systems market, the computer market, or the electronic data processing (or EDP) market. We attach no particular significance to

3.17. The detailed testimony of five witnesses from the companies listed is augmented by the fact that the parties agreed that about 70 "user witnesses . . . would, if called to testify by IBM, testify substantially the same in substance and effect" as those five (Stipulation, dated April 25, 1978).

the name, for semantics do not matter in market definition. What does matter is that major user alternatives and major constraints on IBM's general purpose computer systems are included.

Any definition of the market that excludes the alternatives that the trial record shows exist and are of economic significance will not provide an appropriate vehicle for addressing the question at hand: Does or did IBM have the power to control price and exclude competition? Such alternatives include, in particular, those provided by plug-compatible vendors of processors and peripherals, minicomputers, and leasing companies. The alternatives offered by those products and companies are real world constraints under which IBM had to operate in the pricing and development of its 360 and 370 computer systems and all its general purpose computer products. To exclude such companies and to select from the many alternatives considered by users a "market" consisting of exactly four systems manufacturers is to ignore the purpose of market definition and stack the deck against a reasoned analysis of the question of IBM's power.

Appendix: A Note on Terminals

A related issue to that of the exclusion of vendors of parts of systems is posed by the government's treatment of terminals, which it proposed to exclude altogether whether they were made by systems manufacturers or by others (although some of its market share measurements certainly included IBM-manufactured terminals). It did so ostensibly because industry observers sometimes do not consider terminals to be part of a system, because terminals may communicate with other boxes over telephone lines, and because some of the very numerous companies that supply terminals do not supply complete systems. None of these reasons have much to do with the constraints arising from demand and supply substitutability.[98]

Thus, the correct question to ask in terms of demand substitutability is whether terminals can substitute for other parts of the system. If they can, then terminals constrain IBM's alleged monopoly power over the "systems" defined to exclude terminals. If such substitution possibilities exist, then leaving terminals out of the market is a mistake because to do so leaves out a constraint arising from demand substitutability. Further (even putting aside the direct substitution of terminals for other parts of the system within a given manufacturer's line), if the quality and price of terminals affect the choice between systems, customers can substitute by moving away from systems organized with relatively few or with less attractive terminals toward systems that emphasize the use of terminals or with more attractive terminals. Substitution here involves a reorganization of the way in which the customer's system operates. This type of substitution is as important in its economic effects as substitution by replacement or one-for-one substitution. Such substitution would not be possible if terminals and other system parts always had to be used in fixed proportions, but that is not the case.

Terminals in fact do substitute for other system parts, and the importance of this kind of substitution should not be underestimated. One of the basic choices that customers with several locations face is between various forms of centralized, decentralized, or distributed systems. Users decide on more or less computing power at remote locations, ranging from dumb terminals to intelligent terminals to minicomputers to larger computers, with a corresponding decrease in the size and capability of the central computer installation. As the processing capability of terminals is increased, the load on the central computer is reduced. The equipment to process that work load is also reduced. Terminals substitute for central processing units, and systems in which terminals are of greater significance (that is, value) substitute for systems in which terminals are of less significance.

Terminals are thus necessarily included in the computer systems market. Indeed, terminals and other communications devices are integral parts of computer systems that involve communications capability, as an increasingly large number do today. Terminals perform input and output functions that can otherwise be performed by peripheral devices included in the government's market, such as card readers, card punches, line printers, communications controllers, and processors. Finally, with the evolving structure and organization of computer systems, some computer systems are used as terminals, and terminals have the capabilities to perform increasing amounts of the functions of computer systems. Intelligent terminals, for example, are used to off-load and distribute the processing functions from the central site with the result that the line between terminals and computer systems has become increasingly blurred.

Chapter 4

Market Share

Monopoly power is present when a firm is sufficiently insulated from competitive pressures to be able to raise its prices or slow down the introduction of new technology (either in product or in process innovations) without concern for its competitors' actions because its rivals cannot offer customers reasonable alternatives. It is the ability of a firm to raise prices or market inferior products while excluding competition that constitutes monopoly power. Monopoly power is not present when a firm can keep its business only by means of lower prices or better products than its competitors'—by "superior skill, foresight, and industry." This is the case no matter how large a share of some appropriately defined market the firm may have. In a market properly defined to include all significant constraints on the alleged monopolist, a low market share signals the absence of monopoly power, since the firm's competitors, taken together, are likely to take its business away if the firm attempts to exploit its customers.

The converse is not true, however, for market share can be high for more than one reason. One such reason, of course, is monopoly power. However, a firm may have a large market share by reason of being there first. It may have a large market share by reason of being better. It may have a large market share by reason of being more efficient and therefore able to provide its goods at cheaper prices than its competitors can. It is easy to lose sight of this, but it is crucially important not to do so.

Thus, a firm's large share does not imply power if firms not in the market can readily enter or if existing firms (whatever their share) can readily expand so that customers will have realistic alternatives if the given firm attempts to raise prices or hold back technology. In such a case a large market share does not imply monopoly power, since the firm with a large market share can only maintain it through better products or lower prices. Although a large market share indicates the *possible* presence of monopoly power, it only signals the need for further investigation into the firm's power to raise prices without losing business.

Use of market share as an indicator of monopoly power depends on having a market properly defined. If products are homogeneous and have no close substitutes, market share is a better indicator of possible monopoly power than if products are differentiated and the boundaries of the market are hard to fix. When market boundaries are fuzzy, an overly narrow market definition overstates the share of the alleged monopoly because it excludes products and firms that substantially constrain the firm's behavior. An overly broad market definition, on the other hand, understates the share of the alleged monopolist because it includes products and firms that do not constrain that behavior. It is particularly hard to take account of supply substitutability in market share measures, since firms that could easily make the product but do not already do so are unlikely to be counted. (This makes an analysis of entry particularly important.)

Even if the market is properly defined and market shares correctly measured, market share is only one element of, and not the key to, the analysis of monopoly power. The crucial question is not what market share *is* but what it would *become* were the firm to attempt to exercise monopoly power. This is the question of the ease with which buyers can turn to other sellers and substitute products and the readiness with which competitors will expand output if it appears that monopoly returns are being gained.

A market share measure can be particularly misleading in a young market with much technological change, such as the EDP market. Market share, a statistic that is at best only a snapshot of a continuous, dynamic process, reflects past success and not the competitive process itself or its future results. When competition takes the form of the explosive introduction of new products and new technology, market share measurements are ephemeral at best. As Edward S. Mason states, "It *is* true that innovation in products and processes is of the essence of competition and that in certain industrial areas where the rate of innovation—and consequently of obsolescence—is rapid, market share is essentially irrelevant to a judgment of market power."[1]

Market Share Measurement

Aside from these conceptual problems, the actual measurement of market share is not a simple task. Apart from the questions of market definition discussed earlier, there are inevitable questions of units, choice of time periods, comparability, and so forth, particularly in a market with differentiated products. These problems are difficult and lead to somewhat arbitrary decisions.

Such problems would arise in any market. They are dwarfed in the case of the EDP market, however, by a much more serious problem of a conceptual nature, caused by the simultaneous existence of a large volume of sales and lease transactions. The way in which such transactions ought to be combined to give a measure of market share is not easily determined. As we shall see, any single measure of market share in this market has conceptual difficulties, and the most appropriate solution is to measure, for each year, both IBM's share in net value of EDP equipment shipped in that year and IBM's ownership share of EDP equipment in use. In the absence of these data, revenue is the next best single measure.

Desirable Properties of Share Measures
A share measure of a market for a durable producer good in which financial transactions take a variety of forms should have the following properties to be at all useful:

recognition of the effect of ownership and control of existing equipment;
recognition of competitive capabilities to produce new equipment;
recognition of differences in buyer commitment;
recognition of the period of measurement; and
reflection of important changes in a firm's power.

Recognition of Ownership and Control   Since computer equipment typically does not wear out physically, a machine that has been sold can and often does reappear on the market. That is, the machine itself can be resold, its time or services can be sold, or it can be leased. A sold machine, therefore, is an actual or potential competitor to IBM's new machines in a way that a machine leased from IBM is not. A market share measure should recognize this competition and should register the actual reappearance of such machines on the market.

Recognition of New Production   The purpose of market share analysis is to provide evidence as to whether a firm's competitors would be able to offer its customers realistic alternatives if the firm attempted to raise prices or hold back technology. One source of such alternatives is the stock of existing machines already in the hands of competitors. Another source of alternatives is the ability of competitors to produce new machines. Ideally a market share measurement should measure production capability directly and indicate whether the combination of machines in the hands of competitors and new machines that competitors could produce is substantial enough to offer customers a significant alternative. In practice, production capability is difficult to measure directly, and current production is generally used as a proxy. When this is done, it is important to evaluate the resulting shares in the light of whether it is relatively easy or relatively hard for firms in the market to increase production.

Recognition of Differences in Buyer Commitment   A proper market share measure should treat machines that are leased for a limited time differently from sold machines; the two are not equivalent. Upon expiration of the term of a lease, the customer has the option of returning a leased machine, which may or may not go out on lease again. A customer leasing on a short-term basis, even on a repeated basis, is always open to competitors as a potential lessee. The renewal of an old lease is an important part of the market and in principle is just as much a competitive transaction as the signing of a new lease. So long as the customer retains the option of not renewing a lease, the manufacturer is subject to a competitive risk that is not present with a sold machine. This potential for additional competitive transactions distinguishes a machine on a limited-term lease from a sold machine.

In addition, differential treatment of sold machines and machines on limited lease is necessary to reflect accurately the quantity of computer services transferred in any transaction. In a real sense a sale actually does transfer the entire body of the machine's future services at the time of the transaction. A lease does not do this; instead it transfers one year's worth of the machine's services when a machine goes out on a one-year lease. A market share measure should account for the greater quantity of services transferred in a sale by differently weighting sold machines and machines on limited lease.

Representativeness of the Measurement Period   Market share should be measured over a sufficiently long period to reflect reliably the position of the market participants. For example, the measured share would be wholly unreliable if the time period measured was so short that the sale of a single computer on a particular day could greatly increase a manufacturer's market share compared with its share over a slightly longer period.

Reflection of Important Changes in Power   Most important of all, and implicit in much of what has already been discussed, is the fundamental notion that a market share measure is not an end in itself. If market share is to be useful at all, it must provide an indicator of the *current* power of the firms measured. Market share measures that reflect historical success but not current success or failure are irrelevant to any analysis of monopoly power.

No matter how it is measured, actual market share is a very poor index of power. Suppose that a company's market share is very high but that a small rise in its price would result in a loss of so much business that its market share would then become very low. That would imply a very limited power to raise prices. We are interested, therefore, not merely in the market share measures themselves but in how they would change if the supposed power were exercised.

In the case of computer equipment, the treatment of machines after they have been sold must reflect this concern. The growing stock of sold machines constrains IBM and causes its power to decline over time. Owners of machines have the option of leasing or reselling the machines, leasing time to others, or selling computer services in competition with IBM. They have the further option of retaining old machines instead of replacing them with a new model. Secondhand sales, third-party leasing, and other sales of computer time or services do not have to materialize in actual transactions to provide constraints on IBM. The "overhang" of potential market transactions and deferrals or replacements are sufficient to provide such constraints. This overhang effect, always present in durable goods markets, is intensified in the EDP market by the activities of leasing companies and service bureaus, which provide a mechanism for marketing and enhancing sold machines (or their services). Because of the constraints they impose on IBM, such companies must be included in the relevant market. It is therefore essential that the trend in market share reflect the growth over time in actual or potential market supply from sold machines. (The fact that such measures as revenue end up counting such machines more than once is beside the point. We seek to measure market power, not to do national income accounting.[4.1])

4.1. Despite this, a quite useful adjunct to a strict revenue measure is "value added," which, although difficult to measure, attempts to compensate for the existence of vertical interfirm relationships. A value added measure in the EDP market tends to undervalue the competitive activities of leasing companies and service bureaus and thus to overstate IBM's share of the market in terms of market power. On a value added basis, the "maximum possible IBM share" was 54 percent in 1967 and 42 percent in 1972 (McKie Testimony, p. 236).

Alternative Single Measures of Market Share

In this section, let us assume that what we mean by a "machine" (or "system") is well defined and that it is clear how to measure IBM's share of sold machines and IBM's share of leased machines. Some of the prominent candidates for single market share measures that combine sales and leases are revenue, net shipments, and installed base.

Revenue   This measure is simply the ratio of the inflow of dollars into IBM from sales and leases to the comparable inflow of dollars for the market as a whole. There are some problems with the use of revenue as a single measure of market share because of its sensitivity to changes in the mix of sales and rentals. For example, if IBM were to move from leasing all its machines (having confidently expected them to be leased throughout their entire life) to selling many machines, a revenue market share measure would produce a big bulge in IBM's market share although there would be no effective change in the selling of computer services except for the timing of the payments. Such a temporary bulge in IBM's revenue share did occur in the years 1967–1968, reflecting sales to leasing companies and other users. That increase in sales over leases did not increase IBM's market share in any reasonable economic sense—indeed, it *decreased* any power IBM may have had by transferring ownership and control to others, including competitors—but it did cause a big increase in revenue within a limited period.

It follows that revenue must be measured over a period long enough to be representative. If, for example, one took a short enough period, revenue would, in effect, largely measure machines sold during that period (assuming cash payment[4.2]) because revenues from leased machines would be relatively small. Over a longer period of time, however, this problem diminishes.

To see this, consider the following example. Two companies, A and B, each ship ten computers a year. Every computer has a sales price of $1,000 and a lease price of $200. Company A only sells computers, and Company B only leases them. For the first four years, a revenue measure will show Company A with a higher market share than Company B. The shares will be equal at year five, however, because while Company A will still be shipping its ten computers worth $1,000 each,

---

4.2. A revenue measure is influenced by the terms of payment, which is undesirable in a market share measure. However, this is an unimportant problem if measurement periods are at all long.

Company B will then be receiving rent not only from the computers currently shipped but from computers shipped over the past four years. If computers literally had a five-year life, revenue from then on would show each company with a 50 percent share. Moreover, it is also true that any effect of a shift in the lease-purchase mix (for example, increased selling by Company B) would vanish after five years.

What happens after five years, however, if machines do not evaporate? A revenue measure will then show the share of Company B gradually increasing relative to that of Company A, at least over a period equal to the average length of time the equipment stays on lease. This change in shares, however, is appropriate because the lease customers of Company B are continually redeciding to take the machine from Company B. In that sense, old customers are not different from new ones. Moreover, old machines on lease from the manufacturer are no different from new shipments. Company B's machines can best be thought of as being marketed every period by Company B to its customers.

What happens in this example to the machines of Company A? When Company A sells its machines, it receives all the revenue it will ever receive from those machines, and they pass entirely out of its control. It has done as well as it would have done had it leased them for five years. If those machines then reappear in later transactions on the market, it will indeed be sensible to count them as still in the market but as producing revenue for their *owner* and not for Company A.

As this suggests, one of the advantages of revenue as a measure is that it treats leases and purchases differently. It is entirely appropriate to count purchased machines differently from leased machines. When manufacturers lease computer systems on a short-term basis, they are not selling as much product as if they were to sell the computer systems. The customers to which they lease them may very well turn them in after a year or so. If it takes approximately N years for the lease revenue to be equivalent to the sales price, then a manufacturer leasing the computer for one year is, in a very real sense, only leasing $1/N$ of a computer. The manufacturer that sells the computer, on the other hand, is selling an entire computer, not a fraction of one, and the share measure should reflect the difference.

A further benefit of a revenue measure is that it deals with current activity. If IBM were to attempt to act noncompetitively, the loss of current business, either by cancellation of revenue-producing leases or by the rejection of new IBM proposals, would appear directly in IBM's revenue. In both cases, the increase in the revenues of IBM's competitors would be approximately reflected in their share.

Net Shipments   Net shipments equal gross shipments minus computer equipment returned during the measurement period. This measure weights a newly sold machine and a newly leased machine equally and thereby takes no account of the greater quantity of computer services transferred with a sold machine than with a leased machine. It treats a sold machine as equivalent to a leased machine that unexpectedly evaporates after one year. It also excludes the renewals of leases for leased machines, which renewals should be considered as market transactions. These transactions are treated in a net shipments measure as simply not in the market.

A net shipments measure treats the shipment of a leased machine as equivalent to that of a purchased one even though far less has been sold in the former case. However, when a machine is returned, a net shipments measure counts that return, subtracting it from gross shipments. The loss of an ongoing lease customer will thus show up in such a measure.[4.3] What will not show up directly is the retention of such a customer. When customers retain their machines on short-term lease from year to year, the companies from which they lease those machines are successfully acquiring their business just as much as if they were shipping machines to them for the first time. Both the customer who is in the first year of the lease of a given machine and the customer who renews that lease for the second year are each acquiring one year's worth of a machine. In both cases they are open to competition (before the decision is made). A net shipments measure only counts new customers and counts them as acquiring as much of their machines as if those had been purchased. The renewing customer is not counted at all. Further, the discontinuing customer is counted as sending back a full machine rather than only the next year's worth.

This measure is not fully adequate for the analysis of market power. Consider the following. Suppose that IBM's competitors were limited in capacity and could only ship a limited number of additional machines per year. Further suppose that IBM attempted to raise prices and exploit its customers. In such a circumstance, IBM might find its share of net

4.3. The fact that such returns do not affect *gross* shipments makes a gross shipments market share measure totally inadequate in an industry where much equipment is leased and returned.

shipments very sharply reduced, even dropping to zero, because of the existing capability of competition. Nevertheless, IBM's net shipments share would fail to reflect the fact that its lease customers continued to renew their leases because competitors could not supply them.

The use of net shipments does not necessarily understate IBM's market power. Suppose that IBM had a large share of net shipments but that other companies had a very high share of renewal lease business. Among the constraints on IBM's pricing would be its consideration of the chances of acquiring that business. By raising its price, it might forego such a chance. That would be a serious consideration even if its share of net shipments remained very high. To put it a little differently, an increase in price might make little difference to IBM's share of net shipments but a great deal of difference to its share of the total lease business. In such circumstances, looking at IBM's share of net shipments would lead one to the conclusion that it had a great deal of power because that share was not much affected by the price increase, whereas in fact it had very little power, having lost a very large amount of business it would otherwise have acquired.

Although the use of net shipments ignores the competitive transactions involved in lease renewal, it recognizes the cancellation of leases by subtracting returned machines. However, it does not account for leasing company or service bureau activity. It is a measure of productive capacity of hardware, however, and as we suggest later, it is a useful measure to look at in combination with an ownership share.

Installed Base   This measure of market share takes the total amount of installed computer equipment measured in rental value or purchase value and computes IBM's share as the percentage of the value of installed machines, both leased and sold, manufactured by IBM. In this measure, all machines are credited forever back to the manufacturer[4.4] (and, in practice, old, obsolete machines are usually valued at or above original prices, a practice that we ignore for the present).

Because this measure takes no account of change in ownership and control, it overlooks the fact that a sold machine is out of the manufacturer's power and constitutes potential or actual competition to the

---

4.4. A proper installed base measure would attribute the value of equipment to its current owner, regardless of whether the owner was the manufacturer. The installed base measures used by the government and reported in the industry press do not count machines in this way, however. We thus discuss installed base measures as if necessarily attributing equipment to its manufacturer. The true measure of "stock" share is discussed later.

manufacturer. The result is that it completely ignores the share of the market controlled by leasing companies and service bureaus. With this measure, an IBM machine that was purchased two years ago by a leasing company and has provided $100,000 of lease revenue to that company, would still be counted in IBM's share of the market. This is a very misleading picture of IBM's market share and power, especially considering the increasingly large proportion of IBM machines that are sold rather than leased.

The installed base measure is also wrong because it takes no account of trends in production capacity and installation. The market share of a manufacturer that has produced 1,000 machines over the past ten years is counted the same as that of a manufacturer that has produced 1,000 machines in the past two years. The current market share and the potential power of the second, however, is much greater than those of the first. For this reason, installed base is a particularly inappropriate measure for a young or growing market into which entry is occurring and the competitive positions of the firms are changing.

Indeed, the touchstone question in using market share as any kind of indicator of monopoly power is whether an attempt to exploit customers would lead to a sharp reduction in market share. By this criterion, an installed base measure is an extremely poor way to measure market share. Suppose that IBM were to sell its entire stock of computers and leave the business. Its share of an installed base measure might remain high for a long time, but IBM would have no power. As James W. McKie remarked, the use of such a measure "is equivalent to saying that because Stonehenge still stands, the Druid construction company is still a factor in the market."[2]

Less dramatically, suppose that IBM were to raise prices and attempt to earn monopoly profits. Only current transactions (including current leases) could be affected. Machines produced by IBM and sold long ago would remain out in the marketplace. Even if IBM lost all its current customers from such a price rise, the installed base measure would fail fully to reflect it because it would continue to count in IBM's share the machines previously sold, grossly understating the effect of the price rise and therefore grossly overstating any power. Indeed, the only effect on an installed base measure in such a case would be the loss of revenue from current customers. A share measure based on current revenue would reflect this directly.

Single Measures: Conclusion

None of the single measures just discussed is perfect for combining information on share of sold machines and share of leased machines. Even the best of such measures (revenue) involves an arbitrary choice of the relative weights to be given to sold and leased machines. These difficulties arise because each is an attempt to compress the relevant information into a single number, *the* market share. It would be preferable to examine two measures of share rather than one, recognizing that both measures must be used together to give an accurate picture.

A straightforward approach is to measure IBM's share of sales in a given year and IBM's share of leases outstanding. If the difficulties that we have been discussing arise primarily from the problem of combining leases and sales, why not keep those two items separate and pay attention to both of them? There are two difficulties in doing this in so simple a form. First, a change in the pattern of transactions from leasing to selling could easily change the two measures in a way that would have little to do with market power. Second, and more important, treating the problem in this way would give no adequate recognition to the place of sold machines in the computer market. Competition from machines owned by leasing companies, service bureaus, and ultimate users would not appear in either measure.

A much more satisfactory way of handling the matter takes account of this problem by looking not at sold machines and leased machines as such but at machines being produced (or shipped) and machines being used, a share of computers and a share of the services of those computers.

IBM's share of machines being produced needs no explanation; it measures IBM's net shipments relative to those of other manufacturers.

IBM's share of computer equipment in use consists of the value of all the computer equipment *owned* by IBM divided by the value of all the computer equipment in use. This is where the competition of machines purchased by others is properly recognized. The greater such competition, the lower will be IBM's share of computer equipment in use. This is a true stock share of the kind often used in durable goods industries.[3] It is very different from the installed base measure discussed earlier. If there is a large stock of computer equipment compared to current production capacity *and* a large share of that base is owned by IBM, then the existence of that base would be important in assessing IBM's power over price. Similarly, if IBM's ownership share is low, then the control it has over price is low. That lack of control is what makes the competition of sold machines so important. That is especially true in the EDP market because leasing companies, service bureaus, and others are actively marketing the equipment or services of the sold equipment in competition with IBM.

Using these two measures together avoids the problems that are inevitable when one attempts to force leases and sales into the procrustean bed of a single measure. To the extent that market share measures are useful at all in the analysis of monopoly power, such a twofold measure will thus be substantially better conceptually than any single one.

It must be emphasized, however, that the twofold measure just described really is a twofold one. Neither part can meaningfully be used without the other. To attempt to do so would be to return to the problems of single measures. Unfortunately, sufficient data to derive a time series of these measures do not exist.[4.5] We must therefore use the best of the single measures, revenue. Fortunately, excellent data on revenue are available as a result of a program of depositions ordered by the court (Census II[4.6]). These data comprise much better primary source material than are generally available in complex markets.

IBM's Revenue Share

No matter how one arranges the data to reflect sensible views of who is in the market, the picture that emerges is the same. IBM's share has declined fairly steadily and was well below 40 percent by the 1970s and probably below 30 percent by the 1980s. The very persistent myth, lasting beyond the trial, that IBM had and retained two-thirds of the market is an installed-base-at-original-prices myth of no relevance.[4]

Figures 4.1 to 4.6 graph IBM's share as calculated from Census II. Taking first IBM's share of all reported EDP revenues (figure 4.1), this declined from 78 percent in 1952 to 51 percent in 1961 to 33 percent in 1972. Moreover, from the beginning of 1969 to the end of 1972 IBM's share went from 47 percent to 33 percent, a decline of 14 per-

4.5. It seems clear, however, that IBM's ownership share and net shipments share of a properly defined market would be too low to warrant an inference of monopoly power (JX 4, p. 38; PX 5208, p. 78; DX 9417).

4.6. "Census I" was taken in 1971 in the private suits, first used by the plaintiff's experts in the *Greyhound* case, offered and received into evidence in the *Telex* and *Memorex* cases, and used by the plaintiff's witnesses in the *Calcomp* case. 1,773 companies responded to Census I, although in less detail than the 624 responding to Census II.

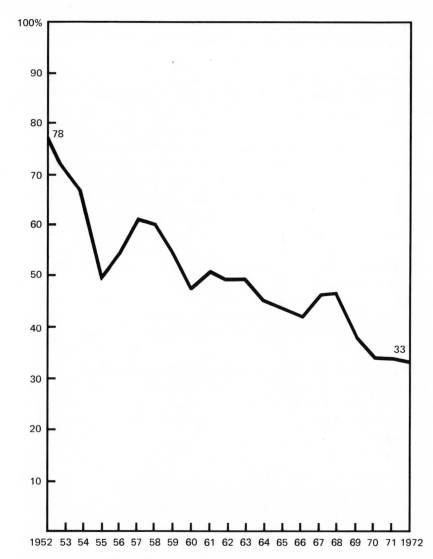

Figure 4.1   IBM's share of all U.S. EDP revenue, as reported in Census II.

centage points in four years. This is inconsistent with the claim that IBM possessed monopoly power.

Further, this sharp decline in share, proceeding generally throughout the entire period, with the exception of bulges corresponding to product cycle deliveries (and in 1967–1968 to increased purchase activity), is not a matter of counting a great many small companies. If one looks only at the 100 companies with highest reported U.S. EDP revenues in 1972 in the Census II depositions (including IBM), IBM's share of revenues from the sale or lease of EDP products and services in the United States follows the same downward trend (figure 4.2): 80 percent in 1952, 53 percent in 1961, and 37 percent in 1972. From the beginning of 1969 to the end of 1972, IBM's share of the EDP revenues of only this group of competitors fell from 50 to 37 percent.

The same picture emerges if we exclude (inappropriately) revenues from separately marketed software and services (such as the revenues of service bureaus) and look only at revenue from the sale or lease of EDP hardware products in the United States. For the same years, IBM's share of such revenues for all reporting companies and for the same 100 companies as before is graphed in figures 4.3 and 4.4, respectively, and is shown in table 4.1 for the years 1952, 1961, 1968, and 1972.[5]

It is possible that these numbers are affected by the fact that some companies (generally not IBM) in the EDP market buy products from other manufacturers and then re-lease or resell them. The revenue from such products probably overstates the economic participation of these firms, since one would often want to count only the value added by the reselling company. However, such effects are not very large at all. For the trial, Raymond J. Dubrowski of Price, Waterhouse prepared estimates that very conservatively eliminated such double counting. (After such a conservative correction is made, IBM's share is overstated.) Excluding the value of products or services acquired from other companies *and also excluding all* EDP revenue generated by leasing companies, service bureaus, time-sharing, facilities management, and maintenance companies, IBM's share of revenues on this "value added" basis is graphed in figures 4.5 and 4.6 and is shown for the years 1952, 1961, 1968, and 1972 in table 4.2.[6]

Such a picture of IBM's share, declining by 1972 to some value between 33 and 45 percent (the higher value corresponding to the most limited version of what is to be included), is generally consistent with what we know from other sources. For example, the sworn depositions on written questions used in the *Telex, Greyhound* and *CDC* cases

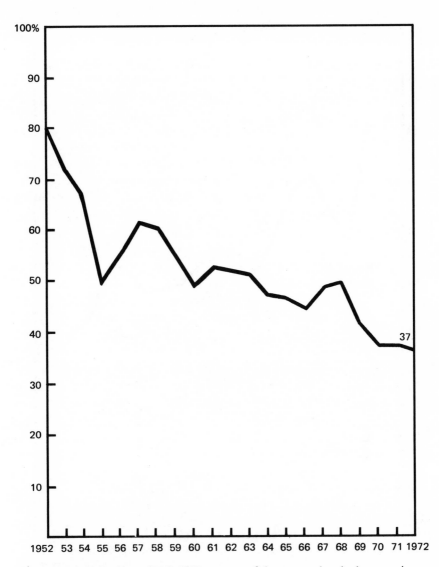

Figure 4.2   IBM's share of U.S. EDP revenue of the top one hundred companies, as reported in Census II.

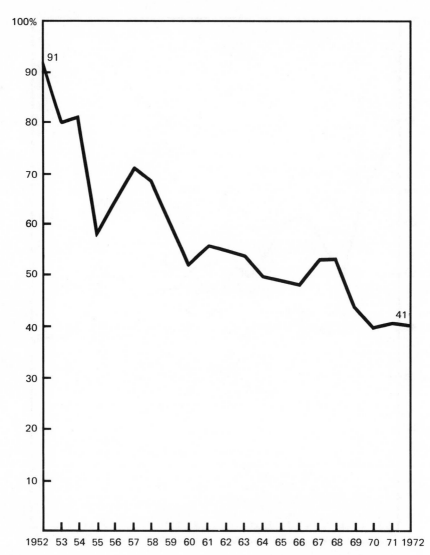

Figure 4.3   IBM's share of all U.S. EDP product revenue, as reported in Census II.

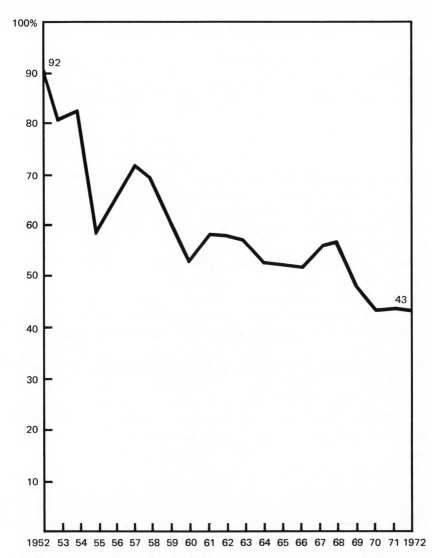

Figure 4.4   IBM's share of U.S. EDP product revenue of the top one hundred companies, as reported in Census II.

Table 4.1

Year	IBM's share (%) of U.S. EDP product revenue (all reporting companies)	IBM's share (%) of U.S. EDP product revenue (top 100 companies)
1952	90.1	92.0
1961	56.4	58.4
1968	54.0	56.9
1972	40.7	43.4

(Census I) show IBM's share of revenue from the sale of EDP products and services in the United States declining from 64.1 percent in 1952 to 35.1 percent in 1970. Calculations on more limited bases yield a roughly similar picture, with IBM's 1970 share lying between 39.6 and 44.9 percent.[7]

Further, there is reason to believe that the decline in IBM's share did not stop in 1972. Since 1976 the industry journal, *Datamation*, has published an annual review of the top 50 (or 100) "U.S. companies in the data processing industry," comparing these firms on the basis of estimates of "data processing revenues." Based on the *Datamation* estimates, IBM's share of U.S. data processing revenues for the "Top 50" companies was 43.6 percent in 1975, 44.3 percent in 1976, 42.6 percent in 1977, and 40.8 percent in 1978.[8] For calendar 1979, IBM's share of the "Top 50" companies' U.S. EDP revenues was 34.4 percent, and its share of U.S. data processing revenues for the "Top 100" companies was 31.3 percent. While such estimates are necessarily less reliable than the Census II estimates and cover far fewer companies, they show essentially the same pattern already observed.[9]

Finally, we may note that the decline in IBM's revenue share does not greatly depend on the inclusion of even as many as 50 companies. The government's industry-expert witness, Frederic Withington, estimated an IBM share that includes the "data processing revenues" of only Univac, Honeywell, Burroughs, DEC, NCR, CDC, and the "plug-compatible mainframe vendors," a small fraction of IBM's U.S.-based competitors in the EDP market. Nonetheless, taking Withington's narrow selection of manufacturers (a selection that includes manufacturers of IBM-compatible CPUs but not manufacturers of plug-compatible peripherals or several systems manufacturers that Withington himself classified as "general purpose"), IBM's share of U.S. data processing revenues "has decreased from 57.2% in 1977 to 54.6% in 1978 to 52% in 1979."[10]

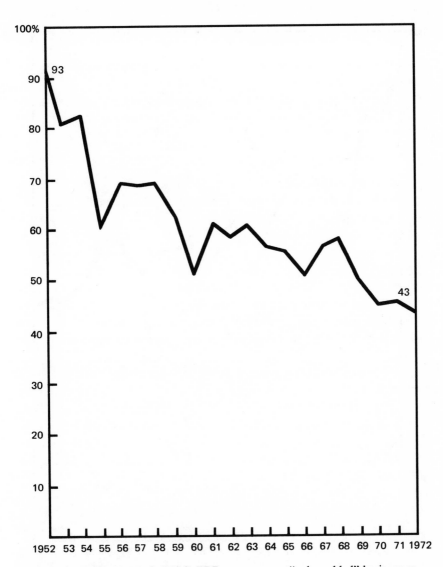

Figure 4.5   IBM's share of all U.S. EDP revenue on a "value-added" basis, as reported in Census II.

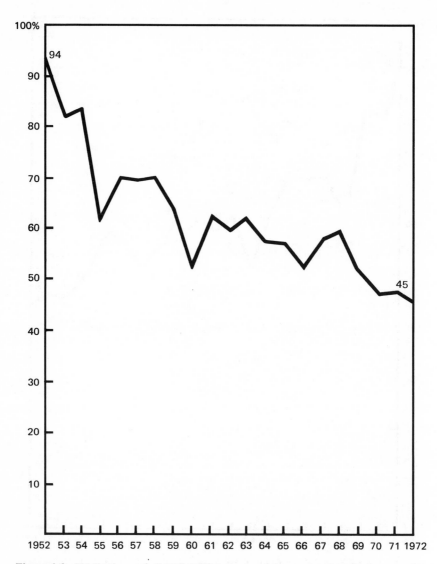

Figure 4.6   IBM's share of all U.S. EDP revenue of the top one hundred companies on a "value-added" basis, as reported in Census II.

Table 4.2

Year	IBM's "value added" share (%) of all reporting companies	IBM's "value added" share (%) of top 100 companies
1952	92.9	94.4
1961	61.4	62.2
1968	58.0	59.3
1972	43.4	45.0

It is apparent that IBM's market share properly calculated (and measured in a number of ways) has been falling steadily over a long period of time and is now down somewhere in the neighborhood of 35 percent or lower. What conclusion can be drawn from this for the question of monopoly power? IBM has the largest in annual revenues of any company in the EDP market, but the record of IBM's share over time and the current level of this share forces one to conclude that monopoly power is not and has not been present.

Since the question one is trying to answer is whether the alleged monopolist would lose substantial business if it tried to raise prices and exploit its customers, the obvious question to ask is whether there are limits on the ability of competitors and entrants to expand. This can be examined by looking at what could possibly hamper them. It can also be examined by going directly to the main questions: Have competitors expanded and has entry occurred? What has or what would happen to market share (properly defined) if IBM were to attempt to raise prices unduly or to offer inferior products?

In fact, competitors can expand and have expanded; in many cases they grew faster than IBM.[11] There are many statements in the record showing that IBM could not retain its business if it tried to offer inferior products or failed to keep its prices competitive. For example, R. B. Curry, vice president of Southern Railway, recognized the competitive pressures on IBM when he wrote to D. W. Brosnan, president and chief executive officer of Southern Railway, on April 17, 1964 (shortly after the announcement of System/360 by IBM), that: "Prices of computers have been coming down while the computer capacities are being increased tremendously. If IBM does not bring out new computers at reduced prices, their competitors take the business."[12]

Withington described the relationship of technology and competition and the pressures this puts on IBM.

Q Mr. Withington, in order to compete effectively in the general purpose computer systems market that you described in your direct examination, must each of the manufacturers of general purpose computer systems keep up with the technology?

A Yes.

Q What happens if any manufacturer of a general purpose computer system, as you presently define that term, fails to keep up with the technology?

A After some period, his products will be unsalable to new customers, and at a later time he will begin to lose his existing ones.

Q And that includes IBM as well as Univac, Burroughs and Honeywell; is that correct?

A It does.[13]

Asked what would happen if IBM "raised its prices," F. Rigdon Currie of Xerox gave the following testimony.

A I believe IBM would lose orders, would lose lease base.

Q And is that because, sir, the selection of computer systems by users is made on price/performance bases?

. . . .

A Yes, on principally price/performance, that's correct.

. . . .

Q IBM by raising the price would have changed the price/performance relationship between its products and those of its competitors in a way adverse to it and that would cause more customers to select IBM's competitors' products rather than IBM, is that your opinion?

. . . .

A Yes, that's my opinion.[14]

Curiously, the government's pretrial briefs demonstrated that IBM had been forced to take competitive action to save its business. To take only one example, the System/360, according to the Antitrust Division, was IBM's response to "competitive inroads that were being made by firms like Honeywell . . . Univac and General Electric," and System/360 "constituted a direct confrontation of IBM's rivals in the systems markets . . . intended as the mechanism to reverse the unfavorable market trend that IBM faced as its markets became increasingly competitive."[15] Indeed, the Antitrust Division viewed IBM's entire history as a series of forced responses to competitive pressures with new products and lower prices and concluded that it saw monopolization.

The conclusion that IBM's share does not imply monopoly power is supported by consideration of the record of IBM's market share over time. IBM's market share has been declining persistently. Further, it has declined during a period in which the price/performance of computers generally, as well as those manufactured and marketed by IBM, has improved to an extent unparalleled in any other market at any time. This strongly indicates that if IBM's price/performance had not improved as fast as it did, IBM would have lost share even faster. The fact that its share has declined and competitors have grown—many of them faster than IBM—shows that monopoly is absent and is consistent with the picture of competition that emerges after a detailed analysis of the other structural, behavioral, and performance factors.

The Government's Analysis of Market Share

The government economists' testimony as to IBM's market share was, of course, not that just given. The differences, however, did not for the most part consist of matters over which reasonable people—let alone trained economists—should differ.

The market share measurements offered by the government were defective as measures of monopoly power or competition for at least four general reasons—aside from issues of data quality. First, they did not measure either the government's "market" or the economically relevant market, the EDP market. Second, they used an installed base measure and counted old machines at original value (at least).[4.7] Third, they credited IBM-manufactured equipment owned by leasing companies and service bureaus to IBM despite the fact that the equipment was used in competition with IBM. Fourth, some of the measures even attributed to IBM the value of competitive plug-compatible peripheral equipment that replaced IBM equipment.

Market Definition
Not surprisingly, the government's market share measures did not reflect the view of market definition taken in chapter 3. For the reasons given, such measures fail to reflect the constraints on IBM. But this is only to be expected. What is surprising is that the government's measures *also* did not relate to the state of competition in its *own* view of the

4.7. It is interesting to note that the complaint discussed IBM's share of shipments and its share of revenues, giving a figure that Census II showed was far too high (Complaint, paragraphs 16–17). By the time of the trial, the government was only interested in installed base measures.

market.[4.8] Thus, for example, the market share figures used by Alan McAdams included all of IBM's System/360 systems in IBM's share despite the fact that McAdams excluded all 360s from his market as of 1971. This is not a small effect. Considering that the only IBM systems delivered in 1971 and included in McAdams's market in 1971 were the 370/145, 370/155 and 370/165, IBM's share of this market in that year might have been quite small. Needless to say, McAdams did *not* include more modern computers made by others with computing power equal or greater to that of the included System/360 machines.[16]

Installed Base

We have already discussed some of the distortions created by the use of an installed base measure, yet this was the measure used by the government's economists. How did they seek to justify its use?

The first claim in this regard was that in a market in which much of the equipment is on lease, an installed base measure directly reflects the fact that customers engaging in lease transactions are making current decisions; therefore, the machines leased by such customers should be counted as part of current share.[17]

It is, of course, quite true that lease customers are part of the current market. Every time a lease is renewed or not cancelled (and this can be as often as once a month), a decision is implicitly taken to continue with the particular vendor involved. This reflects the fact that short-term leasing provides continual opportunities for competitors and for new entrants. But does this make an installed base measure of market share appropriate?

If all computers were leased, then an installed base measure would indeed be appropriate, but only if each computer was valued at its current lease rate, not at original prices. Of course, in that case, an installed-base market share measure would be identical with a revenue measure, for it would measure the value of computer services to users. All computers are not leased, however, and there is a large portion of sold machines.

4.8. We concentrate on share in the alleged "general purpose market." McAdams also presented some installed base calculations for IBM's share of plug-compatible tape and disk drives. The only proper conclusion that can be drawn from those calculations is the natural one that when IBM first introduces a new disk or tape drive, it has a very large share of devices of the new type. That share declines rapidly as others imitate the new device, and IBM's total share of disk or tape drives only remains high through further introduction of better products. See Fisher Testimony, pp. 529–536.

Suppose, on the other hand, that all computers were purchased. In this case it is hard to see why an installed base measure would be appropriate at all. As in every other market, the appropriate measure of market share would be a measure of current output, which in this case would mean a measure of revenue.

Since when all goods are leased an installed base measure is appropriate only because it reflects revenue and when all goods are purchased an installed base measure is inappropriate and a revenue measure appropriate, it is hard to see why a combination of purchase and lease makes an installed base measure rather than a revenue measure appropriate.

As this suggests, the problem with installed base as a measure of market share is its treatment of sold machines, a feature particularly important when old machines do not wear out. Aside from the "Stonehenge" principle involved, which simply makes installed base (at best) react far too slowly to current market conditions, this defect is additionally distorting because leasing companies and service bureaus offer sold IBM equipment in competition with IBM. Installed-base measures treat leasing company machines as being in *IBM's* share forever. That treatment simply does not reflect the competition offered by leasing companies to IBM. It is true that leasing companies are IBM customers when they buy machines. It is also true that they then become IBM competitors when they seek to place machines in competition with IBM. At that point, the machines should be in the leasing company's share and not in IBM's share, for the goal of market share measurement is to assess market power. (The *Alcoa*-related issue of unforeseen constraints was discussed in chapter 3.)

The government witnesses also contended that an installed base measure is appropriate because customers tend to stay with the manufacturers whose machines they have, so that an installed base share shows the share of the market most susceptible to future marketing by a particular manufacturer.[18]

In the first place, to the extent that the statement just made is true (and, as our later discussion of software conversion shows, it is easily overstated), it simply states that installed base share is an appropriate measure because it may tell one something about the future share of revenue. But this itself shows that revenue itself is the primary measure. If revenue figures are available, why use an inferior proxy? If in fact it is true that a high installed base share means a higher share of customers later on, then this will simply show up in a high share of revenue later on. If it is not true, then to count the revenue now by relying on an installed-base measure is obviously wrong. The installed-base measure provides no excuse for not measuring revenue shares directly.

Second, the justification of installed base as a predictor of *future* share leads to severe difficulties concerning the manufacturers of compatible systems or parts of a system. (The government and its economists ignored these difficulties by ignoring such competitors, or, worse, by including their products in IBM's share.) The large number of customers using IBM's operating systems does not imply a great opportunity for IBM alone. It is also an opportunity for IBM-compatible CPU manufacturers such as Amdahl, Magnuson, and National Semiconductor, whose equipment uses the same operating system. Indeed, it is also an opportunity for the manufacturers of plug-compatible peripherals (PCMs). If what the customers want is the IBM operating system, then an installed base measure might say something about future revenues for all sellers offering equipment compatible with an IBM operating system, but this is by no means only IBM; it includes leasing companies, PCMs, and other systems manufacturers that might choose to make themselves compatible with the IBM operating system. The notion that all such machines should be counted as though they were IBM's and therefore somehow contribute to IBM's power is mistaken. Moreover, even if it were true, it would show up in IBM's revenues later on. One should not measure market power by crediting to IBM sales it has not yet made and may never make.

To take an example, Control Data (CDC) offers plug-compatible CPUs and peripherals (that is, plug-compatible systems) that can replace all the products of the IBM system (without apparently ever being in the market as the government and McAdams defined it). To assume that IBM and not CDC or some other plug-compatible manufacturer will always win the business is to obscure the purpose of a market share measurement—to assess what would happen in the market if IBM failed to act competitively.

The use of installed base rather than revenue creates further analytic difficulties. How should older machines be treated? Plainly, an obsolete machine ought not to be valued in the same way that it was when it was new. This is a common problem in economics when one has to find a common valuation or basis of measurement for heterogeneous items. The obvious measure is also the correct one: to value different machines by the prices they can respectively command on the market. A revenue measure does that automatically. An installed base measure *might* do it but would require constant revaluation of the older computers to reflect their falling prices.

Despite this, all but one of the installed base measures used by the government counted older equipment *at full original value.* This would be bad enough in a market with only a limited amount of product evolution, but in the EDP market, it is an analytic disaster. In light of the tremendous technological change which makes small $10,000 machines today the equal of million-dollar machines of ten years ago, it makes no sense to count older machines in a manufacturer's share at all (unless they are on lease from it), much less to count them at full value. Moreover, this is especially true for IBM, which has brought out new products at so fast a rate that more than 80 percent of IBM's Data Processing Division's revenue in 1979 came from products manufactured since 1974.[19]

The single installed base measure used by the government that did revalue old machines made matters even worse. This was a measure produced by Withington, who adjusted the prices of older machines to reflect current "revenue producing value," including the "revenues that a manufacturer may be expected to attain at present and in the future." These revenues consist of "rental payments," "maintenance revenues for all purchased machines," "revenues from expected future sales of add-on peripheral equipment," "revenues that may derive from software applications of systems programs on license by the user," and "perhaps most important of all, . . . the probable replacement value potential of the system installed." For example, in determining the value to be attributed to an obsolete computer such as the 360/30, Withington included in his IBM installed base figures some value attributed to that System/360 Model 30 because of future revenues that IBM may obtain through replacement of the 360/30 computer system in the future by another IBM computer system.[20]

The result of this approach cannot be useful in the economic analysis of monopoly power. At best, if the estimates of the future revenues to be gained from an installed base are correct, such revenues will show up in a revenue measure when they occur. An installed base measure such as this cannot substitute for such a revenue measure by purporting to guess what it will be.

This is not a small matter. As observed earlier, one would expect obsolete systems to be valued at lower and lower prices as better equipment becomes available. The systems values used by Withington, however, can be thought of as being made up of three parts. The first part is the declining actual price of the obsolescent system; the second is the revenue-producing potential described earlier; the third is an adjustment made for additional equipment added on to the system after it was shipped. Yet, although Withington testified that in no event would the average systems value for an obsolete computer system exceed the original list price of that computer system, in fact there were only two cases (the 1401 from 1973 to 1974 and the 7090/94 from 1972 to 1973) in which the systems value as estimated by Withington for an IBM system decreased *at all*. Further, for all 360 products and some other products, the systems value used by Withington for 1976 (the year before his testimony) was substantially above the systems value listed for the first year that the equipment was included. For example, in Withington's estimates, the System 360/30 began in 1967 with a systems value of $380,000 and ended up in 1976 with a systems value of $610,000. The System 360/50 began in 1967 at $1.2 million and ended up in 1976 at $2 million. Yet both of these machines were obsolete by 1976. Withington himself estimated that their market values in January of 1977 were, respectively, 5 percent and 12 percent of the original list purchase prices.[21]

Such measures should never be taken seriously in a great antitrust case as reflective of market power, and the other installed base measures used by the government were not materially better.[4.9]

Another of the justifications given by the government's economists for the use of an installed base measure was that such a measure was appropriate because it could be regarded as a cumulation of net shipments. Since, in most industries, shipments can be taken to reflect a firm's current operations, this would make the use of installed base a measure of those activities that smoothed out short-term fluctuations.[22]

It is true that some installed base measures are sums of all past net shipments. This is not true, however, of an installed base measure that counts other firms' products (plug-compatibles) in the installed base of a particular manufacturer. Further, it is not true of an installed base measure that makes *any* adjustment whatsoever to the prices of equipment once installed, regardless of whether such an adjustment would appropriately reflect the current market value of such equipment. Thus, when installed base measures simply record historical values as of the

---

4.9. In particular, the installed base figures supplied by the International Data Corporation (IDC) are fraught with problems. See Mancke testimony, pp. 890–897, especially the footnotes; for testimony by IDC, see PX 7475: McGovern (Transamerica); and PX 7213: McPherson Dep.

dates of shipments, changes in the installed base from year to year will represent net shipments; when the installed base is revalued, this is not true, however, since the year-to-year change will also include the change in valuation. Such changes in valuation do not reflect any shipment activity whatsoever.

There is a dilemma here. If installed base measures are to count old machines relative to new ones in ways that correctly reflect their relative importance, such measures *must* revalue old machines downward as they become obsolete.[23] In that case, however, such measures cannot be regarded simply as the cumulation of past shipments and, in particular, changes in them do not merely reflect net shipments.

The Inclusion of Plug-Compatible Peripherals in IBM's Share

We discussed earlier the reasons for treating plug-compatible equipment manufactured by independent manufacturers and marketed in competition with IBM as an integral part of the computer systems market. Given this, the natural thing to do is to count independently sold or leased peripherals as one counts any other product in any other market, namely as in the share of the company that sells or leases them. The government and its economists, however, actually suggested that plug-compatible peripherals offered in competition with IBM should be counted in *IBM's* share. Withington's reason for this was ". . . that since these devices are necessarily plug-compatible with IBM systems, they are in some respects part of the IBM base on which future growth can be calculated since IBM is the organization which will evolve the system architecture and system programs concepts which will continue to appeal to those same users, and thus will continue to be a future supplier, perhaps, at some future time getting back the business which it has lost to a plug-compatible successor."[24]

The argument that the measure counts the value of IBM "systems" and that because PCMs attach to IBM's CPUs, their products become a part of an "IBM system" and should be attributed to IBM is a word game ignoring the basic facts of competition. PCM peripherals compete with and replace IBM's peripherals, depriving IBM of revenues and profits on those products. If IBM raised the systems price through an increase in peripherals prices and PCMs replaced IBM's peripherals, under the government's measure IBM's share would not change; it might even go up if PCMs were more successful than IBM had been. Thus, such a measure says nothing at all about market power and distorts what is happening in the market. That is especially true when one considers that the government included PCM peripherals in IBM's systems share despite the fact that PCMs were not even included in the government's definition of the 'systems market and were the *only* competitors of IBM in the government's PCM submarkets. This inconsistency is basic; the same IBM peripherals are in both "markets."

Lee Preston's testimony revealed the definitional nature of the inclusion of PCMs in IBM's share. The questioning started generically asking about the measurement of all peripherals (IBM and non-IBM) "marketed for enhancement of existing systems":

Q ... In terms of taking a systems share of net shipments for the general purpose computer systems market, would you in calculating such a share include the value of tape drives, disk drives, printers, which are marketed for enhancement to existing systems?

A No, I would not include them if I could exclude them given the data available to me.

But then Preston testified that "as a matter of measurement" he would in fact "include the installed peripherals in the installed base value of the system once they are installed." According to Preston, "[o]nce the peripheral is installed as part of an IBM system, then I would include its value in the value of that system, and I would include that as an element of IBM's share of the installed base in the general purpose systems market."[25]

This is an approach to market definition and share measurement that can only reveal the niceties of the categories used by the observer; it can tell nothing about market power.

Another argument that was made to justify the inclusion of PCMs in IBM's share is that plug-compatible peripherals, because they are functioning under the IBM operating system, are particularly susceptible to replacement by IBM equipment. Since the government witnesses intended the installed base measure to indicate such susceptibility, they counted all equipment functioning under IBM operating systems in IBM's share.[26]

Here we encounter head on some of the problems involved in installed base versus revenue as a market share measurement. IBM's installed base share is supposed to measure the advantage that IBM has in replacing equipment functioning under IBM operating systems. Aside from the fact that if IBM is successful in capitalizing on its supposed advantages, this will show up later in IBM's revenues and be measured, it is a strange sort of advantage that also accrues to one's competitors. Indeed, the fact that plug-compatible competitors are able to replace

IBM's equipment says that anyone who wants to be compatible and take advantage of the IBM operating system can do so. (Moreover, those advantages are available to leasing companies as well.) Since peripherals are frequently more than 50 percent of the value of the system, one will be counting a great deal of competitive equipment in IBM's share if one counts PCM peripherals in IBM's market share. Since there can be systems with IBM-compatible CPUs combined with independently manufactured IBM plug-compatible peripherals, there is at least a substantial possibility that IBM may receive no revenue or profit from systems included in its market share and that the supposed advantage of IBM's installed base may be entirely reaped by IBM's competitors. Even without this example and even without IBM-compatible CPUs, this would be true of a very large fraction of a system with PCM peripherals.

The object of market share measurement in the analysis of monopoly power is to give some kind of index of market power. To leave independent peripheral manufacturers out of the systems market is to fail to understand the systems choice (and, for that matter, the peripherals choice). To count their equipment as though it were IBM's is worse; it is totally misleading. If higher IBM systems prices induced users to acquire systems with plug-compatible peripherals, a proper market share measurement should show IBM's loss of business to indicate the constraint on IBM's prices. Attributing the non-IBM peripheral equipment to IBM would of course show no such change.

Withington exposed the absurdity of the inclusion of PCMs in IBM's systems share when he answered "yes" to the following question: "Going back to the question of plug-compatible equipment and plug-compatible central processing units, is it true that the existence of actual plug-compatible competitors for IBM central processing units and peripheral equipment puts a constraint on the pricing of IBM's central processing units and peripheral equipment?"[27] Withington was also asked, "Does the fact that there are manufacturers which manufacture and market plug-compatible peripheral devices and central processing units for replacement of IBM central processing units and peripheral devices mean that IBM is less able to market a product with less price/performance and functionality than its competitors?" He responded, "I think I must say yes . . . the degree of penetration and presence of the plug-compatible manufacturer and the number of them indicates that probably a reaction will occur, if it is within the technical competence of the plug-compatible manufacturer, to an IBM product inferiority, which constrains IBM's freedom to a greater degree than the others."[28] That is obviously right, and it makes no analytic sense to treat that constraint as if it increased IBM's power by including the value of the competitors' equipment in IBM's share.

In sum, the government's and its economists' use of an installed base measure to assess IBM's market power was a distortion of the role of market share in the economic analysis of competition and monopoly. It counted IBM's past successes forever. Older, obsolesent machines were carried in IBM's share at original value (or more), and newer, more capable competitive machines were simply ignored. Plug-compatible competitive equipment that replaced IBM boxes was counted in IBM's share, so that success for an important group of IBM's competitors was attributed to IBM. The *Alcoa*-induced attempt to secure high market share figures ran riot, and serious economics was left behind.

Chapter 5

Innovative Competition: The "Constant Leapfrogging Game"

One of the best indicators of competition is direct evidence of competitive rivalry and reaction. The competitive process can be observed at work through firms driven to maintain current and gain additional business by lowering prices and improving products and by reacting to the price and product improvements initiated by competitors. In a market such as the EDP market, which is characterized by rapid technological change with both product and process (cost-reducing) innovations, the results of the competitive process are better products and decreasing real prices. The competitiveness of the process is demonstrated by evidence that competitors must react to each others' actions and to users' demands and must keep pace with technological change.

In the case of innovative competition, one can describe in some detail the process that is expected to occur if the market is competitive. Consider the competitive interplay initiated by a product innovation. When a new and better product is introduced, customers will be willing to pay more for it (indeed, that is the definition of "better"). It will appear to command a price premium over existing products, but such an appearance is an illusion. Since customers are willing to pay more for it than for existing products, it follows that—properly corrected for the increased quality of the product—price has not gone up. If, at the original prices, customers prefer the new product, then "price/performance" has improved (that is, price, corrected for quality, has gone down).

After the successful new product is introduced, others will imitate it. To induce customers to accept their products, such imitators will have to offer some advantage. Such an inducement can be in the form of lower prices (which the imitators can generally afford, since they will usually experience lower research and development costs than the innovator[1]) or further product improvements or both. Whatever the advantages, on a quality-corrected basis, the imitators will have to offer lower prices than did the original innovator.

With respect to any given product, the initial price differential between imitator and innovator cannot long persist. Customers may at first be unwilling to acquire the product of the imitator because of the increased risks involved in using a product that has not already been field tested, but as the imitators gain experience and reputation, that risk differential will disappear. Provided the products of the imitators are in fact good ones, customers will no longer need as big an inducement as before to try them. As the imitator's products are selected, the innovator will lose business it would otherwise have obtained. Before long, the original firm must reduce prices (or improve its product) or lose increasing amounts of business. Of course, by the time this process works its way out, both the original innovator and the imitators may have been surpassed by still further innovations offering still more product quality per dollar. In a market where innovation is continuing, the process repeats itself.

In short, in such a market, every firm—innovator or imitator—will have to offer a price-per-quality improvement when offering a new product. Every firm will attempt to price below existing products on a quality-corrected basis.

The situation is much the same when process innovation is involved. As technological change reduces costs, the pressure of competition will force firms to pass on such cost reductions to their customers. When technological advance is open to all, no one firm can long refuse to pass on such cost reductions lest it lose business to others that do. Products that appear later, if they offer the same performance as existing ones, can and will be offered at a lower price as new, less costly methods of production are used to make them.

The Pressures of Competition

The trial record is filled with evidence that suppliers in the EDP market feel constantly compelled by competition both to improve their products and to reduce prices—and to react to the improved products and lower prices of competitors. For example, Edwin S. McCollister, director of market development of the international group at Burroughs (and employed at RCA from 1961 to 1971 as vice president of marketing), testified that "competitive conditions in the industry have been such that the manufacturers are always under extreme pressure to get out a new set of equipment and get it into the marketplace and get it installed as quickly as they can."[2]

John J. Hangen, vice president of NCR, testified that "it is necessary to be able to match the products that are available from competitors, and in many cases this [requires] that you have continued development efforts to come up with . . . improved products . . . either from a cost standpoint or a performance standpoint, [that] allow you to compete on a price/performance basis." He agreed that NCR's competitors are "constantly striving to come up with and succeeding in coming up with improved products with improved price/performance" and that "in order to match those competitors it is necessary for NCR to do likewise."[3]

Reginald Jones, chairman of the board and chief executive officer of General Electric since 1972, agreed that "General Electric believe[d] that one of the characteristics of the business computer systems business was that competition constantly forces suppliers to come out with better products at lower prices in order to keep the customers that they had and to get new customers." "[E]very time we went out to sell a computer there were a lot of other people knocking on the customer's door, attempting to sell him a computer." He added, "You had to bring out something that would exceed the price/performance of the existing competition because you knew full well that they were going to be moving ahead of you. It is a constant leap frogging [sic] game."[4]

Winston R. Hindle, vice president and group manager of Digital Equipment Corporation (DEC), wrote that "[t]here is no looking backward in [the EDP] industry as you undoubtedly know. So if one stops to ponder the past and be self-satisfied, the more aggressive competitor will quickly charge past." Hindle agreed that "it is one of the results of competition in the computer business that companies such as Digital Equipment Corp. are constantly forced to come out with new and better products in order to continue to keep the customers they have and in order to get additional customers. I would regard the computer industry as a tough competitive marketplace."[5]

Richard Bloch, formerly of General Electric, testified that "you get to a point in which the price/performance is so improved over equipment of days of yore that it is clear that . . . users are going to move to new equipment, and either you are going to provide that new equipment or your competitors are going to provide it."[6]

These are all statements by officials of IBM's competitors called as government witnesses.[7] The same phenomenon is obvious to customers and industry observers.[8] For example, Joseph Smagorinsky of the National Oceanographic and Atmospheric Administration testified that "[c]ompetition within the industry is as much a spur [to 'exceptional computer developments'] as a development contract. If there is a single manufacturer, then he doesn't have to move any faster than he wishes to move. On the other hand, if he feels he'll be out-marketed by a competitor, then he will try to produce a better product, certainly at a more favorable performance-to-cost ratio at an earlier time."[9]

Donald Hart of General Motors stated that "each manufacturer" faces "very competitive pressures."[10]

Phillip A. Friend of Quantum Science (a consultant to the Department of Justice and originally on its trial witness list) agreed at his deposition that firms in the computer industry "must react to prices and product offerings of other firms." He testified that "[i]n the computer industry competition in price is significant resulting in striving for new products with lower cost components." Further, "[t]here has been a tremendous increase in performance of products." Friend agreed that it is "generally true" that when a manufacturer is confronted with a new product or a lower price, "he is forced to react by introducing a better product or reducing the price of the product presently in the market."[11]

Frederic G. Withington of Arthur D. Little, the government's industry expert witness, wrote in December 1965 that the ability of "[t]he manufacturers to become profitable is strongly affected by the intense competition in the industry. The cost of manufacturing the electronic portions of computer systems has dropped sharply in recent years, but competitive pressures have forced the manufacturers to pass these reductions on to the customer instead of retaining them as increased profits."[12]

Fourteen years later in a report entitled "The World Computer Industry: 1978–83," issued in April 1979, Withington stated that "intense competition" between IBM and the manufacturers of IBM-compatible processors and peripherals will produce "a continuing flow of new products of unprecedented price/performance." He concluded that for the period from 1978 to 1983 "dynamic growth potential is still present in the computer industry" and that "in order to share strongly in such growth . . . the competitors must be increasingly innovative."[13]

It has not escaped notice that IBM is subject to such pressures. As we have seen, immediately after IBM's announcement of System/360, on April 17, 1964, R. B. Curry, vice president of Southern Railway, wrote "Prices of computers have been coming down while the computer capacities are being increased tremendously. If IBM does not bring out new computers at reduced prices, their competitors take the business."[14]

Withington agreed that if "IBM doesn't keep up with the technology and does not introduce equal or better price/performance products [than those] being offered by its general purpose systems competitors . . . and by its plug compatible competitors, . . . IBM will begin to lose its installed base."[15] This is true of all suppliers, even of those producing his narrow definition of "general purpose" systems.

Q What happens if any manufacturer of a general purpose computer system, as you presently define that term, fails to keep up with the technology?

A After some period, his products will be unsalable to new customers, and at a later time he will begin to lose his existing ones.

Q And that includes IBM as well as Univac, Burroughs and Honeywell; is that correct?

A It does.[16]

This view was not merely held outside of IBM. IBM documents show a company recognizing that it must constantly strive for price/performance improvements to meet or beat competition, even when its own new products would have an adverse impact on the sales of its existing products. That theme constantly recurs, perhaps most notably in the planning for System/360 starting in the original SPREAD report of 1961, which predicted the demise of IBM's highly successful new 1400 series and called for the development of the new family.[17]

Thus, IBM Vice President and Group Executive T. V. Learson wrote in July 1963 concerning the General Products Division's reluctance to render obsolete IBM's existing 1401 with the then-planned System/360:

The 101 [announced as the System/360 Model 30] must be engineered and planned to impact solidly the 1401.

I know your reluctance to do this, but corporate policy is that you do it. It is obvious that in 1967 the 1401 will be as dead as a Dodo bird. Let's stop fighting this.[18]

At about the same time, IBM's chairman, T. J. Watson, Jr., wrote, "I think it important to note, however, since we seem to have suffered for a few months or even years because our machines predated the effective competitive machines now in the market place, that we now make these machines good enough so they will not be just equal to competition, for I am sure that once they are announced, our competitors will immediately try to better them. This is all to the good and I am for competition, but I want our new line to last long enough so we do not go in the red."[19]

Writing again in November 1963, Watson stated,

There is a great deal of running about and extra effort being expended in all areas of the IBM Company now because once again we have allowed ourselves to become somewhat non-competitive without recognizing one simple obvious fact. In bringing new machines and devices to the marketplace, our competitors in today's market are simply not going to stand still. We should recognize that in every area, they will take the best we have and immediately start working in a tough, hard-minded fashion to produce something better.

We find ourselves in our present position because we seem to assume our competitors will stand still in certain areas after we announce a superior product. . . .

I believe that whenever we make a new machine announcement, we should set up a future date at which point we can reasonably assume that a competitor's article of greater capability will be announced. We should then target our own development program to produce a better machine on or before that date.[20]

In fact, Watson wrote in October 1965 that IBM's announcement of System/360 was *compelled* by competition. He concluded that "[W]e were so up against the wall saleswise that had we waited another nine months to announce the line we would have lost positions that we could ill afford to lose."[21]

The history of IBM throughout the 1960s and 1970s was one of continued concern with competition and competitive pressure. The competitive constraints and stimuli came from systems manufacturers, plug-compatible peripheral suppliers, leasing companies, service bureaus, "minicomputer" manufacturers, and plug-compatible central processing unit (CPU) manufacturers.[22]

There can, indeed, be more than one interpretation of IBM's concern with competition. Watson's statement that IBM should "target our own development program to produce a better machine on or before" the date by which a competitor announces one surpassing the existing line might be taken as showing evidence of "intent to monopolize." The government did in fact cite his statement as to the pressure to announce System/360 as evidence that the announcement was "premature" and hence somehow predatory.[23] We take up such questions in discussing IBM's alleged anticompetitive actions in chapter 8. Suffice it to say here that a case in which *all* the behavior involved takes the form of a drive to lower prices or improve performance lest business be lost is a very suspicious monopoly case. Conceivably there are circumstances in which a large firm should not be permitted to react to competition;

when such reaction is continual and it is obvious that the firm *cannot* stand still, then it is a mistake to interpret matters as a monopoly, whatever the market share involved. These are not the statements of a monopolist living the "quiet life."

The Competitive Pricing of Computers

The pressures just described have produced a stream of technological improvements that have dramatically reduced the costs of computing as well as greatly expanded the capability and usefulness of computers. While there is no precise way to measure that progress, it is plainly very large on any measure. Here are some simple examples:

Processor speed, as measured by number of multiplications per second, increased by a factor of 1,400 from the IBM 701 announced in 1952 to the IBM 3033 announced in 1977, with the cost per 100,000 multiplications (without adjusting for inflation) falling over the same period from $1.26 to $0.01.

The price of one million bytes of main memory for the IBM 4341, announced in early 1979, was 1/500 of what it was for the IBM 701, and the capacity of main memories has increased enormously.

The storage capacity of magnetic disks, per spindle, increased from 4.4 million bytes in the IBM 350 (RAMAC) disk drive of 1956 to 25.87 million bytes on the IBM 2314 disk drive of 1965, to 100 million bytes on the 3330 of 1970, to 317.5 million bytes on the 3350 of 1975, to 1.26 *billion* bytes on the 3380 of 1980. Data transfer rates for disk drives increased by 136 times from the 350 to the 3350 and by another 2.5 times in the five years from the 3350 to the 3380.

The price of disk storage has also decreased. A dollar of rental bought 6.8 thousand bytes on the 350, 38.2 thousand bytes on the 2314, 145.6 thousand bytes on the 3330, 470.0 thousand bytes on the 3350, and 1.19 *million* bytes on the 3380.

There are many more such examples, which, important as they are, take no account of harder-to-measure qualitities such as reliability, modularity, ease of use, or capability of software, all of which have also improved greatly.[24] It is plain that to continue successfully in the business, firms must keep up with such improvements. Indeed, since such improvements are expected by customers, newer products must offer them if they are to replace older ones successfully in the "constant leapfrogging game."

In this connection, it is illuminating to examine the pricing policies of firms. It was alleged at the trial that IBM has an advantage over the other firms because other firms —to place their products—had to price at a 5–20 percent discount below IBM.[25] Leonard Weiss and Lee Preston, basing their conclusions on hypothetical questions put by the government attorney, testified that this implied a product differentiation advantage for IBM and a barrier to entry.[26]

Such a conclusion is unwarranted for several reasons. At the simplest level, it ignores the fact that IBM was losing market share over most of the period in question (the late 1960s and early 1970s). Thus, accepting the discount testimony at face value, the process of reaction to lower prices that one would expect to see was in fact taking place. Only if one assumes that all competitive markets are always in long-run equilibrium can one believe that the mere fact (assumed) of different prices implies lack of competition. Real competitive processes take time—although, as discussed in chapter 4, the working of the competitive process will be rather obscured if one adopts installed base as the measure of market share.

Second, the testimony as to such discounting was both narrow and rather vague. Prices of different computers are not directly comparable and a correction for quality ("performance") must be undertaken. The witnesses in question, while agreeing that such a correction was required, had not undertaken it save in a very limited way—if, indeed, they spoke precisely at all.

The measures used for such limited corrections were primarily processor speed in instructions per second or the speed of the performance of an application or set of applications per dollar of price. A view of "price/performance" solely in terms of raw hardware speed is very narrow and ignores major aspects of product value of great significance to computer users, such as reliability, the quality of support services and maintenance, the variety and quality of peripherals available, ease of installation and of operation, and software capabilities. Putting hardware comparisons aside for the moment, it is not at all clear that there was any systematic discounting from IBM's price properly considered beyond the general and quite understandable feeling that to win customers from IBM one had to offer a product more attractive than did IBM. One distinct possiblity is that competitors finding IBM with a reputation for reliability and service and with excellent products in dimensions other than pure hardware capability simply found that they had to offer superior hardware capability per dollar in order to compete.

In fact, however, there is another quite simple possibility. In a market characterized by innovative competition, one of the dangers is to take a snapshot of the process frozen at any point in time. To do so is to misunderstand the nature of the market, to treat it as if it were in unchanging long-run equilibrium. Any conclusions that one derives from such a snapshot are likely to be badly misleading.

As discussed earlier, all competitors, including IBM, must, in a technologically competitive world, offer products with price/performance characteristics comparable to or better than those already on the market. *All* new products, if they are to succeed, must be priced in quality-corrected terms below existing ones. The fact that this was true of IBM's competitors when attempting to displace IBM's existing products is not surprising. It would be odd if they did *not* price by reference to the most successful firm in the business.

What distinguishes this situation from that of an IBM price premium (other considerations aside) is whether the same thing was true of IBM itself in introducing new products. If IBM could command such a premium, then it could do so on new products as well as old. If, on the other hand, the pricing testimony simply reflects the necessity to price new products (on a quality-corrected basis) below old ones, then IBM's pricing of new products should exhibit the results of the same necessity.

The Comparison of Price/Performance

With a product as multidimensional and complex as a computer system (or even an individual box), price comparisons are very difficult to make. Yet price by itself means nothing; it is price adjusted for the quality of the product that matters. In practice, full quality adjustment is not possible because of the complexity of the products involved.

A computer system (or product) embodies a number of attributes that the user values to greater or lesser degrees, depending on the user's particular needs. Certain hardware attributes are relatively easy to measure: the time it takes to perform an addition, the number of instructions performed per second (usually expressed in MIPS, million instructions per second), the rate at which data are passed back and forth from CPU to main memory, the capacity of the main memory, the storage capacity of a disk or tape drive, the mean time it takes to gain access to information stored on disk or tape, the rate at which such information can be transferred to or from the CPU or the main memory, the number of lines per second that a printer can print, and many more. Most of these measures are already composites of other measures (the rotational speed of a disk drive, the speed with which circuits operate, the distance that electrical signals must travel, etc.). Further, they are not of interest for their own sake but because they interact to determine the kind of throughput that users can expect to achieve—the amount of work they can perform per hour. Even throughput itself is multidimensional and depends on the mix of problems that the particular computer user has.

Even at the level of such relatively physical measures, the problem of combining them into a quality index to be compared with prices is quite severe. Are MIPS per dollar more or less important than memory capacity per dollar? How should the relative importance of printer lines per minute and disk drive access time be assessed in adjusting prices for quality? While nearly any such measure will show the very sharp improvement in price/performance—the decline in quality-corrected prices—which has dominated the industry, they will all show different rates and different comparisons among machines. Thus, statements about percentage differences in price between IBM and "comparable" products of its competitors can at best be taken as very crude approximations.

The problem becomes even more severe when we leave relatively easy-to-measure hardware characteristics that generally form the bases for performance comparisons.[27] Wider attributes of computers are of great value to users. A computer system provides users not merely with raw throughput but also with a range of functions and ease of use permitting them to solve differing arrays of problems with differing facility and to organize their business around data processing in different ways. To an important extent, these attributes of a computer system pertain to its operating and other software. Given the hardware characteristics, how easy is it to use or manage the hardware and human resources of the customer in productive ways? How much programming effort is required? How easy is it to detect errors or to stack jobs in batch operation or to operate in time-sharing mode? These attributes are all of importance to users, yet not only is it difficult to weigh their importance against each other or against the hardware characteristics, it is difficult to describe these largely software-related characteristics as measurable quantities themselves.

The same difficulty occurs to an even greater degree when we consider some of the less tangible attributes of a computer system. How, for example, should the attributes of modularity be valued? How valuable is the ability to perform scientific- and business-oriented applications with equal facility? How valuable is it that the system being considered is a part of a particular compatible family? These attributes are all hard or impossible to quantify yet are plainly important to many users.

Similarly, a computer system's reliability and serviceability are part of its quality. These can, in part at least, be measured statistically in retrospect. But users acquire systems with some expectation about the degree of risk that the computer systems will break down and some expectation as to what will happen if they do. Those expectations will be based at least in part on customers' past experience with the vendors of the system and on the vendors' reputations. Such intangibles are also involved in customers' assessments of the likely assistance they will get from the vendors in configuring systems that will suit their data processing needs or in altering systems when those needs change. Yet these attributes, while hard to quantify, are also part of the quality of product for which the customer pays and for which prices must be corrected to make sensible comparisons.

Let us put all these considerations aside for the moment and examine the simpler but still very difficult problem of correcting prices solely for the quality of hardware performance—the construction of a price/performance measure. This is still a very complex task. We shall describe how, in principle, it should be systematically done using statistical methods. The results of such a study are to be preferred to impressionistic statements, and the difficulties involved illustrate the greater difficulties involved in any other type of price/performance comparison.

Even restricting attention to measurable hardware characteristics, a computer system is multidimensional. Naturally, if only one characteristic mattered—processor speed, for example (in millions of instructions per second—MIPS)—price/performance calculations would be straightforward. One would calculate the amount of that characteristic per dollar—MIPS/$—and compare machines on that basis. The fact that different machines had differing values of the characteristic in question would not present insurmountable difficulties.

Even in such a case, however, it is possible that one would have to make some choices as to what is to be compared. Suppose that processor speed is the only characteristic. In general, it will not be true that there is a particular IBM machine offering precisely the same processor speed as does a particular Burroughs machine, for example. Rather, the Bur-

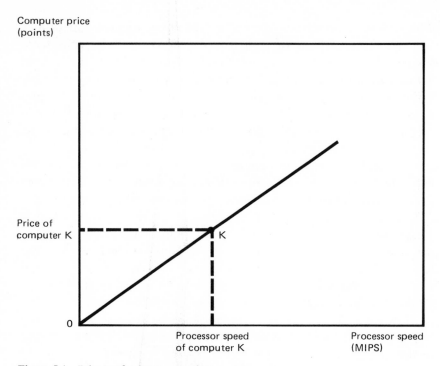

Figure 5.1   Price/performance as a slope.

roughs machine may fall between two IBM machines by that measure.[5.1] The purpose of making a performance correction is to interpolate between the points represented by the IBM machines to construct, in effect, the price IBM would have charged if its machine had the same processor speed as did the Burroughs machine. Naturally, if all IBM machines had the same processor speed per dollar, such interpolation would be trivial.

Some diagrams may help to make clear what is involved. In the following figures, processor speed is measured on the horizontal axis and computer price on the vertical one. A particular point such as point *K* in figure 5.1 represents a combination of processor speed and price. The price per unit of speed ($/MIPS) for the computer represented by

5.1. In more realistic situations, this sort of thing is not only common, it occurs as the deliberate policy choice of manufacturers. Thus, Beard of RCA testified as to RCA's policy of placing the computers of its Spectra line between different computers of the System/360 in terms of performance (Beard, Tr. 10121; see Tr. 10106–07; see record evidence cited in the Historical Narrative, pp. 1331 (NCR), 1332 (Magnuson)).

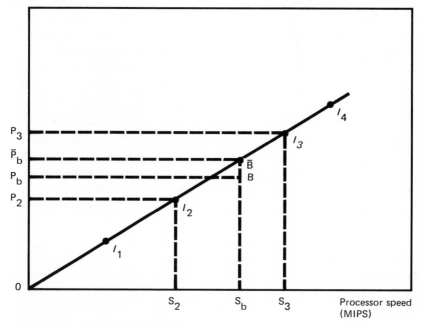

Figure 5.2   Interpolation of price/performance: the simplest case.

point K is the slope of the line connecting K and the origin. The steeper that slope, the more expensive is the computer per MIPS (the lower is the price/performance).

In figure 5.2, it is supposed that all IBM computers have precisely the same price/performance measured in this way, that is, they offer precisely the same relationship between processor speed and price over all available speeds and differ in performance only as to speed. The points corresponding to IBM computers have been labeled I_1, I_2, I_3, and I_4 and, since they represent the same price/performance relationship, all fall on the same straight line through the origin. In the example, a Burroughs machine is also depicted, represented by the point B. It has processor speed S_b, which falls between the processor speeds of two IBM machines I_2 and I_3; these speeds are denoted in the diagram S_2 and S_3, respectively. Similarly, the price of the Burroughs machine, denoted by P_b, falls between the prices of the same two IBM machines P_2 and P_3, respectively.

In this simple case, it is easy to compare the price of the Burroughs machine to those of IBM. Since all the IBM points fall on the same straight line through the origin, it is a reasonable (indeed, the only possible) inference that had IBM offered a machine with the speed of the Burroughs machine S_b, it would have priced it so that the corresponding point fell on the same line as the other IBM points. Such a point is represented by $\bar{B}$. The corresponding price, denoted $\bar{P}_b$, can be read off the diagram. Naturally, in this example, that price is higher than the price of the actual Burroughs machine P_b; this corresponds to the fact that the actual Burroughs machine lies below the IBM line and hence, in this example, offers better price/performance than the IBM machines and costs less than a "comparable" IBM machine would. But, in the example, there is no actual comparable IBM machine; the "comparable" machine is the interpolated construction represented by $\bar{B}$.

The situation is a bit more complicated in figure 5.3. The IBM and Burroughs points are denoted as before. Now, however, although the IBM points all lie along a straight line, that line does not pass through the origin. By examining the slopes of the lines connecting successive IBM points with the origin (dashed lines in figure 5.3), we see that as we move to higher-speed machines—from I_1 to I_4—price/performance rises. The higher-speed machines of the line involve fewer dollars per MIPS than do the lower-speed ones.

In this situation, consider the Burroughs machine represented by the point B. As before, it has speed S_b and price P_b between those of two IBM machines I_2 and I_3. However, unlike the case in figure 5.2, the Burroughs machine does not offer price/performance unambiguously superior to that offered by IBM. While B represents better price/performance than I_1 or I_2, it represents poorer price/performance than I_3 or I_4.

In these circumstances it is not so plain that a meaningful price/performance comparison can be made. Customers considering the choice of machines will be choosing between B and one of the IBM machines. They will make the choice that best suits their needs. Customers choosing I_3 or I_4 will get more performance per dollar than customers choosing B; customers choosing I_1 or I_2 will get less. Not all customers will choose I_4—the machine with the best price/performance—because it is the machine with the highest uncorrected price. Customers that do not need the high-speed performance represented by I_4 may very well choose one of the other machines, even though the price/performance of such

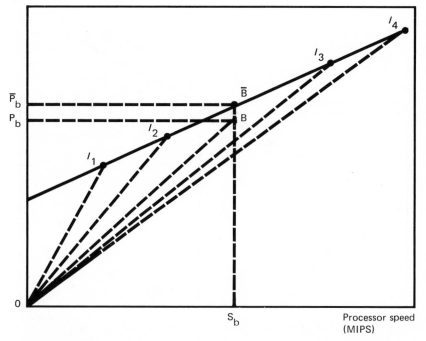

Figure 5.3   Interpolation of price/performance: a more complex case.

machines is lower. Thus, since total cost matters, B may be chosen over I_3 or I_4 at lower price/performance because it represents an opportunity to save money by giving up the performance afforded by I_3 or I_4. Similarly, I_1 or I_2 may be chosen over B even at lower price/performance.

Thus it is not obvious whether B should be considered to offer better or poorer price/performance than does the IBM line. Nevertheless, since all the IBM points fall on a straight line, it is easy to interpolate and ask what price IBM presumably would have charged had it chosen to offer a machine with speed S_b, the speed of the Burroughs machine. The point representing such an interpolated machine is given by $\bar{B}$ and its price by $\bar{P}_b$. Since $\bar{P}_b$ is greater than P_b, reflecting the fact that B lies below the IBM line, we might conclude that IBM would have charged more for a machine of speed S_b than did Burroughs and that Burroughs should be considered as having better price/performance than IBM in this example.

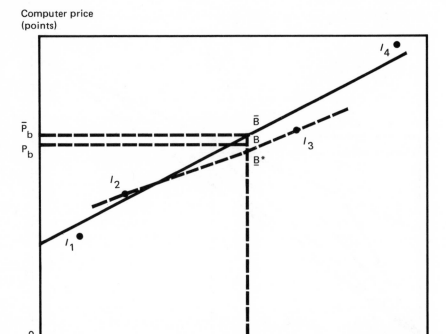

Figure 5.4   Interpolation of price/performance: "closest" points or multiple regression.

So far, all IBM points have fallen exactly on a straight line, and this has made interpolation to find the constructed Burroughs point, $\bar{B}$, both clear and easy. Now, however, suppose that the IBM points, while falling reasonably close to a straight line do not lie exactly on one. (Generalization to a smooth curve is simple.) Such a situation is depicted in figure 5.4. In this case, the IBM points fall close to, but not on, the solid line. Again we must decide whether the Burroughs machine B, with speed S_b and price P_b, offers better or worse price/performance than that offered by IBM. Again this is not a question with an unambiguous answer—B offers better price/performance than does I_1 or I_2 but worse price/performance than does I_3 or I_4. Putting that aside as before, we now face a new problem. If we seek to construct the point, $\bar{B}$, that represents the price IBM would presumably have charged for a machine with speed S_b, how is this to be done?

One possibility would be to interpolate between the points represented by I_2 and I_3. This would result in the point B^* in the diagram and would yield the result (since B^* is below B) that IBM offered better price/performance than did Burroughs. On the other hand, instead of interpolating using the line connecting I_2 and I_3, one might do so using the solid line—the one nearest to which all the IBM points lie. If one does this, one obtains the point $\bar{B}$, which lies *above* B, suggesting the conclusion that IBM offered poorer price/performance than did Burroughs. Obviously, it matters which choice one makes.

Two comments should be made about that choice. First, even with a unidimensional view of performance, one might argue that IBM price/performance ought to be derived from the line that best reflects all the processors rather than the particular relationship between just two— that the line reflects a pattern of the whole family with minor deviations occurring for individual points. One should use all the information in all the data to locate the solid line and estimate $\bar{B}$.

This argument, however, presumes that all such information is relevant. If we had reason to suppose, for example, that the relation between price and speed were totally different for low speeds than for speeds near S_b, one would not use information about low-speed machines. (In the diagram, this is plainly not the case. The low-speed machine I_1 lies quite close to the line through the other observations.) Similarly, information that there were reasons for a particular machine being priced unusually high or low would lead one to use the data for such a machine with caution, if at all. Only when machines can be expected to be similar—drawn from the same family with no special attributes—can one safely combine the data for them.

Second, in the very simple case depicted in figure 5.4, one can identify the two IBM processors (I_2 and I_3) that are "closest" to the Burroughs machine in terms of performance because performance is measured by one variable. In a more realistic case, with more than one attribute of performance, it will not always be clear which two IBM processors are the "closest" to B.

A customer who acquires a computer acquires all of its characteristics. If we are to correct price for quality as seen by the customer, we must somehow combine all these characteristics into a single index, letting each characteristic take on the relative importance it has in the customer's eyes. In the simplest case, in which customers simply add the values they implicitly assign to each characteristic, this is a matter of determining the weight to be assigned to each one; in more complex and realistic cases, in which the value customers feel they receive from a particular characteristic depends on the level of another characteristic (if the importance of disk drive access time depends on CPU speed, for example), the matter is even more difficult.

Obviously, we do not know the values that customers implicitly assign to computer characteristics. The construction of a quality measure from the user's point of view is thus not an easy task, particularly since there is no reason to believe that different users view matters in the same way. Two methods of proceeding are available but unattractive. First, one can simply *assume* the way in which different characteristics are to be combined, but this is arbitrary and begs the question. Second, one can try to combine hardware (and some software) characteristics into a single index of "throughput" by running benchmark tests in which the times taken by different computer systems to perform a given series of tasks are compared. Benchmarking is fairly common in the industry, but suffers from the fact that the mix of jobs used is not necessarily typical for any customer; indeed, different job mixes are used for different customer types and by different testers.[28] In any event, data on benchmark tests are not readily available in a form that would allow performance comparison among enough computer systems to answer the question concerning pricing. This means we must use statistical methods to perform an interpolation. The optimal method— multiple regression—is well-known.[29] By regressing computer price on various performance attributes, we can both use all the information efficiently and also solve the problem of how to combine the attributes into a single index that can then be used to make price/performance comparisons.

It is important to understand the limitations of such a procedure, however. There are two reasons why such a regression should not be interpreted as estimating implicit "prices" for performance characteristics in terms of user valuation, as has been done for other durable goods.[30] The first and more important reason has to do with the nature of the computer industry and with the very hypothesis (that of "leapfrogging") that we are seeking to test. When markets are in long-run equilibrium, regressions of price on attributes can measure the way in which customers value those attributes—the trade-offs that customers are just willing to make. Such regressions can also simultaneously measure the costs of providing those trade-offs as seen by firms.[31] When markets are not in equilibrium, such interpretations are unwarranted.

Consider the computer market, which has never been close to long-run equilibrium in its entire existence. If it is true that new products tend to offer better price/performance to displace or to compete with older products, then since older, obsolescent products do not instantly disappear and are not instantly repriced, we should see a price/performance relationship for new products that differs from that for old ones. To put it differently, if we wish to test the hypothesis that new products are on the advancing price/performance frontier and old products within it, then we can only estimate the position of that frontier using new products; we cannot do so by a regression using data on both old and new products.

Further, if the introduction of new products continually changes the frontier, as manufacturers compete for customers, we cannot expect the frontier itself to represent user valuation of performance characteristics. Rather, at any one time it represents the pricing policy of the manufacturers involved (which may, of course, involve *their* estimates of user valuation). Hence, when we estimate that frontier at a given moment, we must do so using the machines of a particular manufacturer (in the present instance, IBM). The results can then be used for our original purpose of interpolation, but should not be interpreted beyond that. To use data for more than one manufacturer in estimating such a price/performance surface would be to defeat our purpose.

The second reason for caution in interpreting such regression coefficients as user valuations is simpler. We cannot give an exhaustive list of important characteristics. It is likely, therefore, that we shall leave out some that are correlated with others we include. The coefficients of the included characteristics will then include the effects on price of the excluded ones. So long as our purpose is interpolation, this does not matter greatly. With multiplication time highly correlated with addition time, for example, it will not matter whether we use addition time, multiplication time, both, or some combination for interpolation. To interpret the coefficient of addition time in such an example as the value placed by users on addition time itself would be totally unreasonable.

We must thus content ourselves with our original modest objective —interpolation on IBM's price/performance surface to enable comparisons with the machines of other manufacturers. This requires the use of data on all IBM machines introduced at approximately the same time. We can perform such an analysis for at least one important moment in IBM's history, namely, when IBM introduced a whole line of machines, the System/360 announced in 1964.[5.2]

The Price/Performance of System/360

In principle, regression techniques are applicable to the full complexity of quality correction—for software, reliability, and intangible characteristics as well as for hardware performance. In practice, however, that is not feasible. Precise data on some elements of quality, such as maintenance, are lacking, while it is not even clear in principle how to measure others, such as modularity or flexibility of use. The same problems exist with the functions provided by software.

We are thus compelled to concentrate on hardware characteristics only. This means that the price/performance comparisons made will generally be biased in favor of a higher price for IBM. This is because IBM generally provided more complete and higher-quality services than did some other manufacturers, more complete modularity, and better reliability and maintenance. It made no separate charge for so doing.[32] Note that a similar upward bias applies if customers are willing to pay (and IBM can charge) for the lower risk associated with IBM because of IBM's past record. Quality corrections using only hardware characteristics cannot adjust for such phenomena. Thus, if one found from the statistical analysis that IBM sold at a higher price on a hardware-corrected basis, one would then have to decide how much of that price stemmed from nonhardware elements, including deserved reputation, before reaching any conclusion. Since we find that IBM was definitely *not* a high-priced firm even on a hardware-corrected basis, we can reject *a fortiori* the proposition that it commanded any *undeserved* price premium.

Moreover, even restricting attention to hardware, it was only possible to perform the analysis for CPU/memory combinations and not for computer system configurations as a whole. In particular, the price/performance of peripherals is not included. Since, for at least some peripherals in the period studied (the middle 1960s), IBM offered devices pretty clearly superior in price/performance to those of its competition (printers and especially disk drives, for example), the inability to include

---

5.2. The reverse comparison—interpolating on a different manufacturer's price/performance surface for comparison with IBM—is not possible, at least for the same period. No other manufacturer introduced so broad a line at one stroke.

such devices will substantially understate the performance of the IBM systems.[33]

The reasons for leaving out peripherals are as follows. The boxes that make up a computer system and whose prices when added together become the "price" of that system can be configured in a great many ways. Depending on the configuration chosen, the individual performance characteristics of the boxes combine in different ways to affect the performance of a system. Thus, it is not obvious how these characteristics should be thought to affect the system price. Further, it is not at all plain what relevance one would give to the price at which IBM would have offered a system configured in a way quite different from its actual systems. System/360, for example, was predicated on the use of disk drives with the performance of the IBM 2311 and later the 2314. It is not clear what meaning, if any, to attach to a comparison between a competitor's system with no disk drives and an IBM system when IBM's solution to the same customer's data processing problems would have involved disk drives.[5.3]

Further, it is a mistake to think of computer system "prices" as such. A computer system does not have a single price. Its price to the customer is the sum of the prices of the boxes that make it up (and the prices of separately priced software and services that the user must either acquire from a vendor or produce himself). Since such boxes can be configured in a large variety of ways and since there is both box-to-box and system-to-system competition, pricing at IBM is invariably done on a box basis.[34] Such pricing takes account, as it must, of the effect on the total cost and performance of systems configured in various ways, but while there may be a regular relationship between the price of a box and the characteristics of that box's performance, there can be no such regular relationship between the fictitious price of a system and the characteristics of the boxes that constitute it except for one derived from the box-price/box-characteristic relationships.

This means that one can hope to accomplish hardware-corrected price comparisons on a box basis at best. The obvious comparisons to make are those of processor/memory combinations. Further, these are the only comparisons that involve enough data to enable studies of the sort about to be reported to be made. Finally, at least for the introduction

5.3. Of course, if we knew that a particular IBM configuration "corresponded" to a particular competitor's configuration, this would be no problem. But this is where we came in. Configurations do not correspond in this fashion. It is the need to compare the prices of products with *different* characteristics that is the whole problem being addressed.

of System/360, an analysis of peripherals is not required. For example, there was only one principal disk drive originally offered by IBM with System/360—the 2311. On every price/performance measure, it was an improvement over all existing drives, and with only a single data point, there is no way to extract from the data the way in which such measures ought to be combined.

We thus restrict attention to the evaluation of the price/performance of CPU/memory combinations. We concentrate on the introduction of System/360 and compare IBM's price/performance on this very limited basis with that offered by Burroughs, Control Data Corporation, General Electric, Honeywell, NCR, RCA, and Univac. These were the firms named by the government as manufacturers of "general purpose computer systems" as of the time of System/360 and thus fit the allegation that IBM priced above other firms in the government's "market." The results show very clearly that even on such a limited basis, System/360 was an immense price/performance improvement, offering much better price/performance than did IBM's earlier systems or those of IBM's competitors. Further, they show the inexorable effect of innovative competition on prices—a steady decline—until IBM's System/360 had itself been overtaken in price/performance in the "constant leapfrogging game."[5.4]

Data for 25 IBM CPU/memory configurations included in the government's market were used to estimate a price/hardware-characteristics relationship. The configurations used were for the 360/20, 360/30, 360/40, 360/50, 360/65, and 360/75. All configurations were used for which there was a lease price given in the General Services Administration (GSA) price list for fiscal 1966 or 1968 (published in mid-1965 and mid-1967, respectively).[5.5] The processors involved constitute all the processors envisioned in the original planning for System/360 (the SPREAD Committee Report),[35] except for the processors of the Model 90 Series, which the government excluded from its market. They were all announced in 1964 and constitute all 360 processors announced

5.4. Unfortunately, it does not appear possible to perform a similar analysis for System/370. By the time of the introduction of that family in 1970, different manufacturers had unbundled software and services to a greater or lesser degree, making price comparisons difficult. Further, by that time, CPUs had themselves become more complex, and it is difficult to tell from the available data either what some of the relevant characteristics are or what is or should be included in the data for a particular CPU. Some data do not seem available at all.

5.5. The GSA price list comes out at the beginning of the fiscal year, that is, in the middle of the preceding calendar year.

during 1964–66, with the exception of the Model 90 Series, the 360/ 44 and the 360/67 (all excluded from the government's market).[5.6] They are thus all the System/360 processors announced during 1964–66 that the government described as "general purpose electronic digital computer systems," and therefore the ones for which, according to the government, IBM's supposed price premium should be most pronounced.

In addition to its exclusion by the government, the 360/44 ought not to be included in this analysis since it was deliberately developed to offer better price/performance characteristics than the rest of the line in terms of raw hardware performance and thus represented a departure from IBM's usual price/performance surface.[36] This shows up quite clearly if the results for the included System/360 processors are used to evaluate the price/performance of the 360/44. The 44 appears well below the common price/performance surface, offering about a 40 percent price/performance advantage over the rest of the line in terms of the hardware performance measures used. (That difference is significant at the .0001 percent level.) To have included the 360/44 would have been to use a point known to be unsuitable for interpolation (and to have made System/360 look even better).

Similarly, even had the government included the 360/67 in its market, the 360/67 ought to be excluded from the present analysis. In terms of the processor/memory characteristics used in the study, it was identical with the 360/65 but carried a higher price because of time-sharing capabilities not possessed by the 360/65. Since we are not able to take account of time sharing (except by treating the charge for time sharing as the difference in price between the 360/67 and the 360/65), there was no point in using the 360/67 in the sample.

Whether the 360/90 Series should properly have been included if one ignores the government's market definition is a harder question. However, it appears doubtful that the performance measures used would adequately measure the performance of the Model 90s. Further, these computers were developed somewhat differently from the rest of the family, as we discuss in chapter 8.

It is also not completely clear that the inclusion of the small 360/20 is entirely appropriate. This machine, announced in November 1964, was not quite fully compatible with the rest of the line and, more

5.6. This ignores the 360/60, 360/62, and 360/70 processors announced in April 1964, but superseded before delivery by the 360/65 and 360/75, which had faster memories.

important for our purposes, was oriented in terms of decimal, rather than binary, arithmetic. We therefore performed the analysis in alternative ways (to be described in detail), allowing for such decimal orientation and also leaving out the 360/20 altogether. The results are very insensitive to such choices.

For all non-IBM computers that the government characterized at the beginning of the trial as "general purpose electronic digital computer systems,"[37] price comparisons were made for all CPU/memory combinations for which prices could be found in *either* the GSA price list for fiscal 1966 *or* the GSA price list for fiscal 1968. Results for both sets of prices are given in table 5.1. There are two matters that need comment here. First, in interpreting comparisons made with the fiscal 1966 lease prices for non-IBM computers, it must be remembered that no adjustment has been made for the fact that the interpolated IBM lease prices are for fiscal 1968, while IBM raised its lease prices and lowered its purchase prices by 3 percent in calendar 1966 (the "3×3" price change). Thus, the interpolated IBM lease prices were actually 3 percent *lower* in fiscal 1966 than appear in table 5.1.

Second, the earliest prices used for competitors' machines (for fiscal 1966) were those in effect well *after* the announcement of System/360 — after competitors had had time to react. Since competitors did react to System/360,[38] the numerical results of table 5.1 must be adjusted if one is to interpret them in terms of price/performance as it existed in April 1964 — the time of the original System/360 announcement. We return to this when we discuss the conclusions to be drawn.

The performance measures used were a measure of memory size and two measures of speed. They are defined as follows:[39]

BSZ   memory size in thousands of bits;

ADDT   the time taken by the CPU to do a five-digit fixed-point (binary) addition (including the time necessary to retrieve the numbers being added from storage and to store them and their sum) in microseconds;

BUS   a measure of the rate of data transfer between memory and CPU in bytes per second.

(We explain later the reasons for believing that a different choice of variables would not lead to materially different conclusions.) A log-linear form was used.[5.7]

5.7. The use of logarithms means that it makes no difference whether one uses a measure such as additions per second or seconds per addition as a variable. This is a considerable convenience. Since the fit was very good and only interpolation was required, we did not look further.

One problem deserves comment. As already mentioned, the 360/20—the smallest processor in the line—was a decimal-oriented machine, and it is thus not clear that binary addition time is the appropriate measure to use for it. Further, the 360/20 binary addition time was either 450 or 1,332 microseconds depending on the length of the words being added. Several regressions were run as follows: leaving out the 360/20; using a 450 microsecond addition time; using a 1,332-microsecond addition time; using the 360/20 decimal addition time of 675 microseconds; using an obviously enormously low figure of 180 microseconds suggested by Alan McAdams; introducing a dummy variable equal to unity for 360/20 observations and zero otherwise.

It can be shown that the last procedure, by its special treatment of 360/20 observations, makes the result independent of the addition time used for the 360/20. Further, if *all* differences between the 360/20 and the larger processors in the price/performance relationship are attributed to the interpretation of addition time, the results can be used to estimate that addition time that makes the 360/20 fall on the same price/performance surface as the other machines.[5.8] When this is done, the addition time estimated is 431 microseconds or 362 microseconds, respectively, depending on whether or not the BUS variable is included. These estimates are close to (and not significantly different from) the 450 microseconds figure, but the hypothesis that 180, 675, or 1,332 microseconds is correct can be rejected at extremely high significance levels.

In any event, all these methods gave results for price/performance comparison purposes that are only trivially different. The principal difference is that the BUS variable has a significant coefficient when the higher addition times are used but not otherwise (it is close to significant at 450 microseconds). Further, when addition times far from 450 microseconds are used, there is, as there must be, evidence of a

---

5.8. Let $M = \log$ ADDT. With the dummy variable, d, the regression contains terms $\alpha M + \beta d$. A change in the 360/20 addition time used from M_{20} to M^*_{20} (with M called M^* after the change) merely rewrites this as $\alpha M^* + \{\alpha(M_{20} - M^*_{20}) + \beta\}d$, so that only the coefficient of the dummy variable is affected, and that in the obvious way, the change of variables being nonsingular. Further, since if the coefficient of d were zero, there would be no need to distinguish the 360/20 from the rest of the line, the estimate of β/α can be interpreted as the appropriate correction to the logarithm of 360/20 addition time originally used, M_{20}.

separate effect associated with the 360/20.[5.9] In consequence, we give the results only for the case of a 450-microsecond addition time.[40]

The estimated regressions for 450 microseconds are

log price = 7.358 − 0.425 log ADDT + 0.445 log BSZ

$\quad\quad\quad\quad\quad$ (0.222)   (0.022)$\quad\quad\quad\quad\quad$ (0.024)

$\quad\quad\quad\quad\quad$ (t = 33.2)(t = −19.1)$\quad\quad\quad$ (t = 18.5),

R^2 = 0.9963,

$$(5.1)$$

log price = 7.053 − 0.376 log ADDT + 0.444 log BSZ + 0.055 Log BUS

$\quad\quad\quad\quad\quad$ (0.274)   (0.035)$\quad\quad\quad\quad$ (0.023)$\quad\quad\quad\quad$ (0.031)

$\quad\quad\quad\quad\quad$ (t = 25.7) (t = −10.7)$\quad\quad\quad$ (t = 19.3)$\quad\quad\quad$ (t = 1.76)

R^2 = 0.9967,

$$(5.2)$$

where the figures in parentheses are standard errors and t-statistics. The coefficients have the expected signs, and the fit is extremely good. Since the discussion and our results differ only trivially if (5.2) rather than (5.1) is used, we shall use only (5.2) as the estimated equation from now on.

These results are quite suitable for our purpose of interpolation. Indeed, the probability that the results on price/performance given in table 5.1 are due to chance is vanishingly small; the estimated differences in price/performance are far greater than can be explained by random variation around the plane given by the regression equation.[5.10]

Such reliability is important not only in itself but for the question of the dependence of the results on the particular variables used to represent hardware performance. Suppose that one were to use a different measure of hardware performance. If that measure is correlated with IBM's System/360 prices (and if it is not, there is no point in using it here), then it *must* also be highly correlated for System/360

5.9. There is no other evidence of a processor-associated effect leading to autocorrelation in the disturbances.

5.10. McAdams's suggestion that multicollinearity between addition time and memory size destroys the possibility of accurate estimation needs no further comment given t-statistics as large as those involved here (PX 7409-A: McAdams Surrebuttal Narrative Testimony, pp. 291–295).

with the three variables used previously, which together explain 99.67 percent of the variation in the logarithms of System/360 prices. Further, since so much of the variation is already explained, the use of an additional measure could contribute nothing. Thus, in terms of interpolating on IBM's price/performance surface, we need look no further.

Despite this, there is a possibility—although not a very good one—that the use of different variables would matter in our results on price/performance below. For this to be true, any new variable in question would have to be systematically very closely related to the variables actually used for System/360 computers, but *not* so related for competitor computers. Further, the new variable would have to affect the pricing of competitor machines in ways *not* accounted for by the included variables. This is not impossible. The performance of a computer of relatively unusual architecture—such as the CDC 6600 with its array of peripheral processors—may not be captured by the variables used.[41] It is doubtful that such effects are widespread or systematic in the comparisons to be given, however. The variables used are highly correlated with other readily available measures. While the performance of a particular computer—such as the CDC 6600[5.11]—may be misestimated, any phenomenon as supposedly widespread as a higher IBM price ought to be so plain—if real—that it will show up when performance is measured in this way.

In fact, no such picture emerges. Table 5.1 lists the results company by company (for prices both as of the beginning of fiscal 1966—mid-1965—and the beginning of fiscal 1968—mid-1967) when the estimated System/360 equation is used for interpolation. The results are expressed as the ratios of the actual competitor prices to the calculated IBM prices in percent. Thus a value less than 100 indicates a higher IBM quality-corrected price (poorer price/performance for IBM) and a value greater than 100, a lower IBM quality-corrected price (better price/performance for IBM). If the hypothesis that IBM can and does price above its competitors were true, then the results should show numbers *less* than 100 for competitors' machines.

The listing is arranged by manufacturer, and the fiscal year at whose beginning the CPU involved first appeared in the GSA price lists is shown in parentheses. (The first fiscal year for System/360 was 1965.)

5.11. The CDC 6600 does not appear in the analysis, since it was not listed by the government as "general purpose."

Table 5.1 Price/performance comparisons with System/360

Machine	Fiscal year of first appearance in GSA price list	Price/performance ratio, 1966	Price/performance ratio, 1968
Burroughs			
5500	1965	153 [147[a]]	153 [147[a]]
300	1966	287	264
2500	1967		90
3500	1967		90
CDC			
3100	1965	57	67
3300	1967		93 [90[a]]
GE			
225	1962	191	
215	1964	194	
425	1964	78	
435	1964	114	
415	1965	71	74
435/7	1968		119
405	1968		70
425/7	1968		114
Honeywell			
800	1959	185 [160[b]]	
400	1960	307 [266[b]]	
1800	1963	165 [143[b]]	
1400	1964	281 [243[b]]	
200	1965	123 [106[b]]	131 [113[b]]
2200	1966	152 [132[b]]	162 [140[b]]
120	1966	120 [104[b]]	122 [106[b]]
1200	1966	124 [108[b]]	137 [119[b]]
4200	1966	157 [136[b]]	152 [131[b]]
8200	1967		150[c][130[b,c]]
NCR			
315	1962	230	
315/100	1965	179	179
315/RMC	1965	139	123
RCA			
301	1961	219	
3301	1965	123	127
70/15	1966	62	62
70/25	1966	55	55

Table 5.1 (continued)

Machine	Fiscal year of first appearance in GSA price list	Price/performance ratio, 1966	Price/performance ratio, 1968
70/45	1966	96	99
70/55	1966	76	78
70/35	1966[d]	93	96
70/46	1968		124
Univac			
Univac III	1961	171	
490	1961[d]	197	
1107	1961[d]	272	
490A	1964	185	
1050 III	1964	217	
491	1966	142	149
494	1966	71	70
1108	1966	92	93
9200	1967		57
9300	1967		72

a. Alternative estimate assumes interleaving capability of memory always efficiently used as in multiprocessor environment.

b. Honeywell used a 6-bit instead of an 8-bit word. Alternative estimate assumes memory size should be measured in words rather than bits.

c. There were two Honeywell 8200s, a character-oriented processor and a word-oriented processor. The price/performance ratio for the former is 105 [92[b]] and that for the latter is 211 [183[b]].

d. First appearance of machine in GSA price list was in a supplement to that list in the indicated fiscal year.

The ratios presented are geometric averages for all the CPU/memory combinations using the same CPU.[5.12]

First consider the numbers as of fiscal 1966. The principal conclusion is plain. With one possible exception (the GE 425), *there was not a single computer system admitted by the government to be a "general purpose electronic digital computer system" that appeared in the GSA price lists earlier than System/360 and offered superior price/performance to that of System/360 even based on post-System/360 prices.* This is true even *without* taking account of the superior peripherals and the increased modularity, flexibility, compatibility, and other features that helped to make System/360 so successful. When IBM introduced System/360, it obviously priced the computers of that family *below* the offerings of its competitors.

This statement is not a reflection of chance fluctuations. Using standard statistical tests, the probability that the pre-System/360 competitive computers were really offered at the same or better price/performance than System/360 and that the results we have just observed were due to chance is less (and usually *far* less) than one in a thousand for every computer system listed in those years. (These statements refer to the geometric averages given.)

Even the one apparent exception to the result, the GE 425, is more apparent than real. The non-IBM prices used were those of the GSA price list for fiscal 1966; the IBM prices were for fiscal 1968 including the "3 × 3" price change of 1966. For a comparison as of the announcement of System/360 we must correct for the "3 × 3" price change and, more important, for the cuts of 8–13 percent that GE made in its prices for the 425 when System/360 was announced.[42] When this is done, the ratio for the GE 425 changes from 78 to 93, a figure not significantly less than 100 at the 5 percent level. (A similar calculation for the GE 435 increases the ratio to 131 from 114.)

Not only was the price/performance of System/360 superior to all these earlier competitor machines, but it represented a substantial improvement over IBM's own earlier lines. Comparisons similar to those given previously yield ratios of 200 or more for every preexisting IBM computer still on the GSA price list in fiscal 1966 (and there is only one computer—the IBM 7040—even close to 200).

5.12. It is worth remarking that although table 5.1 presents comparisons for computers without taking into account charges for use beyond 176 hours a month, the conclusions do not change when extra use charges are taken into account.

System/360 thus offered a substantial price/performance improvement over everything that was available prior to it. Indeed, T. V. Learson appears to have underestimated matters when he wrote in July 1964 that "NPL [System/360] was a price reduction of 30–50 percent so that competition is forced to come along with us."[43] Learson made that statement after CDC and GE in particular had sharply reduced prices in response to System/360. As already observed, those reduced prices are already reflected in the fiscal 1966 prices used in table 5.1.

A fuller picture of the competitive reactions can be obtained from the results in table 5.1 using prices from the GSA price lists for fiscal 1968 and including the additional machines that first appeared in the fiscal 1967 and fiscal 1968 price lists. The machines introduced by fiscal 1965 by Burroughs, Honeywell, NCR, and RCA all offered inferior price/performance to System/360 even at 1968 prices. Moreover, NCR failed to introduce additional computers even by fiscal 1968 (mid-1967). Honeywell introduced several additional computers with substantial price/performance improvement over its pre-1965 machines, but also never matched the System/360 level during this period—a period lasting about three years after IBM announced System/360. Burroughs and Univac introduced machines inferior to the price/performance of System/360 but by fiscal 1967 (mid-1966) and fiscal 1966 (mid-1965), respectively, had introduced machines with superior price/performance to that of System/360 on this limited hardware-corrected basis.

GE responded to System/360 by reducing prices. As a result, GE's 400 Series, announced slightly earlier than System/360, offered roughly similar price/performance to that of System/360 at fiscal 1966 and fiscal 1968 prices. In time for the fiscal 1968 price list, GE introduced additional systems also falling on both sides of the System/360 price/performance surface. CDC sharply reduced prices, giving it an edge with the 3100, and then introduced the 3300 in 1967 at just about the System/360 level.[44]

RCA introduced its Spectra series in 1966—a family designed to be compatible with System/360. The results for the Spectra series show almost a consistent price/performance edge over System/360, although the RCA computers were not delivered until one to two years after System/360 and not in quantity until early 1967. Even here the advantage was greatest in the smaller computers (the 70/15 and 70/25), which "were relatively low cost, low margin systems" on which RCA did not put "marketing emphasis."[45] The 70/35 and especially the 70/

45 offered negligible (and statistically insignificant) improvements over the earlier System/360 (none at all in fiscal 1968 for the 70/45 when the "3×3" price change is taken into account).[5.13]

Thus, even taking account of the price reductions and introductions of new computers, System/360 not only offered clearly superior price/performance than did earlier computers but continued to offer price/performance superior to most computers being delivered through at least 1966. If the government's contention that others were forced to price at a discount relative to IBM were correct, we should see few if any ratios greater than 100 at least from 1964 on. This is very far from the case. *Even without accounting* for System/360's superior peripherals, functions, modularity, reliability, and compatibility, the introduction of System/360 represented a tremendous improvement over virtually all existing products. In addition, such comparisons show very clearly the downward trend of prices in the market. Far from being the high-priced firm, IBM was the leader in offering price/performance advances.

Such a result is not a surprise. Customers in the computer market are far from stupid—indeed, they are very sophisticated.[46] This is not a market for impulse buying of relatively inexpensive consumer goods. It is a market whose customers include, first, the federal government itself and, second, most of the nation's major corporations. Further, for even the smallest customers, there are trade publications and consultants able and willing to assist in the very important choice of a computer system. In such circumstances, to believe in irrational brand loyalty leading to a large price advantage is to denigrate the intelligence of those making computer-procurement decisions. IBM could not have had the success it did—especially with System/360—without offering its customers superior value.

IBM itself understood that the System/360 was a major advance. An internal IBM memorandum of February 24, 1964, concluded that System/360 "will have an advantage over all existing systems offered by major competitors." Paul W. Knaplund, who in 1964 had the responsibility for organizing the presentations on System/360 considered by top management, testified that "price/performance comparisons were made within IBM utilizing assumed System/360 configurations compared against the best of competitors' announced systems. . . . Those comparisons showed System/360's price/performance generally to be

5.13. Even for fiscal 1966 prices, the improvements estimated for the RCA 70/35 and 70/45 are not statistically significant.

superior to the best known competitive systems and substantially superior to the best of IBM's older computer systems." At the same time, those comparisons "substantially understated the advantages of System/360 to IBM's customers and prospective customers" because the analytical methods used in computing price/performance did not adequately take into account the value System/360 offered with respect to (1) disk storage, (2) compatibility, (3) improved reliability, and (4) software support."[47]

With System/360, IBM replaced its own earlier computers, which were being made obsolete by competitors, and offered—even within the narrow hardware dimensions considered previously—a large price/performance improvement. When all of the dimensions of System/360 were considered, there was no doubt in the marketplace about the enormous achievement of IBM. As Withington reported in October 1964, "With the introduction of their System/360 equipment, IBM established the new price-performance standard for equipment within the computer industry for the next several years," an opinion he reiterated during his testimony.[48]

It is clear from all of this that the allegation that others must price below IBM and that IBM somehow has a higher price is a myth, at least for the events here considered. Price/performance improves over time. In addition, the price/performance of new machines surpasses that of older machines even after price reductions on the earlier products. These are the necessary outcomes of innovative competition. IBM—like all other manufacturers—was forced to improve or suffer losses, falling behind in the "constant leapfrogging game." In turn, IBM's competitors were forced to respond, just as IBM was forced to act. If they could, they priced their later computers below IBM, just as IBM had priced its System/360 computers below the prices of its competitors' earlier computers. Some competitors succeeded in doing this, forcing IBM to respond again. Some succeeded partially, accomplishing it for some but not all of their computers. Some never succeeded in the period covered by these results. IBM's "power" over price was the power possessed by any efficient firm or technological leader—to keep prices *down* (or performance up) and force others to go along if they wished to stay in the competitive race. That sort of power is not monopoly.

Chapter 6

Entry and Barriers to Entry

In the competitive process, poor price and product performance by some incumbent firms leads to the entry of new firms and the expansion of competitors or both. As a result, business is bid away from the original firms. The effective operation of the process of entry and expansion in response to incentives caused by the failure of incumbents to act competitively is the antithesis of monopoly power; it is the circumstance of blockaded entry that gives rise to such power. Monopoly power is by definition the ability to control (that is, to raise) prices *without* inducing entry and expansion. A "barrier" to entry is something that interferes with the competitive process, which prevents new firms from entering *when there is a profit incentive to do so.*[6.1] Barriers to entry are factors or conditions of the market that give the incumbent firm a *persistent* advantage over new entrants, so that new entry will not be attracted even though the incumbent earns economic profits.[6.2] Thus, the incumbent is sheltered or protected from the competitive pressures of potential entry; the constraint placed on an incumbent by the prospect of new entrants is absent.

It is important to understand that a barrier to entry only exists when an incumbent firm can *refrain* from competing without inducing entry. The fact that firms already in the market compete vigorously with each other and are expected to compete with new entrants is not a barrier; it is a symptom of competition.

Not all "advantages" possessed by an incumbent result in barriers to entry. In order to be a barrier the "advantage" must be one that cannot be reproduced by an entrant with effort or expenditure comparable to that expended by the incumbent. Thus, not everything that

6.1. Our understanding of barriers to entry has benefited greatly from conversations with C. C. von Weizsäcker as well as from his writings. See C. C. Von Weizsäcker, *Barriers to Entry: A Theoretical Treatment* (Berlin, Heidelberg, New York: Springer-Verlag, 1980). 6.2. We shall discuss the definition of "economic profits" and the "economic rate of return" at length in chapter 7. It is important to keep in mind that such profits represent the excess over all of the costs necessary for the production of the products and services in question, including a return on the capital already invested.

makes entry by a new firm costly or beyond the reach of some or even many firms constitutes a barrier to entry. The fact that entry into a business requires some investment of money, time, skills, and other intangibles may make entry difficult, but does not mean that there are barriers. That is just as true when the investment is large in absolute terms as when it is small. The fact that a plant has to be built, a distribution network set up, employees hired, and other skills and equipment acquired—all of which may require a substantial invest-ment—does not in itself constitute an economically relevant barrier to entry as long as the incumbent firm also had to make such an investment of money, time, and skill or would have to make a comparable current investment to expand.[6.3]

The current accounting profits earned by incumbent firms include a return on their past investment in plant and equipment. Entry into a business (for incumbents as well as potential entrants) typically involves a period of time in which the plant is being built and in which current revenues do not exceed current costs. If the firm is to be successful, that period will be followed by a later one in which current revenues do exceed current costs. The economic rate of return on that process must be considered as a whole. The question concerning economic profits is whether, after properly attributing the profits to the initial investment, the rate of return being earned on the whole venture in-cluding the investment costs of entry is above a competitive rate (after adjustments for risk). That question cannot be answered by examining only the *current* accounting profitability of firms in the business and ignoring the costs of the investments that led to those profits.[6.4]

A barrier to entry exists only if there are factors or circumstances of the market that enable the economic rate of return—calculated to take account of risk and the timing of costs and revenues—to exceed a competitive rate without attracting entry. Suppose, for example, that all that is involved in entry is the high cost of initial investment to build the plant. If potential entrants fail to enter because the profits that they eventually expect to earn after the plant is built are not sufficient

6.3. The need for a large investment may, however, be associated with the phenomena of economies of scale or imperfections in the capital market, which can constitute barriers to entry under some circumstances. We discuss this later.

6.4. As explained at length in chapter 7, such accounting measures as return on sales or the ratio of accounting profits to stockholders' equity tell us nothing about whether economic profits are being earned and therefore nothing about whether a more than competitive rate of return exists for any firm in the market.

to yield a competitive return on the entire investment, *including* investment in the plant, then there is no barrier to entry. Rather, the competitive process is doing its job. This situation involves no difference between incumbent firms and potential entrants. Large plants must be built by both. To do so, both must expect eventually to earn sufficient return on that investment. The fact that incumbent firms have already built their plants only says that we are observing them in a different stage of the process. *A barrier to entry only exists where incumbent firms have some persistent advantage over potential entrants.*

It is important to note that this remains true even when the process of plant construction and entry is lengthy (which is not the case in the EDP industry). When future market conditions are correctly forecast by all, enough plant construction will take place to make the economic rate of return no more than normal when that return takes account of the waiting time between investment costs and ultimate return. After the initial plants are built, this will mean a period when price is above *short-run* marginal cost. If future market conditions are correctly forecast by a few firms but not by all, these firms may reap the rewards for their superior foresight by a period of profits lasting until others can get in. When demand expands in ways unforeseen by anybody, incumbent firms will earn windfall profits until new entry occurs. In all these cases there are no barriers to entry. The competitive process might be aided by better forecasting, but it would surely not be aided by a policy, say, of subsidizing plant construction by latecomers. Such a policy would expropriate the rewards whose prospect induced the initial firms to enter. Time is money, and there is no more reason to call a long delay time a barrier than so to call the need to build a plant.

The need to provide and finance a lease base in the EDP industry is also no different analytically from the need to provide and finance a plant. Incumbent firms have already done that; new firms have yet to do it. As with investments in plant and other assets of production, the question is whether incumbents can earn economic profits on the whole process, including the costs of acquiring a lease base, without inducing the entry of others. There is no reason to suppose that such is the case. Both incumbent firms and entrant firms must finance lease bases if they are to offer customers the opportunity to lease their products. If customers demand leases, such financing is part of the real investment cost of meeting that demand. The financing of the lease base, like the construction of a plant, is necessary to provide services that the customer values. The fact that incumbent firms may have a cash flow from a previous lease base is no more relevant than the existence of any other source of funds.

The same principle applies to the analysis of whether the reputation of incumbent firms is a barrier to entry. Suppose that, at identical prices, customers prefer the products of incumbent firms to the products of new ones, even though those products appear to an outsider to be equally good. This may superficially appear to be a barrier to entry, since potential entrants apparently must offer a lower price to get customers to buy their products. Nevertheless, that price difference does not prove that a barrier to entry exists. When customers buy a product, they do not buy merely the physical thing involved. Rather, they buy with it some degree of assurance that the product will work, that it will last a certain amount of time, that it will suit their particular needs, and that the maker will stand behind it. For simple products, like bread, such aspects, while present, may be relatively unimportant compared to those directly related to physical characteristics. For complex products, like computers, they can be very important.

Customers who prefer the products of an incumbent manufacturer to those of the new entrant may well do so because they are buying the assurance of quality, suitability, and service that comes with the reputation of the incumbent manufacturer. That reputation can be the result of years spent in the business and may have required a substantial investment to acquire and maintain. The product of a new entrant may, in fact, turn out to be as technically suitable as the product of the incumbent for customers' needs, but it may be associated with more uncertainty and risk. Even though outside technical experts may rate the two products as technically equal, they will not be equally good to customers unless they believe that such evaluations remove all uncertainty not only about technical performance but about the collection of services and assurance that they are buying when they buy the product.

If customers put high value on the reputation of the manufacturer, then manufacturers will find it profitable to invest in acquiring such a reputation. Just as profits have to be calculated as a return on total investment including the investment in plant, so they must be calculated on the entire investment, including the investment in reputation-building and goodwill. Such investments in intangibles are just as real as physical investments in plant and equipment. Potential entrants that have yet to build a reputation are not thereby barred or deterred from entering. They would only be so barred if incumbent firms had an advantage in establishing a reputation that could not be duplicated by new entrants;

that is, if for some reason it was easier for the first firms than for later ones.

It is plain that in the EDP market, the burdens of establishing customer confidence and a reputation for reliability and service were much more severe and the risks of failing were greater for the pioneering entrants than they were for later entrants. Indeed, later entrants had (and have) an advantage over IBM and other pioneers. Whereas IBM and others had to convince customers that a new and unfamiliar product was in fact suitable for their needs and had to assume through short-term leasing and bundling (discussed later) the risks that something would go wrong, later entrants did not have to do so and could take advantage of the success of IBM (and others) in that regard.

When new firms first enter a business and produce products physically similar to those of the incumbents, those products may sell at a price disadvantage as customers continue to pay for the reputation of the established firms. Over time, that price difference will tend to disappear as customers gain experience with the new firms' products. As this happens, incumbent firms will have to reduce their prices or improve their products or see their business disappear. This is the story of IBM and the independent peripheral manufacturers. When independent peripheral manufacturers began offering equipment imitative of IBM equipment, they did so at a price discount because customers otherwise would not experiment with them. As their reputations grew, they achieved substantial success, and IBM was forced to lower its prices or lose business.[6.5]

Similar issues are involved in the entire analysis of entry under innovative competition. A firm invests in research and development and, after some time, produces a new product. It earns substantial accounting profits on that product, considered as an excess of revenues over current cost. Other firms may be temporarily prevented from entering the production of that product because of the need to find out how to make

---

6.5. Even when competitors have established a reputation, some lower prices may remain necessary in an innovatively competitive market for an imitative firm to induce customers to take its version of a new product. That product will typically be available only some time after the innovative product it copies. The risk that it will not operate properly will therefore be greater than for the already tested product of the innovator that it seeks to replace. Imitators can reduce customer uncertainty by establishing a track record with earlier products, but they may not be able to eliminate entirely the risk that their new product will not be a successful copy. This is not a barrier to entry; it is a reflection of the choice of a strategy of entry through imitation rather than innovation and of the fact that imitators have lower investment costs than do innovators.

it. (In the EDP market that temporary lag is short and getting shorter.) Nevertheless, that fact does not constitute a barrier to entry.

This case has some features not present in this discussion so far, although the basic principles are the same. One must first consider whether the original firm is in fact earning economic profits when investment in research and development is properly taken into account. So far as the innovator is concerned, investment in research and development was just as much a part of the investment necessary to produce the goods as investment in manufacturing plants was. The difference in this situation, however, is that the investment necessary for others to get into the business is quite likely to be *less* than the investment that was required for the incumbent firm to enter. A product once invented need not be invented again if it can be imitated. Nevertheless, it costs potential entrants something to get into the business because, for example, they may have to reverse-engineer the product to learn how to produce it. Obviously, this is not a case in which the incumbent firm has a permanent advantage relative to potential entrants; indeed, the reverse may very well be true. Assuming no patent protection, the most that an efficient entrant would ever have to spend is the investment to rediscover the product—an investment that the incumbent has already undertaken—and even then the risks may be less since the feasibility of the innovation has already been established. If, in fact, it is possible to reverse-engineer the product, then the new entrant is likely to be able to produce the product with a substantially *lower* investment than that made by the incumbent firm.

Thus, not every apparent advantage constitutes a barrier to entry. Those that do arise from natural or nonreproducible advantages of incumbents over potential entrants. For example, cost advantages stemming from access to superior resources, such as exceptionally fertile land or mineral deposits, from geographic proximity to sources of supply or to customers, or from exclusive access to technology are highly unlikely to be replicated effectively by entrants and so may confer enduring cost or pricing advantages on incumbents.

Cost advantages that are not barriers may stem from superior productivity, due in turn to skillful management, employee dedication and morale, or innovative research and development. Similarly, as we have seen, pricing advantages may stem from incumbents' reputations for reliable products and service or other factors differentiating their products from those of entrants. In these circumstances, entrants may not be able immediately to replicate the characteristics of incumbents and may therefore suffer temporary cost or pricing disadvantages until they evolve effective organizations, establish their own reputations, or otherwise differentiate their products. The need to establish an efficient organization, reputation, or product preference means that entry may require a greater capital investment than it might otherwise. As with any investment required for entry, however, that additional investment is not a barrier to entry unless the investment required of entrants is greater than that which incumbents have had to make to attain their status.

As this discussion should make clear, an analysis of barriers to entry must be done over time, not for a moment in time. It is only from a perspective over time that the analysis can take into account, as it should, the amount of investment made by incumbents before the new entrant comes in and the erosion over time of any temporary advantages that the incumbent may have when a newcomer first enters.

The History of Entry, Growth, and Expansion

Throughout its history, the EDP market has had substantial and continuing entry at an ever increasing rate. That entry has been coupled with the rapid expansion of many existing participants. The evidence shows that the competitors that must be taken into account in assessing the constraints on IBM number not three (as the government contended) but at least in the hundreds. All but a small percentage of those competitors entered the EDP market for the first time in the 1960s or 1970s. For example, in Census II, of the 617 companies reporting U.S. EDP revenues in 1972, only 98 reported such revenues as of 1961.[1]

The list of companies competing with IBM is very long and necessarily includes many companies that entered the market in the 1960s and 1970s using various approaches: companies offering "parts" of systems; companies offering computer systems of a variety of sizes, including so-called minicomputers; software companies; leasing companies; systems integrators; and service bureaus and time-sharing companies. A partial list as of 1980 was given in table 3.1.

Many competitors have grown faster than IBM, and collectively their growth rate has outstripped IBM's.[2] Consequently, as seen in chapter 4, IBM's share of the EDP market has declined significantly and persistently since 1961. Entry and growth of IBM's competitors have been facilitated by a variety of factors.

First, the rapid growth of the market facilitates entry because an entrant need not displace an existing competitor's equipment in order to establish an initial position or toehold in the market.

In less than thirty years, the EDP market has grown from nothing to one of the largest in the world. In terms of annual revenues, it passed the billion dollar mark by 1961, more than tripled in size between 1961 and 1967, and doubled again between 1967 and 1972.[3] Since 1972, that growth rate has continued. The trade publication *Datamation* published estimates of total data processing revenues for the "top 50 U.S. Companies in the Data Processing Industry" for the years 1975 through 1979. Those estimates (using worldwide data processing revenues for the firms involved) suggest another increase of around 100 percent in the size of the computer market in only four years, with a total size worldwide (current dollars) of more than $43 billion in 1979. On average, the market grew in the 1960s and the 1970s at compound growth rates of 20 percent or more, meaning that it doubled in size every three to four years.[6.6]

The EDP market's sustained, dramatic growth shows no sign of abating. The government's industry expert Frederic Withington wrote in his April 1979 report, "The World Computer Industry: 1978–1983," that the computer industry is today entering what "should be . . . one of the most dynamic growth periods in its history." Burroughs, in its 1979 annual report, stated that "[t]his is a dynamic industry, and we have barely scratched the surface of its long range potential," and Sperry Rand, in its 1978 annual report, "estimate[d] that only a small fraction of the applications that could be computerized today are in fact computerized. The result is a sizeable pool of potential computer customers." Edward J. Mahoney, deputy director of the division of financial and general management studies, United States General Accounting Office, estimated in 1974 that only one or two percent "or perhaps even less" of the possible applications of computers had actually been implemented "so that I see nothing but a dramatic continued increase for the industry."[4]

6.6. While exact calculation is impossible, the U.S. EDP revenues reported by the 72 companies in Census II that were also among the top 100 data processing companies listed by *Datamation* in 1980 (including IBM) increased from $1,321,230,000 in 1966 to $4,653,270,000 in 1972, representing a compound growth rate of over 23 percent (DX 8224). By 1979, the U.S. data processing revenues of those 72 companies as reported in *Datamation* had reached $16,580,600,000 (DX 13945). Comparing 1966 with 1979 gives a compound growth rate of over 21 percent.

Second, the rapid rate of technological change that has characterized this market has continually created opportunities for firms to enter or expand by coming up with new and better ways to satisfy customer needs. This has, of course, put pressure on existing firms.

Technological change, coupled with changes in system design, such as increasing modularity, created opportunities for companies to compete by offering box-for-box plug-compatible replacements for products offered by suppliers of computer systems. In particular, the modular design of IBM's System/360, coupled with its extraordinary acceptance by customers, contributed in substantial part to the entry of companies offering plug-compatible replacements for parts of IBM systems.[5]

Similarly, improvements in circuit technology and other product innovations have contributed to the increasing importance of distributed processing and the increasing use of combinations of small but powerful processors as an alternative to larger processors, creating competitive opportunities for new entrants as well as for existing firms.[6] In Withington's view, "technological innovation in the general purpose computer business" (even as he defined it) is "at least as rapid today as at any period in the past and more rapid than at some periods." (He had earlier agreed that "technological change in the computer industry has proceeded at about as rapid a rate as users can absorb.")[7]

Third, the fact that a significant portion of IBM computer products have always been leased, especially on very short lease terms, rather than purchased by customers has facilitated the entry and growth of competitors. The leasing of IBM computer systems has meant that it has been easier than it otherwise would have been for new entrants, and existing competitors, to replace installed IBM equipment because the user could readily return the IBM equipment and avoid further lease payments. (The government's contention that leasing is actually a barrier to entry is flatly incorrect, as discussed later.)

Fourth, entry into the computer market has been facilitated by the fact that companies have a broad range of opportunities to enter on a small scale with a limited product line and, upon achieving a "toehold" position in the market, can use that as a basis for further expansion. Many entrants, such as CDC, DEC, or Data General, have done this with tremendous success. This entry strategy has enabled many companies entering the EDP market to become profitable very quickly and to remain profitable while in the midst of very rapid growth.[8]

Fifth, entry into the EDP market is facilitated by the fact that a new entrant need not do everything itself. An entrant can easily acquire parts and components from a third party. If it wants to enter by offering complete systems, it can acquire most (or even all) of the parts of those systems from others. It can obtain silicon chips from semiconductor houses and software from software companies; it can take advantage of the marketing capabilities of other companies by selling some of its products to systems integrators or leasing companies (as PCM suppliers have done); it can even contract for maintenance to be provided by third parties such as SORBUS or COMMA. In sum, an entrant initially can attempt to implement an innovative idea while taking advantage of the specialization achieved by other suppliers. (Examples are given later.) Once the entrant is established, it can begin to assume more and more of those functions itself. That fact has made entry into the market substantially easier than it was when IBM and Sperry Rand initially entered in the early 1950s.[9]

Sixth, companies have been able to use expertise or capabilities acquired in a related field to facilitate their own entry into the computer market. Examples of such related fields include business or office equipment (for example, IBM, Sperry Rand, Burroughs, NCR, Wang); components, especially semiconductors (RCA, Intel, Texas Instruments, National Semiconductor); and communications (AT&T, ITT, Northern Telecom). In addition, of course, many successful entrants have been founded by persons who gained their expertise working for existing computer suppliers, especially IBM, and then left to form their own firms.[10]

Finally, a seventh factor facilitating entry into the computer market is the existence of sophisticated customers who make procurement decisions on a tough-minded, return-on-investment basis and are constantly prepared to examine the alternatives available to satisfy their data processing needs.[11] Sophisticated customers quickly become aware of and are receptive to new, promising alternatives. In certain cases particular customers have played important roles in encouraging and promoting the growth of particular entrants and the development of new technology.[12]

The very large number of entrants into the computer market is apparent even if one focuses only on the most artificially narrow "market" alleged by the government: the market for "general purpose computer systems" as described by Alan McAdams and based in part on the government's industry expert Withington.

When Withington first testified in 1977, he offered his "rigorous" definition of "general purpose" and said that in addition to IBM, Sperry

Rand, Burroughs, and Honeywell (the only firms McAdams included in his market), three other firms (DEC, Data General, and Hewlett-Packard) had expanded their product lines upward so that their largest systems "essentially" had "general purpose capability" and any difference said to exist between their systems and a full general purpose system, as Withington defined it, was "mostly a semantic one." When Withington returned to the witness stand in June 1980, however, he testified that the number of companies manufacturing computer systems marketed in the United States that met his "rigorous" definition had grown to ten, and "possibly" thirteen companies: Burroughs, Sperry Rand, Honeywell, DEC, Data General, Hewlett-Packard, NCR, Hitachi, Fujitsu, Datapoint and "possibly" Wang, Prime, and Tandem.[13]

In addition to firms that met his "rigorous" definition, Withington said that firms that manufactured small business computers and thus had a "base . . . of their own customers . . . could grow up to their own versions of general purpose systems." In 1977 Withington identified thirty established manufacturers marketing small business computer systems to end users in the United States.[6.7] In 1980, however, he testified that "I am told that somewhere between sixty and seventy companies purport to offer small business systems in the United States today." Similarly, Withington acknowledged that there were additional foreign firms that could "enter" that market just as Hitachi and Fujitsu have done.[14]

Finally, companies that currently manufacture only parts of systems, such as the IBM-compatible CPU or plug-compatible peripheral suppliers, must be considered potential suppliers of "general purpose computer systems" by Withington's "rigorous" definition because by merger, acquisition, joint venture, or internal expansion those suppliers could begin marketing complete computer systems instead of just CPUs or peripherals and indeed some have done so.

Of course, a "market" with such rapid entry is one drawn so arbitrarily narrow as to take no account of supply substitutability. Even if one ignores this, the evidence of entry and growth and the large number of potential entrants is inconsistent with existence of monopoly power in that "market." That evidence is even more compelling when the market is properly defined and the full evidence of entry and growth is reviewed.

6.7. That list included ten of the thirteen companies identified in 1980 as suppliers (or "possible" suppliers) of general purpose computer systems, as rigorously defined. It did not include Tandem, Hitachi, or Fujitsu (DX 2595).

It is thus most unlikely that there have been serious barriers to entry into the market. An examination of the factors that the government contended are such barriers (economies of scale, capital requirements, leasing, conversion costs, bundling, and maintenance[6.8]) shows this very clearly and also shows that such contentions resulted from a total misunderstanding of what a barrier to entry is.

The Alleged Entry Barriers

Economies of Scale
The government's chief economic witness, McAdams, testified that among the "major barriers to entry" into the manufacture and marketing of general purpose computer systems was "the scale of operations which are required in order to achieve efficiency in the manufacturing and marketing of a full family of bundled systems, and that scale appears to be in the range of at least ten percent of the marketplace as identified by a series of different manufacturers." Similarly, Leonard Weiss judged "very tentatively" that the evidence indicates "that you need to have 5 to 15 percent of the general purpose market to be efficient in this industry." To Weiss this implied a "very high scale barrier to entry" into the general purpose computer systems "market."[15]

In a static market, manufacturing economies of scale (or similar economies in marketing and service) are the only ones that can arise. In a market characterized by technological change there may also be economies of scale in research and development so that larger firms with larger research and development establishments are able to make advances in ways that smaller firms find it harder to achieve. These two types of scale economies have very different effects. Static economies of scale, as in manufacturing, can under some circumstances provide barriers to entry if they are large enough relative to the size of the market. This is not generally true of economies of scale in research and development, which can be quite substantial without causing entry barriers.

Economies of scale may affect entry in several ways. First, the advantages of efficient, large-scale operation may make it necessary to invest in a large plant or large amounts of research and development.

6.8. Access to technology or skilled personnel is not a barrier to entry in the EDP market. Technology is freely available, and personnel circulate among firms. See Mancke Testimony, pp. 752–766. Many of IBM's competitors were founded by former IBM employees. We have already discussed brand loyalty (apart from conversion costs) in chapter 5.

As explained earlier, such a necessity by itself is not a barrier to entry. Second, the necessity for large-scale operation may require large amounts of capital, and imperfections in the capital market, if they exist, may under certain circumstances provide a barrier to entry.

Apart from these points, it is well understood that when sunk costs are incurred by incumbents, economies of scale in manufacturing can be a barrier to entry.[16] To take the simplest example, suppose that the technology of producing a homogeneous product is such as to make production impossible below some minimum output per year, $\bar{x}$, and that marginal cost above $\bar{x}$ is constant and equal to average cost, c. Consider the demand for the product at a price equal to c, say $D(c)$. If $n \leq D(c)/\bar{x} < n + 1$, where n is an integer, then it is clear that no more than n firms can profitably operate. With n strictly less than $D(c)/\bar{x}$, n firms will be able jointly to cut output to $n\bar{x} < D(c)$ and raise price above c without attracting entry. Of course, their ability to do so will depend on their ability to coordinate their actions; this ability will tend to be less if n is large than if it is small. Further, the extent to which price can be raised above c will tend to be less if n is large and $\bar{x}$ is small relative to $D(c)$ than if n is small and $\bar{x}$ large relative to $D(c)$. What matters in all this is the effect of economies of scale relative to the size of the market—not $\bar{x}$ alone, but $D(c)/\bar{x}$.

As this example illustrates, the importance of economies of scale as a barrier to entry does not depend merely on how large a firm has to be to take advantage of those economies. It depends on the relationship between the minimum efficient scale and the size of the market as measured by the volumes demanded at remunerative prices. Consequently, the likelihood that economies of scale will be a barrier to entry is less in large markets than in small ones.

Further, the effect of economies of scale as a barrier to entry disappears in growing markets. In the example given, if demand were to grow over time, more and more firms would enter if prices were raised. Barriers arise from economies of scale when potential entrants believe that the addition of their output will "spoil the market" by driving price to unremunerative levels. Where the market is growing, there will be more and more room for such additional output.

One important feature of this example requires discussion. We assumed that output below $\bar{x}$ units was literally impossible so that entrants could not expect incumbents to cut output below that figure. In more realistic situations things happen more flexibly; while there may be a minimum efficient volume of output, a reduction of output below that volume will only raise average costs slowly. In such a case, potential entrants can consider coming in at a scale smaller than minimum efficient size, taking minor losses and expanding as the market grows. The special assumption of no output being possible below the minimum efficient scale is therefore an extreme one in which economies of scale act most sharply as a barrier to entry. Even then, that barrier becomes of less and less importance for larger and larger markets. It will disappear entirely for quickly growing markets.

The analysis of economies of scale in research and development is altogether different. Suppose that a large research and development establishment is required to make certain kinds of major advances. That will generally mean that the firm with such an establishment must also be large enough to spread the costs of research and development over a large output. The existence of such a firm may be required for rapid technological progress, but that requirement need not provide a barrier to entry. Unlike the case of static economies of scale, there is no necessity for potential entrants to start out large—that is, so large that their entry would depress the price to unremunerative levels. Instead, when technological advances are made by the larger firm, others can learn to imitate them,[6.9] generally with less research and development expense than that needed to achieve the innovation. In the process of innovative competition, the advantage of any innovator only lasts until others can imitate or surpass the original innovation, and even if a large research and development establishment is required to innovate, it will generally not be required to imitate. Thus, even if the market does not have room for more than a few firms large enough to support efficiently large research and development facilities, there may still be ample room for effective additional competitors that rely at least in part on an imitative rather than an innovative strategy.

Further, even though large research and development expenditures may be required for certain kinds of major innovations, it does not follow that they are required for all innovations. In a market characterized by technological change and growth, there will always be room for good ideas, particularly if the possession of these ideas enables a firm to gain a toehold and grow to a larger size. Moreover, while economies of scale in research and development may enable large firms to

6.9. Imitation is possible unless the large firm's innovations are protected by patents. Patents, however, are not a factor in the computer market. See Mancke Testimony, pp. 752–766.

make large changes in products or technology, it may be possible once those changes are made for smaller firms to pursue smaller changes, again perhaps taking advantage of the pioneering research and development of the larger firms. Neither smaller innovators nor imitators need enter at large scale.

In such a situation, economies of scale in research and development provide no permanent advantage constituting a barrier to entry. In order to remain ahead of smaller firms—both innovators and imitators—the firm enjoying such economies must continue to pursue its research and development efforts to offer improved products. These scale economies do not offer shelter from competitive pressures. Whatever economies of scale in research and development exist thus provide no barrier to entry even though the existence of firms large enough to take advantage of them may be required to maintain the pace of technological advance.

There is, to our knowledge, no direct evidence of the extent of economies of scale or minimum efficient size in the EDP market or in the "market" defined by the government. However, there are good reasons for believing that economies of scale do not constitute barriers to entry. A large number of firms of different size employing a wide variety of strategies have entered the EDP market, grown rapidly, and succeeded in achieving healthy profitability. This is plain from looking only at firms that have met or may possibly meet the "rigorous" criteria defined by Withington for "general purpose computer systems" suppliers and may thus enter the government's narrow "market." Data General, Prime Computer, and Tandem are examples.

Data General, formed in 1968, had $1 million of revenue in fiscal 1969. Its worldwide revenues increased to about $53 million in fiscal 1973, and in fiscal 1979 revenues reached $507 million. Data General turned profitable in 1970 and has remained profitable since that time, earning nearly $50 million in net profits in fiscal 1979.[17]

Prime Computer was formed in 1971 and shipped its first product in 1972. Prime's revenues grew from $12,000 in 1972 to $6 million in 1974 and $153 million in 1979. Prime became profitable in 1975 and has remained profitable, earning nearly $17 million net profit in 1979.[18]

Tandem was formed in 1974 and shipped its first computer system in 1976. Since that time, Tandem's revenues have grown from $581,000 in fiscal 1976 to nearly $56 million in fiscal 1979. Tandem became profitable in 1977 and has remained so, earning nearly $5 million net profit in fiscal 1979.[19]

Tandem is an illustration of a company that has chosen to take advantage of the economies of others in assembling its products. Thus, Tandem does not manufacture its own peripherals but acquires them from others, explaining that "[v]ertical integration of peripherals would not improve our margins at present, and would take resources away from our end-user marketing and support efforts. Our strategy is to concentrate resources on product development, marketing and support of our customers, and to build a sound base of satisfied customers as rapidly as possible while maintaining good profitability. At some point in the distant future, however, the economies of vertical integration could change."[20]

This strategy of entry while acquiring parts or whole boxes or services from others has been widely used.[21] Of course, the position that this is not *really* entry because the firm involved does not spring full-blown into actual production of a line comparable to IBM's is merely playing with definitions.

What then were the government economists thinking of when they concluded that 5–15 percent of the market was required for successful entry into the "market for general purpose computer systems" as defined by McAdams? They based this conclusion largely on certain testimony from GE, RCA, and Xerox witnesses, which they interpreted to mean that those companies needed 10 or 15 percent of the "general purpose computer systems market" "to be successful," to be "efficient or to attain stability or something of that sort."[22] That reliance was misplaced for several reasons.

In the first place, the supposed requirement for a share of 10 or 15 percent was apparently based on the assessment of the revenue generation necessary for profitable operation in "the general purpose market," as differently defined by each witness *and* with a strategy of participation in that market on an across-the-board or full-line basis in order to be "number two." Thus, Richard Bloch testified that the GE APL Plan goal of achieving the number two position in the industry, which required a 10 percent share of annual shipments, was based on "the technique by which we were going to attack across the board the entire general purpose business field."[6.10, 23]

6.10. Note that Bloch, unlike the government's economists, measured the 10 percent share goal in terms of "annual shipments." This is a far cry from a 10 percent share of *installed base*, which is the way the government and its economists measured the market. The calculations given later assume that it is size of shipments and not installed base that matters for economies of scale.

Successful entry and effective competition are possible in the EDP market without a full-line product offering, however. Further, it is possible to be an effective and profitable participant in the market without being "number two." Hence the estimates used by the government economists do not reflect the minimum size required for efficient operations. Even if it were true that the market only had room for up to ten full-line suppliers because of scale economies and size requirements associated with full-line supply, there would still be ample effective competition in the market and potential for the addition of new entrants of lesser size offering a narrower spectrum of products and services. Those "smaller" participants, whether offering a smaller selection of computer systems or only parts of systems, exert significant competitive constraints on the "full-line" system manufacturers.

In addition, there is no agreement in the trial record as to the necessity of 10 or 15 percent of the market for profitable operation even assuming across-the-board participation. J. W. Rooney of RCA testified that he did not understand why it was believed that obtaining a 10 percent share of some market would make RCA profitable. Looking back, Rooney concluded that "you do not have to have a 10 percent share of the market to be profitable" and that RCA could have conducted its affairs in such a way that its computer systems business could have been profitable without that share.[24] Indeed, Edwin S. McCollister of RCA testified that it was increasing emphasis on attaining share at RCA after 1968 that "deemphasized control of expenses and achieving a profit, and the end result is that the expenses in the RCA computer division mounted to the point where they contributed significantly to RCA's withdrawal from the business."[25]

Similarly, there is no evidence that Xerox considered such a percentage goal as a requirement for success, let alone for efficient scale of operation. Indeed, Xerox appears never to have taken such a goal seriously.[26] It certainly cannot be concluded that the failure of GE, RCA, and Xerox in the EDP market was due to a failure to attain large enough scale (as opposed to a failure to keep up with the pressure of innovative competition).[6.11] The successful history of small-scale entrants shows such a conclusion to be unwarranted.

Put all this aside, however, and suppose that some percentage goal of 5–15 percent was a minimum scale requirement about 1970. As

6.11. The history of the three exits is set forth in the Historical Narrative, pp. 488–618, 1125–1144. In each case the firm involved failed to have a new product line ready when its old one grew obsolete, and there were management difficulties.

discussed earlier, the question of whether scale economies in a particular market represent a barrier is dependent on the relationship between the production volume required to achieve those economies and the percentage of the available market demand represented by that output. Therefore, a rapid rate of growth of demand in a market can make the importance of scale economies transitory. Rapid growth of demand will encourage the entry of firms that may not initially produce at minimum efficient scale but that anticipate capturing enough of the new business to enable them to reach that size.

This point can be dramatically illustrated in the context of the conclusions of McAdams and Weiss. Let us assume that the minimum efficient scale of operation in the EDP market in about 1970 could be approximated as an output equal to about 10 percent of the market (however defined). Absent evidence that changing technology has caused such minimum efficient scale to grow as the market has grown, the minimum scale as a percentage of the market has shrunk. We estimated earlier that the EDP market has about doubled every four years since 1966. If in fact minimum efficient scale required obtaining 10 percent of the market as measured by annual output in 1970, that scale would be achieved with less than a 5 percent share of annual output by 1975 and with about a 2 percent share of annual output by 1980.[6.12] As our earlier discussion suggests, this is too small to be an entry barrier. It is not plausible that a potential entrant in a market as dynamic as this one (the EDP market or the government's alleged market) would be deterred from entering because it expected its addition of 2 percent to the market to break prices down below remunerative levels, even if IBM could somehow get the other firms in the market to restrict their outputs so as to keep prices above costs.

Perhaps the major analytical problem presented by the government's allegation that incumbents in the "general purpose computer market" are protected by barriers to entry resulting from scale economies is that the source or nature of the alleged scale economies were not identified. From the testimony and examples (RCA, GE, and Xerox) referenced

6.12. This estimate ignores inflation, which in more ordinary markets would have caused about a doubling in revenue with no change in physical output. Nevertheless, it is clear that in the EDP market, there has been a strong trend toward more output per dollar rather than less as in much of the rest of the economy. Consequently, on the assumptions of a scale requirement of 10 percent in 1970, and no changes in the techniques of production that increased the minimum efficient scale, the scale requirements would have shrunk by 1980 to at most 4 percent and perhaps well under 2 percent of the market.

as support for the claim, the government appeared to assert that the "large-scale" requirement is the result of a full-line approach to innovating, manufacturing, and marketing, with its attendant demands for research and development, product planning, manufacturing facilities, and a significant degree of vertical integration. That vision of the necessary scale of operation was premised on a fallacious view of the "requirements" necessary to be "in the market." The government economists defined a market made so narrow by the imposition of such a broad range of requirements for inclusion in the market that there is necessarily insufficient room for very many suppliers meeting those artificially broad requirements. Economies of scale were imposed by definition, and entry at smaller scale was defined away.

As already discussed, such market definition requirements are far too restrictive to recognize most of the important competitive constraints on IBM. Similarly, although the scale requirements for a firm to duplicate IBM at an efficient per unit cost may be large, such duplication is not necessary in order to be an effective competitive constraint or to be a successful entrant into a properly defined market. The errors of market definition lured the government and its economic witnesses into errors of identifying and measuring barriers to entry. That is one of the dangers of a market definition formed without attention to economic principles.

Capital Requirements
The government claimed that "the cost and availability of capital" was among the "most pronounced" of the "absolute cost barriers" to entry: "Capital is readily available to IBM, and, to a lesser extent, the other mainframe manufacturers, but hard to come by for potential new entrants at any price."[27] McAdams further asserted in effect that prospective entrants could enter his market only as full-line suppliers financing a lease base and that the capital required to enter on such a basis was so great as to constitute a barrier to entry. Similarly, Weiss tentatively concluded that if capital requirements were on the order of $1 to $2 billion (which he thought the evidence suggested), then those requirements, especially given what he called the "lease character of the market," were probably large enough to constitute a capital cost barrier to entry ("if," as he put it, "there is a capital cost barrier in any industry"), since "there are relatively few firms that can raise a billion or two billion dollars."[28]

There is substantial disagreement among economists as to whether capital requirements can *ever* constitute a significant entry barrier when there exists a highly developed capital market in which a multiplicity of individuals and organizations continually vie with each other to provide capital service to profitable enterprises.[29] This is because *differences* in capital *costs* are required for there to be an entry barrier. The existence of a capital barrier to entry is dependent on an actual capital cost differential between the entrant and the incumbent rather than on any absolute amount of capital required to enter the market. The mere need to raise capital to build a plant, finance a lease base, engage in research and development, or otherwise participate in the industry is not in itself a barrier to entry; these costs must have been borne by incumbents as well and must still be borne by them to expand. There is no inherent reason why start-up costs for incumbents will be any lower than those for new entrants that can often take advantage of technological progress made by incumbents.

In the absence of differences in absolute dollar requirements, a capital barrier to entry can only come from differences in the costs of obtaining the capital needed. Despite the apparent intuitive appeal of differences in the cost of capital as a barrier to entry, however, the existence of such differences is very doubtful, especially when differences in risk are properly recognized. The superficial impression suggesting that such differences in capital costs exist derives from the assumption that incumbents possess two advantages. First, as ongoing enterprises, they generate cash flow from depreciation charges and retained earnings, which permits them to undertake substantial investment without recourse to external financing. Second, as established firms, they may be considered more creditworthy by financial institutions than new enterprises, and their securities (both debt and equity) may be considered less risky by investors. Granting the validity of those assumptions for the moment does not, however, establish that incumbents have capital cost advantages over new entrants, for new entrants may well be, and frequently are, established firms in other markets. As such, they share whatever capital advantages accrue to incumbents as established firms.

Moreover, a firm that finances its expansion from retained earnings does *not* have a zero cost of capital. By leaving the earnings in the firm, its owners are foregoing the opportunity to invest in other assets or enterprises. In effect, the cost of money to the stockholders becomes the cost of capital to such a firm.

Even if incumbents and potential entrants do face different capital costs, there may be no barrier to entry involved. One source of difference in capital costs stems from differences in risk. As in all areas of economic analysis, interest rates must be adjusted for risk if different situations are to be made comparable. That a relatively risky borrower must pay a higher interest rate than a relatively safe borrower does not itself show a real difference in capital costs. It reflects the fact that the nature of the loan being made is not the same. Incumbents may be able to obtain funds on more favorable terms than can new entrants because investment in established firms with proven track records in a given market is likely to be less risky than investment in firms newly entering the market. Such differences in risk reflect actual differences between firms. In periods of agricultural growth, Caterpillar Tractor's ability to finance an additional assembly plant at rates more favorable than the authors can does not constitute a barrier to entry. Caterpillar knows much more about the heavy machinery business than we do and is far more likely to use the funds profitably.

A correct perception that new entrants are riskier than incumbents is not itself an entry barrier.[6.13] Present incumbents were compelled, at some time past, to overcome a similar perception of risk on the part of investors in order to obtain capital. Many present incumbents entered the EDP business as pioneers, unsupported by any past record of industry performance, and faced the prospect of substantial development costs in an embryonic industry. Current entrants, by contrast, offer the promise of investment in an established, healthy industry and are able to draw upon the existing mass of technological achievement and readily available engineering expertise.

The issue of correct risk assessment by the capital market is similar to that of justified reputation in the eyes of customers, considered earlier. Suppose that entry is considered likely to be profitable because the profits eventually to be earned will justify the initial capital investment required. If there were no risk, one would expect investors to be able to perceive this and entrants to be able to obtain capital. When there is risk, both the entrants and those who provide funds to them must be compensated for that risk, and the entrants will find it harder or more expensive to borrow than they would in the absence

6.13. It is true, however, that the perception that a new entrant is likely to be driven out by a predatory monopolist can be an entry barrier. Predatory acts are discussed in chapter 8.

of risk. That is not a barrier to entry. Of course, opinions differ as to risk, and a potential entrant is likely to think its venture less risky than outside investors do, but the issue of barriers to entry is one of whether investors reasonably evaluate the risks associated with incumbent firms and entrants and accurately reflect those assessments in their behavior.

If investors do not do this, then the capital market is imperfect in the sense that entrants are at a borrowing disadvantage relative to incumbents in a way that does not merely reflect risk assessment. This raises the question of whether such capital market imperfections in fact exist, and economists disagree on whether there are significant capital market imperfections and hence on whether there are in fact capital barriers to entry in *any* part of the economy.[6.14] That disagreement centers on whether new or small firms are at a disadvantage relative to established large ones. But there is no evidence whatever that capital market imperfections give incumbent firms in one area an advantage over large firms established elsewhere seeking to enter that area. Hence, even if capital market imperfections do exist and constitute capital cost advantages for incumbents over small or newly established firms, entry by established firms from other markets is generally sufficient to ensure competitive behavior (and certainly sufficient in the EDP market).

The difficulty of quantifying differences in capital costs adjusted for risk—the only correct measure of a capital barrier—has led to the use of the absolute amount of capital required for entry as a crude indicator of the likelihood that a barrier exists. That approach was adopted by McAdams and Weiss, as summarized earlier; however, their estimates were far too high.

Such overestimation stemmed from more than one cause. For example, the $2 billion figure used by Weiss was drawn from an estimate by Withington of the total value of the installed base of computers that an entrant would need within five or six years. But the actual investment required to build up such a base would be far less than the market value of the equipment, since revenues would be received from leases and sales over the five- or six-year period of the buildup of the base. A second inflated estimate of about $1 billion dollars was produced by McAdams from an overestimation (without discounting) of the losses

6.14. Another possible imperfection is thought by some to exist in that exceptionally large single amounts of capital may cost proportionately more to raise than smaller amounts. However, that imperfection, if it exists, would have the same impact on incumbents and entrants.

GE and RCA were said to have incurred, including their "anticipated" losses for the future. Such figures are overstatements of the facts.[30]

Once one eliminates the obvious errors from which the numbers in the billions derive, one finds estimates that at best suggest a cost of $200 to $300 million for a firm to develop an entire general purpose computer system product line (as defined by Withington), create a nationwide marketing and service organization, and begin production and marketing.[31] Even this figure is greatly overstated as a measure of the capital requirements for entry. There is no reason that a new entrant needs to spring on the market with the product line that Withington defined as "the minimum necessary degree to be credible" or to match every product offering made by IBM. Firms can and do begin on a more modest scale and, if successful, expand. Virtually every participant in the market entered in that way, including IBM. The first cause of the government's mistake about entry requirements was its market definition, which defined away any such thing as small-scale entry. The error in estimating capital requirements was thus another consequence of a market definition formed without regard for economic principles.

Even assuming such a restrictive market definition, the proper measure of the barrier to entry is derived by looking at the costs faced by the most likely potential entrants. If the "market" is defined by the rigorous set of requirements propounded by McAdams, then the most likely potential entrants are the suppliers of computer systems that fall short of one or more of McAdams's tests. To take one of the simplest examples, McAdams required that a firm both lease and sell and decided that DEC, Data General, and Hewlett-Packard should be excluded from his market because they apparently did not lease. Thus, even assuming McAdams's assumptions about those firms to be correct, the capital barrier from the standpoint of those potential entrants would be the cost of offering their products on lease. Given the variety of ways in which that can be and is done (for example, through leasing companies and financial intermediaries) and the costs of financing a lease base, even if it is done by the manufacturer itself, capital requirements are indeed small (and identical to those faced by the incumbents). They cannot constitute a barrier to entry.

Similarly, McAdams included NCR and CDC in his narrow market in 1971 but excluded them in 1977. He also testified that the Data General and Hewlett-Packard products offered in 1977 "might well be" included in his definitions as of 1970. Evidently, then, these companies failed to meet the market definition in 1977 because of the additional requirements that arose over time. Withington estimated that the costs of meeting those additional requirements would be about $50 million. Thus, even accepting all of the government's and McAdams's assumptions, one can identify explicitly from those statements four potential entrants separated from the "rigorous" "general purpose systems market" by not more than $50 million. Indeed, by 1980 Withington testified that NCR, Hewlett-Packard, and Data General were all marketing products that met his definition of general purpose. In addition, Withington recognized that there were today perhaps sixty to seventy manufacturers of "small business systems," and they appear to be well placed for future entry.[32]

Once we leave the never-never land of verbal game-playing with market definitions, it is apparent that the capital requirements for becoming a competitor of IBM are not high. Many, many firms have entered the EDP market as suppliers of less than complete computer systems and, necessarily, less than a full family of such systems. Many of these entrants have over time become suppliers of broad ranges of EDP products, and some have become suppliers of families of general purpose computer systems. Indeed, the government's view of the genesis of the EDP market entrant springing full-grown into the marketplace had no historical precedent until perhaps the mid-1970s, when companies like Tandem and Prime effected entry in that sort of dramatic fashion and with far less investment than Withington postulated.[33]

Hardware entrants can avoid capital outlays for product development by purchasing readily available components and computer products from a large number of vendors that stand ready to supply them. This was done in the 1960s by SDS, for example. These purchases are common, involving "every computer system manufacturer," according to Withington. For example, RCA purchased peripheral equipment from a number of suppliers, curtailing its own peripherals development because it "did not want to expend all the money that would have been required to continue to develop all its own peripherals . . . they felt that they could best utilize their financial resources . . . by utilizing outside sources who were developing these peripheral devices."[34]

The phenomenon is not limited to hardware manufacturers or hardware acquisition. Applied Data Research (ADR) developed "the interfaces to special display equipment" and built "software," then went on to sell "the system as one unit. . . ." Formation was described as possessing "unique capabilities in the development of highly complex EDP systems utilizing the wide variety of available computer componentry and hardware in cost effective ways." The company eventually began producing IBM-compatible CPUs. Winston Hindle of DEC testified that his company sold PDP-11s to original equipment manufacturer (OEM) customers that would, in turn, write their own applications programs and then market the PDP-11 systems with the application programs to the end user.[35]

Companies can also reduce capital requirements by selling to independent marketers. By so doing, they are able to avoid the expense of large marketing organizations. For example, in the early 1970s, National Semiconductor marketed its products through STC, Itel, and Memorex, and Intel marketed through CIG and Itel and later sold some part of its products through Telex and third-party leasing companies. AMS memories were marketed by Memorex, CDC, CIG, and Itel. Memorex marketed to a number of OEM customers. It did so to acquire cash with which first to begin marketing directly to end users and then to develop its own systems.[36]

By combining one or more of these techniques, companies were and are able to enter the computer market with relatively limited resources, manufacturing or marketing first a single product or service. They can then expand their product offerings if they so choose. They have done so using a variety of financing devices to reduce capital needs still further. Such devices have included acquisition for high price-earnings ratio stock (CDC); sale and leaseback (Honeywell); and arranging financing through leasing companies (Telex and DEC).[37]

Clearly, the government estimates of even $200–$300 million far exceed the capital requirements for entry into the market when either the market is correctly defined or the requirements even for the government's own narrowly constructed market are measured properly for purposes of assessing barriers to entry. In his classic work, *Barriers to New Competition*, published in 1956, Joe S. Bain judged capital requirements in excess of $100 million to be "very large." He said that requirements of that size might constitute a barrier to entry.[6.15] Assuming that there exists a magnitude at which capital requirements become large enough possibly to raise a barrier to entry, that magnitude is certainly related to the size of the economy and to the supply of external

6.15. Joe S. Bain, in *Barriers to New Competition* (Cambridge: Harvard University Press, 1956), pp. 157–158, also remarked, however, "as to how much more difficult it is to raise 100 million dollars than 1 million, or how much differential disadvantage is thereby imposed on the entrant as compared to established firms, we may speculate, but we do not have much reliable information on this point."

funds. Thus, Bain's estimate of "very large" requirements for 1956 must be adjusted to reflect the relevant changes that have occurred since that time in both the value of the dollar and the size of the economy. From the mid-1950s, when Bain wrote, to the late 1970s, the price level rose 2.5 times and real gross national product more than doubled. Therefore, the combined effects of inflation and economic growth suggest that $500 million might be a more appropriate indicator of a "very large" capital requirement today. Similarly, the annual volume of external funds raised by nonfarm, nonfinancial corporations has risen to approximately seven times its level in the mid-1950s, suggesting that Bain's standard of $100 million should be translated into about $700 million in today's economy. Only the most extreme estimates in the record are "very large" by these standards, and those estimates are greatly exaggerated, as already explained. Thus, capital requirements for entry are not "very large" by Bain's standard.

Moreover it has historically been relatively easy for computer companies to raise funds. Particularly during the period of stock market growth in the late 1960s, the "go-go" years, computer-related companies were the darlings of the market and could raise funds on terms that failed to reflect the full risk involved. And this was not merely a matter of raising money from small unsophisticated investors.[38]

We have been discussing actual capital investment needs. We repeat that using the magnitude of capital requirements as an indicator of possible capital cost barriers to entry creates a danger that the mere existence of capital requirements will themselves carelessly be taken to be barriers and that the amount required will be taken to be the size of the barrier. Such usage is very misleading. New entrants into the market must ordinarily build a plant; hire workers, salesmen, administrators, and managers; arrange for supplies of components and raw materials; and do many other things. This is no more than incumbents had to do when they entered. Such requirements for entry, including capital, are necessary for all entrants, old and new, and do not in themselves provide cost or pricing advantages to incumbents over new entrants. To be sure, incumbents have already incurred the costs of entering when new entrants are considering entry and therefore may superficially appear to have a current cost advantage. But if incumbents were to raise prices to levels above their own costs, *including a normal return on the capital costs of entry,* they would surely attract new entrants in the absence of actual barriers to entry. A competitive price covers costs including a normal return on the capital costs of entry, and incumbents cannot charge a higher price merely because capital is required to enter. They can only do so if they have a cost advantage over potential entrants in obtaining that capital. There is no evidence in the record showing that entrants into the EDP market (or the government's "market") have higher capital costs than incumbents in general or IBM in particular.

However one looks at it, capital requirements have not been a barrier to entry in the computer market. This is important, for, as we shall see, essentially all the other barriers suggested by the government reduce to a requirement for capital.

Leasing as a Barrier to Entry

The government suggested that leasing has in some sense been forced on the marketplace by the fact that IBM has offered its products on short-term leases. This was said to have created a barrier to new entry by increasing risks and capital requirements.[39]

Leasing has a natural economic function. The allocation of the risk of obsolescence differs between a lease transaction and a sales transaction. The owner of a computer bears that risk. If a computer is purchased, the risk of obsolescence is borne by the customer; if the computer is leased for a short time, that risk is borne by the lessor. A variety of other possible contractual arrangements allocate risks differently between the supplier and the user.

Another risk involved in a computer transaction arises from uncertainty as to the future data processing requirements of the user. Users who purchase computers accept more of the risk that the computer may prove unsuited to their changing needs than do lessees. Of course, purchasers have some flexibility if their requirements change. If their needs exceed their forecasts, they can rent additional equipment or computer time or services. If their needs fall short, they may be able to sell time on their systems directly. However, to the extent these alternatives do not provide enough flexibility, purchasers who find themselves with unsuitable computers face the transaction costs of selling that equipment. By leasing computers, users can shift the risks of such costs from themselves to the lessors. Different lengths of lease terms and different cancellation provisions allocate that risk in differing proportions between the lessor and the lessee.

There is also the risk that the computer will not work or will be often out of service. Purchasers of computers bear that risk unless they also purchase separate maintenance contracts. When a computer is leased, however, that risk is automatically assumed by the lessor. This provides a very strong incentive for manufacturers to maintain their own leased computers.

Finally, someone has to finance the computer. If a computer is purchased, the customer has to provide or arrange for the financing. If it is leased, the manufacturer or other lessor must do so. Again, there are transactions that fall in between.

All of these factors provide reasons why many computer users should and do rationally prefer to lease computer systems rather than to buy them. Those reasons are particularly strong because of rapid technological change that increases the risk of obsolescence and because the great growth in the usage of computers can make users relatively uncertain about their future needs. Users base the purchase versus lease decision on a careful consideration of such factors together with the relative prices for purchasing and leasing.[40] There are, however, reasons to expect EDP manufacturers to be more willing than customers to accept some of the risks involved, and therefore to expect to see frequent lease transactions in the EDP market.

Manufacturers are likely to be in a better position than the ordinary computer customer to evaluate the risk of obsolescence. They know what is being developed in their laboratories; they will have some idea of developments elsewhere. It is the manufacturers' business to know about these things. The users, on the other hand, are generally not in the data processing business themselves and are not so well placed as manufacturers to assess the likely course and speed of technological change. They may be, therefore, much more uncertain than a manufacturer about the risk of obsolescence. Even if all parties have the same expected rate of obsolescence, manufacturers are likely to view the situation as less risky than users, because they are more certain about those expectations.[6.16]

Next, consider the risk that a particular computer will prove unsuited to a particular user's needs. Here again, manufacturers are much more likely to accept that risk than are users. If users purchase computers and then find those computers unsuitable, they must generally go to the trouble of selling them and acquiring new ones or of buying or

6.16. It is instructive in this regard to note that IBM in 1964 rejected a suggestion of its treasurer, K. N. Davis, that it place the risk of technological change on the user by refusing to lease *any* System/360 equipment. Customers would not have accepted System/ 360 so readily under such conditions and IBM was compelled by competitive necessity not to do so (Historical Narrative, pp. 346–347).

selling computer time. Users, in general, are not particularly well placed to market computer systems without a broker. Manufacturers, on the other hand, are in the business of matching up computer systems with customers. Because manufacturers are dealing with many users at once and with many different computer products, they can act themselves as efficient brokers. That a particular computer may be a mismatch for a particular user will be offset by the strong possibility that there will be another user dealing with and known to the manufacturer for whom the computer will be useful.

This is not just a reason why manufacturers should be willing to be lessors when users would prefer to be lessees. It is also a reason why third-party lessors arise and why some customers, who are themselves big enough to find within their organizations users for computers that become unsuitable for particular needs, choose to purchase rather than lease. We thus find leasing companies and used equipment brokers competing in the EDP market. We also find the federal government itself (the largest user of computers) setting up elaborate arrangements for the reutilization of computers within the government as well as establishing a fund (the ADP Fund) to enable the government to purchase computers from manufacturers and lease them to government users.[41]

The third kind of risk—that the computer will fail to work—is also one that manufacturers are likely to be more willing to bear than are users. Manufacturers have more information than users about how likely it is that a computer will do what it is supposed to do. They are also better placed than users to set up maintenance organizations.

These considerations all point to the conclusion that leasing is common in the EDP market because it is an effective way to allocate risk and is demanded by customers.[6.17]

With that background let us look at the government's position on leasing. We have already seen that leasing is not a barrier to entry. The necessity (if it is a necessity) of investing in a lease base is no more a barrier to entry than is the necessity to invest in a plant. Incumbents

---

6.17. There are also tax considerations that provide incentives for leasing. Thus, when a computer is purchased, profit to the manufacturer is taxed immediately. The contribution of that profit to the purchase price can only be deducted by the buyer as part of depreciation, bringing tax benefits over several years. When a computer is leased, on the other hand, the taxable profit to the manufacturer is also an immediately taxable loss to the lessee. Peter A. Diamond has pointed out to us that under reasonable assumptions, this means that the manufacturer and customer can jointly gain by leasing rather than selling.

have no special advantage in such investment, and capital costs, as we have seen, are not a barrier. The provision of leases to customers is the provision of something that they demand and are willing to pay for. It is no different in that regard from the provision of any other aspect of a product. Only if IBM could somehow "force" unwanted leasing on customers would this not be true (and even then no barrier to entry would be created unless IBM had a permanent cost advantage in providing leases).

Moreover, assuming that IBM had a strong preference for lease, how could it enforce that preference on its customers? Under its consent decree, entered into in 1956 in settlement of an earlier case, IBM could not refuse to sell. Had IBM wanted to make users lease, it would thus have had to lower the cost of leasing relative to purchasing. Since customers differ in their attitudes toward the risks discussed earlier, lowering the lease price relative to the sale price would, in general, induce an increasing number of users to lease rather than purchase. Thus, a manufacturer that wished to do so could induce most of its customers to lease by charging a sufficiently low lease price relative to the purchase price.

It is very important to realize, however, that the reverse is not true. By raising the lease price relative to the purchase price a manufacturer cannot induce more and more computer users to purchase rather than lease. If customers prefer to lease, neither IBM nor any other manufacturer can prevent them from doing so. This is because of the possibility of arbitrage between purchasing and leasing. It is obviously possible for third parties to purchase computers from the manufacturer and then lease them in competition with the manufacturer. That is the business of leasing companies. It is, just as obviously, not possible for third parties to lease machines from manufacturers and then sell them in competition with them. Thus, a manufacturer that raises his lease price relative to purchase price will find that there comes a point at which users no longer deal directly but switch to leasing from leasing companies. This will force the manufacturer to lower the lease price relative to the purchase price or otherwise lose a large number of lease customers. *In a competitive market, certain levels of the lease price relative to the purchase price are simply not sustainable because they will be arbitraged away by leasing companies.*

This quite competitive phenomenon is exactly what happened to IBM in the late 1960s and is part of the story of the leasing companies. IBM's "3 × 3" price change which raised lease prices and lowered purchase prices, occurred at a time (September 1966) that was otherwise propitious for leasing companies because of the Investment Tax Credit, the ease of raising capital, and the anticipated long life at remunerative prices of System/360. Leasing companies entered and arbitraged the difference between IBM's purchase and lease prices. Leasing company offerings lowered the average lease prices users paid, thus raising the ratio of purchase to lease prices in the market—the natural result of competitive arbitrage. When IBM priced its System/370 and later equipment, it was forced to take such competition into account.[42]

Thus, certain mixes of lease and purchase business *cannot* be induced by prices. High customer purchase/lease business mixes are not sustainable because the relative prices that would otherwise induce such mixes also induce entry by leasing companies, making those relative prices untenable. Given the many other factors influencing leasing company profitability in 1966, the fact that such companies found it profitable to enter and grow rapidly following IBM's price change in late 1966 suggests that the proportion of leases to sales in IBM's business was previously about as low as it could get and be sustained.

Hence, both because manufacturers ought to be more willing than customers to bear the risks associated with owning computers and because of the possibility for arbitrage between purchasing and leasing created by leasing companies, it is not surprising to observe a high percentage of lease transactions by end users in the EDP market. It would be surprising to observe anything else, since leasing accommodates users and their attitudes toward risks.

Indeed, if leasing were not desired by users, other manufacturers would have a grand opportunity to sell computers when IBM was trying to force customers to lease them. If leasing were not desired by users, other manufacturers could not be forced to lease. Customers who preferred to purchase but to whom IBM attempted to keep leasing would be glad to have the opportunity to shift their business to manufacturers willing to sell rather than lease their computers. IBM cannot force customers to lease and so block the entry of other competitors that would prefer to sell to those customers.[6.18] *Unwanted* leasing cannot be a barrier to entry, and *desired* leasing obviously is not one.

Moreover, if IBM's lease customers are induced to lease by low lease prices, where can IBM earn monopoly profits? The answer must be

6.18. DEC, Data General, and Amdahl all entered the market with a sales-oriented strategy. Note that Amdahl produces IBM-compatible CPUs (Mancke Testimony, pp. 404–405, 806–808).

from purchase customers, if anywhere. The government, in advancing this theory, referred to it as apparently "paradoxical."[43] It is stranger than apparently paradoxical; it cannot be true. Aside from the implausibility of supposing that IBM has monopoly power that arises from forcing leasing on the preponderance of its customers while all the monopoly profits come from the customers that do not accede to that pressure, purchase prices simply cannot involve any element of exploitation if lease prices are low. Any customer in such a situation could avoid the exploitation and the capital requirements by leasing instead of purchasing. With lease prices competitively constrained, purchase prices must also be constrained, a fact reflected in IBM's pricing of System/370 to take account of leasing competition and to secure a reasonable number of purchases (as discussed in chapter 8).[44]

Thus, leasing does not constitute a barrier to entry. The desire of customers to lease provides no advantage to incumbent firms over entrants any more than does the necessity to manufacture the product. Leasing may increase the capital requirements for doing business, but capital requirements do not form a barrier to entry. Leasing does have an effect on entry, however. Short-term leases leave customers accessible to new entrants to an extent that purchase does not. Under short-term leases, customers bear neither the risk of capital loss nor the burden of reselling the computers. They can return their computers to the vendors whenever they wish. As a result, customers are constantly open to new competition. A lease-oriented market, therefore, is one that positively encourages entry, not one that discourages it.[6.19]

Conversion Costs

The government claimed that "the lack of transferability of software from machines of one manufacturer to those of another has constituted a substantial barrier to entry."[45]

Users of computers acquire combinations of hardware and software to suit their computing needs. Part of what they must acquire is the software, which they can get from computer manufacturers, user groups, or software houses, or by writing it themselves. The costs they have incurred in the past are sunk costs; the relevant test for users in selecting

---

6.19. This salutary effect of short-term leasing on entry was recognized by the government in its claims as to IBM's Fixed Term Plan that one- and two-year leases deter or prevent entry by "locking up" customers (chapter 8). This is flatly inconsistent with the claim that short-term leases are also an entry barrier. Purchases would "lock up" customers more completely than long-term leases.

computers is what costs are to be incurred or can be avoided in the future. Conversion costs arise when a change in a customer's application or equipment needs requires a change in software. Because of the costs of writing software, users will not normally choose to undertake such a change unless they see corresponding net benefits, generally in the form of increased performance, more function, or lower prices.

Software costs are conceptually no different from the costs that exist when users have purchased some or all of their hardware or any other durable good. To convince a customer to switch, the seller of a new durable good must always persuade the user that the benefits of changing are sufficient to justify the cost of acquiring the new equipment as opposed to remaining with the old one which, having been acquired in the past, has no further acquisition cost. Hardware "conversion" is often less costly in the case of computers than in the case of some other durable goods, since many users lease their computers. Software, however, is commonly owned by users rather than leased, that is, the costs of acquiring or writing it have already been incurred.

The Magnitude of Conversion Costs   For conversion costs (which the government called "software lock-in") to create a barrier to entry, they must give some persistent cost advantage to the incumbents. The size of any such barrier is thus not the *absolute* cost that a competitor must incur to convert users to its products or the price at which it must sell to induce users to acquire its products but the *difference* between that amount and what the incumbent must spend or the price it can charge. The nature of conversion costs, however, is not a matter for facile generalization.

Software conversion expenses can arise whenever a user changes application programs to run in a new systems environment. Such changes often involve changes to a different system of the same manufacturer. In addition, other major changes in a user's computing environment can give rise to conversion expenses. Such expenses can arise when a user changes operating systems, changes the mode in which applications are processed, or changes from a centralized to a decentralized processing approach. The actual costs of conversion vary widely, depending on the circumstances of the individual user, the applications, and the user's technical expertise, and depending on the vendors involved, their equipment, and available conversion aids. Conversion from one to another computer of the same manufacturer can be more expensive than conversion to a computer of a different manufacturer.[46]

Firms in the computer industry have eased conversion problems by directly assisting users with their reprogramming, by providing conversion aids, or by offering various degrees of compatibility with installed equipment.[6.20] Conversion aids commonly used include emulators, which are generally microcode devices allowing one machine to act as if it were another; simulators, which accomplish the same result less efficiently through software; and translators, which are programs assisting the translation of software written for one machine into language acceptable by another. For example, (1) In the mid-1960s Honeywell successfully displaced IBM 1400 computers with its 200 Series computers through the use of the LIBERATOR "automatic program conversion package." (2) At the same time, GE displaced IBM 1401 and 7000 Series computers with its GE 400 and 600 Series by designing hardware and software to facilitate conversion and by providing both a piece of hardware called the "7090 Simulator" and a 1401 compatibility feature. (3) IBM's 360 computers were incompatible with IBM's predecessor systems, so IBM facilitated the conversion to 360 by providing emulation devices, simulation programs, and translators. (4) Between 1965 and 1970, RCA pursued an initially successful strategy of attacking IBM's installed base by designing its Spectra Series computers to be compatible with IBM's computers and making it as easy for a user to move to RCA as to move up within the IBM line. (5) Since the mid-1970s, a large number of IBM-compatible CPU manufacturers have appeared, including Amdahl, Magnuson, National Semiconductor, and CDC, offering CPUs that can be used as direct replacements of IBM CPUs with little or no software conversion costs. Of course, manufacturers have often chosen to offer compatibility between successive products of their own. Thus, IBM's System/360, System/370, 3000, and 4300 Series have all been software-compatible.[47]

Interestingly, in the early 1970s Xerox offered conversion to XDS machines for a fee, converting seventy to eighty customers from various compatible machines. Xerox's costs for forty of these conversions rep-

6.20. It also appears that conversion costs have tended to diminish over time as more users have done more programming in higher-level languages that are largely machine-independent. At least users who choose to do so can provide for ease of future conversions with such languages (J. Jones, Tr. 78878). The use of higher-level languages has been facilitated by the increasing memory sizes and speeds and decreasing hardware costs available to users (Enfield, Tr. 19943–47; see also Historical Narrative, pp. 1522–1525).

resented only 4.83 percent of the value of the Xerox equipment installed and only 3.75 percent after Xerox's charges to users for conversion services are accounted for.[48]

Whatever the case may be with respect to the costs of conversion, it is clear from the record that users in fact regularly incur those costs and convert. They do so because the benefits of the new equipment are thought to outweigh the costs of conversion and any other costs from the replacement. Thus, Donald Hart of General Motors, describing several conversions his department had undertaken, wrote that "[c]onversion costs must be taken into account when changing computers; however, in retrospect, the value of each of the . . . changes far exceeded the cost[s incurred]." Withington estimated that in each of the three periods, 1955 to 1963, 1964 to 1970, and 1971 to 1977, between 60 and 90 percent of all users of "general purpose" systems converted from one manufacturer's system to that of another, converted to an incompatible system of the same manufacturer, or converted to a new operating system of the same vendor. Moreover, these figures do not include those who "converted" without substantial software change to plug-compatible peripherals or CPUs.[49]

Are Conversion Costs a Barrier to Entry?   In any durable goods market, suppliers that wish to induce users to purchase or lease their products must offer some improvement over what users already have. If a user has a computer installed that the supplier is attempting to replace, one factor in the user's evaluation of the attractiveness of the replacement offer will be the software costs, which depend in part on whether and to what degree the user must change software or write all new programs instead of continuing to use existing programs. As we have seen, suppliers can make their offers more attractive to the users in several ways. They can simply write the new programs for the users; they can provide conversion aids such as emulators; or they can design their computers to be compatible with the users' existing computers. Even if they do none of these, they can convince users to replace existing equipment and bear the conversion costs themselves by offering sufficiently improved performance and price.

Assuming first (for the sake of argument only) that an entrant must effect the displacement of currently installed equipment of other vendors in order to obtain any business at all, does conversion represent a barrier to entry that shelters existing vendors from the threat of new entry? It does not. An existing manufacturer planning new products must consider the question of software conversion with respect to its existing customers just as an entrant must do if it wishes to persuade an incumbent manufacturer's customers to switch to its computers. The incumbent manufacturer has the same alternatives as the entrant. Both can attempt to design a new computer that achieves a price/ performance level adequate to stay up with competition and is also fully compatible with the incumbent's previous equipment. In that case, the ability to innovate and utilize new technology will be circumscribed by the requirements of compatibility.[6.21] Alternatively, the incumbent manufacturer or the entrant can offer an improved but incompatible computer and provide emulators. Another possibility is that the incumbent manufacturer or the entrant can offer an improved but incompatible computer along with conversion aid and assistance.

Both the incumbent and the entrant are equally faced with the situation that the user has already invested in software. If the incumbent manufacturer introduces a new system that is incompatible with previous systems, the user choosing to install the new system will have to undergo a conversion. The entering vendor can also produce an incompatible computer, in which case the conversion to the computer of the entering vendor need be no more difficult than the conversion to the incumbent's new system. Alternatively, if the new entrant introduces a system compatible with the incumbent's prior computer or if conversion aids permit users to use their old programs on the entrant's system without modification, conversion to the new entrant's system can be easier than installing the incumbent's new system. This is what happened when IBM introduced the System/360. Conversion from predecessor IBM computers to 360 was no less difficult and probably more difficult than conversion to the Honeywell 200 or the GE 600 computers or the Univac 1108.[50]

In designing System/360, IBM opted to make the various computers in that line compatible with one another. *If it chooses that strategy, a new entrant facing this situation has to do no more than IBM did to achieve that compatibility.* Thus, as observed earlier, RCA adopted a strategy of designing its Spectra family so that users of IBM's System/ 360 could run their programs on a Spectra computer essentially without modification. Conversion from second generation IBM computers to RCA was no more difficult than conversion to System/360, and System/

6.21. This was a factor, for example, in IBM's development of System/370 (Historical Narrative, p. 885).

360 users could migrate to Spectra as easily as they could upgrade within the System/360 line. This compatibility strategy has been followed most recently by a number of manufacturers that have introduced a variety of IBM-compatible CPUs, and entire IBM-compatible systems, that span virtually the entire IBM 370, 4300 and 3000 Series performance spectrum. These manufacturers not only permit users to retain their investment in software but effectively acquire software by "piggybacking" on the efforts and costs incurred by IBM to develop software for IBM systems. This is a cost advantage for the entrant.[51]

Thus, in inducing users to change, as opposed to stay with, existing hardware, new entrants, at worst, merely have to do what the incumbents may have already decided to do. Both new entrants and incumbents face precisely the same choices and problems—and investments. It appears, in fact, that compatibility is becoming easier to achieve. At the same time, it may be that the difficulty of achieving the price, performance, and function improvement that the market demands of new products is increasing for incumbents choosing to remain compatible with prior product lines. An incumbent may thus enjoy no advantage over a new entrant with respect to the need to convince the users of the incumbent's older machines to install its newer equipment or with respect to the methods available to encourage that installation. Under these circumstances, conversion costs cannot be a barrier to entry.[52]

Note, in particular, that the incumbent can have no barrier-to-entry advantage because it already produces computers compatible with the customer's software and the entrant has yet to do so. Such a situation merely reflects the fact that the incumbent has already made the investment and done what the entrant has yet to do, and that is to build a product that will work with software in which the customer is willing to invest. This is no more a barrier to entry than the fact that the incumbent already has a plant and the entrant has yet to build one.

Indeed, in the EDP market, entrants may have an advantage over incumbents. They have the advantage of being imitators in innovative competition. By entering after users have already acquired software and by providing either emulation or full software compatibility, new suppliers can provide users with software for their hardware at a lower total cost than that of the software used with the users' original hardware. To take the starkest example, Amdahl and other IBM-compatible CPUs run software that either users, IBM, or third parties have written. The IBM-compatible CPU manufacturers (or the manufacturers of plug-compatible peripherals) can take advantage of the efforts expended to develop software for IBM computer systems.[6.22]

This analysis is reinforced upon examining whether conversion "liberates" IBM from the constraints of competition. Consider what would happen if IBM were to attempt to raise its prices to users of its hardware that have already invested in the necessary software and are, according to the government, "locked-in." IBM's ability to do this is constrained, in the first instance, by the probability of attracting competitors that would provide conversion aids or software-compatible hardware (including leasing companies offering IBM-manufactured hardware at reduced prices). Indeed, it is possible today to have a system composed entirely of IBM-compatible devices with no part of the system being of IBM origin except the operating system. Because of such compatibility, IBM users are *less* "locked-in" than the customers of other suppliers, and IBM is *more* constrained than other suppliers are.

Moreover, in order to take advantage of conversion costs, an incumbent would have to charge a higher price to existing customers than to new ones. In order to do this, IBM would have to raise the prices to new users once they had become IBM users. Naturally, such discriminatory price increases could only affect lease customers. Incumbents would thus either have to give up all hope of acquiring new customers or price discriminate by enticing new customers with low prices, while raising prices on hardware already on lease. Such a policy could not succeed for very long, for users, observing such a pattern, would take account of the likelihood of later rental charge increases in considering from whom to acquire hardware in the first place.

In any event, to take advantage of conversion costs, it would be to IBM's advantage to make movement among its own systems as difficult as possible so that it could price discriminate between old and new customers. But this is the opposite of what IBM did. In introducing the 360, IBM was among the first to provide compatibility among the computer systems it offered and thus to make it easier for customers to move from one system to another.

6.22. McAdams, of course, by requiring participants in his "market" to meet Withington's "rigorous definition" of "general purpose," thereby defined away one of the principal strategies whereby an entrant can eliminate any conversion cost—that of compatibility with an existing manufacturer. Since entrants choosing to be compatible with IBM software are not counted in McAdams's market, all entrants must—by definition—offer equipment incompatible with that of IBM. But this is the sort of tortuous logic that follows from an artificial market definition obscuring the facts.

It is interesting to note in this regard that with the announcement of 360, IBM not only made it easier for customers to move between its own systems but created an opportunity for switching to other suppliers' systems. With IBM supplying a family of compatible systems, other manufacturers wishing to be software-compatible with IBM's entire customer base could do so by providing compatibility with any one of the family. Had IBM not provided compatibility among so many of its systems, other suppliers would have had to provide software compatibility with many different systems in order to become software-compatible with IBM's customer base. In providing a large compatible family with a common input/output interface in System/360, IBM thus increased opportunities for both suppliers of IBM-compatible CPUs and suppliers of plug-compatible peripherals.

The point here is that to take advantage of "conversion costs," suppliers must be able to exploit their old customers. They cannot do so by facilitating conversion, and if they fail to facilitate conversion, other suppliers will take advantage of the opportunity and will do so themselves.[6.23]

In fact, IBM does not discriminate between new and old customers. Its hardware prices are the same to all users, new and old, converting and nonconverting. Competition for new users prevents IBM, as well as other suppliers, from exploiting any advantage that conversion costs might give it with respect to its existing customers. Consequently, the competitive pressures of other incumbents and potential entrants on the prices and product performance of IBM in its offerings for new installations (that is, installations that do not replace existing equipment and for which there are no conversion costs) necessarily act as constraints on IBM's offerings for replacement of existing IBM (or non-IBM) equipment, since the same prices and products are involved in both situations.

Only if one adopts the greatly mistaken assumption that, for the most part, all uses and users of computing equipment have been found

6.23. In this connection, the story of the Honeywell 200 and its LIBERATOR is illuminating. Had IBM desired to take advantage of conversion costs, it would have made it difficult for users of its highly successful 1400 series computers to convert to 360 systems and it would have raised rental charges on the 1400 series computers. It could not do this because of competition. For example, in December 1963, a few months before IBM announced System/360 (April 1964), Honeywell announced its H-200 computer with its LIBERATOR, which allowed the H-200 to emulate the IBM 1400 series, and users began to convert to the H-200 (Historical Narrative, pp. 619–620). IBM thus had to provide compatibility between the 360 and the 1400 series by providing 1400 emulation on System/360 (Beard, Tr. 9956–58, 10231–32; Enfield, Tr. 20020–24; Case, Tr. 73048–49; PX 3647, p. 2).

and that a new entrant must succeed in displacing currently installed equipment in order to enter and grow can one even begin to take seriously the notion that conversion costs are a barrier to entry. Even then, as we have seen, such a notion would be incorrect.

Bundling

The practice of "bundling" is the provision by hardware manufacturers of certain software and support without separate charge from the hardware. There is general agreement on the salutary effects of the practice of bundling on computer users and on the growth and development of the market for computers. Nevertheless, the government asserted that the practice constituted a barrier to entry into the market.[53]

The government claimed that bundling "significantly increas[ed] the breadth of goods and services a would-be competitor had to supply to this market before he could be considered an effective participant," thereby leading to increased capital requirements for entry. In addition, bundling allegedly "inhibited the development of a computer support services industry," which would have facilitated the "entry of new systems manufacturers by providing the support capacity which the potential competitors found necessary to offer in order to compete with IBM." According to McAdams, bundling "has tended to deprive users of specialization. Each of the systems manufacturers has had to have a substantial amount of generalized capacity." This, according to Lee Preston, raised technical and financial requirements for entry and made difficult "toehold" entry when an entrant begins by offering specialized functions or products and then expands.[54]

Apart from the claim that barriers to entry resulted, the government claimed that bundling software and support services gave IBM the ability to discriminate among its customers so as to thwart competition: "Because IBM could vary the amount of support services it provided any given customer without a resulting change in price, IBM was able to meet competitive threats merely by increasing the size of the bundle of services offered. . . . In so doing, IBM could subsidize certain competitive accounts at the expense of those accounts not needing or desiring the services IBM could provide."[55]

Curiously, however, these claims about bundling were limited to a short period of time—from 1965, when bundling was said to have ceased being "necessary from the perspective of the user," to 1969, when IBM unbundled, having announced its intention to do so in late 1968.[56]

Bundling and the Growth of the Market   The elements that were offered without a separate price were nonhardware elements, such as education, software, and systems design services.[6.24] Originally, this support had to be provided by manufacturers in order to market their equipment to users taking the risk of accepting a new, unfamiliar, and expensive object, the computer. "The sale itself, however, was considered the 'computer hardware,' while all other services provided were specified simply as support for the 'sale.'"[57]

In the earliest days, the support and services necessary to operate computer systems effectively simply would not have been available to a wide base of customers unless offered by the manufacturer. Moreover, users were interested not only in the price of the hardware they were acquiring but in the total cost of performing their data processing tasks effectively and reliably. Bundling offered users "a predictable cost that they could budget against," and they "also knew that the undefined problems that existed in data processing, in their computing world, would be covered as well." Thus, bundling was a useful marketing approach for a manufacturer—offering what customers wanted and were willing to pay for. Accordingly, virtually "[a]ll the computer manufacturers marketed on a bundled basis" from at least the time of Univac I. "Free programming support, free programs, and free user education became expected clauses to any hardware leasing or contractual arrangement."[58]

User demand for bundled software and support continued during the period of the introduction of the new and complex third-generation hardware and software during the mid- and late-1960s. New lines and new ways of doing things were being introduced, requiring customer training, programming, and systems design services.[59] IBM encountered such requirements with the introduction of its System/360 line. In January 1964, F. P. Brooks, one of the fathers of System/360, foresaw the problems that the advances incorporated in that family of computers would cause with respect to user education: "[t]he breadth of System/360 and the number of innovations, particularly in gross systems concept, will require substantial lead time between announcement and proper installation. . . . The sheer amount of new abilities, new options, new specifications, and new prices will require time for the customer to assimilate. A major education program for IBM field personnel and

6.24. IBM also maintained the stock of computers that it owned and leased to customers without charging separately for such maintenance. Maintenance issues are discussed later.

customers must intervene between announcement and successful installation."[60]

Thus, while the long life of the architecture of System/360 would ultimately make it possible for IBM to unbundle as users became familiar with that architecture, the sharp increase in complexity as users moved from second-generation equipment to System/360 made the years immediately following System/360's introduction in April 1964 a particularly inopportune time at which to do so (contrary to the government's claim about the 1965–1968 period). Users were being trained and retrained to use far more complex equipment in increasingly sophisticated ways than had hitherto been possible. Withington wrote in 1968 that

Programmers and system analysts are in inadequate supply. . . . The advanced, integrated applications many users wish to implement are novel and very complex and require much more creative, high-level system analysis than the simpler, second generation applications did. . . .

The increasing complexity of the third generation hardware and software (a necessary corollary to its increased capability) makes it difficult for the average user to understand and use. It may take longer than it used to for users to fully exploit the equipment they are currently installing: many users will not be able to use anything larger or more complex for a number of years.[61]

Other manufacturers also experienced and responded to the increased user demand for support in the 1960s; indeed, some of them remained bundled later than did IBM. Honeywell even responded to IBM's 1969 unbundling announcement (which it believed would be regarded as a price increase) by increasing its own prices slightly and advertising its offering of "the same old bundle of joy."[62] By responding to user demands for bundled services, vendors provided the assurance that users required as computers became rapidly more sophisticated and complex and more and more users began to use them. Vendors accepted the responsibility of ensuring that their equipment would operate efficiently and suit user needs and relieved users of the risk that their systems would not work. Until third-generation architecture had stabilized and users had been educated and were accustomed to computer use, it was natural to provide that assurance without separately charging for it.[63]

Bundling was thus a crucial element of the growth of the market and continued to be desired by users in 1965–1968. Do the facts suggest that it was a barrier to entry?

Systems Engineers   At IBM, the provision of bundled support began before the installation or even the acquisition of a computer by the customer. The systems engineer (SE) assisted in the preparation of the proposal made to the customer. The IBM sales representatives drew on them for technical support. Systems engineers worked with customers to define requirements, design the system configuration, and develop approaches to applications problems. They also engaged in customer education and training and in programming. This work would sometimes continue after installation, since systems engineers were responsible for "making sure that the customer was indeed implementing the targeted applications, the business applications, and doing the job properly and being of whatever assistance we could to make sure that the machine was . . . performing properly."[64]

Thus, much of the SE support offered on a bundled basis represented part of the task of IBM's marketing of its own computers; this was true of other manufacturers as well.[65] To the extent that such support services constituted marketing efforts and support for the manufacturer in its marketing of complex products, it is obvious that such services could not be charged for; they represented marketing costs to the manufacturer that would be recovered (if at all) in the product prices if the manufacturer was successful.

The amount of SE services assigned to a particular account before or after installation did not vary in any simple way. IBM's John Akers testified that IBM's systems engineers "were a scarce resource within the branch office" and that SEs "were allocated on the basis of how much assistance a particular customer needed at a particular time; the degree of experience that the customer had; whether or not that customer perhaps required additional educational effort because he or she was installing a new computer system or computer system for the first time." Systems engineers were assigned to customers on the basis of "who needed the work done and what had to be done to make it a successful installation."[66]

One would expect such variations. Computer manufacturers provided users with systems engineering services to familiarize users with their computers and to ensure that those computers functioned properly in solving customer problems. They were an important part of the process of minimizing risks so as to induce customers to acquire computer systems in the first place and to learn how to use them and expand them later on. But, by relieving customers of such risks, IBM, like other manufacturers, accepted the risks. By giving users "a predictable cost that they could budget against," the manufacturer took over the uncertainty in cost resulting from unforeseen variation in user needs. This necessarily led to variation among accounts. In particular, large accounts in terms of revenue might not require more systems engineers than did smaller ones unless they were also more complex—and complex in relation to the abilities of the customer's own data processing personnel.[67]

It was, indeed, the sophistication of the customer's personnel that was important for IBM's future expenses. Since, by bundling, IBM and other manufacturers assumed the obligation (and the substantial cost) of assisting customers to operate in a useful and efficient manner, these manufacturers stood to gain if, in the course of providing that assistance, they could also educate customers so that they would not require such assistance in the future. In the long run, this could be accomplished in part by the provision of increasingly sophisticated operating systems relieving customer programmers of a number of complex tasks. It could also be accomplished directly through systems engineers' training of customer personnel in both the use of the advancing software/hardware combinations and the tasks that had not yet been taken over by software. It was in IBM's interest to provide customers with the resources needed to make them self-sufficient, and this provision was made to all customers even if it might actually require more resources to be provided to some than to others at any particular time.[68]

To subsidize some accounts at the expense of others by offering accounts open to competition, a relatively large number of systems engineers would have been self-defeating. It would not have led to fully satisfied self-sufficient customers in the "subsidized" accounts. Further, by offering less assistance than needed to the "subsidizing" accounts, IBM would be leaving them dissatisfied and open to competition as well.[69] The fact that some customers actually required more services than did others only reflects the fact that in an uncertain situation, outcomes will be different. We shall return to this later.

The policy of promoting self-sufficiency of customers, however, carried with it an end to the practice of not charging separately for such services. When enough customers became self-sufficient and when changes in hardware and software ceased to require them to be taught very new ways of operating, it was no longer necessary to bundle. By increasing self-sufficiency in customers, IBM created a growing group that did not require the bundle. The exact date on which that group was sufficiently large that it made sense to unbundle and provide the formerly bundled services at separate charges for those who wanted them is a matter of judgment. In IBM's judgment it came in 1969.[6.25]

6.25. IBM announced its intention to unbundle in December 1968, before the complaint

Software and Software Companies   As the EDP market developed in the late 1950s and early 1960s, systems vendors had to meet a demand for increasingly sophisticated software. That demand increased enormously in the mid-1960s when the supply of a sophisticated operating system became necessary in order to succeed. Operating systems and other manufacturer-supplied software were provided at no separately stated charge. Further, user groups such as SHARE and GUIDE exchanged user-written software.[70]

Despite this, a large and flourishing group of software houses entered the market starting in the late 1950s. That group grew rapidly throughout the 1960s, a period during which IBM and most other systems manufacturers bundled software. Such firms began as contractors, assisting hardware vendors in the creation of operating systems and went on to offer software products directly to users, who at all times have done the lion's share of programming. Writing in 1966 "to state the opposition of the Department of Justice to the issuance of patents on computer programming methods," which would have promoted charges for software, Donald F. Turner, then assistant attorney general in charge of the Antitrust Divison, described the situation eloquently:

The computer industry is one of the most dynamic in the American economy, in terms of absolute as well as relative growth, and further rapid expansion is anticipated. . . . Current investment in programming or the "software" portion of the computer industry, is approximately equal to the equipment or "hardware" portion, and should surpass it in the very near future. Growth in the software portion of the computer industry has been facilitated by a remarkably free and easy exchange of ideas, concepts and programs. One of the notable features of the programming industry, indeed, has been the widespread establishment, sponsorship, and universal acceptance of joint user groups to facilitate the exchange of programs and algorithms. As a result, for the past twenty years, almost all basic ideas in computer programming have been available openly to all computer users.

One of the major policy arguments advanced for extension of patent protection to computer programs is a supposed need to encourage individuals and companies to invest in programming development. But it is difficult to conceive how the field of programming could have grown faster, or that its past growth has been hampered in any meaningful fashion by a lack of investment funds. *If anything, the current*

---

in *U.S.* v. *IBM* but well after the start of the Antitrust Division's investigation. The extent to which the possibility of litigation weighed in the unbundling decision is a matter of pure speculation.

free interchange of programs has led to an extraordinarily efficient use of scarce programming talent and has kept needless duplication of existing programs and techniques to a minimum. Furthermore, many small software companies have achieved financial and technical success by producing more efficient versions of widely used manufacturer-developed programs. These more efficient versions of operating programs benefit other software producers, computer manufacturers, computer users, and the general public. In the light of past experience, any step which could upset the vital interchange of programming materials should be approached with the utmost caution.[71]

Even so, the "field of programming" was about to grow even faster. By 1965, there were approximately 40 to 50 independent suppliers of software. Between 1965 and 1969, the number of software suppliers "exploded" in a period described by government witness Lawrence Welke as "the flowering of the independent software industry." Welke estimated that by 1968 there were approximately 2,800 software vendors. This entry and growth of software vendors was stimulated by the development and introduction of System/360 because of the "increased complexity of the hardware technology, as well as the software technology." Users ordering System/360 needed help in planning for and converting to the new hardware and software, and "this, in turn, caused a demand that was reflected back onto the software firms." Also, during the period of the introduction of System/360, "people expanded the use of computers and put more and more applications on," which required more programming. By the late 1960s, the most successful independently supplied software products were competing against IBM programming that was not separately priced, providing savings through higher efficiency.[72]

Bundling cannot in fact have significantly restricted the number and growth of independent software companies in such a way as to hamper hardware manufacturers, as the government claimed. By the time of IBM's unbundling in 1969, there were a large number of software houses providing contract programming, and revenues from that source were much greater than from independent software products being marketed to end users. Contract programming was not affected by the tradition of not charging users separately for software, and it was precisely the ability to secure contract programming that entering hardware manufacturers wanted and on the government's theory were not able to obtain.[73]

Was Bundling a Barrier to Entry?   The facts thus squarely contradict the claim that bundling was a barrier to entry because it forced hardware vendors to provide all the supporting services and software themselves instead of being able to contract to obtain them from independent suppliers. Hardware manufacturers, including entrants, could and did contract with such suppliers, thus providing customers with the necessary software without producing it in-house. Between 30 and 50 percent of the systems software developed for third-generation computers was developed by independent software suppliers.[74]

There were also firms whose entry was facilitated by the very practice of providing operating software at no separately stated charge. Suppliers of plug-compatible peripheral equipment for attachment to IBM systems, for example, did not have to provide system control programming for their devices because the IBM operating system was available to them and in the public domain. Moreover, when Amdahl and other manufacturers of IBM-compatible CPUs began in the mid-1970s, they did not have to provide any operating software at all.

In any event, assuming that there was a necessity to provide users with the complete set of hardware, software, and services to fill their needs, this would not be an entry barrier. A barrier to entry is something that gives incumbent firms a persistent advantage over potential entrants. If, in order to "force" others to bundle, IBM had to bundle itself, then IBM had to meet the same requirements as did anyone else. This proposition is no different from the proposition that the provision by IBM of covers to its boxes or peripheral equipment was not a barrier to entry. To the extent that customers desired such things, demanded them from IBM and others, and chose to do business with firms which met those demands, there were no costs incurred by potential entrants that were not also incurred by IBM.[75]

Customers demanded that manufacturers of hardware provide software, support, and maintenance in the EDP market because such things were essential to data processing and not otherwise available. Thus, even assuming that there were a necessity to provide these things in-house, as was not the case, that necessity would not amount to a barrier to entry any more than the requirement to provide hardware, unless incumbents have a capital or other cost advantage.[6.26] We have already seen that this was not so.

6.26. The most likely source of such an advantage lies in economies of scale discussed earlier. In principle, such economies do exist in software, but the entry of small software houses shows that they cannot matter here. (Economies of scale in maintenance, which present a similar issue, are discussed later.) Note that some other vendors remained bundled after IBM unbundled in 1969.

As users became more sophisticated and were willing to bear the risks themselves, firms seeking to fill the software needs of users appeared—as one would expect in a competitive market. It was thus simply not so, as Preston suggested, that bundling made "toehold" entry impossible, for entrants did not have to offer everything themselves or, if they did, produce it all in-house. Of course, the government failed to recognize such entry because it *defined* its market in a way that did not count "in" anyone less than a miniature copy of IBM.

Could bundling have been a barrier in some other way? Suppose, contrary to the conclusion reached here, that IBM subsidized accounts that competition threatened at the expense of "unthreatened" accounts. This would not constitute a barrier to entry (in the absence of a capital barrier), for entering firms could do the same thing. Moreover, a barrier to entry exists only when the incumbent can raise prices or offer inferior products without inducing entry. Hence, for bundling to have been a barrier to entry, IBM would have had to have the ability to block entry in those accounts in which it did *not* give a great deal of service. For that to have been true, there would have to have been some barrier apart from the giving of service. In short, bundling in and of itself cannot constitute a barrier to entry even if all firms had to bundle. In order for there to be such a barrier to entry, there must be something that made it less costly for IBM to bundle than for others.

In any case, IBM could not "force" other firms to bundle. Only the demands of customers could do that, and IBM could not force the bundle on unwilling customers without encouraging entry. If a significant number of customers would have preferred not to buy the bundled package but to purchase only hardware or only hardware and some software, then, by bundling, IBM would have made it *easier*, not harder, for new hardware suppliers to enter and take those customers away. Similarly, if IBM subsidized some accounts by providing them services while forcing others to pay for services they did not want, the latter accounts would have been particularly susceptible to competition by suppliers that would sell them only the wanted goods and services. Such a strategy was initially followed by DEC and SDS and, to a lesser extent, by CDC, all of which later found it profitable to increase the amount of software and support they offered.[76]

Likewise, computer manufacturers, other than IBM, already in the market, were already providing a full line of services. If the bundle had not been desired by some of IBM's customers, those other manufacturers would have found it easier to offer less of a bundle, price some items separately, reduce their hardware prices, and take away those customers. In addition, those manufacturers could have marketed their products and services on both a bundled and an unbundled basis, giving users a choice. Yet most other manufacturers bundled.

Note the importance of this. The bundling-equals-barrier argument about the necessity of providing all the support IBM offered might (if correct) provide a reason why all manufacturers had to offer software and services with their hardware. But, even accepting that argument, it provides no reason why such manufacturers had to provide a full line of software and services *at no separate price*. Indeed, if the bundle had been used by IBM to discriminate between customers, then other manufacturers would have found it profitable to offer separately priced items rather than bundling themselves. There is no reason that everybody else had to do something because IBM did, unless customers demanded it. The fact that other manufacturers chose to do business on the same basis as IBM is the best possible proof that that basis was indeed one designed to serve customer needs.

Indeed, when IBM unbundled in 1969, not all firms did so. Some firms perceived the very real possibility that they could thereby obtain an advantage over IBM by offering to retain the risks that customers would now have to assume themselves if dealing with IBM. It was not obvious in 1969 which was the best way to respond to customer needs.[77]

Was Bundling Price Discrimination?   Even though bundling was not a barrier to entry, did differences in the amount of services provided to different accounts evidence monopoly power? Was bundling a form of price discrimination?

In the first place, price discrimination does not show "monopoly power," although it may show some market power. Further, to the extent that bundling shows market power in this way, it follows that any firm that bundles has market power, not just IBM. However, such variation in support is not in fact price discrimination in any meaningful sense.

The reason for this is clear if one understands the difference between risks viewed *ex ante* (before the outcome of a risky event is known) and risks viewed *ex post* (afterwards). In providing the bundle, manufacturers accept risks concerning the proper installation and use of their products. In effect, they are providing a warranty for customers. Not very surprisingly after the event, it may turn out that some customers appear to benefit more from that warranty than do others. That is the nature of the acceptance of responsibility for the outcome of uncertain events. After those events become known and are no longer uncertain, some of them may turn out to be favorable and others unfavorable. That some customers turned out not to need the bundled software and support as much as others is only a reflection of this fact.[6.27]

It follows that bundling could have involved price discrimination only if classes of customers differing as to the risks involved could be distinguished *in advance*. So far as we can tell from the trial record, this was not possible. (It appears to have been difficult even to classify customers into such groups *ex post*.) Moreover, if risks could have been classified in advance, it would have been easy for other manufacturers to bid away the low-risk customers of IBM by offering to accept fewer risks (by providing fewer services) at a lower price, since, presumably, they could have figured out which were the low-risk customers. In this respect, the situation differs from the bundling case in *United States v. United Shoe Machinery Corp.*, in which there were no other competitors. The claim that bundling was price discrimination is at odds with the claim that it was a barrier to entry. Both claims cannot be true; in fact, neither is.[78]

Summary   The fundamental fact about bundling is that it provided customers with assurance that their systems would work and satisfy their needs. By bundling, the manufacturer, not the customer, assumed the risk involved in making that happen. No doubt, manufacturers would have preferred not to have to do this; however, until a sizeable group of customers became "self-sufficient" and able and willing to absorb such risks for themselves, competition required that manufacturers absorb such risks if they wished to sell or lease their computers to the majority of users. Over time, such self-sufficiency did develop, partly due to the experience customers gained under the bundled arrangement. This led first to the ability of such firms as DEC or SDS to offer their equipment to technically sophisticated users without a lot of support services or software, and then, as the "self-sufficient" group

6.27. Of course, the fact that the software and services involved were offered at no separately stated charge gave those customers that did turn out to need them every incentive to ask for them. Like all manufacturers accepting such risks, IBM felt the burden of meeting those demands (PX 2804A, pp. 1, 2; PX 2805A, p. 1; PX 4053, p. 1; PX 1748, p. 11), which undoubtedly contributed to IBM's desire to promote self-sufficiency in its customers.

became even larger, to general unbundling by IBM and eventually by other manufacturers.

No doubt, if all companies in the early days had agreed among themselves to charge separately for support services and software, customers, having no choice, would have been compelled to accept such arrangements, but the market would not have developed as fast as it did. Since customers were more willing to take equipment when manufacturers assumed the risks involved, by bundling, than when they did not, a marketing opportunity was created. Only a noncompetitive market could have avoided the pursuit of that opportunity first by one or two firms and then by all competing for the customers' business. Some manufacturers undoubtedly would rather not have bundled but felt that they had to do so in order to compete with IBM. Competition, while conferring benefits on customers, is often disliked by those who have to compete. That does not make it a barrier to entry.

Maintenance
The analysis of maintenance practices involves some of the same issues as that of bundling. The government alleged that the practice of providing maintenance with no separate charge on leased equipment (IBM separately priced it on sold equipment) resulted in a restriction on the entry and growth of independent maintenance vendors so that "computer systems manufacturers competing with IBM have been forced to provide maintenance internally." In the government's view, new systems manufacturers have been deprived of the cost benefits that would allegedly flow to them as a result of the existence of regional maintenance firms of optimal scale that "could provide the same level of service to customers of all systems manufacturers."[79]

There are a number of reasons for computer hardware manufacturers to assume the maintenance responsibility for their own leased equipment. "Excellence in maintenance is critically important" to users because of the disastrous impact that extended periods of downtime have. In addition, the manufacturer must consider the effects that inadequate maintenance would have on the asset when it is returned from lease. Presumably for these reasons, a number of systems manufacturers in addition to IBM choose to provide maintenance on their own equipment as part of the rental agreement and at no separate charge.[80]

Moreover, independent computer maintenance companies have in fact entered and grown, offering maintenance services on a broad geographic basis to IBM and non-IBM users. These companies have competed for the maintenance of purchased computers, including computer equipment leased by leasing companies to end users. Partly because of the increase in leasing company purchases, the number of the available IBM-manufactured computers on which maintenance was separately priced was substantial and growing in the second half of the 1960s. By the mid-1970s, such independent maintenance service was available in or near every major city, aided in part by IBM cooperation.[81]

No doubt, independent maintenance companies would have preferred also to maintain IBM's leased computers. The complexity of the contractual arrangements that would have been involved, however (performance bonds, specification of type and speed of response to service calls, assurances as to parts, etc.), is the sort of thing that makes vertical integration efficient. In addition, the provision of in-house maintenance leads to continued input from customer needs into product development plans. Thus, it is not surprising to find that hardware manufacturers often provide their own maintenance even though independent contractors exist and that some new manufacturers, after an initial period of using such a contractor, elect to develop their own maintenance capability.[82]

Put all this aside, however, and consider the possibility that by separately pricing the maintenance of its own leased equipment, IBM would have facilitated greater growth by independent maintenance companies that would have achieved regional economies of scale, which could then have been transferred to the maintenance of the computer products of new vendors. There are two possibilities to consider, depending on whether the efficiencies involved in maintenance—the spare parts and skills of the field engineers involved—can be transferred between manufacturers. We shall call the case in which they cannot be so transferred "manufacturer independent."

It appears evident that spare parts must be manufacturer-dependent, if not, indeed, machine-dependent.[6.28] Different manufacturers use different parts in their machines. This means that the economies of scale involved in the inventory of spare parts are economies within a single manufacturer. One could not obtain those economies by servicing the machines of several manufacturers. Servicing the machines of manufacturer A and manufacturer B requires the same spare parts inventory regardless of whether the same organization services both.

6.28. If such economies are machine-dependent, then no manufacturer, including IBM, gains any advantage from the size of its installed base of older machines when maintaining its newer models.

It is not so obvious whether the services of field engineers are manufacturer-dependent. This has to do with whether training and experience on one manufacturer's machines can be transferred and used in the maintenance of other manufacturers' machines. Such transference need not be direct; an engineer trained to maintain the machines of manufacturer A may be better able to learn to maintain the machines of manufacturer B in less time than an engineer starting from scratch. However, Withington testified that when a company acquires the lease base of another company, "[t]he maintenance of the machines is a distinct and different problem from maintenance of the acquirer's existing ones" and the maintenance force that serves the newly acquired equipment "must be maintained as an independent and separately trained force indefinitely thereafter."[83]

To the extent that economies of scale in maintenance are manufacturer-dependent, IBM's provision of maintenance on its leased computers could have no influence on entry. Customers acquiring computers from companies other than IBM wish to have those computers maintained. The computers have to be maintained either by the manufacturer, by the customer, or by third parties such as independent maintenance organizations. In any case, someone has to bear the cost of maintaining them, and one would expect those costs ultimately to be passed on to customers. This is so regardless of whether the manufacturer itself maintains the computers. In the manufacturer-dependent case, the fact that IBM maintains its leased computers is of no relevance. If IBM had not done so, others, including third parties, maintaining IBM computers would not have obtained any advantage transferable to the maintenance of other manufacturers' computers. That is what manufacturer-dependence means. Even had IBM entirely contracted maintenance out to third parties, manufacturer-dependence would imply that this would have assisted in no way in providing maintenance for the equipment of other manufacturers.

On the other hand, to the extent that whatever economies of scale can be achieved in maintenance are transferable among the equipment of various manufacturers, independent maintenance houses can achieve those economies by maintaining the equipment of several manufacturers together with the large base of purchased IBM equipment and thereby provide entering vendors with an independent maintenance resource on which to draw. Furthermore, economies that result from the transference of field engineering training and skills to the maintenance of the equipment of different manufacturers can be captured by independent maintenance houses (or other manufacturers) regardless of whether IBM maintains its own assets. All that is required is the hiring away of IBM's customer engineers, as COMMA (an independent maintenance house) did at the time of its entry.[6.29, 84]

Thus, in either case, IBM's policy of protecting its own assets by maintaining them itself could not be a barrier to entry. Indeed, it was not. The maintenance by IBM of its own computers did not keep independent maintenance houses from arising. Hardware manufacturers seeking to enter could and did contract with such houses, although many hardware firms—like IBM—preferred to maintain their own assets themselves.

To summarize, the history of entry shows that barriers to entry into the EDP industry (or even the government's narrow "market") are unlikely to have been substantial. Analysis of the barriers alleged to have existed bears out this conclusion. These alleged barriers were not barriers at all.

6.29. This assumes that the set of other manufacturers' equipment plus the set of IBM equipment owned by users or by leasing companies is large enough to achieve any regional economies of scale. This is a very large base of machines.

Chapter 7

Profits

We have already seen that market share measures, at their best, are but crude indicators of monopoly power, requiring careful analysis of their sources. The question naturally arises whether there is any other simple way to identify monopoly. At first sight one such way seems to be available. Simple economics appears to teach that a monopoly earns profits while competitive firms do not. Hence it is tempting to conclude that one can identify monopoly by looking at profits. As we shall see, the government's economists yielded to that temptation and testified extensively as to IBM's high accounting rate of return (profits divided by either stockholders' equity or total capitalization) as compared to other firms.

There is considerable support for such a procedure in the economics literature. Led by Leonard Weiss (whose testimony will be discussed), a large number of studies have investigated the relation between accounting profit rates and variables representing industry structure. In such studies, high accounting rates of return have been interpreted as indicating noncompetitive levels of profit; in the case of a single firm, this would be monopoly profit.[1] Further, high accounting profits have been directly interpreted in industry studies in this way.[2]

Despite this history, the facile identification of high accounting profit rates with monopoly is unwarranted. In part, this is due to practical problems well-known in the literature (and partially recognized in theory—but not in practice—by the government's economists); in part it is due to less well-recognized problems of principle. Indeed, while the phenomena in question are discussed in some of the literature and have even entered testimony in at least one other antitrust case,[3] their importance has not been fully appreciated. This is no light matter, for, as we shall see in this chapter, the problems involved are so large as to make *any* inference from accounting rates of return as to the presence of economic profits, and a fortiori monopoly profits, totally impossible in practice.

Theory and Measurement

The difficulties with the inference of monopoly profits from high accounting profit rates begin with two facts. Accounting profits differ from economic profits, and not all economic profits are monopoly profits. The difference between accounting and economic profits may be preliminarily summarized as follows. Accounting profits consist of gross revenues less the costs that appear on the books of the firm, including depreciation. Economic profits, on the other hand, involve a different definition of costs in which the cost attributed to each factor is its opportunity cost, the amount which the factor could earn elsewhere. In particular, as seen in chapter 2, such costs include the return on capital necessary to induce the owners of capital to take the risks involved in investing in the business. Other opportunity costs not appearing on the books of the firm may also be involved.

The reason for such a definition (which will be considered at greater length) is that it gives to economic profits the role they play in economic analysis, namely, of signaling that more resources should be devoted to a particular industry. We have already considered that role in chapter 2; now we must explore it more extensively before returning to the definitional question.

The Role of Economic Profits

The proposition that economic profits are not earned in competition is false. That statement is true only as regards positions of long-run competitive equilibrium. To concentrate only on such situations is to lose sight of the fundamental role played by profits and is particularly dangerous in analyzing an industry characterized by continual change.

Long-run equilibrium requires either that demand, costs, and technology all be unchanging or that changes in them be completely and accurately foreseen. If either set of requirements prevails, competitive equilibrium necessarily implies the absence of economic profits—positive profits would induce entry and expansion until the economic profits were eliminated and losses would induce exit and contraction until the losses were eliminated. Economic profits are, however, consistent with long-run equilibrium in the presence of monopoly, which requires barriers both to the entry and the expansion of competitors in order to exist. Those barriers prevent the expansion of supply that causes prices to drop until economic profits disappear. However, even firms in competitive markets earn economic profits temporarily until incumbents and entrants have adjusted to conditions of demand, cost, and technology.

Merely to state that profits disappear in long-run competitive equilibrium is to observe only the theoretical end result of the role that profits play in competitive markets. Further, it is to concentrate on the least important aspect of that role in real-world competitive markets, which may *never* be in long-run equilibrium. The important fact about economic profits concerns not their disappearance in equilibrium but their role in the adjustment processes that are expected to lead toward equilibrium positions. Economic profits are the incentives that cause firms to act—thus, they are the ultimate mechanism that allocates resources to productive uses; compels firms to be efficient; stimulates innovation, skillful management, and responsiveness to user demands; and persuades firms to take risks where the benefits of success outweigh the risks. In a competitive economy, such private benefit-cost calculations also reflect social benefits and costs.

Thus, unforeseen or inaccurately forecast changes in demand, costs, or technology cause economic profits (or losses) in competitive markets. When demand expands faster than producers have anticipated and provided for, prices rise to ration available supply. In addition, incumbent firms earn economic profits. These profits provide the signal and the incentive for incumbents to expand capacity and for new firms to consider entering. The economic profits attract capital and other resources from other activities. That is a desirable result because the presence of the profits is evidence that society values additional output from the market more than the output that would be lost in other markets as a result of the transfer of resources to be employed in this market. If market demand grows very rapidly relative to the economy as a whole, incumbents and new entrants alike, even in the aggregate, may for some time be unable to grow fast enough to keep up with demand because of inevitable frictions that exist in the adjustment process. In that case, economic profits will continue to exist to attract additional investment until supply as a whole catches up with demand.

Similarly, unforeseen cost reductions, while they ultimately lead to price reductions, also increase the profits of those who first make them. The resulting profits provide the signal and incentive to expand capacity to satisfy the increased quantity demanded at the equilibrium output implied by the lower costs.

Obviously, technological change in the form of new products or processes can be an important source of the unanticipated increases in demand and reductions in costs that generate economic profits, even in competitive markets. Profits in a competitive market accrue to the innovator and more generally to those that attempt to meet customer demands and find cheaper and better ways of doing so. Profits also induce increases in supply and provide the incentive and reward that lead firms to develop and introduce new products and processes. After each successive change in demand and supply, market forces will impel the adjustment process toward equilibrium, but new disruptions may lead to new forces of adjustment long before equilibrium has been reached.[7.1]

One normally expects differences in the profitability of different firms in a real competitive market. Those that through skill or luck respond best to changes in demand will do better than the others and earn more economic profits. The first firms to implement cost reduction techniques or to make product or process innovations will also be the ones rewarded with more economic profits. In general, those firms that innovate achieve particularly efficient management organizations, more effectively predict user needs, and—for any or all of these reasons—serve those needs better will be rewarded by profits for doing so. The existence of economic profits in a market, however, does not mean that all firms will enjoy such profits. Those firms that are less energetic or skillful than others may earn lower profits or suffer losses.

Economic profits are a signal that more resources should be applied to a given activity. In a competitive market, the prospect of profit induces old firms to expand and new firms to enter. One result of this is that, in equilibrium, competition bids profits away. The actual dissipation of profits only happens in equilibrium, however, and equilibrium may not in fact be reached. That is particularly true in innovative competition, in which new developments continually occur. In such competition, profits are the incentive provided to the innovator for successful innovation. They are the rewards for being better than other

7.1. Recognizing that competitive firms may earn profits while the market adjusts toward equilibrium, it might be thought that average profits over periods of five to ten years can be taken as an indicator of competition or monopoly. Under this assumption, one would infer a lack of competition if profits averaged over a five or ten year period are "high" by some standard. Even ignoring all the problems discussed later, such a procedure cannot deal with the existence of profits in competitive disequilibrium. It assumes that "high" and "low" years will somehow cancel out, but there is no warrant for this. When new opportunities are constantly arising, all years may yield "high" profits.

firms in producing products that suit customer needs, being efficient, or having the foresight and skill to develop and serve new market opportunities. While such profits only persist for the innovator so long as others do not successfully do the same things, a market with a continual history of innovation, development, and growth is likely to be a market with a history of economic profits, for it is a market that probably has not yet reached equilibrium.[7.2] Economic profits can persist under competition if disequilibrium persists.

Economic profits also exist in monopoly, but there they continue to exist after long-run equilibrium has been reached. Monopoly profits are the economic profits that arise from an artifically imposed scarcity of the product, that is, from the decision of the monopoly not to produce more output even though customers stand ready to buy more at prices that would more than cover marginal cost. Economic profits may include monopoly profits, but the existence of economic profits does not mean that monopoly profits are being earned. If one seeks to identify monopoly profits, one must first find economic profits and then discover their cause. Only to the extent that economic profits come from a decision to restrict output or output quality (in effect, to raise prices and exclude competitors) are they monopoly profits.

Accounting Profits and Economic Profits

Even in the absence of monopoly and disequilibrium, however, "profits" may still appear on the books of competitive firms. This is because such "accounting profits" do not correspond to economic profits, which are defined so as to play the central role discussed. Since accounting data are the only directly available data, it is very important to understand the difference between accounting and economic profits. There are two kinds of issues involved: the differences between accounting profits and economic profits in dollars and the difference between accounting profits and economic profits as profit rates.

7.2. Only when new opportunities fail to arise can we be be sure that the competitive system actually has a tendency to approach equilibrium. For a formal discussion of the stability theorem involved, see Franklin M. Fisher, "Stability, Disequilibrium Awareness, and the Perception of New Opportunities," *Econometrica* 49 (March 1981), pp. 279–317, or Franklin M. Fisher, *Disequilibrium Foundations of Equilibrium Economics* (Cambridge: Cambridge University Press, 1983).

Opportunity Costs and Risks

The analysis even of the theoretical case of competitive equilibrium only shows equilibrium profits at zero when an appropriate definition of costs is used. That result requires defining costs to include a "normal" return on capital—a return on capital just large enough to keep the current amount of capital in the business without any incentive for contraction or expansion. In other words, costs are defined to include the "opportunity cost" of capital—the return that the capital could make elsewhere, including an allowance for differences in risk. With no return, or too small a return on capital used in a particular business, there would be incentives to employ that capital in areas promising greater returns. Therefore, a certain level of accounting profits is necessary to keep the capital employed in that business. The proposition that the zero profit point is the equilibrium point for competitive markets thus requires that one include part of what accountants call "profits" in what economists call "costs." In practice, this is sometimes dealt with in a slightly different way. One examines accounting profits, which implicitly include the necessary return on capital, calculates a return on capital, and attempts to decide whether or not that return is above or below a "normal" return.

The inclusion of the opportunity cost of capital in costs rather than profits, however, is only one example of the attribution in economics of a portion of accounting profits to a cost, namely, to an implicit payment to a factor of production. There are other such examples as well; these are generally known as "rents."

Suppose that, in a competitive market, one firm happens to have a particularly advantageous location for its plant, being located close to its source of raw materials, for example. Suppose that other firms cannot acquire equally advantageous locations. In such a case, the firm in question will earn accounting profits, even in equilibrium. Its accounts will show that its average costs are less than those of its competitors.[7.3] As a result, it will earn accounting profits (revenues minus costs) when its rivals do not. Such accounting profits are not economic profits, however; they are economic rents.

The accounting profits in this example arise not from the activity of the firm in its production business but from its advantageous location.

7.3. This will not generally be true of its marginal costs. In equilibrium, the firm in question, like all competitive firms, will operate where marginal cost equals price, and it will be the same price for all firms. This may imply a larger output for the advantageously located firm than for the others.

Thus, one ought to think of the firm as both a landlord and a manufacturing firm. As a landlord, it has the choice of either renting the advantageous location to itself or renting to another manufacturer. What should the rental price be? It should be the difference between what the firm can expect to make at another location (zero in equilibrium) and what it can expect to make if it has this location—the accounting profits made by the original firm. If the original firm does not choose to rent the advantageous location to one of its rivals, then it is forgoing money it could otherwise make. In contemplating rational decisions about its business, the firm should value the land at its *opportunity cost*, the amount it could get for the land by renting it elsewhere. Just as the opportunity cost of capital appears (implicitly) in accounting profits but not in economic profits, the opportunity cost of another factor of production (the land) appears in accounting profits but not in economic profits. In terms of the economic analysis of competition, such opportunity costs are properly included in costs and not in profits in this example. In such cases, accounting profits here contain an "unimputed rent," that is, an element of rent that properly belongs to a factor of production but is not imputed to that factor on the firm's books.

There are sources of rents other than advantageous locations. For example, a firm that makes a process innovation and reduces its costs will make accounting profits. One way of regarding those profits is as accruing to the innovating or technology-changing activities of the firm. So far as the manufacturing activity is concerned, these accounting profits contain unimputed rents, for the firm could sell or lease its discovery to others for the difference it would make in their costs. Hence, by retaining the innovation itself the firm forgoes the opportunity of earning such money. Even if it does lease its innovation to others, one must think of the firm's own manufacturing activity as paying the same lease price for the innovation if one is properly to attribute profits to the different activities of the firm.

In general, rents (which may reflect economic profits in other activities) differ from profits in production because they do not signal a need for an expansion of production activities themselves. They arise instead from a scarcity of some underlying factor, land or particular skills, for example. If factor owners and firms are not the same, competition for scarce factors is likely to make such unimputed rents imputed unless—as is possible in an efficient management system—the rents reside in a large team rather than in any small group of individuals. When the firm itself owns the scarce factors, such imputation will not take place, for firms do not generally keep their books so as directly to reflect their opportunity costs. Rents that remain unimputed form part of accounting profits but not of economic profits.

Depreciation

The costs that firms experience include some costs properly attributable only to specific, short-run time periods. The wages paid a production worker, for example, constitute payment for his services during the period for which he is paid. Generally, however, the firm will have other costs attributable to benefits or services spread out in time. Principal among these will be the cost of its capital assets, that is, of its capital stock.[7.4] Thus, the physical plant or the production machinery of the firm is generally acquired at one period of time but yields benefits over an extended period. It is particularly relevant for the computer market that the capital stock also includes the stock of equipment owned and out on lease with customers. The issue for profit calculations is how to take the costs of such plant and equipment properly into account.

To understand the problem, consider the obvious alternative of expensing all such costs as they occur, that is, of treating the costs of plant and equipment as though they were just like any other costs incurred in a particular year. To do so would give quite a misleading picture of profits. It would show a large downturn in profits, perhaps losses in the year of the investment expense. It would show relatively high (and sometimes very high) profits thereafter. Yet such high profits in later years could not have been achieved had the investment expense not been incurred, for the capital equipment invested in will still be in use. Thus, it is sensible to attribute the investment costs to the years of useful life of the plant or equipment in question, treating some of the costs as being incurred in every year. Such spreading of investment costs corresponds to the fact that benefits from the investment are earned in different years; it is the source of "depreciation."

What is a proper attribution of capital costs over the years of useful life? As we shall see, except for its effects on taxes, depreciation is not an issue in the evaluation of the economic rate of return, to be defined.

7.4. "Capital stock" does not refer to the securities issued by the firm. It refers to the stock of capital assets that the firm has—for the most part, the collection of plant and equipment in which the firm has invested.

In general, however, one can say that since the purpose of spreading such costs is to match them with the benefits they bring, depreciation schedules ought to reflect the time structure of such benefits. That will generally be impossible to do exactly; more important, the books of actual firms generally cannot be expected to do it very well at all. The time profile of benefits resulting from a capital investment may have quite a complicated shape. For example, benefits may first rise and then fall. But actual firms are restricted in their depreciation accounting by generally accepted accounting principles and the tax code and follow certain fairly simple depreciation formulas (straight-line, declining-balance, or sum-of-the-years' digits, for example). Depending on the different depreciation schedules adopted by particular firms, their accounting profits, which subtract depreciation from gross profits, will differ.

Does that difference mean that firms that choose a more accelerated form of depreciation are understating their profits relative either to firms with less rapid depreciation schedules or to economic profits? Certainly not. Such comparisons depend on what the true time profile of benefits actually looks like. If all firms being compared have identical or similar time schedules of benefits, then (*and only then*) might it be said that firms choosing to depreciate quickly have understated their profits relative to firms that choose to depreciate slowly. Even then, it may simply be the case that firms that choose slower depreciation methods are overstating their profits. (Moreover, as we shall see, even such a comparative statement is *not* true of the effects of depreciation on the relative economic profit rates of return of firms, and it is economic profit rates of return that count in assessing the presence of monopoly profits.)

This does not mean that one can get a clearer picture of profits by ignoring depreciation altogether and adding it back into accounting profits. To do so is to ignore investment costs altogether—to treat all capital equipment as though it were free. Nor can it be said that such a procedure gives a better picture of the relative status of different firms using different accounting methods than is obtained with depreciation left in. For example, if one firm uses relatively capital-intensive, automated methods and another firm uses less capital-intensive methods, ignoring depreciation by adding it back simply understates the costs and overstates the profits of the relatively capital-intensive firm to a greater extent than it understates the costs of the less capital-intensive firm. It will have that effect even if both firms use the same method of depreciation. Depreciation represents a real and important element of cost. One cannot ignore it.

The reason that depreciation creates a problem is, as we have seen, a matter of timing. Such matters of timing lie at the heart of the problems surrounding attempts to estimate profits as a rate of return. They arise for a fundamental reason—the firm operates over time, and its activities in one period (capital investments) have effects in another. Because of this, it is necessary to depart from the simplistic model of profit maximization with no regard to time and to consider the more general version in which time is an important variable. In this more accurate version, profit maximization becomes the maximization of present discounted value.

Present Discounted Value[7.5]

Suppose that an opportunity will pay the authors X_t dollars t years from now in each year from year 1 through year T. Suppose that the interest rate is r, with interest compounded once a year.[7.6] The present value of such a stream of payments is given by

$$\text{present value} = \frac{X_1}{1 + r} + \frac{X_2}{(1 + r)^2} + \cdots + \frac{X_T}{(1 + r)^T}. \tag{7.1}$$

Any alternative whose present value is more than this amount will enable us by borrowing and lending at interest rate r to achieve a higher payment in every year than X_t, the payment in such a year given in the above stream. Similarly, the alternative described in equation (7.1) is superior in this very strong sense to any opportunity with a smaller present value.

Plainly, it is sensible to value opportunities offering streams of payments over time at their present values. To decide whether a given investment is worthwhile, one compares the present value of the stream with the initial cost of the investment. The investment is worth making if and only if its present value exceeds the cost. The maximization of present value (by accepting opportunities when present value exceeds cost) is the generalized version of profit maximization by firms—appropriate when decisions have repercussions over time.

7.5. The ensuing discussion of present discounted value and the economic rate of return is an elementary exposition. It is intended primarily for non-economists. Alas, sad experience leads us to believe that it may also be useful for some economists.
7.6. More general cases are readily treated.

It is important to understand how present-value calculations are made in investment decisions. As a result of a particular investment, with initial cost C, the firm experiences a change in its revenue and cost streams. The net difference between the changes in revenue and those in costs is a stream of net benefits that flows from making the investment. These are the X_t of equation (7.1). Such benefits may be quite complex, for they represent all the changes resulting from the investment. When the investment is large, these may involve very long-lasting effects. (The decision of IBM to invest in the development of System/360, for example, was not a marginal decision. Its repercussions continue to this day and into the future.) Yet whether benefits are complex or simple, the evaluation of an investment requires estimation of those benefits and a computation of their present values to reduce the benefit stream to dollars of a common date—the date of the initial investment. If that present value is greater than the initial cost C, or equivalently if the present value of all benefits and costs including the initial cost is positive, the investment is worth making.

It is worth noting here that depreciation plays a role in such calculations only because of the tax treatment of depreciation—a benefit. Aside from this, there is no need to count depreciation explicitly; the necessity to make replacement expenditures will show up in the costs of those expenditures themselves, subtracted from the benefit stream when they occur and discounted back to the time of the initial decision.

Now, in discussing the proposition that profits will be zero in competitive equilibrium, we noted that this requires a definition of costs that includes the opportunity cost of capital. Contemplating the long run, the firm must count among its costs the necessity of paying interest (or forgoing receiving it) on the funds tied up in the capital used in production during the period for which the profits are calculated. This is precisely the same computation involved in using the interest rate to discount future benefits and to arrive at present value. For example, if the interest rate is 10 percent and an investment of $100 will just bring a $10 return plus the release of the $100 at the end of that time, then that investment has a zero present value—that is, the present value of the benefits stream ($110/1.1) less the capital cost ($100) is zero. This is equivalent to saying that the $10 earned over the original cost of capital represents just the return (10 percent) required to pay the interest charges (the opportunity cost of capital) so that there are zero economic profits.

In long-run competitive equilibrium, the present value of the future profits of every firm will be zero, subtracting the capital value of each firm's assets in the initial period. If present values were greater than zero, then there would be an incentive for expansion and entry; present values less than zero would imply an incentive for contraction and exit. This is the full statement of the disappearance of economic profits in long-run competitive equilibrium.

So far, this discussion has been silent about risk. An interest rate that simply reflects the direct costs of borrowing and lending money is not high enough to reflect the risk involved in tying up funds when returns are uncertain. Hence, for risky ventures, the firm should use a discount rate r that exceeds its actual borrowing costs by an amount sufficient to compensate for risk. This will result in its refusing some propositions that have a positive present value (net of investment costs) at the underlying interest rate because such prospects have a negative present value when the interest rate is adjusted to take account of risk. Propositions that would barely pay off will not be worth taking if they are risky.

By what amount should the interest rate be adjusted upward for risk? It is not possible to say in numerical terms. In general, the most one can say is that risky enterprises should (and will) use a higher discount rate than should (and will) less risky ones.

The Economic Rate of Return

The concept of present value holds the solution to properly measuring profit *rates* in the analysis of competition or monopoly. Investments whose benefits come later than costs will not be worth making at high rates of interest, but may be worth making at low ones. *The economic rate of return on an investment is that interest rate at which the present value of the benefit stream from the investment would just equal its initial costs and the investment just be worth undertaking.*[7.7] Maximization of present value becomes equivalent to the undertaking of those investments with an economic rate of return above the actual interest rate (adjusted for risk). Economic rates of return greater than interest rates (adjusted for risk) correspond to positive economic profits.

7.7. If an investment has periods of negative benefits coming later than positive ones, the economic rate of return is not unique. In that case, which we assume away in what follows, dealing with profit rates at all is a mistake, and the accounting rate of return does not fare better just because it is uniquely defined.

This definition corresponds to incentives to entry. When a potential entrant perceives the economic rate of return to be earned by entering as greater than the normal return—the risk-adjusted return it could make by investing elsewhere in the economy—it will wish to enter, for its cost of capital is the opportunity cost of not investing in other activities. If the economic rate of return on entry exceeds that cost, then the present value of entering will be positive, being negative if the economic rate of return on entry falls below that cost of capital. Thus, to ask whether there is an incentive to enter is to ask equivalently whether the present value of entering is positive, given the entrant's cost of capital (including an adjustment for risk), or to ask whether the economic rate of return exceeds that cost of capital. The latter corresponds to asking whether prospective profits are sufficiently high to provide an incentive to entry. It is thus the economic rate of return (adjusted for risk) that is equalized in long-run equilibrium in a competitive economy.

As this suggests, the concept of the economic rate of return applies to the firm as a whole as well as to individual investments. Consider the firm at any given moment. To define the economic rate of return on the firm's activities from that moment on, consider the new activities that the firm will undertake. Those activities involve a stream of expenditures, including capital expenditures, and a stream of returns as a result of them. The economic rate of return on those activities is the interest rate at which the activities would just be worth undertaking in the sense that the present value of the stream of net returns (revenues minus expenditures) would be zero. In effect, the future activities of the firm, not already committed, are treated as a single investment. As with a single investment, if the economic rate of return on the firm's future activities is above the cost of capital adjusted for risk, those activities will be worth undertaking; someone perceiving that this will be true for him will find an incentive to enter. *This is the meaning of positive economic profit.*

Note again that except for its effects on taxes, the depreciation schedule used by the firm plays no role in the definition of the economic rate of return. Indeed, the depreciation of capital itself plays no role except insofar as it requires later capital expenditures to replace worn-out or obsolete equipment. Those expenditures are treated as they occur. This is because present-value calculations take direct account of the timing of such investment expenditures and the benefits associated with them.

The "Normal" Economic Rate of Return

The fact that the economic rate of return, adjusted for risk, is equalized in long-run equilibrium in a competitive economy might lead one to believe that one can find economic profits by comparing the economic rate of return of a particular firm to some "normal" or average rate of return in the economy as a whole. If one is also willing to make judgments about disequilibrium, it might then be possible to identify monopoly profits. It is important to realize that this cannot be done easily. Aside from the difficulties associated with calculating the economic rate of return for a particular firm (let alone all firms), which we shall discuss at length, this is because the phrase "adjusted for risk" is a nontrivial caveat and, moreover, disequilibrium cannot be ignored.

Even if all markets were competitive and, what is more, even if all markets happened to be in long-run equilibrium at the moment of calculation, one would see substantial variations in economic rates of return. Firms in relatively risky markets would earn a higher rate than firms in relatively safe markets. Further, since in practice most markets will *not* be in long-run competitive equilibrium, some economic rates of return will be higher than normal, even given appropriate adjustments for risk, and entry and expansion should occur. Some will be lower than normal, adjusted for risk, and contraction and exit should occur. The identification of a "normal" rate of return for the economy as a whole will not be possible; even for a particular market, it will not be an easy task. It will require considerably more than simply averaging the rates of return of some or many firms or markets.

Calculating the Economic Rate of Return

Even these difficulties, however, pale into insignificance beside the problems associated with a direct calculation of the economic rate of return for an individual firm—a calculation already presumed in the preceding comments on how the normal rate might be calculated.

To see the problem involved, consider again the definition of the economic rate of return. That definition involves not only valuing the expenditures and returns achieved by the firm in the past but also the stream of expenditures and returns that it will achieve in the future. This is a necessary complication. The entire reason for making rate-of-return calculations in the first place is that expenditures made at one time have consequences at later times. Firms earning profits now are earning them in part as a result of decisions made and expenditures undertaken in past years. Firms making expenditures now do so not merely for the profits (if any) they will bring in the year of the expenditure but in the expectation of a resulting stream of later returns. Direct calculation of the economic rate of return requires knowledge of the entire stream of expenditures and returns starting with the moment when the computation is made, including times yet to come.

Obviously, it is not possible to do this directly. To do it, not only would one have to know about future events, but one would have to have very detailed information on the time pattern of past expenditures and receipts. Unless one wishes to go back to the beginning of the life of the firm, this in itself is a complex matter since the returns involved will be returns additional to those the firm would have made had it not pursued the new activities whose return is being valued. Further, even if one goes back to the beginning of the life of a firm, the information involved is typically not available, and a complete computation would require such information through the end of the life of the firm, an event that has not yet occurred for most firms of interest.

Does the absence of the ability to make such direct calculations rob the concept of the economic rate of return of all value? Not at all. Firms, in making decisions, *must*, in one way or another, consider the cost of capital; they must and do make present-value calculations. Of course, there is an important difference between these calculations and those that an outside analyst might wish to make. Firms make decisions about present opportunities: whether to invest in one project; whether to discontinue another. Those decisions are forward looking. A firm makes those decisions without regard to past expenses or sunk costs. Thus, a firm has no need to ask whether it is earning or has earned a positive economic rate of return (economic profits) as an entity; its only interest is whether, over some future period, particular decisions will be profitable (have a positive present value, given the cost of capital). If firms expand and undertake new activities, we can presume that they expect those activities to have economic rates of return greater than their costs of capital adjusted for risk. If they refrain from engaging in new activities or contract activities already begun, then their economic rates of return, as perceived by them, must fall short of their costs of capital adjusted for risk—the returns they could earn elsewhere. The fact that an outside analyst finds it difficult to calculate the economic rates of return involved does not mean that the firms involved cannot and do not in effect take them into account in their investment decisions.

That fact, however, is not much comfort for outside analysts wishing to use economic rates of return as a test to decide whether particular on-going firms earn economic profits at a given time. Nevertheless, the economic rate of return is the correct rate of return concept and the *only* correct concept by which economic profits can be judged. It is the only valid concept of profits on which the theory and the resulting predictions about firms' behavior and market outcomes are based. One must be especially skeptical of efforts to prove propositions or to test hypotheses from the theory centered on economic rates of return with empirical data that do not reflect those rates of return.

Accounting Rates of Return: Measurement Problems

One class of measures of profit rates that depend on relatively available data and can readily be computed is the class of measures used in much of the empirical literature, measures of "accounting rates of return." Although differing in detail, the measures in this class all take some measure of current accounting profits and divide it by some other magnitude, generally a measure of the capital invested in the firm as reflected by accounting records. Typically, the capital measure so used is either stockholders' equity or total capitalization (a measure of the total value of the firm's capital assets). As we shall show, *accounting rates of return do not yield helpful information about economic rates of return and hence permit no inference whatever concerning monopoly profits.* This is true even if all the serious measurement issues presented by accounting rates of return are resolved.

Before we get to such a demonstration, however, it is desirable to consider very briefly some of the better understood "measurement" and definitional issues involved in accounting rates of return, as these will occur again in a discussion of the testimony of the government's economists. Throughout it must be kept in mind that accounting rates of return are useful as an indicator of profitability only insofar as they yield information about the economic rate of return on capital.

1. Accounting rates of return on *sales* are of no use in this regard. High rates of return on sales can yield low rates of return on capital if there are large investments required to achieve them—for example, if heavy investments in research and development are needed. Rates of return on sales will not be equalized in competitive equilibrium.

2. Even accounting rates of return on capital involve a choice of denominator—either stockholders' equity or a measure of total capitalization. There are reasons for deciding either way. A firm can acquire its capital assets through either equity or debt. The computation of the

accounting rate of return on total capitalization seeks to find the return to the firm on its capital assets independently of how those assets are financed. Under certain conditions (which are unlikely to be approximated in the real world), it can be shown that the firm will be indifferent as to whether the money is raised by equity or debt. In such circumstances, comparisons of rates of return between firms ought not to depend on the particular choice the firm has happened to make.[4]

In the real world, however, the firm may very well care about how it raises funds. The firm is in the business of earning a return on the capital invested in it by stockholders. From this perspective, the raising of funds by the issuance of debt and the consequent interest payments are merely part of the mechanism through which that return is earned and should be treated as any other set of receipts or expenditures.

3. In using either denominator, the issue arises of how to take account of inflation. If profits are in current dollars, the use of book values for the denominator will yield misleadingly high rates of return simply because the value of the firm's capital has been understated. Correcting for this is not simple if one is to compare different firms whose capital assets have different age structures.

4. The numerator of the accounting rate of return also presents problems. These are the problems discussed previously concerning the difference between accounting and economic profits, and we need not discuss the rent-opportunity cost issues further.

5. The treatment of depreciation does require further discussion, however, for it presents a serious issue in the computation of accounting rates of return (although not in the proper computation of the before tax economic rate of return). The accounting rate of return focuses on a particular moment and does not properly attribute the benefits accruing from the capital stock to the time period in which they belong. Instead, it compares capital stock and profits in a particular year. Because of this, as discussed, whatever the "true" rate of depreciation, firms that take relatively fast depreciation will, other things being equal, show lower dollar profits than will firms that use relatively slow depreciation schedules.

Contrary to the assertion of the government economists,[5] *this does not mean that, other things being equal, firms that take relatively fast depreciation will have lower accounting rates of return than firms that take relatively slow depreciation.* The depreciation practices of the firm enter the denominator as well as the numerator of the accounting rate of return. The book value of the firm's capital assets consists of the original value of those assets less depreciation already taken on them. A firm that chooses a relatively rapid depreciation schedule will, other things being equal, show a lower book value for its assets and a lower value of stockholders' equity than will a firm that chooses a relatively slow depreciation schedule. Hence, the firm choosing a rapid depreciation schedule rather than a slow one reduces both the numerator and the denominator of the accounting rate of return relative to a firm making the opposite choice. The complete effect of such a choice on the accounting rate of return may be to drive that rate either down *or up*. As will be shown by example, more rapid depreciation will lower the accounting rate of return if and only if the rate of growth of the capital stock is above the accounting rate of return; otherwise it will raise it. Rates of growth below accounting rates of return are the rule, not the exception, however. Thus, one cannot conclude in comparing firms that a firm with a relatively rapid depreciation schedule should have its profit rate adjusted upward.

It is yet a greater error than this to suppose that one can remove the effects of different accounting practices on the accounting rate of return by adding depreciation back into profits to obtain a measure of so-called cash flow to be divided by stockholders' equity or total capitalization (a procedure adopted by Alan McAdams, as will be discussed). To add depreciation back into profits and divide by either one of the two denominators is to add depreciation back into the numerator but not to take it out of the denominator. This *must* raise the accounting rate of return and *must* falsely show firms choosing a relatively rapid depreciation schedule to have a high accounting rate of return even if a symmetric treatment of depreciation for all firms would show this not to be the case.

6. The treatment of so-called intangibles such as advertising or research and development expenses may also involve adjustments to both the numerator and denominator of the accounting rate of return—adjustments that are difficult or impossible to make in practice. Since research and development is very important in the computer industry, we focus on that example.

Research and development (R&D) expenditures, like expenditures on capital equipment, are investments that bring benefits over an extended period of time, not just in the year in which they are made. Therefore (although this presents no problems at all for the economic rate of return) in attempting to determine the accounting rate of return, one should not treat the costs of R&D as a subtraction from profits in the year in which they are incurred. Rather, they should be treated as a capital expenditure bringing later returns and amortized according to some depreciation schedule.

Accounting rules have forbidden capitalization of R&D expenditures since 1975. In the years prior to 1975, companies differed in the way they treated R&D expenses. For tax or other reasons, many companies (including IBM) expensed R&D, treating R&D expenditures as an addition to costs and therefore as a subtraction from profits in the year in which the expenditures were made. Even when companies capitalized R&D, it is not plain that their method was appropriate for the analysis of economic profits. Indeed, the appropriate method is not evident. If R&D expenditures are considered a capital investment, then some estimate of the depreciation of the "stock" of R&D capital must be assigned to later years. But the rate at which old R&D depreciates is even less certain and likely to be more complicated than the rate at which capital equipment depreciates. It is true that by expensing R&D, firms presumably depreciate R&D too quickly (taking total depreciation in one year, in effect) relative to the benefits derived; but firms that capitalized R&D in the past may have taken depreciation too slowly by that standard.

As with any depreciation adjustment in comparing firms, going from faster to slower depreciation of R&D—and, a fortiori, going from expensing to capitalizing R&D expenditures—affects both numerator and denominator. We use the latter extreme case to show that the result (as for any depreciation) depends on the rate of growth of the stock of what is being depreciated relative to the accounting rate of return of the firm.

Suppose, first, that the firm expenses R&D. Suppose that its accounting profits before such expenses are equal to 10 and that the denominator of the accounting rate of return (either total capitalization or stockholders' equity) is equal to 50. Suppose further that its R&D expenses in a given year are 5. Then, expensing R&D, the firm will have an accounting rate of return of $(10 - 5)/50 = 10$ percent.

Suppose that an otherwise identical firm capitalized R&D and depreciated it at the rate of 1 per year. This would make the numerator of its accounting rate of return 9, since only R&D depreciation and not R&D expenses would be subtracted. However, not only would the numerator be greater than in the former case, so would the denominator. The denominator now would include the value of the firm's accumulated stock of R&D assets. Suppose, for the moment, that accumulated stock was worth 40. The firm capitalizing R&D expenditures would then have an accounting rate of return of 9/(50 + 40) = 10 percent, as before.

Suppose, however, that the second firm's accumulated stock of R&D was worth 25. In that event, the firm would have an accounting rate of return of 9/(50 + 25) = 12 percent. Or suppose that the firm's R&D assets were worth 50. Then the accounting rate of return would be 9/(50 + 50) = 9 percent

Thus the effect of going from expensing R&D to capitalizing it can change the accounting rate of return in either direction. The interesting point in the above example is that at which the value of the accumulated stock of R&D is equal to 40 because that is the point at which the ratio of the net current additions to R&D (4 = 5 − 1) to the value of accumulated R&D (40) is precisely the same as the accounting rate of return when R&D is expensed (10 percent). Thus, if the rate of growth of the stock of R&D is *greater* than the accounting rate of return when R&D is expensed, then capitalizing rather than expensing R&D will *increase* the accounting rate of return. If the rate of growth of the R&D stock is *less* than the accounting rate of return when R&D is expensed, then capitalizing rather than expensing R&D will *decrease* the accounting rate of return.

In order to determine the effect on the accounting rate of return of different accounting practices for the treatment of R&D expenditures, as compared to some appropriate capitalization of those expenditures, one must make a judgment as to the rate of growth of the value of R&D considered as an asset. This requires looking not merely at whether R&D expenditures are increasing over time but directly at the relation of such expenditures to the value of the R&D asset, *taking proper account of the depreciation of R&D*. Such proper depreciation is impossible to evaluate, and it is therefore not generally possible to tell in which direction expensing rather than properly capitalizing R&D drives the accounting rate of return. As in the treatment of depreciation of physical assets, however, it is *not* the case that expensing R&D necessarily lowers the accounting rate of return.

Accounting Rates of Return: The Basic Conceptual Problem

These problems, great as they are, are dwarfed in importance by the fact that the accounting rate of return is *conceptually* the wrong measure. Accounting rates of return take profits in a particular year and divide them by a measure of the value of the firm's capital assets in that year. But the nature of a capital investment is that it brings in returns in years later than that in which it is made. This is what makes it different from a current expense. Thus, the profits in a particular year involve the returns due to past investments and not directly to the capital stock that happens to be in place in that year. When current investment is occurring, that investment will bring in returns in the years to come and not merely (if at all) in the year in which the investment is made.

It follows that to take the profits of a particular year and attribute them to the capital stock in place in that year is to provide a measure that is not in itself a correct measure of the economic rate of return—the only correct measure that can be used in assessing economic profits. Further, as we shall see, the relationships between the accounting rate of return and the economic rate of return are very complex. They depend both on the time shape of returns from investments and on the rate of growth of the firm's capital stock.

The misleading nature of the accounting rate of return (the full extent of which will be exhibited) in attributing current profits to capital stock associated with later profits cannot be cured by taking averages over time. Moreover, the problem is exacerbated if the value of the capital stock in the denominator of the accounting rate of return (either total capitalization or stockholders' equity) is taken as of the *end* of the year in which the profits are earned, since investments made during a year, particularly in the latter part of the year, can have little or no effect on the profits earned during that year.

A simple, but unrealistic, example (more realistic ones will be given later) illustrates the problem. Suppose that a productive machine costs $100. Suppose further that as a result of investment of the $100 in the machine at the end of a particular year (year 0), a stream of returns is obtained as follows. In year 1 the machine is still coming on-line, and there are no returns—the additional revenues, if any, being just balanced by the additional costs of having the machine. Starting in year 2 and for every year thereafter, the net benefits from having the machine are worth $39. This goes on forever; the machine does not depreciate.

In this example, it is easy to show that the economic rate of return is 30 percent. At that interest rate, $100 at the end of year 0 is equivalent to $130 at the end of year 1, and this in turn will yield at 30 percent interest payments of $39 for every year thereafter. On the other hand, the accounting rate of return will depend on the rate of growth of the firm. To see this, we calculate the accounting rate of return on the book

Table 7.1

Year	Profits ($)	Beginning-of-year capital stock ($)	Accounting rate of return (%)
1	0	100	0
2	39	200	19.5
3	2×39	400	19.5
4	4×39	800	19.5

value of the capital stock as of the beginning of each year for the easiest case of a constant rate of growth. (Results in terms of end-of-year assets or stockholders' equity can be derived from these; they are quantitatively but not qualitatively different.)

Suppose first that the firm only invests in a single machine and then stops. The book value of its capital stock will then be $100 forever, and after the first year, its profits will always be $39, yielding an accounting rate of return of 39 percent rather than 30 percent. Suppose, on the other hand, that the firm grows quite rapidly, *doubling* its capital stock (not its investment) every year. The results are in table 7.1.

Plainly, the accounting rate of return will be 19.5 percent forever. The accounting rate of return on end-of-year assets will be even farther from 30 percent, namely, 9.75 percent, and no amount of time averaging will cure this. It is not hard to show that in this example the accounting rate of return on beginning-of-year assets will coincide with the economic rate of return of 30 percent if and only if the firm also grows at a 30 percent rate. This is a particular case of a general theorem.

The Main Propositions

The following results are proved in the appendix to this chapter and will be exemplified.[7.8]

1. Unless depreciation schedules are chosen in a particular way, so that the value of any past investment is always calculated as the present value (at an interest rate equal to the economic rate of return) of the stream of benefits remaining in it[7.9]—a choice that is totally unlikely to be made—the accounting rate of return on a particular investment

7.8. Many of these results are not new, but the size of the effects involved does not appear to have been appreciated.

7.9. Such a "natural" depreciation formula—which we shall term "economic depreciation"—was first suggested by Harold Hotelling in 1925. See Hotelling, "A General Mathematical Theory of Depreciation," *Journal of the American Statistical Association* 20 (September 1925), pp. 340–353.

will differ from year to year and will not, in general, equal the economic rate of return on that investment in any year.

2. The accounting rate of return for the firm as a whole will be an average of the accounting rates of return for individual investments made in the past. The weights in that average will consist of the book values of those different investments, which in turn depend on the depreciation schedule adopted and, particularly, on the amount and timing of such investments.

3. Unless the proportion of investments with a given time shape remains fixed every year, and unless the firm simply grows exponentially, increasing investments in each and every type of asset[7.10] by the same proportion for every year, the accounting rate of return to the firm as a whole cannot even be expected to be constant, let alone equal to the economic rate of return.

4. Even where the firm does operate in such an unrealistic manner—the case most favorable to the accounting rate of return—the accounting rate of return will vary with the rate of growth of the firm and will not generally equal the economic rate of return.

5. The only reliable inferences concerning the economic rate of return that can be drawn (and only in such an unrealistically favorable case) from examination of the accounting rate of return stem from the fact that the accounting rate of return and the economic rate of return will be on the same side of the firm's exponential growth rate. If the accounting rate of return is higher than the growth rate, then the economic rate of return is also higher than the growth rate. If the accounting rate of return is lower than the growth rate, then the economic rate of return is also lower than the growth rate. If the accounting rate of return equals the growth rate, and in this case *alone*, the economic rate of return will be equal to the accounting rate of return.[7.11]

6. Even in the unrealistically favorable exponential growth case, the accounting rate of return depends *crucially* on the time shape of benefits, and the effect of growth on the accounting rate of return also depends on that time shape. In particular, it is not true that rapidly growing

7.10. Two assets are said to be the same "type" if they yield the same time shape of benefits.

7.11. It is worth pointing out that these results apply to accounting rates of return on total assets, not directly to accounting rates of return on stockholders' equity. Further, they apply to accounting rates of return on beginning-of-year, not end-of-year or yearly average, assets. As the later examples show, the problem of making inferences from accounting rates of return on end-of-year (or average) assets is even worse—if possible—than when beginning-of-year assets are used.

firms tend to understate their profits and slowly growing firms tend to overstate them. The effect can go the other way.

7. All these results apply both to before-tax and after-tax rates of return.

The Likely Size of the Effects

The differences between the accounting and economic rates of return can be quite large—large enough to account for all or most of the variation in accounting rates of return in the American economy. To show this, we consider examples, concentrating on after-tax rates of return. In these examples, the corporate tax rate is assumed to be 45 percent and (in most examples) the after-tax economic rate of return is fixed at 15 percent, while growth rates, depreciation methods, and the time shape of benefits are allowed to vary.[7.12] Very large variations in the accounting rates of return are readily generated.

Consider an investment whose benefits begin immediately and last for six years following the time shape exhibited in column 2 of table 7.2. For convenience we refer to this shape as the Q-profile. (It was— quite erroneously—suggested by McAdams as typical of IBM's experience with System/360 after he objected to other examples.[6]) The figures in column 2 are scaled to produce an after-tax economic rate of return of 15 percent on an initial investment of $100 when sum-of-the-years' digits depreciation over a six-year life is used. The remainder of the table shows the calculation of the corresponding accounting rate of return each year.

Plainly, the after-tax accounting rates of return vary substantially. They never equal the after-tax economic rate of return (15 percent) and exceed it in every year that has positive net profits. Actual firms do not generally exhibit such variation in their accounting rates of return because the averaging effects of growth, as it were, attribute

---

7.12. Fifteen percent was roughly the average *accounting* rate of return in United States manufacturing corporations in 1978 (*Economic Report of the President, 1979*, pp. 279–291). If accounting and economic rates of return tended to coincide, 15 percent would be a reasonable choice for the economic rate of return. Since the rates do not generally coincide, the choice is immaterial. Choosing a lower economic rate of return would reduce the range of accounting rates of return in the results that follow (for the *same* examples) but would not affect the conclusions.

With a fixed capital investment, a given time shape of gross profits before depreciation and taxes results in different after-tax economic rates of return for different depreciation methods. To fix the after-tax economic rate of return for a given time shape, in the examples, the height of the gross profit benefit stream is adjusted proportionally to produce the desired after-tax economic rate of return.

Table 7.2 After-tax accounting rates of return (%) for the Q-profile (6-year life; no delay) (after-tax economic rate of return, 15%; tax rate, 45%; sum-of-the-years' digits depreciation)

Year	Gross profits (cash flow before tax)	Depreciation	After-tax profits	Beginning-of-year net assets	Accounting rate of return (beginning-of-year assets)	End-of-year net assets	Accounting rate of return (end-of-year assets)
1	23.3	28.6	(5.3)	100.0	(5.3)	71.4	(7.4)
2	44.1	23.8	11.2	71.4	15.7	47.6	23.5
3	51.9	19.0	18.1	47.6	38.0	28.6	63.3
4	40.5	14.3	14.4	28.6	50.3	14.3	100.7
5	20.2	9.5	5.9	14.3	41.3	4.8	122.9
6	7.8	4.8	1.7	4.8	35.4	0	Infinite

profits from past investment to the book value of investments whose profit results are yet to come rather than to the declining book value of old investments.

While such an averaging effect tends to stabilize the accounting rate of return, that magnitude is still a hodgepodge devoid of information about the economic rate of return. This point is illustrated by table 7.3, which presents asymptotic accounting rates of return assuming constant exponential growth for three different versions of the Q-profile, each with the same tax rate (45 percent) and after-tax economic rate of return (15 percent).[7.13] The first version (table 7.2) has no delay between investment and the beginning of the benefit stream, and depreciation is taken over the resulting six-year life. The second version has a seven-year life, including one year's delay between investment and initial return. The third has an eight-year life, including a two-year delay between investment and initial return. Except for the lag at the beginning and differences in scale, the gross-benefits stream is the same in each case. The top half of the table gives accounting rates of return on beginning-of-year assets; the bottom half gives accounting rates of return on end-of-year assets.

Several things are apparent from this table. First, the accounting rates of return only equal the true economic rate of return of 15 percent when the growth rate is also 15 percent and when the accounting rate of return is measured on beginning-of-year assets. Otherwise the accounting rates vary from 7 percentage points below to almost 11 percentage points above the economic rate of return.

Second, it is not true that more rapid depreciation, other things being equal, tends to understate accounting rates of return. In this example, when the rate of growth is below 15 percent, declining balance and sum-of-the-years' digits depreciation produce a higher accounting rate of return than does straight-line depreciation for given growth rates, time profiles, and economic rate of return. The effect is reversed when the growth rate exceeds the economic rate of return of 15 percent. This illustrates the general proposition discussed previously: More rapid depreciation *increases* the accounting rate of return (measured on beginning-of-year assets) when the growth is less than the economic rate of

7.13. In these examples, exponential growth takes place by repeated investment in the same type of product; that is, all investments have the same time shape of benefits. This is obviously an unrealistic assumption but one that is more likely to produce equality between accounting and economic rates of return than are more realistic ones. See the appendix to this chapter.

Table 7.3 Asymptotic accounting rates of return (%) on three versions of the Q-profile (tax rate, 45%; after-tax economic rate of return, 15%)

Growth rate	6-year life (no delay)			7-year life (1-year delay)			8-year life (2-year delay)		
	Straight line	Declining balance	Sum-of-years' digits	Straight line	Declining balance	Sum-of-years' digits	Straight line	Declining balance	Sum-of-years' digits
Beginning-of-year assets									
0	15.2	17.8	18.1	18.1	21.3	22.0	21.0	24.7	25.9
5	15.2	16.9	17.0	17.0	19.1	19.4	18.9	21.1	21.7
10	15.1	15.9	15.9	16.0	17.0	17.1	16.9	17.9	18.1
15	15.0	15.0	15.0	15.0	15.0	15.0	15.0	15.0	15.0
20	14.8	14.1	14.1	14.0	13.2	13.1	13.3	12.4	12.3
25	14.7	13.3	13.3	13.1	11.5	11.4	11.7	10.1	9.9
30	14.5	12.5	12.6	12.2	10.0	9.9	10.3	8.0	7.8
End-of-year assets									
0	15.2	17.8	18.1	18.1	21.3	22.0	21.0	24.7	25.9
5	14.5	16.1	16.2	16.2	18.1	18.5	18.0	20.1	20.7
10	13.7	14.5	14.5	14.6	15.4	15.5	15.3	16.3	16.5
15	13.0	13.0	13.0	13.0	13.0	13.0	13.0	13.0	13.0
20	12.4	11.8	11.8	11.7	11.0	10.9	11.1	10.3	10.2
25	11.7	10.6	10.7	10.5	9.2	9.2	9.4	8.1	7.9
30	11.1	9.6	9.7	9.4	7.7	7.6	7.9	6.2	6.0

return and *decreases* the accounting rate of return when the growth rate exceeds the economic rate of return. By theorem 7A.2 in the appendix, the changeover point is also where the growth rate equals the accounting rate of return on beginning-of-year assets. Since this is the only point about depreciation that we wish to demonstrate in these examples, we provide only results for sum-of-the-years' digits depreciation in later tables.[7.14]

In all the examples in table 7.3, firms growing at rates greater than the economic rate of return of 15 percent have accounting rates of return on beginning-of-year assets less than that economic rate of return, while those growing at rates less than 15 percent all have accounting rates of return on beginning-of-year assets greater than the economic rate of return. (So simple a relationship does not hold if the accounting rate of return is based on end-of-year assets.) Contrary to what might be expected, this qualitative relationship provides no practical basis for adjusting accounting rates of return so that they will accurately reflect economic rates of return.

For example, table 7.3 shows that firms that use sum-of-the-years' digits depreciation and grow at 5 percent have accounting rates of return on beginning-of-year assets ranging from 17.0 to 21.7 percent. Thus, even for firms with the same growth rate and depreciation method, the required adjustment varies from 2 to 6.7 percentage points depending upon the time profile of benefits. Clearly, the time profile, depreciation method, and growth rate must all be known before accounting rates of return can be adjusted to reflect economic rates of return.

In the foregoing examples, for a given time shape, faster-growing firms have lower accounting rates of return than slower-growing ones with the same economic rate of return. Even if this were a universal phenomenon, it would not provide a way to adjust accounting rates of return to reflect economic rates of return since different firms will generally have different time shapes and, therefore, require different adjustments. The difficulties are even worse in practice because the accounting rate of return can actually *rise* with the growth rate, causing

7.14. There is one additional point about depreciation that we shall not bother to exemplify. Since the depreciation method chosen affects the time shape of the after-tax benefit stream, the relationship of after-tax accounting rates to the growth rate is particularly sensitive to the depreciation method. It can even happen that faster growth increases accounting rates of return for one choice of depreciation method and decreases them for another—all for the same pretax benefit time shape and the same after-tax economic rate of return. This makes adjustments for growth even harder to make than appears from the examples that follow.

slower-growing firms to have their economic rates of return *under*stated. Thus, even the strong assumption that firms have the same time profile is insufficient to permit adjustment of accounting rates of return; the specific profile must also be known in order to make inferences about the ranking of economic rates of return.

To demonstrate this phenomenon, consider the results of altering the original Q-profile (the one with a six-year life and no time delay) by spreading the last year's gross profits out evenly over five years (years 6–10) instead of having them all in year 6. table 7.4 shows that this small change in the profile produces an increasing relationship between the growth rate and the accounting rate of return. The earlier results for sum-of-the-years' digits depreciation are reproduced for ease of comparison.

Focusing on the first column of results ("10-year life (no delay, last-year spread)"), we see that the accounting rate of return on beginning-of-year assets actually begins by rising with the growth rate, reaching the value of the economic rate of return (as it must) at a 15 percent growth rate, and then going slightly above it before falling back again. (It is a special feature of this particular example that these values are all close to the economic rate of return of 15 percent.) The behavior of the accounting rate of return on end-of-year assets is different. This magnitude falls with the growth rate (in this example), but it exhibits still another phenomenon. As opposed to the previous example, where the accounting rates of return on both beginning-of-year and end-of-year assets were above the economic rate of return of 15 percent for low growth rates and below it for large ones, here the accounting rate of return on end-of-year assets starts *and finishes* below the economic rate of return of 15 percent. There is *no* rate of growth for which the accounting rate of return on end-of-year assets equals the economic rate of return of 15 percent.

The impossibility of making inferences about relative profit rates should be obvious even within the confines of these examples, all of which represent only relatively slight variations on the same profile. *Every one of the firms exhibited in table 7.4 has the same underlying after-tax economic rate of return. Yet their after-tax accounting rates of return on end-of-year assets vary from 6.0 to 25.9 percent.* (Here and later, the results for beginning of year assets are similar.)

Further, it is impossible to infer anything about relative profitability by attempting to adjust for growth rates. For example, each row of table 7.4 involves firms with the same growth rate, so that there is

Table 7.4 Asymptotic accounting rates of return (%) on four versions of the Q-profile (tax rate, 45%; after-tax economic rate of return, 15%; sum-of-the-years' digits depreciation)

Growth rate	10-year life (no delay; last year spread)	6-year life (no delay)	7-year life (1-year delay)	8-year life (2-year delay)
Beginning-of-year assets				
0	13.9	18.1	22.0	25.9
5	14.5	17.0	19.4	21.7
10	14.8	15.9	17.1	18.1
15	15.0	15.0	15.0	15.0
20	15.1	14.1	13.1	12.3
25	15.1	13.3	11.4	9.9
30	15.0	12.6	9.9	7.8
End-of-year assets				
0	13.9	18.1	22.0	25.9
5	13.8	16.2	18.5	20.7
10	13.5	14.5	15.5	16.5
15	13.0	13.0	13.0	13.0
20	12.6	11.8	10.9	10.2
25	12.0	10.7	9.2	7.9
30	11.5	9.7	7.6	6.0

Table 7.5 Before-tax benefit streams from an investment of $100 (after-tax economic rate of return, 15%; tax rate, 45%; sum-of-the-years' digits depreciation)

Year	X-firm ($)	Y-firm ($)
1	90.2	107.0
2	27.1	10.7
3	18.0	10.7
4	9.0	10.7
5	9.0	10.7
6	9.0	10.7

nothing to adjust for in comparing them; yet, except for the special row corresponding to the point where the growth rate is equal to the true after-tax economic rate of return, the after-tax accounting rates of return continue to vary. For the row corresponding to 5 percent growth, for example, after-tax accounting rates of return vary between 13.8 and 20.7 percent. For the row corresponding to 25 percent, they vary between 7.9 and 12.0 percent. Further, it is not correct to say that slow-growing firms have accounting rates of return that overstate their economic rates of return, while fast-growing firms have accounting rates of return that understate them. Continuing to use accounting rates of return on end-of-year assets, the firm just introduced ("10-year life (no delay, last-year spread)") has an accounting rate of return that understates its economic rate of return at all levels of growth. If one uses beginning-of-year assets, it has accounting rates of return that tend to understate its economic rate of return at low rates of growth and (slightly) overstate it at higher ones.

Moreover, the phenomenon of accounting rates of return increasing with the growth rate can be considerably more marked if we use other profiles. Table 7.5 shows the before-tax benefit stream (corresponding to an initial investment of $100, an economic rate of return of 15 percent, and sum-of-the-years' digits depreciation over a six-year life) for two other profiles labeled "X-firm" and "Y-firm", respectively. Table 7.6 shows the after-tax accounting rates of return for these firms when they grow exponentially at various rates. The after-tax accounting rate of return on beginning-of-year assets rises rather rapidly with the growth rate. The after-tax accounting rate of return on end-of-year assets also rises with the growth rate. However, as was also the case for the variation on the Q-profile examined earlier, it does not reach the economic rate of return of 15 percent.

Table 7.6 Asymptotic accounting rates of return (%) for X-firms and Y-firms
(economic rate of return, 15%; tax rate, 45%; sum-of-the-years' digits depreciation)

Growth rate	Beginning-of-year assets		End-of-year assets	
	X-firm	Y-firm	X-firm	Y-firm
0	12.9	12.5	12.9	12.5
5	13.6	13.3	13.0	12.7
10	14.3	14.2	13.0	12.9
15	15.0	15.0	13.0	13.0
20	15.7	15.8	13.0	13.2
25	16.3	16.6	13.0	13.3
30	16.9	17.3	13.0	13.3

Can the Conceptual Problem Be Overcome?

That the accounting rate of return—after-tax as well as before-tax—is
a misleading measure of the economic rate of return is evident from
examining cases of single projects such as shown in table 7.2. The cases
in later tables are unduly *favorable* to the accounting rate of return in
that they mask its behavior by averaging. That averaging effect is
achieved by the quite unrealistic assumption that investment by the
firm always brings in the same time shape of returns and that the firm
grows each year by increasing its investments at the same percentage
rate. Even on such favorable terms, it is impossible to infer either the
magnitude or direction of differences in economic rates of return from
differences in accounting rates of return. This is because such inferences
require not only correction for growth rates, but *also* knowledge of the
time shapes of returns.

The level and behavior of the accounting rate of return are very
sensitive to the type of time shape used. Even within the Q-profile
example, the rates vary depending on when the time shape begins and
how the last few years are spread out. There is every reason to suppose
that firms differ in the time shapes of their investments and that a
particular firm's investments differ among themselves. Thus, comparing
accounting rates of return among firms in order to make inferences
about monopoly profits is a baseless procedure.

This conclusion can be most dramatically demonstrated by juxta-
posing accounting rates of return for firms with different time shapes
and *different* economic rates of return. When this is done, it is easy to
see that firms with *higher* accounting rates of return can have *lower*
economic rates of return. Table 7.7 gives after-tax economic rates of

Table 7.7 After-tax economic rates of return (E) and asymptotic accounting rates of return on end-of-year assets (A) for eight time shapes (tax rate, 45%; sum-of-the-years' digits depreciation)

Time shape	Growth rate 0%		Growth rate 5%		Growth rate 10%	
	E	A	E	A	E	A
Q-profile, 8-year life (2-year delay)	13.0	21.6	16.0	22.6	17.8	21.2
Q-profile, 7-year life (1-year delay)	14.0	20.2	17.0	21.6	18.8	20.9
One-hoss shay, 6-year life (no delay)	15.0	20.0	18.1	21.4	19.7	20.7
One-hoss shay, 4-year life (no delay)	16.0	19.8	19.0	21.3	20.0	20.289
Q-profile, 6-year life (no delay)	16.1	19.6	19.05	21.2	20.05	20.287
Q-profile, 10-year life (no delay; last-year spread)	18.0	16.9	20.0	18.5	22.0	19.8
X-firm	19.0	16.2	21.0	17.8	23.0	19.2
Y-firm	19.2	15.8	21.2	17.4	23.2	18.9

return and after-tax accounting rates of return on end-of-year assets for three growth rates (0, 5, and 10 percent), and for each of the six time shapes already discussed as well as two other "one-hoss shay" time shapes.[7.15] For *each* growth rate, the examples are chosen so that the eight firms represented are ranked in *ascending* order of economic rates of return and in *descending* order of accounting rates of return — a complete reversal even with growth rates constant.

Examination of Table 7.7 shows again that no inference about relative after-tax economic rates of return is possible from after-tax accounting rates of return. For example, the lowest after-tax economic rate of return in the table is that for the Q-profile with an eight-year life at a zero growth rate. For that firm, the after-tax economic rate of return is 13 percent. Yet, its after-tax accounting rate of return on end-of-year assets is 21.6 percent, the second-*highest* accounting rate of return in the table, and a value well above that of 15.8 percent for the Y-firm at zero growth, corresponding to a 19.2 percent economic rate of return. The 21.6 percent accounting rate of return so encountered is even above the 18.9 percent figure obtained for the Y-firm at 10 percent growth — a figure that corresponds to an economic rate of return of 23.2 percent, the highest in the table, and more than 10 percentage points above the economic rate of return of 13 percent for the Q-profile with an eight-year life at zero growth. Similar examples of reversals occur throughout the table.

Nor can one eliminate these effects by correcting somehow for differences in rates of growth. The table as constructed exhibits a reversal of the ordering of economic and accounting rates of return with the rate of growth held constant. Rate-of-growth effects have thus *already* been removed from each pair of columns to an extent beyond that which one could hope to achieve in practice. Moreover, it is not true that faster-growing firms should have their accounting rates of return adjusted upwards relative to slower-growing ones. Consider the comparisons between the Q-profile with a ten-year life at zero growth and the Q-profile with an eight-year life at 5 percent growth. The faster-growing firm has an accounting rate of return (22.6 percent) already greater than that of the slower-growing firm (16.9 percent), but its economic rate of return (16.0 percent) is *below* that of the slower-

7.15. The "one-hoss shay" time shapes have a constant return (no lag) for four and six years, respectively, and zero returns thereafter. The term *one-hoss shay* comes from Oliver Wendell Holmes's poem "The Deacon's Masterpiece," in which a carriage gives service for one hundred years and a day and then disintegrates all at once.

growing firm (18.0 percent). Adjusting the faster-growing firm's accounting rate of return *upward* relative to that of the slower-growing one will make things *worse*, not better, even though other examples go the other way.

Accounting Rates of Return: Conclusions

As all of this makes clear, there is no way in which one can look at accounting rates of return and infer anything about relative economic profitability or, a fortiori, the presence or absence of monopoly profits. The economic rate of return is difficult—perhaps impossible—to compute for entire firms. Doing so requires information about both the past and the future, which outside observers do not have, if it exists at all.[7.16] Yet it is the economic rate of return that is the magnitude of interest for economic propositions. Economists (and others) who believe that analysis of accounting rates of return will tell them much (if they can only overcome the various definitional problems that separate economists and accountants) are deluding themselves. The literature that supposedly relates concentration and economic profit rates does no such thing, and examining absolute or relative accounting rates of return in order to draw conclusions about monopoly profits is a totally misleading enterprise.

Thus, for a number of reasons—the differences between accounting and economic profits, the treatment of depreciation, the capitalization or expensing of intangibles, and especially the fundamental conceptual differences between the accounting and economic rates of return—one cannot use accounting rates of return to infer the presence of economic profits or even to rank firms by profitability. Further, the presence of economic profits in a disequilibrium world does not imply the presence of monopoly profits. The hope that one can look at accounting rates of return (or, more generally, at any typically available profits data) and make any reliable inference—let alone a simple inference—about the presence or absence of monopoly is a dangerous will-o'-the-wisp. Monopoly profits can only be inferred from a serious and detailed analysis of the underlying structural phenomena that indicate the presence or absence of monopoly.

7.16. If we made the strong assumption that the same time shape of returns held for all investments made by a given firm throughout its life, then it might be possible to recover that time shape by regression of gross returns on a distributed lag of past investments. We are indebted to Zvi Griliches for this suggestion.

The Position of the Government Economists

Despite this, the government's case against IBM rested in part on an analysis of profits using accounting rates of return. McAdams, Lee Preston, and Weiss all testified in this regard, with Preston and Weiss using return on stockholders' equity and McAdams return on total capitalization (end-of-year assets). McAdams also presented figures on return on sales, which are totally irrelevant.[7]

It must not be thought that such testimony was peripheral. While all three economic witnesses backed away from relying on profits, calling profit evidence "confirmatory," in fact such evidence played a central role. McAdams's market definition, on which, as we have seen in earlier chapters, so much turned, was based on an "iterative procedure" in which a potential market was explored and found to be correct when supposedly high profits within it did not produce entry. Yet, as we saw in chapter 6, the "market" was constructed so as to define away entry, and the profit evidence thus remained the only nondefinitional item leading to the conclusion.[8]

Such profit evidence, which all related to accounting rates of return, would, as we have seen, have been meaningless at best in terms of yielding information concerning economic rates of return, let alone monopoly profits. Yet not only were the government economic witnesses apparently unaware of the conceptual issues raised previously, but they also, for the most part, gave only lip service at best to the treatment of the many other problems of measurement and definition involved in using accounting rates of return. Preston and Weiss used accounting rates of return totally unadjusted in any way; McAdams did make adjustments and, as we shall see, made matters even worse.

A brief examination of Weiss's testimony will show what was involved. Weiss was aware of some of the problems associated with accounting rates of return,[7.17] in particular, the capitalization of intangibles. Yet, despite the obvious importance of R&D expenditures in the computer industry relative to other industries, he made no attempt *in fact* to adjust for this. Rather, he offered a direct comparison of unadjusted accounting rates of return between IBM and 47 other companies taken

7.17. In fact, Weiss's understanding of the "measurement" problems was not always correct. Weiss testified (Weiss, Tr. 70645, 70589) that *any* growth in assets will lead a firm with rapid depreciation to understate its accounting rate of return relative to a firm using a slower depreciation method. As seen earlier, this is simply wrong as a matter of arithmetic.

from the top of the *Fortune* 500. He calculated as "excess profits" the extent to which IBM's accounting rate of return exceeded the average for the other 47 firms. Similarly, Preston compared IBM's unadjusted accounting rate of return to the average for all U.S. corporations.[9]

To conclude that such comparisons show the presence of monopoly profits requires one to disregard completely *every* issue raised in this chapter. It assumes that all markets are in long-run equilibrium and equates economic profits with monopoly profits. It equates accounting profits with economic profits. Further, it assumes away differences in risk, problems of the treatment of depreciation, and, as noted, the important issue of the treatment of intangibles. And it does all this in addition to ignoring the fundamental issue that the accounting rate of return is *at best* uninformative about the magnitude of interest, the economic rate of return.

It is not surprising that one can easily reach absurd results by such calculations. On the same basis, one would have to conclude that the firms earning above-average accounting rates of return in the tables given earlier in this chapter are earning "excess" profits. Leaving artificial examples aside, about one-third of Weiss's 47 firms had accounting rates of return above the average; by the same reasoning, they also were earning "excess" profits. Moreover, an analysis by Richard B. Mancke of firms with accounting rates of return *higher* than IBM's shows the absurdity of conclusions reached in this way.

Mancke examined all firms on the Standard and Poor's COMPU-STAT primary file for which data were available for at least seven years, during 1962–1975 (the period used by Weiss). He found 480 whose average accounting rates of return for that period exceeded that of IBM. The list included Royal Crown, 7-Up, and Dr. Pepper, as well as Coca-Cola; Emery Air Freight and Purolator, Champion Spark Plug, Quaker State Oil Refining, Maytag and Whirlpool, Caesar's World, Tampax, Alberto-Culver, and McDonald's and Gino's. It strains credibility to believe that all of these firms (let alone all the others on the list) enjoyed monopoly profits.[10]

One would suppose that adjustments in accounting rates of return were more likely to be made when comparing firms in different industries than in the same industry, but this was not the case with the testimony of the government economists. Their interindustry comparisons involved no adjustments whatever. By contrast, upon calculating accounting rates of return for IBM and other computer firms, McAdams was surprised to see less of a difference than he had anticipated. He then undertook a series of adjustments designed to "unmask" the "true profitability of IBM." The principal adjustments were as follows:[11]

First, McAdams, unlike Weiss and Preston, preferred to use return on total capitalization rather than return on stockholders' equity "to take out the effect of the differences between the ways in which different firms finance themselves as a factor which might explain why it was that some of them were showing very high cash flow returns in a way that I had not anticipated they would." While there are reasonable arguments in favor of such a measure, it will perhaps come as no surprise that IBM carried very little debt in the period analyzed, so that the effect of going from stockholders' equity to total capitalization was to reduce the accounting rate of return for other firms relative to IBM.[12]

Second, McAdams did not stop there. Observing that IBM was holding large amounts of cash and financial securities, McAdams decided to remove these assets and their relatively low returns because he "wanted to see the underlying earning rate on the operating assets of the corporation as compared to the financial assets which I feel perform in a way which is so different from the way in which the corporation itself performs in marketplaces that I wish to remove its influence."[13]

The holding of those financial assets was a part of the way in which IBM did business. The cash needs associated with the development of System/360 had indicated a need to hold liquid assets for the development of successor projects and expansion (aside from the general need to finance a lease base of computers, which the government and McAdams elsewhere described as a barrier to entry). In fact, by the late 1970s, after McAdams's testimony, the cash reserves had largely been reduced. Holding reserves for use in the business is a part of the cost of doing business and cannot be separately treated without a demonstration that it is extraneous to the business.[14]

Of course, such adjustments resulted in an apparently higher rate of return for IBM. It is worth remarking that McAdams failed to make any similar adjustment for such relatively riskless assets in the course of a later, totally erroneous attempt to show that IBM was not engaged in a risky business, so that adjustment for risk could not explain IBM's apparently high profit rate.[7.18]

7.18. McAdams calculated the "beta" for IBM in the capital asset pricing model, but made a major computational error vitiating the results. See, PX 7409: McAdams Rebuttal Narrative Testimony, pp. 264–266 and 271–277 and DX 15010: Fisher Surrebuttal Narrative Testimony, pp. 83–97.

Third, to adjust for the effects of different depreciation practices, McAdams added depreciation and amortization back into profits. Yet such a procedure ignores the fact that depreciation represents a real cost of doing business and cannot be set arbitrarily to zero. Further, this adjustment does not in fact take out the effects of different depreciation practices. As discussed previously, it removes depreciation from the numerator *but not the denominator* of the accounting rate of return. This *guarantees* that, other things being equal, firms with relatively rapid depreciation schedules will falsely appear to have relatively high rates of return because such rapid depreciation will cause the denominator of the measure to be relatively low for such firms. It should come as no surprise to the reader that IBM takes relatively rapid depreciation so that this adjustment raised IBM's accounting rate of return relative to those of others in the industry simply as an arithmetical artifact.[7.19, 15]

Even ignoring the fundamental conceptual difficulty with the accounting rate of return, one sees that the testimony of the government economists was at best simplistic and at worst extremely misleading. Given their willingness to reach conclusions from such comparisons, it is not surprising that the conceptual difficulty with the accounting rate of return—its noninformativeness about the economic rate of return—was not a matter of which the government economists were aware.

In fact, the government's economists failed even to recognize that the economic rate of return was the magnitude of interest in measuring profits. Three years after his original testimony, Weiss testified in early 1981 (after seeing a version of the analysis just set forth),

[D]own to this fall, I had thought of the internal rate of return [the economic rate of return] as something that the business schools did to help their students learn to think or something, and I didn't take it very seriously. . . .

. . . .

. . . I certainly acknowledge that until this fall I did not feel I needed to think about the internal rate of return at all. Since this fall I realized that I must, and surely I put it on my reading list. I am going to do it in a week or two in my own classes.[16]

McAdams stated, "The economic rate of return is mechanically derived. It has no normative characteristics."[17]

7.19. Even removing depreciation from both the numerator and denominator would not be correct, for IBM tends to use more capital-intensive methods than do other firms in the industry.

Conclusions

There is no question but that IBM is a successful and profitable firm. Indeed, it is probably a highly profitable firm (although it is less certain whether it is more profitable than are other expanding computer firms). All that can be at issue, therefore, is the source of such profits. By the government's theory, they stem from monopoly; by an alternative view, they are the rewards for innovation and the bearing of risk and include rents for past achievements.

Yet if IBM is profitable whether or not it is a monopoly, there can be little point in elaborately manipulating data to show such profits. Such manipulation can be justified only by a belief that all profits are necessarily monopoly profits, and this, in turn, requires a belief that all markets can be treated as if they were in long-run equilibrium.

Such a belief, indeed, underlay much of the government's case, but it was especially important here. Only a belief that *all* markets (not just the computer market) are in long-run equilibrium can even begin to justify the sweeping comparisons of rates of return across industries to which the government economists testified. Indeed, such comparisons, even were they comparisons of economic rates of return, would require a belief not only in long-run equilibrium but in equality of riskiness across industries and firms.

Of course, the comparisons involved were not of economic rates of return at all; they were comparisons of accounting rates of return, which are uninformative. To reach their conclusions from such data as to IBM's alleged monopoly power thus required the government and its economists to ignore major problems of algebra and accounting as well as basic conceptual difficulties in the differences between accounting and economic concepts with similar names. Worse, it required them to ignore the fundamental role of profits in a dynamic economy.

Appendix

Before-Tax Analysis: The Accounting Rate of Return on Individual Investments

We begin our analysis of the problem by considering the before-tax accounting and economic rates of return on a single investment. Later we shall consider the firm as being made up of a series of such investments, which may be (but need not always be) of the same type.

The after-tax case is treated subsequently and shown to be isomorphic, although more complex.

An investment may be thought of for heuristic purposes as a "machine" costing $1. If this is invested at time 0, the firm experiences a stream of net benefits as a result. Such benefits include all changes in revenues and costs (other than initial capital costs) that accrue to the firm as a result of making the investment. The flow of such benefits at time θ is denoted $f(\theta)$.[7.20]

The economic rate of return on a machine, r, is that discount rate which makes the discounted value of the benefit stream equal to the capital costs of the investment. In other words, r satisfies:

$$\int_0^\infty f(\theta)e^{-r\theta}\, d\theta = 1. \tag{7A.1}$$

We assume that the integral in (7A.1) is monotonically decreasing in r, so that (7A.1) has a unique positive solution. This will be true provided that the negative portion of the net benefit stream (if any) precedes the positive portion. This is the usual case.[7.21]

Now the firm adopts a depreciation schedule for this machine. Let $V(\theta)$ denote the book value of the machine as of time θ. Then $V'(\theta)$ is the rate of depreciation at θ, where the prime denotes differentiation. Plainly, $V(0) = 1$, and it makes sense to suppose that $V(\infty) = 0$, although this latter condition is not really needed.

Accounting profits attributable to this machine at time θ will be equal to net benefits less depreciation. We can think of the accounting rate of return for this machine as the accounting rate of return that the firm would have if this were its only asset. Denoting that rate $b(\theta)$,

$$b(\theta) = \frac{f(\theta) + V'(\theta)}{V(\theta)}. \tag{7A.2}$$

The first question that comes immediately to mind is that of when $b(\theta) = r$ for all θ within the life of the machine. We prove that this will occur if and only if the depreciation schedule adopted by the firm

---

7.20. The time origin is arbitrary. The flow of benefits is assumed to depend on the age of the machine only. Thus an investment at time t brings in benefits of $f(\theta - t)$ at time $\theta \geq t$. Time dependence of the benefit stream can be handled below by thinking of it as equivalent to investment in different kinds of machines at different times.

7.21. If (7A.1) has more than one solution, then the economic rate of return is ill-defined and there is even less point in considering whether the accounting rate of return yields information about it.

always values the machine as the discounted value of the future benefit stream, discounting at the economic rate of return r.

THEOREM 7A.1 $b(\theta) \equiv r$ if and only if

$$V(\theta) = \int_{\theta}^{\infty} f(u)e^{-r(u-\theta)}\, du. \tag{7A.3}$$

Proof
a. Suppose (7A.3) holds. Differentiating with respect to θ yields

$$V'(\theta) = -f(\theta) + rV(\theta), \tag{7A.4}$$

which when substituted in (7A.2) yields $b(\theta) = r$.
b. Suppose $b(\theta) \equiv r$. Then, from (7A.2)

$$V'(\theta) \equiv rV(\theta) - f(\theta). \tag{7A.5}$$

This is a linear differential equation with an additive forcing function $-f(\theta)$. Its solution is therefore in the form

$$V(\theta) = Ce^{r\theta} + z(\theta), \tag{7A.6}$$

where $z(\theta)$ is any particular solution of (7A.5) and C is a constant to be determined by the initial conditions. However, by part (a) of the proof, the integral on the right-hand side of (7A.3) is a particular solution of (7A.5). Hence, $z(\theta)$ can be taken as that integral. Do this and note that $z(0) = 1$ by (7A.1), the definition of the economic rate of return. Since we have $V(0) = 1$, setting $\theta = 0$ in (7A.6) yields $C = 0$, and the theorem is proved.

Thus, even when the firm has a single simple investment with no ambiguity about marginal versus average economic rates of return, the accounting rate of return will not equal the economic rate of return except for a particular choice of a depreciation schedule—a choice we may term "economic depreciation."

The reason for this is not hard to find. The book value of the firm's assets reflects the investment expenditures made in the past less the depreciation already taken on them. The benefits for which such investments were made are at least partly in the future. Yet the accounting rate of return takes gross profits before depreciation as the benefit flow that happens to be currently occurring. Unless depreciation is chosen so as to reflect the change in *future* benefits in the appropriate way, there is no reason to suppose that the result of such a calculation should equal the economic rate of return, and theorem 7A.1 shows that the two will in fact generally not be equal.

Will firms tend to adopt an "economic depreciation" schedule yielding book value as in (7A.3)? This is pathologically unlikely. In the first place, out of equilibrium, firms will not discount the future at the economic rate of return. Moreover, except in the simple Santa Claus case of $f(\theta) = ke^{-\lambda\theta}$ which corresponds to exponential depreciation or other similarly special cases corresponding to straight-line or other standard depreciation methods, the benefit stream from investment when plugged into (7A.3) will not yield depreciation schedules anything like those used by actual firms to optimize after-tax profits (given the schedules permitted by the Internal Revenue Service) or like those used for non-tax-reporting purposes. Real investments will almost invariably have complicated time shapes for their benefit streams. Further, even relatively simple shapes yield economic depreciation schedules that are quite far from accounting ones. To see this, one need only observe that if $V(\theta)$ satisfies (7A.3), there is no reason that $V'(\theta)$ must always be negative. Indeed, if the time stream of benefits starts low and then has a hump a few years out, taking economic depreciation would require writing up the value of assets for the first few years. Yet there is nothing bizarre about such an example.

We must, therefore, with pathologically unlikely exceptions, expect that the accounting rate of return on a particular machine will generally not equal the economic rate of return, r. (How far off it can be is demonstrated by examples.) This should make us suspect that the same thing will generally be true of the firm as a whole, and we now go on to explore that question.

Before Tax-Analysis: The Accounting Rate of Return for the Firm as an Average

It is fairly plain that the best hope for an accounting rate of return equal to the economic rate of return will occur if all investments made by the firm are exactly alike, since otherwise (as will be shown) changes in the mix of investment types will change the accounting rate. So we begin by considering the case in which all machines are like the machine just described.

It now becomes necessary to distinguish calendar time, denoted t, from the age of the machine, denoted by θ. We let $I(t)$ be the value of investment made at t (equals the number of machines purchased). Let

$K(t)$ denote the book value of the firm's assets at t and $\pi(t)$ the value of its accounting profits at t. Then

$$K(t) = \int_{-\infty}^{t} I(u)V(t-u)\,du = \int_{0}^{\infty} I(t-\theta)V(\theta)\,d\theta, \qquad (7A.7)$$

where $\theta = t-u$. Similarly,

$$\pi(t) = \int_{-\infty}^{t} I(u)\{f(t-u) + V'(t-u)\}\,du \qquad (7A.8)$$

$$= \int_{0}^{\infty} I(t-\theta)\{f(\theta) + V'(\theta)\}\,d\theta = \int_{0}^{\infty} I(t-\theta)V(\theta)b(\theta)\,d\theta$$

by (7A.2).

Hence, letting $a(t)$ be the firm's accounting rate of return at t gives

$$a(t) \equiv \frac{\pi(t)}{K(t)} = \frac{\displaystyle\int_{0}^{\infty} \{I(t-\theta)V(\theta)\}b(\theta)\,d\theta}{\displaystyle\int_{0}^{\infty} \{I(t-\theta)V(\theta)\}\,d\theta} \qquad (7A.9)$$

so that we have proved

LEMMA 7A.1   At any time t, the accounting rate of return for the firm as a whole is a weighted average of the individual accounting rates for its individual past investments, the weights being the book values of those past investments.

It should be obvious that this result would also be true if machines were not always of one type.

We now ask whether such an average will equal the economic rate of return. First consider whether the average can even be independent of t. This can happen in two ways. First, $b(\theta)$ might be independent of θ. We know from theorem 7A.1 that this will happen for $b(\theta) \equiv r$ only for the case of economic depreciation already discussed which we rule out. It is easy to show that $b(\theta) \equiv q \neq r$ is impossible, for a proof essentially the same as that of theorem 7A.1 would show that $b(\theta) \equiv q$ if and only if

$$V(\theta) = Ce^{q\theta} + z(\theta), \qquad (7A.10)$$

where

$$z(\theta) \equiv \int_{\theta}^{\infty} f(u)e^{-q(u-\theta)}\,du. \qquad (7A.11)$$

But $V(0) = 1$ so that $C = 1 - z(0) \neq 0$ if $q \neq r$. Then (7A.4) yields $V(\infty) = \pm\infty$ depending on $q \gtrless r$, and this is not possible.

The other way in which $a(t)$ might be independent of t would be if the relative weights in the average did not change over time.[7.22] In this case,

$$\frac{I(t_1 - \theta)V(\theta)}{I(t_2 - \theta)V(\theta)} = k, \tag{7A.12}$$

whence

$$\frac{I'(t_1 - \theta)}{I(t_1 - \theta)} = \frac{I'(t_2 - \theta)}{I(t_2 - \theta)} \tag{7A.13}$$

for all (t_1, t_2). Evidently it must be the case that

$$I(t) = Me^{gt} \tag{7A.14}$$

for some constant growth rate g.

The remainder of our investigation will concern the case of exponential growth with the scale factor M set equal to unity. This case is the most favorable to accounting rates of return approximating economic rates of return since in its absence accounting rates of return will not even be constant, even though the economic rate of return is well defined and constant.

Before-Tax Analysis: The Effect of the Growth Rate on Exponential Growth

We are now dealing with a case in which the accounting rate of return is (at least asymptotically) constant and given as

$$a = \frac{\displaystyle\int_0^\infty \{e^{g(t-\theta)}V(\theta)\}b(\theta)\, d\theta}{\displaystyle\int_0^\infty \{e^{g(t-\theta)}V(\theta)\}\, d\theta} \tag{7A.15}$$

where a denotes the (asymptotic) constant value. This is still a weighted average of the accounting rates of return on individual investments. Plainly, the growth rate g affects the weights. Since the accounting rates

7.22. For a *given* distribution of $b(\theta)$, there might be other possibilities, but these would be even more special than the case of economic depreciation already discussed. The statement in the text is true if $a(t)$ is to be constant despite unknown variations in $b(\theta)$ with θ.

of return on individual investments will almost always not be constant in view of theorem 7A.1, changes in the weights will usually affect the average.

We now study such effects and ask, in particular, what inferences can be drawn concerning the economic rate of return r from knowledge of the accounting rate of return a and the growth rate g without information on the time shape of benefits $f(\cdot)$ since the latter information is plainly never available from the books of the firm—even assuming it is known in detail to the firm's forecasters.

The first thing to say in this regard is that while (as we shall show) there exist values of g for which $a = r$, these values will be the exception. One cannot expect accounting and economic rates of return to coincide even in the most favorable case of exponential growth and a single investment type except by the merest accident. What information *can* be gleaned from the accounting rate of return is analyzed here.

It will be convenient to set up the problem a little differently from the analysis already given. Let $\pi^*(t)$ denote the gross profits of the firm before depreciation. Let $\delta(t)$ denote total depreciation taken at time t. Let $K^*(t)$ denote the *undepreciated* value of the firm's capital stock. Let $D(t)$ denote the total depreciation already taken on that stock. Finally, let $a^* \equiv \pi^*(t)/K^*(t)$, so that a^* is the accounting rate of return that would be observed if there were no depreciation. The following relationships hold:

$$a = \frac{\pi^*(t) - \delta(t)}{K^*(t) - D(t)}, \tag{7A.16}$$

$$\pi^*(t) \equiv \int_{-\infty}^{t} e^{gu} f(t-u)\, du = \int_{0}^{\infty} e^{g(t-\theta)} f(\theta)\, d\theta \tag{7A.17}$$

$$= e^{gt} \int_{0}^{\infty} e^{-g\theta} f(\theta)\, d\theta = e^{gt} \pi^*(0),$$

$$K^*(t) = \int_{-\infty}^{t} e^{gu}\, du = \frac{1}{g} e^{gt}, \tag{7A.18}$$

$$\delta(t) = \int_{-\infty}^{t} e^{gu} V'(t-u)\, du = \int_{0}^{\infty} e^{g(t-\theta)} V'(\theta)\, d\theta = e^{gt}\delta(0), \tag{7A.19}$$

$$D(t) = \int_{-\infty}^{t} \delta(u)\, du = \int_{-\infty}^{t} e^{gu}\delta(0)\, du = \frac{\delta(0)}{g} e^{gt}. \tag{7A.20}$$

Evidently, we have proved

LEMMA 7A.2 $\delta(t)/D(t) = g$.

We now study the effects of g on a^*.

LEMMA 7A.3

a. If $g = r$, then $a^* = r = g$.

b. $d \log a^*/d \log g < 1$.

c. a^* and r are always on the same side of g. That is,

$a^* < g \leftrightarrow r < g$,

$a^* = g \leftrightarrow r = g$,

$a^* > g \leftrightarrow r > g$.

Proof

a. By using (7A.17) and (7A.18),

$$a^* = g\pi^*(0) = g \int_0^\infty e^{-g\theta} f(\theta) \, d\theta. \tag{7A.21}$$

If $g = r$, then $\pi^*(0) = 1$ by the definition of the economic rate of return (7A.1), whence $a^* = g = r$.

b. From (7A.21),

$$\log a^* = \log g + \log \pi^*(0), \tag{7A.22}$$

but examination of $\pi^*(0)$ shows that it is necessarily decreasing in g since it is the discounted integral of future benefits from a single machine discounted at the rate g. Thus, $d \log a^*/d \log g < 1$.

c. These statements follow directly from a and b.

Using lemmas 7.A2 and 7A.3, we can now proceed to the main result of this section for the magnitude of interest, the accounting rate of return, a, itself.

THEOREM 7A.2 a and r are always on the same side of g. That is,

$a < g \leftrightarrow r < g$

$a = g \leftrightarrow r = g$

$a > g \leftrightarrow r > g$

Proof. By definition, $\pi^*(t) = a^* K^*(t)$. By lemma 7A.2, $\delta(t) = gD(t)$. Substituting in (7A.16) gives

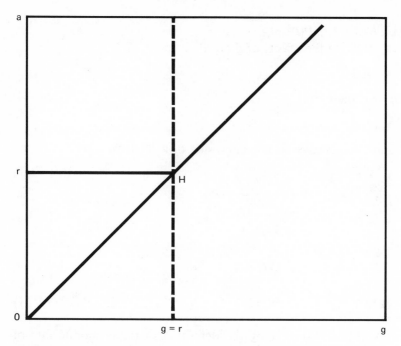

Figure 7A.1 Regions for the relationship of the accounting rate of return and the growth rate.

$$a = \frac{a^*K^*(t) - gD(t)}{K^*(t) - D(t)} \underset{<}{\overset{>}{=}} g \qquad (7A.23)$$

accordingly as $a^* < g$, $a^* = g$, or $a^* > g$. The desired result now follows from lemma 7A.3.

A diagram may be illuminating here. In figure 7A.1, the growth rate is measured on the horizontal axis and rates of return on the vertical axis. The 45-degree line indicates where growth rates and rates of return are equal. Theorem 7A.2 states that the accounting rate of return must be above the 45-degree line to the left of the dashed line at $g = r$; it must pass through H, the point of intersection of the dashed line and the 45-degree lines; and it must be below the 45-degree line to the right of the dashed line.

Can we say more than this? The answer is in the negative without information on the time shape of benefits $f(\cdot)$. In particular, it is *not* the case that the direction of change of a with respect to g is signed. Nor is it true that r must lie between a and g. These facts are exemplified in the text.

After-Tax Analysis

These same results apply to the analysis of the relationship between the after-tax economic rate of return and the after-tax accounting rate of return. This is obvious if the depreciation schedule used is not that used for tax purposes; in that case, the effect of taxes is to change the benefit profile $f(\cdot)$, with the analysis the same as before given the new benefit profile. Moreover, the same thing is true if tax depreciation is used. To see this, let α be the tax rate $0 < \alpha < 1$ (assumed constant for simplicity). Let r' denote the after-tax economic rate of return. Then r' satisfies

$$\int_0^\infty \{(1 - \alpha)f(\theta) + \alpha d(\theta)\}e^{-r'(\theta)}\, d\theta = 1, \tag{7A.24}$$

where $d(\theta)$ denotes depreciation on an asset of age θ and $f(\theta)$ continues to denote its *before*-tax benefits.

This reflects the fact that the choice of a depreciation schedule $d(\cdot)$ affects after-tax returns.

Define

$$f^*(\theta) = \{(1 - \alpha)f(\theta) + \alpha d(\theta)\}. \tag{7A.25}$$

We now show that the analysis of the before-tax case applies directly to the after-tax case with $f^*(\cdot)$, the after-tax benefit schedule, replacing $f(\cdot)$, the before-tax benefit schedule.[7.23]

To see this, observe that the denominator of the accounting rate of return (whether total capitalization or stockholders' equity) will be the same before and after taxes. The numerator in the after-tax case, after-tax profits less depreciation, will be

---

7.23. A word about the treatment of inflation seems appropriate here. In the before-tax analysis, it does not matter whether we work in real or nominal dollars (so long as we are consistent). In the after-tax case, however, the fact that depreciation deductible for tax purposes must be in nominal terms appears to raise some difficulty. That difficulty is only apparent. Suppose that we begin by working in real terms. The nominal nature of the depreciation deduction plus the effects of inflation affect the depreciation schedule measured in real terms. We show, however, that any after-tax case with *any* depreciation schedule is isomorphic to some before-tax case. The effects being considered will, of course, influence *what* that before-tax case is, but they will not alter the existence of such a case. While the nominal nature of depreciation (like any other factor affecting the depreciation schedule) will affect what the numerical value of the real after-tax accounting rate of return is, it will not change our results.

$$\int_{-\infty}^{t} (1-\alpha)\{f(t-\theta) - d(t-\theta)\} I(\theta) \, d\theta$$

$$= \int_{-\infty}^{t} \{(1-\alpha)f(t-\theta) + \alpha d(t-\theta)\} I(\theta) \, d\theta - \int_{-\infty}^{t} d(t-\theta) I(\theta) \, d\theta$$

$$= \int_{-\infty}^{t} f^*(t-\theta) I(\theta) \, d\theta - \int_{-\infty}^{t} d(\theta) I(\theta) \, d\theta.$$

$$(7A.26)$$

But this is the *same* numerator as would be encountered in the before-tax analysis for a firm with the same depreciation schedule but *before-tax benefits $f^*(\cdot)$*. For such a firm, r would be the *before*-tax economic rate of return. Hence analysis of the after-tax case is identical to that of the before-tax case with an appropriate adjusted definition of the benefit schedule. All previous results apply to it.[7.24]

7.24. It is interesting (and revealing of the full unity of the before-tax and after-tax analysis) to note what happens in the case of "economic depreciation" examined earlier. In that case, it turns out that the (pathologically unlikely) choice of an "economic depreciation" schedule involves the *same* depreciation schedule whether "economic depreciation" is chosen before or after tax. Assets are valued at the present value of all remaining benefits either before or after tax; it makes no difference. Further, the choice of depreciation schedule makes the after-tax economic rate of return, r', relate to the before-tax economic rate of return, r, in the natural but—except with this depreciation schedule—not inevitable way: $r' = r(1 - \alpha)$.

To show these things, return to the differential equation (7A.5) from which we derived the formula for economic depreciation in the before-tax case.

$$V'(\theta) = rV(\theta) - f(\theta).$$ $$(7A.27)$$

Consideration of the before-tax analysis shows that if and only if $V(\cdot)$ satisfies this and $V(0) = 1$, then

$$V(\theta) = \int_{\theta}^{\infty} f(u)e^{-r(u-\theta)} \, du,$$ $$(7A.28)$$

the present value of future benefits.

Now, choose $V(\cdot)$ and hence $d(\cdot)$ to satisfy (7A.26) and therefore (7A.25). Then

$$(1 - \alpha)V'(\theta) = r(1 - \alpha)V(\theta) - (1 - \alpha)f(\theta).$$ $$(7A.29)$$

and

$$V'(\theta) = r(1 - \alpha)V(\theta) - \{(1 - \alpha)f(\theta) + \alpha d(\theta)\} = r(1 - \alpha)V(\theta) - f^*(\theta)$$ $$(7A.30)$$

since $d(\theta) \equiv - V'(\theta)$. But this is in the same form as (7A.5). Hence, as in (7A.6),

$$V(\theta) = \int_{\theta}^{\infty} f^*(u)e^{-r'(u-\theta)} \, du + Ce^{r'\theta}$$ $$(7A.31)$$

with $r' \equiv r(1 - \alpha)$. Here, C is a constant of integration; however, $C = 0$, since (7A.26) shows that $V(\infty)$ is finite. Since $V(0) = 1$, we have:

$$1 = \int_{0}^{\infty} f^*(u)e^{-r'u} \, du,$$ $$(7A.32)$$

which shows that r' is the after-tax economic rate of return. From (7A.26) and (7A.29) with $C = 0$, $V(\theta)$ is both the before-tax and the after-tax present value of the remaining benefit stream at θ, whence "economic depreciation" is the same in both cases. See Paul A. Samuelson, "Tax Deductibility of Economic Depreciation to Insure Investment Valuations," *Journal of Political Economy* 72 (December 1964), pp. 604–606.

Thus, in after-tax analysis as in before-tax analysis, there is no reason to believe that differences in the accounting rate of return correspond to differences in economic rates of return. Our computer examples show the effects can be very large; the belief that they are small enough in practice to make accounting rates useful for analytic purposes rests on nothing but wishful thinking.

Chapter 8

Anticompetitive Behavior and IBM's Actions

Whatever view of the market one takes, it is apparent that IBM is the largest firm in it. The question of what actions such a firm can take to preserve its position—of what acts should be permitted under the *Alcoa-United Shoe* standard—is an important one for antitrust policy.

Anticompetitive conduct must differ from action that would be expected to occur under competition. It follows that not every action that "damages" competitors is anticompetitive. In a competitive market, less efficient, less responsive, less innovative competitors will always suffer. In particular, firms facing the prospect of lost business are expected to cut prices in order to acquire business if it will increase their profits. Some or all of the business so acquired might otherwise have gone to competitors. Yet, such price cuts are not anticompetitive, even though less efficient firms might be forced to give up profits in order to match the new prices or even go out of business because they cannot match those prices profitably.

Note that this analysis is unaffected by the price cutter's awareness that lowering price may drive out particular competitors. All firms intend one result of their competitive acts to be the acquisition of business that otherwise would have gone to their rivals. Nevertheless, when they are forced to reduce price in order to avoid losing business and profits, their actions in the face of such threats are precisely the behavior that competition is expected to cause. Such actions should not be treated as anticompetitive. Similarly, the design and introduction of new, profitable products is not anticompetitive just because it inconveniences particular competitors. Ultimately, the marketplace will decide if there is benefit to a design choice; this is especially true where the new product offers an additional option. The provision of new and better products, like the lowering of prices, often injures competitors in the sense that it deprives them of business, which is its purpose under competition.[1]

Anticompetitive conduct is conduct that makes no sense without the monopoly profits that can be made only after competition is reduced or driven out by the monopolistic reduction of output or of output quality to achieve unjustifiably high prices. Conduct that brings profitable higher sales cannot be anticompetitive regardless of how uncomfortable it makes competitors.

The following conditions must be present to find that conduct is anticompetitive:

First, the conduct must be other than that encouraged by and consistent with the competitive process. The subjective intent of a company is difficult to determine and will usually reflect nothing more than a determination to win all possible business from rivals—a determination consistent with competition.

Second, the conduct must also be substantially related to the maintenance or acquisition (or attempted acquisition) of monopoly power, in that it must have (or be expected to have) the effect of destroying or excluding competition.

The first prong of this test is a matter of necessity if aggressive competition is to be encouraged. The inherent uncertainty of a rule that would require businesses to respond to competitive stimuli subject to the later judgments of others that the responses were too much or too little would have an inevitable dampening effect on competition. Activities such as lowering prices (if not below cost, as explained later), introduction of better products, dissemination of pricing and product information, and adoption of improved design concepts or more efficient means of production are incidents of the competitive process that benefit customers. To premise their legality on an inquiry into the specific motivations or subjective intent of the firms that engage in such conduct (when it is clear that all firms engaged in competition attempt and intend to win as much business as they can) or on retrospective evaluation of whether there were more "desirable" alternative actions that could have been chosen, would be to elevate competitors above competition and threaten the entire competitive process for the sake of those who are not intended to be its beneficiaries and at the expense of those who are.

The reason for the second prong of the test is self-evident: if the act is ineffectual (and expected to be so), it is irrelevant, except perhaps as a proof of lack of monopoly power on the part of the actor. Since the first prong of the test may be difficult to apply, it is well to be aware that failure to pass the second is dispositive.

Predatory Pricing and Limit Pricing

A predatory price is a nonremunerative price set in a deliberate attempt to drive out or discourage (actual or potential) competitors. The firm that sets such a price is undertaking a deliberate loss in order to earn monopoly profits once competitors have been eliminated. In this sense, predatory pricing is consistent with long-run profit maximization. But without the prospect of future monopoly profits from subsequent price increases, which will more than make up for initial losses, "predation" is an activity that would not be undertaken by a rational, profit-maximizing firm.

Consider a firm that makes an innovation by discovering a new product. During the period after the discovery and before others learn how to make that product, the innovating firm may earn high profits. When imitators enter and begin to produce the same or similar products, they may be able to offer those products at lower prices, since they can learn from the innovator's experience and thus avoid incurring the same research and development costs. In this situation, customers will turn away from the innovating firm if it attempts to keep its price high. Faced with this circumstance, the original innovator will have to lower its price or lose business. It is the lowering of price that competitive entry is supposed to accomplish.

It may be that, as the original firm is forced to lower its price, some of the imitators will no longer find it profitable to remain in the business. These will be the less efficient firms whose costs were too high to make profits except at prices near the original pre-entry price. Nevertheless, such exits do not in themselves make lowering of the price predatory. This is a fully competitive story even if the original innovating firm consciously realizes that by lowering price it will drive out competitors. It *must* lower its price in this situation or lose business to others. Lowering the price may mean lower profits than it would earn if it could keep price up and *not* lose business, but this is not an available option. In the circumstances described, profits will be greater if prices are lowered than if they are maintained, and the original firm will inevitably acquire business that would otherwise have gone to its rivals.

In this example, the reduction in price was economically inevitable. The original firm was forced by competition to reduce price or lose business and profits. The threat of such loss of business and profits is the prod that competition uses to compel certain behavior. It would be a great mistake to treat as predatory the very actions that competition is designed to compel.

What then would make such a price reduction predatory? A predatory price must be one that makes no sense except as an action taken to destroy or exclude competition. Thus, a predatory price must be a nonremunerative price whose only object is to force out a competitor, after which prices can be raised. The price has to be so low that setting it will return a profit to the firm only if the price is later raised and monopoly profits are earned after competitors have been driven out.

It follows that a predatory price must have the property that the additional revenues that flow from selling at that price are less than the additional costs incurred in order to make the sales. In the simplest case of a single unchanging good, this means that marginal revenue must be less than marginal cost. Demand curves that do not slope up indicate that price is no greater than marginal revenue, and this in return implies that a predatory price must be below marginal cost. Whether the appropriate marginal cost is short or long run depends on whether the firm has excess capacity.

Since marginal cost is hard to estimate, it may be necessary to use surrogates, such as average variable cost, to apply such a test in practice;[2] the analytically correct standard ought not to be in doubt, however. For an act to be predatory, the additional revenues that stem from the act (not counting later monopoly profits) must be less than the costs that would be avoided by refraining from the act—"avoidable costs."

To take a more complex example, consider the case of a firm contemplating a new program of product development. At various decision points in the process, the firm will have incurred some costs in the past. Such costs are sunk costs and do not enter into a profit-maximizing decision. The costs that do enter into such a decision are those that would be avoided if the firm did not go forward with the program. Similarly, certain revenues enter into a profit-maximizing decision. These are the revenues that the program will bring in if it goes forward over and above those revenues that the firm will receive if the program does not go forward. To be predatory, the decision to proceed in this instance must be made in the expectation that the additional revenues will not cover the avoidable costs. If the firm reasonably expects such costs to be covered, then the program is remunerative, and the decision to go forward is not predatory.

The lowering of prices or the introduction of better products are two activities that competition is supposed to compel. As long as prices are set above avoidable costs, there is no waste of social resources by the firm setting such prices, and the only firms that will be unable to match them and may eventually be driven from the market are less efficient firms. These are results that competition encourages. Pricing below avoidable cost, on the other hand, may eliminate equally or more efficient actual or potential rivals, not just less efficient ones. It can have no legitimate purpose, for its sole justification is driving out competitors so that prices can then be raised and monopoly profits earned. Such pricing leads to an improper allocation of resources and, eventually, to higher prices. Both of these results are inconsistent with competition. They constitute anticompetitive conduct if they are not merely the result of accident or miscalculation and actually have (or are expected to have) an anticompetitive effect.

Note that in this view, a large firm, even a "dominant" firm, would be allowed to engage in "limit pricing," reducing its prices to a still remunerative level when attacked by competition in order to retain business and thus market share. *It is a mistake to believe that a large market share is equivalent to monopoly.* When such a share can only be maintained by reducing prices toward (but not beyond) costs or introducing better products, monopoly power is absent and competition is doing its job.

It may be objected, however, that while permitting such pricing will lead to prices lower than the short-run monopoly price, it may also result in prices above the long-run competitive price. But consider the consequence of making it "anticompetitive" for a firm with monopoly power to price above the perfectly competitive equilibrium price (long-run marginal cost) but below the short-run monopoly price (where profits are maximized as though competitors would never exist). Such a policy would condemn as "predatory" price cuts that are *less* deep than others that are *not* considered predatory. Further, given the difficulty of deciding or proving what long-run marginal cost actually is, such a policy would in practice make firms hesitate to cut prices at all—as competition would require them to do. This would effectively require the firms involved to hold up an "umbrella" over entrants regardless of whether the entrants are efficient. It would thus keep innovative and efficient firms from reaping the rewards of their efficiency. Under such a policy, an innovator would be faced with a Hobson's choice as soon as an imitator could produce the same product at a cost below the short-run monopoly price even if that cost were far above that of the original innovator. The innovating firm would either have to set its price at the short-run monopoly price, allowing the inefficient imitator to take the business, or else it would immediately have to set its price at long-run marginal cost. In either case, the original innovator would lose the fruits of the innovation. This is a recipe for stifling progress by removing the incentives for pursuing it.[8.1] It stands in contrast to the behavior expected under competition, where, as imitators become more efficient, the price drops to the level of *their* costs, eventually falling to the long-run marginal cost of the original firm if it remains the most efficient one or below that level if it does not remain so.

In sum, first, actions of a kind to be expected under competition are not predatory even if competitors are damaged by them. In a competitive environment, gain for one firm very often means a loss for others.

Second, for an action to be predatory, it must be expected to be unprofitable. In such a computation, monopoly profits later to be earned by raising prices after driving out competition are not to be counted.

Third, in order to be predatory, an action must not only be unprofitable in itself, it must also reasonably be expected to exclude competition so that monopoly profits can be earned later. We add this because of the uncertainty involved in later deciding whether a certain action was in fact expected to be unprofitable. When long-run decisions and forecasts are involved, it may not be easy to tell whether they were deliberately unprofitable.[8.2] When the firm undertaking them cannot reasonably have expected to earn later monopoly profits after driving out competition, it is unreasonable to conclude that the actions were predatory even if, with the benefit of hindsight, they appear to have been unwise.

8.1. Leonard Weiss was well aware of such problems in his trial testimony (Weiss, Tr. 70296, 70924–25). Not surprisingly, Alan McAdams favored such a policy (McAdams, Tr. 61681–89; see also 65237–40, 65250).

8.2. It is for this reason that Phillip Areeda and Donald F. Turner emphasize the difficulty of using long-run decisions—particularly investment decisions—as a measuring stick, preferring instead to look at the short-run (P. Areeda and D. F. Turner, "Predatory Pricing and Related Practices Under Section 2 of the Sherman Act," *Harvard Law Review* 88 (1975), pp. 218–220.) It is not necessary for us to consider their view that such long-run analyses would generally be unworkable in practice and that a general rule based on them would prompt potential abuse in the form of "the threat of baseless but costly litigation." In this case the evidence is clear that IBM's practices were not predatory under either rule.

The System/360 Issues

According to the government, virtually all of the System/360 computer products that IBM introduced in and after 1964 and marketed for the remainder of the 1960s were anticompetitive product introductions or "fighting machines." The entire System/360 line announced on April 7, 1964, and a number of individual System/360 products announced at different points in time thereafter were alleged to have been "premature announcements." In addition, the 360/90 series, the 360/67, and the 360/44 were alleged to have been predatory product introductions with prices deliberately set below cost. These claims reach virtually every aspect of IBM's computer business in the mid-1960s and imply that IBM should have totally restructured the conduct of its business during that period of time so as to delay or not to make new product announcements for some unspecified period of time. On its face, this bespeaks a total misunderstanding of the economic analysis of competition and monopoly; after all, the introduction of new products is usually a sign of competition, not monopoly.

The 360/90 Series as a Predatory Pricing Action
The Model 90[8.3] program begun in 1961 was the successor to a series of "super computer" development efforts that IBM had undertaken during the 1950s. Each of those programs had helped advance the state of the art in computing. The Model 90 program was an effort by IBM to "push technology" and build "the most powerful computer" possible at the time.[3]

There were a number of reasons why such attempts to "stretch" the state of the art were undertaken by IBM, including substantial pressure from leading edge customers; a sizeable business opportunity as well as a chance to promote the nation's interest if such demands could be met; the promotional value and added sales that would result from being able to lay claim to providing the world's most powerful computer; the ability to attract the best young talent to work on such advanced projects; and the very valuable "technological fallout" that would result for future development efforts.[4]

With the increasing publicity in 1963 devoted to Control Data Corporation's announced but undelivered 6600 computer system, IBM's

---

8.3. We refer to these machines as "Model 90s." The machines involved were the 360/91, 360/92, and 360/95. Only the 360/91 and 360/95 were ever produced, the 360/92 being superseded by the 360/95.

industry leadership in large-scale, state-of-the-art computers was called into question. In response, IBM management attempted to determine how IBM could "catch up to and surpass CDC in the area of very high performance computer systems" and accelerated the Model 90 program (then called "Project X"). Even so, the program had not "progressed far enough to warrant a general announcement" along with the rest of the 360 Series in April 1964, although a footnote to the System/360 announcement advised customers that development of the Model 90 was in progress. The Model 90s were announced in August and November 1964.[5]

Delivery of the first of the Model 90s was made nine months late, primarily because IBM encountered unexpected problems in the Model 90 circuitry. Each of the systems, however, performed well and to customers' satisfaction and passed all government-imposed acceptance tests. Nevertheless, while the technological fallout anticipated from the program did materialize, the Model 90s were unsuccessful despite price reductions that attempted to make them more competitive. Only fifteen Model 91s were manufactured (four for internal use); two Model 95s were manufactured "specially" for NASA.[6]

In the meantime, CDC manufactured more than two hundred 6000 series computers, including ninety-four Model 6600/6700s. By CDC management's own account, the 6600 was "particularly" successful, and, after the 6600 was delivered, CDC was able to "dominate" the field in large computers from 1964 to 1969. Moreover, from 1964 to 1972, CDC's revenues and gross profits from the sale and lease of 6600s exceeded CDC's targets. As IBM's Paul Knaplund testified, "They [CDC] certainly beat us."[7]

Nevertheless, the government contended that the 360/90 was "prematurely" announced and predatory. We postpone analysis of the prematurity issue and now consider the latter contention, that: "The IBM Model 90 series is a classic example of a fighting machine. Its primary function was to stop Control Data and eliminate the potential competitive threat that that company posed to IBM's monopolization of the marketplace."[8]

At issue is whether IBM believed at the time of announcement that its avoidable costs on the Model 90 program would exceed the revenues that the program would return and would thus be justified only by the alleged monopoly profits to be earned after CDC was "stopped."

IBM could not have expected to "stop" CDC. At the time of the announcement of the Model 92 (later replaced by the Model 95) in

August 1964, the professional forecasters within IBM estimated that the potential in the United States for sales of computer systems of the size and power of the Model 92 was about seventy. Those same forecasters projected that at the prices announced in August 1964, IBM would install twenty-four Model 92 systems in the United States, and IBM's marketing arms only committed themselves to placement of twenty-four such systems worldwide. It is hard to conclude that an action expected to achieve one-third of the potential business for that size system was also expected to drive CDC or any other competitor out of business.[8.4] As we have seen, the CDC 6600 was in fact a remarkably successful product. CDC's EDP revenues more than tripled from 1964 to 1969, from about $150 million to about $570 million.[9]

The pre-announcement financial analysis of the Model 92, done in accordance with IBM's standard full-cost recovery methodology, showed that IBM expected to earn profits of about $10 million on the Model 92 System as a whole, including peripheral equipment that was not otherwise expected to be sold or leased by IBM. The same analysis showed, however, that with respect to the Model 92 central processing units and memory alone, using IBM's standard full-cost recovery methodology, IBM's projected cost would exceed its anticipated revenues.[10]

That analysis did not purport to be an indication of the incremental revenues and avoidable costs associated with the Model 92 announcement. It contained as program costs of the Model 92 processing unit and memory the costs of advanced development work that IBM would have undertaken even if it had not decided to announce the Model 92 and large amounts of fixed overhead that would have been incurred even without the Model 92 program. On the other side of the equation, the analysis ignored completely the substantial "fallout" benefits to future products that could result from the advanced research and development efforts on the Model 90.[11]

IBM was well aware that such technological benefits could be expected from the Model 90 program and that there were thus powerful reasons for undertaking it, even if accounting computations did not properly attribute such benefits to the credit side of the ledger. At just this time (1964), IBM was coming to a full realization of the technological fallout of its earlier development of STRETCH, a large machine that had appeared to lose money but was now paying off first in terms of the 7090 and the 1400 series and then in terms of System/360 itself.[12]

8.4. Note that the contention (raised by Alan McAdams) that the IBM forecast of 360/90 placements was artificially high merely reinforces this if true.

Thus, IBM management recognized that it was particularly inappropriate to measure the potential profitability of the Model 90 program by using IBM's usual full-cost recovery approach and looking only at the central processing unit and memory. The optimum approach would have involved quantifying and including the anticipated fallout benefits, but it was recognized within IBM that such quantification would have been "so speculative in content as to be almost meaningless."

Instead, IBM went part way toward a correct calculation by ignoring such benefits but not counting costs of development programs and other expenses that would be incurred regardless of whether the Model 90s were produced. On this basis, the central processing units (including memory) were expected to recover costs, and the systems as a whole were expected to earn profits of approximately $30 million. Subjecting the figures to intensive and conservative review years later, Sidney Davidson, Arthur Young Professor of Accounting at the University of Chicago (who was called as an IBM witness), agreed that the system was reasonably expected to be profitable on this basis.[13]

Further, the fallout benefits cannot be ignored. They were expected on the basis of IBM's past experience to be substantial, if unquantifiable, and, in fact, they materialized. The Model 90 program produced technological benefits of use in later products, including the solution of the "cracked stripe" circuitry problem and developments in thin film technology, monolithic circuitry, transistor technology, interconnection technology, and machine organization. In addition that program kept IBM from appearing to abandon leading-edge powerful processors, a gain in terms of its image with customers and personnel morale and retention. Since the program as a whole was expected to be profitable even without such benefits, it must have been so with them.[14]

At the trial, Alan McAdams took the position that one ought not to count the profits that IBM expected to earn from additional memory and input/output devices that would be attached to the Model 90 CPUs and would not otherwise be placed. He argued for the exclusion of such profits on the ground that IBM's production facilities were overloaded with a backlog of orders so that peripherals produced for Model 90 systems simply displaced *in production* peripherals for other systems.[15]

This argument is incorrect on two counts. First, the backlog in production facilities was unforeseen when the announcement the 360/90 was being considered. That backlog stemmed from the explosion in demand for the other models of System/360, and the Model 90s were in any case a small fraction of IBM's anticipated output. The decision to announce the Model 90s thus properly counted the additional peripherals.[16]

Second, even putting this aside, the contention that Model-90-stimulated peripherals would not have contributed to IBM's profits is analytically incorrect. Suppose it to be true, for example, that disk drive plants were operating at full capacity and that there was a backlog of orders. Suppose further (contrary to fact) that IBM anticipated this in August 1964. A future order for a disk drive from a 90 series customer would only lengthen the queue for disk drive delivery—it would not (as McAdams suggested) replace another disk drive. This means that while the profits from production of a Model-90-related disk drive would not simply be additional, they would not be offset entirely or even largely by the loss of profits on another disk drive, even if the factory were badly backlogged. They would only be offset to a minor degree by the amount of interest involved in the fact that the profits from the displaced disk drive were postponed.[8.5]

There are two circumstances in which this analysis would not be correct. One such circumstance would be that in which the marginal increase in waiting time consequent upon the production of the 360/90-related disk drives for customers with orders behind those drives in the queue was sufficient to cause those customers to cancel their orders. There is no evidence that anything of the kind happened, and the forecast for the 90 series was too small for it to have been expected to happen.[17] Second, if the backlog could have been expected to be *permanent*, then the production of additional 90 series-related disk drives would have permanently increased waiting times, as the postponed disk drives postponed others, and so forth. In that event, the foregone interest would indeed have a present value exactly equal to the profits from the 90 series-related disk drives. For this to have happened and to have been relevant to IBM's decision, however, IBM would not only have had to anticipate in August 1964 the backlog that emerged a year or so later but would have to have expected that backlog to last forever or at least long enough to make the postponed interest effect more than negligible. This is highly improbable. Such interest effects—mere matters of the timing of receipts—were certainly negligible

---

8.5. Such interest effects could not have been very large. In the mid-1960s, interest rates were much lower than in the early 1980s. The average prime rate in 1964–66 ranged from 4.5 to 5.6 percent (see *Economic Report of the President*, Washington, D.C.: U.S. Government Printing Office, 1981, p. 308).

and would sensibly have been neglected in the light of the uncertainties surrounding forecasts of this nature.

In sum, the development and announcement of the 90 series carried with it a number of quite substantial indirect economic benefits, which IBM anticipated and took into account in deciding to proceed with the program (although of course not in bookkeeping terms). Such a program might very well have been expected to go forward under competition, even if accounting for direct revenues and costs showed a loss. Even without consideration of such indirect benefits, however, the Model 90 program was expected to yield revenues that exceeded avoidable costs. In such circumstances, the decision to announce the 90 series could not have been predatory. Not only was the 90 series not priced below cost but it neither drove out nor could it have been expected to drive out CDC.

The 360/44

Within months after the announcement of System/360, IBM management began receiving reports from the field that "although many users found the System 360 products adequate for data acquisition and data reduction, some felt that a general purpose processor more tailored to those specific applications would be required." Pressure for development of a system to meet those user needs mounted in 1964 and 1965 as IBM Models 40 and 50 were repeatedly beaten by CDC and SDS systems with sparer systems software but faster throughput that permitted them to "outprice" and "outperform" IBM's offerings in the "Intermediate Scientific Area." The Model 44 development was undertaken to provide users with a system that could offer better throughput per dollar than the Models 40 and 50 for "data acquisition, data reduction and certain scientific calculations."[18]

To achieve the cost reductions and performance improvements necessary to offer such a system, IBM had to hard-wire certain of the Model 44's instructions and eliminate some others from the repertoire available with previous 360s. This meant that the 360/44 would be faster and cheaper than it otherwise would have been, but at a sacrifice of functional richness and full compatibility with the rest of the 360 line.[8.6] Thus, it offered users exactly the kind of trade-off of price/performance for function that they were choosing in selecting CDC and

8.6. Optional full compatibility at extra cost was made available (see evidence cited in Historical Narrative, p. 414, fn.**).

SDS systems over 360/40s and 360/50s. Nevertheless, the Model 44 was not particularly successful, and within a few years after its announcement in August 1965, it had failed to achieve anything like the number of sales forecast for it at the time of announcement, being quickly surpassed by competitors.[19]

Let us review these facts in the light of expectations in a competitive market. One firm (IBM) offers products that are rejected by some users in favor of competitive products with somewhat differing characteristics. Under innovative competition, that firm has two choices if it wishes to win more business: lower the prices of existing products or introduce new products that duplicate or improve upon the characteristics of products that particular users are selecting in lieu of those existing products. If those characteristics are of value mainly to a particular group, while others are satisfied with the existing products, then the product-introduction option will be the more profitable one. In this instance, IBM took that option, introducing a new product that would offer users the same kind of trade-offs of performance (that is, throughput) for functions that were being offered by the firms (such as CDC and SDS) that were successfully winning the business of those customers. Those firms responded in turn with new, better performing products of their own. They were successful; IBM was not. Users were given more options and the ability to obtain better products for their dollar.

As with the Model 90, the government again raised claims of "premature" announcement (discussed later) and predatory pricing:

[T]he 360/44 was simply another IBM fighting machine designed to stop specific competitive threats and maintain IBM's overall monopoly position.

. . .

[The Model 44 was] clearly aimed at preventing the growth of CDC and SDS in their respective markets, and at forestalling the entry of these companies into the general purpose market by undermining their potential resource bases.[20]

The government did not claim, however, either that the Model 44 was priced below avoidable cost as a program or that IBM was successful in its alleged aim to "prevent . . . the growth of CDC and SDS." We have already reviewed CDC's extraordinary growth during the alleged period of predation. SDS's growth during this same period was even more spectacular. Its revenues rose from $20.5 million in 1964 to $100.7 million in 1968—almost five-fold. SDS's profits also increased in each of the years 1964 through 1968. SDS, which had been founded in 1961 with an initial capitalization of $1 million, was acquired by Xerox in 1969 for approximately $980 million worth of Xerox stock.[21]

There is no dispute concerning the fact that the Model 44 program was expected to be profitable. The argument that it was predatory turns entirely on the proposition that production of 360/44s displaced production of *more* profitable 360/40s and 360/50s in IBM's backlogged facilities. We have already dealt with such arguments. While some problems were foreseen early in the program, by the time of the 360/44's announcement in August 1965, it was believed that production capacity would be adequate. Further, at best only small interest costs were involved.[22]

In short, the Model 44 may not have been particularly successful, but it was surely not predatory. It was neither expected to be unprofitable nor did it have any discernible effect on the ability of companies like CDC or SDS to compete with IBM.

The 360/67

"Time sharing" refers to the use of a single computer by a number of people simultaneously, each appearing to command the entire computer. System/360 was planned from its inception to have some time-sharing capability, and some such capability was in fact provided. Shortly after the 360 announcement, however, it became clear that many highly sophisticated customers with advanced time-sharing requirements were rejecting as inferior the particular time-sharing approach implemented with 360, primarily because that approach did not include a facility known as dynamic address translation or dynamic relocation hardware ("relocate"), which was believed to be essential for time sharing.[8.7] Losses to GE at MIT's Project MAC and at Bell Labs and the prospect of other potential losses spurred IBM to deal with the problem.[23]

These developments were viewed with great concern within IBM. Nathan Rochester of the Time Shared Task Force stated in the fall of 1964 that

System/360 has been almost universally rejected by the leading time sharing investigators. Time sharing systems are likely to render obsolete systems that are not based on time sharing. Therefore, there is a legitimate worry that System/360 may not be a resounding success unless proper steps are taken.

8.7. Relocate hardware provides a "means for interrupting a program at an arbitrary point, moving it out of main memory, proceeding with the interruption, bringing the interrupted program back into memory at a new location, and starting it again" (PX 1194A, p. 3).

. . .
There is much more at stake than these few prestige accounts. What is at stake is essentially all computing business, scientific and commercial. . . . [We] may find eventually that many of the best programmers will refuse to work at an installation that does not offer time sharing or offers inferior time sharing.[24]

The research group of the task force echoed Rochester's concern: "There is a very strong probability that the 'computing utility' will be *the* way of all scientific computing in a few years, and a good possibility that it will capture a substantial part of the commercial market as well. IBM cannot afford to overlook a development of this scope. *We are currently in danger of losing all contact with the leading developers of this concept.*"[25]

Indeed, as IBM's Scientific Computing Department saw it, the entire market was at stake. The choice of time-sharing equipment by prestigious, scientifically oriented accounts was expected to affect system selection among many more users, both scientific and commercial. Companies with a variety of backgrounds, including experience in "military" and real-time systems were seen as ready to step in and supply users' requirements; and improved time sharing was anticipated to intensify competition from service bureaus. If these predictions were right, every dimension of the market would be affected.[26]

At the same time, IBM's customers were sending clear signals to IBM "loudly and with great conviction" about their needs with respect to time sharing. The sales force recognized and reported to management that IBM's failure to meet those demands would cause "a great deal of churning of [IBM's] installed base, that is, the return of products that IBM had installed because of the requirement for a new capability in a computing system."[27]

IBM had already received a number of requests for proposal (RFPs) from highly sophisticated customers (such as MIT's Lincoln Laboratory and the University of Michigan), and it was decided that IBM could enhance its understanding of advanced time-sharing requirements by responding to these requests and to the needs of a limited number of highly knowledgeable users. IBM's work with those customers, however, only served to intensify the pressure that other users were applying on IBM. Many others viewed themselves as equally sophisticated, complaining to IBM that they did not wish to be treated as "second-class citizen[s]" and demanding that IBM propose time-sharing systems to them as well. As that pressure built, IBM yielded and made proposals to a number of additional organizations.[28]

In March 1965, IBM announced the System/360 Models 64 and 66—which were superseded in April by the improved Model 67—for "limited bidding." The bidding restrictions were removed with the full announcement of the Model 67 in August 1965 for delivery in 1966. During this entire period, IBM went to great lengths to ensure that customers understood both the developmental nature of the program and that "things would change as they went along."[29]

As things turned out, IBM had little difficulty with implementing the Model 67's hardware (including dynamic relocate), but ran into far greater problems with development of the associated operating system, TSS, than had been anticipated. As a result, by the fall of 1966, IBM began advising users that it might be forced to decommit certain TSS functions and announce delays in delivery schedules. Customers were kept fully informed of the problems that IBM was experiencing. Although IBM delivered Release 1 of TSS in October 1967 (it had been scheduled for delivery in June 1967), it was not until April 1969 that IBM was able to deliver a "substantially improved" version of TSS, which was "considered to be an excellent software programming system."[30]

The Model 67 was not a marketing success; the initial problems with TSS prevented use of the system for all but "experimental, developmental or instructional use." Moreover, at about the time the TSS problems were ironed out, System/360 was superseded by the announcement of IBM's next generation of computers, System/370. The experience and technology developed on the Model 67 program, however, was invaluable to IBM in later years, as the virtual storage function capability of the 67 was incorporated "in almost exactly the same way" into 370. Thus, as the Model 90 program had, the 360/67 program provided substantial benefit to future IBM products in the form of technological fallout.[31]

IBM had no choice. It was being told by customers that time sharing was the "wave of the future" and by its own people that all of its business was at stake if user demand for time sharing was not met. GE was already offering a product that many of the most advanced users found preferable to System/360 for time sharing, and many other companies had already begun or were expected to begin offering such capabilities. IBM customers, in turn, were pressing the company to provide a product solution for advanced time sharing. Only if IBM had monopoly power would it have been able to ignore such competitive pressure and customer demand. Under competition, the threat of significant business loss demanded a product response from a rational, profit-maximizing firm. (Indeed, such a response by IBM was both expected and encouraged by the government agency (ARPA) that sponsored MIT's Project MAC, whose award of a contract to GE sparked IBM's effort.)[32]

Nevertheless, the government asserted both that the 360/67 was prematurely announced and that it was predatorily priced with the program "expected to incur a loss or at best show a very low profit rate." The predation was said to have been aimed at GE and CDC, and the 360/67 was "merely another example of an IBM fighting machine designed to preserve IBM's monopoly power."[33]

The growth of CDC during the late 1960s has already been discussed. GE sold much of its computer business to Honeywell in 1969, but its partial exit, as its chairman testified, had nothing to do with acts of IBM. GE's difficulties instead stemmed from inadequate product development that led it to fall behind in the "constant leapfrogging game." A company with substantially greater annual revenues in the mid-1960s than those of IBM, GE also had extended commitments in nuclear reactors and jet engines, which it found more profitable than computers. While it did experience difficulties with its time-sharing systems, these were because of inherent technical problems and not because of the 360/67.[34]

The 360/67 thus had no "victim." It also was not priced below cost. The final pricing review in August 1965 projected a worldwide profit of $21.7 million. That analysis allocated to the Model 67 some but not all of the expected cost of the TSS program, since at the time IBM had another CPU under development that would use TSS (apart from the use of similar software in later machines). However, even if all the then-expected costs of TSS had been allocated to the Model 67, it would still have been projected to be profitable. The theory, advanced by McAdams, that the 360/67s displaced in production (not demand) more profitable 360/65s needs no further discussion. Indeed, there is no evidence that such production trade-offs were expected.[35]

Even apart from this, the Model 67 program offered the prospect of substantial fallout benefits—benefits that were anticipated to accrue and did accrue to future products, in particular to System/370. Such benefits added to the quantifiable profitability of the program. On the cost side, because of the urgent need for time-sharing capability, it is apparent that IBM would have had to develop time-sharing technology regardless of whether the Model 67 was announced in August 1965.

Thus, many of the research and development expenditures on the Model 67 hardware and software were not truly "avoidable" costs that would not otherwise have been incurred. For example, IBM had committed itself to designing time-sharing software well before the decision to announce the Model 67 and would have had to follow through on that commitment regardless of whether the Model 67 was announced for general availability.[36]

Technological fallout, moreover, was only one of the indirect benefits expected to flow from the Model 67 program. As we have seen, IBM was under intense pressure for time-sharing development from a number of very prestigious users, including the federal government. As IBM Chairman Frank Cary testified, "[S]ome of our very, very best customers wanted it. . . . [W]hen customers . . . like AT&T and the Federal Government and the universities and General Motors Research . . . ask us to respond, we certainly at least try to respond to them. And we didn't undertake that with any thought that we weren't going to be able to do it."[37] Further, more was seen to be at stake than the direct business of these prestigious accounts. A failure to keep up with the state of the art in time sharing as perceived by such users was predicted to have repercussions on IBM's entire business, affecting its ability to attract and retain both customers and personnel.

Such predictions—echoed by IBM's customers and marketing forces— meant that *not* to develop time sharing in the form demanded by customers was to risk incurring very large losses. To engage in such development—*even if the direct revenues from the central machine involved* (the Model 67) *would not repay the total development costs*— would be far more profitable than to refuse to do it. Such a profitability calculation does not involve any trace of monopoly profits to be made after competition is driven out; it is a calculation of competitive necessity. IBM plainly believed that it had either to engage in time-sharing development as its customers were demanding or fall behind—possibly forever—in the competitive race. This cannot be predation.[8.8]

8.8. It is worth remarking that a similar analysis applies to the government's claim that the offering of discounts to educational institutions was predatory because it was below cost and designed to influence the later decisions of students brought up on IBM machines (Amended Complaint, paragraph 20(d); Plaintiff's Pretrial Brief, pp. 184–188, 258–286). The only witness who testified as to this suggested that such an effect was weak at best (Morse, Tr. 39065–66, 30976–77). Even if such a "twig is bent" effect were strong, competition would lead to such discounts, since the full benefits of the placement of computers in educational institutions would include not merely the direct revenue but the additional profits resulting from the later decisions of former students.

The Premature Announcement Claims

The government maintained that the announcements of the 360/90, 360/67, 360/44 and, indeed, the entire 360 line, were anticompetitive because they were "premature." It is not easy to state rules as to when a product announcement is premature or when such prematurity is anticompetitive. In general, there is no reason to inhibit the time when a firm announces or brings products to the marketplace. Customers will be the final arbiters of the product's quality and the firm's reputation. Broken promises and unattractive products can be expected to lead quickly to a loss of credibility and sales.

Product announcements in the computer industry involve the release of relatively formal descriptions of new products and their properties. When such formal announcements are made, prices are stated and order taking commences. There is no doubt that IBM, like all or virtually all other firms in the market, regularly announces products in this way as much as a year or so before they are available to customers. It does so, indeed, while they are still under development. This is a natural practice. Customers installing a new computer system need a substantial amount of lead time to make their decisions, plan for the changeover or for the rearrangement of their organization, and prepare the site for the computer. To announce products only when they are ready to be shipped to customers is to ensure a non-negligible lag between the time products are ready for customers and the time customers are ready for them. Hence, some lag between announcement and the date of first customer shipment is required so that orders for the first part of the production run can be secured. In the presence of such good reasons for a lag between announcement and shipment, can announcement of a product not fully developed be anticompetitive?[38]

Advance announcement of truthful information about products cannot be anticompetitive. Indeed, such announcement is procompetitive; competition thrives when information is good. To see this, suppose that IBM did not announce the availability of a product until first customer shipment and that competitors and customers based their plans on guesses about the products IBM would produce. When IBM actually came out with the product, those competitors and customers who had guessed wrong would be damaged.

The only question, therefore, is whether IBM made its product announcements in good faith. In announcing products not yet fully developed, IBM was making a forecast about its ability to deliver. As anyone who has ever engaged in research knows, there comes a time in any research project when one can say with some certainty what sorts of things will be available as the output of the project, even though those things are not yet fully developed. One can also forecast the time at which development will be completed. These forecasts can be made even though there remain problems not yet solved. Of course, in making such forecasts, one is sometimes wrong. When IBM made announcements, it announced what it wished customers to believe and what it itself believed. If those announcements of its belief were made in good faith, then it was imparting information to customers and competitors as to what it expected to do. Even if it was later unable to do those things, the imparting of such information can only aid competition. Only deliberate falsehood could possibly be anticompetitive here, and that is highly improbable since a firm that practiced such tactics would acquire a tarnished reputation that would ill-serve it in the future.

Note in this regard that it is not evidence of the "prematurity" or anticompetitiveness of an announcement if, as McAdams testified, "the essential motivation for the announcement was the pressure of competitors in the market." The pressure of competitors is expected to force the introduction of new products.[39]

The Announcement of System/360 on April 7, 1964

In 1961, IBM began planning what became System/360.[40] It cancelled development of its 8000 series (a successor to the successful 7000 series), which was already well underway, as not sufficiently technologically advanced and began development of a single compatible family of processors. It did so despite the fact that it had just introduced the 1400 series, which was proving by far the most popular system introduced up to that time.[8.9] The SPREAD committee, whose report in December 1961 formed the basis for System/360 planning, saw very clearly that unless IBM had new products developed and delivered by 1965, competition would succeed in surpassing it, replacing the 1400 series (and the 7000 series) and leaving IBM behind. It therefore recommended *as early as December 1961*, at the start of System/360 planning, that the first of the new processors be announced in the first quarter of 1964.[41]

The development of the New Product Line (NPL), which became System/360, was fraught with risk as to achievability and user ac-

---

8.9. By end of 1966, IBM had installed over 10,000 1401s, by far the largest number of any system that it had ever shipped (PX 1900, p. 7).

ceptance. It required an enormous commitment of money and manpower; virtually all of IBM's data processing resources over a number of years were devoted to the program, a commitment that became known as "you bet your company." Development and manufacture of System/360 became a worldwide interdivisional effort. IBM's annual research and development expenditures rose from $175 million in 1961 to $275 million in 1964. Over $100 million was estimated for programming alone—an estimate that was exceeded by more than $25 million.[42]

To meet the requirements for the new Solid Logic Technology (SLT) components used in System/360, IBM literally had to become "in a very short time, the largest component manufacturer in the world." IBM established a components division in 1961, and right up to the 360 announcement continued to open new plants and expand existing facilities throughout the world for the purpose of manufacturing the anticipated SLT components needed in the New Product Line.[43]

IBM made such commitments and took the attendant risks despite the fact that the New Product Line would adversely affect its existing products, many of which were on lease. It recognized that if it did not do so, others would. Thus, IBM Vice President and Group Executive T. V. Learson directed in July 1963 that

The 101 [announced as the System/360 Model 30] must be engineered and planned to impact solidly the 1401.

I know your reluctance to do this, but corporate policy is that you do it. It is obvious that in 1967 the 1401 will be as dead as a Dodo bird.[44]

The SPREAD Committee Report, which had predicted rapid displacement of IBM's then-planned and existing systems, however, had been overly optimistic about the competitiveness of IBM's pre-System/360 offerings. Competitors began "leapfrogging" over IBM's existing second-generation (transistor-based) product line with announcements of newer models of computer systems in 1962, 1963, and early 1964. Those announcements brought home with even greater force the need to make System/360 better than competitive products or have it face rejection by users. CDC's 6600 and 3600 and Honeywell's H-200 were viewed as especially formidable competitors. In particular, the success of the Honeywell H-200, announced in early December 1963, led IBM's marketing personnel in the Data Processing Division to press for the earliest possible announcement of System/360—even earlier than the mid-March announcement date planned as of early 1964.[45]

IBM clearly needed System/360 to remain competitive. Because of the massive resources applied to the 360 program from its inception in 1961, by December 1963 development of the line was "on or ahead of the schedule called for two years earlier in the SPREAD report." Both Data Systems Division (DSD) Vice President Bob O. Evans, who had "worldwide responsibility for coordination of the development" of System/360, and Frederick P. Brooks, who was manager of the New Product Line from 1961 to 1964, were recommending announcement in the first part of 1964, pointing out the need for the unprecedented step of announcing the entire family at once to assist customer planning.[46]

IBM followed its standard practice of having "top management review, with each responsible department, the readiness of the product and the risks involved." The decision was made to announce on April 7, 1964. All departments whose efforts were required to provide the product features and services offered in the System/360 announcement supported this decision; however, IBM's Product Test Department did not. To understand the implications of this requires understanding what role was played by this department in IBM's announcement procedure.[46]

The Product Test Department in IBM was not the only group in IBM that tested the hardware and software associated with its computer products, including System/360. Independent of this department, product testing was conducted within the components division, the development divisions, the manufacturing groups, and the field engineering (or customer service) division. Product Test operated within IBM in addition to the other groups that had product testing duties and responsibilities. It acted as a devil's advocate, independent of the group that had designed and built the machine. Its role was to perform a "technical audit" and point out problems yet to be resolved, so that management would be satisfied in deciding to announce a product that there was a workable plan in place to resolve such problems. As high officials of the Department of Defense later told G. B. McCarter, the head of Product Test, this was a system unique in the industry. It provided extra assurance beyond the industry norm. Thus, as McCarter wrote in 1967, "[j]ust because we [Product Test] don't support a certain machine doesn't mean it won't work. . . . It just means that we found a list of problems, and were able to assist management with the data on which they can base their final decisions."[48]

Thus, an announcement without the formal concurrence of Product Test did not signify that IBM did not expect to be able to deliver to customers what was announced. Indeed, IBM had announced a number of products in this way prior to 1964, including the 1403 printer, which turned out to be one of the most successful products it ever announced. It was able to do so precisely because it adopted procedures that were meant to ensure—and indeed did ensure—that its announcements would be as accurate as possible. Such procedures included the possibility of announcement without the support of Product Test so long as there was an agreed-on plan to resolve the problems Product Test had called to management's attention and took into account the fact that many further tests occurred after announcement.[49]

The announcement of a product still in development is an announcement of a product with problems yet to be overcome. Until those problems are overcome, it is natural to find people pointing them out as obstacles, particularly people whose job it is to do so. Otherwise, those problems could not be overcome. If there were no such problems, the announcement would not be a forecast of what would be delivered in a year or so but a statement of what was ready for immediate delivery, which IBM and other computer industry announcements do not purport to be.

Given Product Test's assignment to be conservative about problems, IBM was faced with a trade-off. In general, if it announced products before Product Test was ready to concur, it ran a somewhat greater risk of announcing products that it might not be able to deliver on schedule. On the other hand, if it only announced products when Product Test was ready, then it ran a somewhat greater risk of delaying the announcement of products that, as things turned out, could have been announced and delivered. IBM was dealing with a process in which announcement was to be made before full certainty could be achieved. By waiting longer before announcement, IBM could make its forecasts more certain but might sacrifice business from customers who would go elsewhere, not knowing about IBM's products. To make the announcement too far in advance might produce gains in those respects but would make the forecasts less certain, leading to customer dissatisfaction if such forecasts turned out wrong. By assigning to Product Test a devil's advocate role, IBM's management undertook procedures (unique in the industry) to ensure that it made those decisions intelligently.

What conclusions can be drawn, then, from the evidence that IBM felt under considerable pressure to announce various products, in particular to announce the System/360 on April 7, 1964? Such pressure is exactly what one expects to see in an industry in which competition proceeds through the introduction of better products. In such an industry, a company that does not improve its product line is left behind. Having the 360 under development, it was in IBM's competitive interest to respond to those pressures by letting customers know about it. Had IBM been a monopolist in 1964, it would not have needed to hurry.

If the System/360 announcement was not a departure from IBM policy, was it "premature" in any other sense? If so, when would it have ceased to be premature? The government suggested no way to test this, and it is hard to see either how to construct such a test or why one is necessary given the reputation risks associated with not fulfilling promises. We can, however, look at the specifics of the 360 experience.

By the standards of the industry, System/360 was in a far advanced stage of development by the time it was announced. For example, CDC followed a practice of announcing machines "before the development and testing was completed"; the GE 455 and 465 were announced but never got past "the point where a prototype existed on the manufacturing floor" and were never delivered; "[a]t the time of the announcement of the Honeywell 8200 the development of the machine had not begun"; although the RCA Spectra 70 was announced in December 1964, the first prototype did not exist until "around the middle of 1965." By contrast, at the time of announcement of the System/360, engineering models of all the processors had been built; full instruction set compatibility across all the processors had been achieved; a complete processor had been built and demonstrated to prove the feasibility of the new SLT circuitry; thousands of SLT modules had already been produced; all, or almost all of the memories had undergone technical evaluation testing; microprogramming and multiprogramming had been tested on one of the processors; four estimating, forecasting, and pricing cycles had been completed; and the componentry, systems, and product testing program already completed was more extensive than the entire testing program previously undertaken by IBM for any system. The 360 announcement was not premature by comparison with industry practice in terms of lag time between announcement and delivery.[50]

Finally, there were excellent reasons for not waiting for Product Test's full concurrence. The innovations of the standard interface and compatibility features of the new family meant that it was unnecessary to test all possible combinations of processors and peripherals. Such tests would then have been required under Product Test's existing procedures and, given the number of products involved, would have taken an extremely long time "while the rest of the corporation stood still," a fact recognized by 360's developers.[51]

The announcement of April 7, 1964, involved processors, peripherals, and software. In particular, IBM announced the first five processors of System/360—the processors envisaged in the original SPREAD report more than two years earlier. These became the processors of the 360/30, 360/40, 360/50, 360/65, and 360/75 systems. The smaller 360/20 was announced in November 1964, and other models (including the 360/90, 360/44, and 360/67) were announced at different times.

All of the processors announced on April 7, 1964, were shipped on or before the dates estimated for them, although some of them were superseded by faster memory versions before delivery. Those versions, the 360/65 and 360/75, however, were delivered to customers on or before the dates planned for their predecessors. The unforeseen overwhelming demand for the machines did lead by October 1966 to an immense order backlog, but well before that time there was an enormous expansion of plant facilities and labor force. Only an unforeseen technical difficulty with the production process for SLT circuitry in June 1965 (over a year after announcement) caused the schedule to slip 60 to 120 days, and that was immediately announced to customers.[52]

IBM did experience problems with the development of OS/360 (the most advanced of the five operating systems announced with System/360), which led to significant schedule slippages and meant that some customers received the full announced capabilities of their operating system later than originally planned. However, these problems occurred despite the fact that Product Test "cumulatively did more testing of OS/360 than . . . ever . . . before for any set of programs for a particular system" and despite the belief expressed by IBM's programmers before the 360 announcement that they could produce OS/360 "in the way that it was originally intended." IBM's problems in this respect were hardly unique. At least Burroughs, Honeywell, RCA, Univac, and Xerox also misjudged the enormous complexity of developing and testing advanced operating systems to be used in a very wide variety of configurations and operating environments.[53]

IBM placed top priority on the solution of these unforeseen problems, with about 5,000 man-years going into design, construction, and documentation of OS/360 between 1963 and 1966. According to government witness Alan Perlis, then chairman of the Department of Computer Science at Carnegie-Mellon University, "when the system finally worked, it had properties that were beyond about any other operating system around." Long before that, however, IBM had delivered four other operating systems for use with System/360. Those systems were well received, and one of them, DOS, which was twenty-five to fifty times as complex as the systems software for the 1401, was particularly widely used and highly rated.[54]

The announcement of the original models of System/360 and the explosion of demand that followed placed very severe strains on IBM. There was a need for great expansion of facilities and labor force, for solution of unforeseen technical problems, and for new capital. Not surprisingly, in looking back, the decision to go ahead did not always seem wise. Thus, for example, IBM Chairman Watson wrote in October 1965 that "[b]y the Spring of '64 our hand was forced and we had to, with our eyes wide open, announce a complete line—some of the machines 24 months early, and the total line an average of 12 months early. I guess all of us who were thinking about the matter realized that we would have problems when we did this, but I don't think any of us anticipated that the problems would reach the serious proportions that they now have."[55]

Regardless of whether Watson's 1965 assessment was right—and the full path of events shows it was not—the issue is the same. What matters is whether IBM made its announcement in good faith, not whether it experienced unanticipated problems that made it regret that announcement.[56]

The Model 90 Series, Model 67, and Model 44 Announcements
Interestingly, despite its claims of "prematurity,"the government did not claim that in announcing System/360 IBM "believed or had reason to believe that it was unlikely to be able to produce and market such products within the announced time frame" or that "IBM misrepresented to customers or potential customers the characteristics, delivery date, capabilities, and/or specifications." It did, however, make such claims concerning the Models 90, 67, and 44, which were also said to be "premature" (as well as predatorily priced).[57]

The Model 90 Series   Development of the Model 90 program began within IBM in 1961 and was greatly accelerated after the announced but undelivered CDC 6600 computer received a spate of publicity in the summer of 1963. In that year, users, including United States government agencies, requested that IBM, CDC, and other suppliers disclose information and make proposals on their advanced computer capabilities. In late 1963 and early 1964, IBM discussed the Model 90 development program with eighteen potential users but did not propose price and delivery terms until after the System/360 announcement in April 1964, when unsuccessful proposals were made to the Bettis and Knolls Atomic Power Laboratories.[58]

It should be noted that during this time IBM declined to announce the Model 90 series at least twice: once in connection with the general announcement of System/360 in April 1964 (that announcement contained a short footnote stating that IBM was developing the Model 90) and once after a review of the program by IBM's Corporate Operations Board in early July 1964.[8.10] Between April 1964 and the August announcement of the Model 92, "significant engineering, cost estimating, forecasting and financial analysis work was done" on the program. A major factor in that period bearing on the technical readiness of the Model 90 series for announcement occurred when IBM management received information from the United States National Security Agency that the circuitry, known both as ACPX and ASLT, on which the Model 90s depended, was feasible.[59]

The computers were announced on August 17, 1964, on a "special" contracts basis only, because of their acknowledged state-of-the-art nature. Product Test did not support the announcement because it could not perform its standard "announcement testing," but it was clearly understood that the program was developmental in that it would involve working with customers to understand their needs. This in turn required disclosure to customers at an earlier stage than Product Test would ordinarily support. Even so, the Model 90s were much further along than some of the machines announced by IBM's competitors. At announcement, a data flow model to test the proposed circuitry had been initiated; circuit performance in floating point arithmetic and machine cycle time had been measured; measurement of arithmetic performance using less advanced ACP circuits had been completed; the logic organization of the machine had been specified; the feasibility of the circuitry had been established; the basic timing and critical loop circuit performance had been determined; and "enough specific problems had been simulated to assure . . . that the committed *basic* parameters had adequate safety factor and [the] overall goals in performance had a reasonable chance of being achieved."[60]

8.10. IBM also did not announce its very successful 360/20 until November 1964 because it was judged not to be technically ready for announcement in April (Knaplund, Tr. 90488–89; JX 38, p. 296).

The Model 90s, which were not particularly popular, passed all governmental acceptance tests and performed to the satisfaction of users. Their first delivery was delayed nine months by unforeseen substantial problems in the circuitry, which arose despite the passage of the feasibility tests conducted by the National Security Agency.[61]

The Model 67   The story of IBM's development of time sharing with the 360/67 has been told earlier, and only a few points need be mentioned here. First, the project was regarded as developmental, and IBM worked together with certain particularly sophisticated users. As pressure built up from other customers, IBM also made proposals to them, still on a limited bidding basis. During the entire period before the removal of bidding restrictions in August 1965, customers "understood that the Model 67 was a research and development project and that things would change as they went along."[62]

At the time of full announcement of the 360/67 in August 1965, Product Test issued a "formal" nonconcurrence but believed the program to be in "good shape." Nevertheless, in the following year, unanticipated problems with the operating system (TSS) built up rapidly, the number of lines of code approximately doubling. Even so, the first release was expected to be "relatively solid in terms of schedule," which had promised delivery of that first release in June 1967. In fact, problems continued to mount, and in the fall of 1966, customers were informed that the schedule would be delayed and that certain functions might be "decommitted." Only in April 1969 did IBM finally deliver a version of TSS that was "considered to be an excellent software programming system" that "essentially did perform and accomplish almost all the things that were in the original specification."[63]

There is no doubt that IBM greatly underestimated the difficulty of producing a sophisticated time-sharing operating system. Such difficulties were similarly unforeseen by many others making similar attempts. In particular, GE never delivered the 645, the machine promised to MIT's Project MAC, realizing that what it had on its hands was "a research project and not a product." Not until after GE sold most of its computer operations to Honeywell in 1970 was the MULTICS time-sharing operating system delivered as originally promised—three years late.[64]

The 360/44   The only basis for the government's prematurity claim for the 360/44 was the nonconcurrence of Product Test. We have explained this issue earlier and need only add that, in 1967, over a year before the complaint and before the government's investigation started, McCarter, the head of Product Test, chose the 360/44 as the prime example of a success for Product Test's role in IBM's announcement procedure.[65]

Premature Announcement: Conclusion   There is no doubt that IBM sometimes underestimated development difficulties. This was particularly true for operating software, OS/360, and TSS. Some such errors, however, are an inevitable price paid for the benefit to customers and suppliers of announcement before development is complete. There is no reason to suppose that IBM was ever deliberately deceptive; on the contrary, it took extraordinary pains to guard against such errors. There is also no reason to suppose that failure to deliver as promised goes unpunished in the marketplace or that the trade-offs in the announcement decision should be or can be sensibly regulated by the threat of antitrust litigation.

Acts Supposedly Directed at Leasing Companies

As discussed in chapter 3, leasing companies constrain IBM's prices in two ways: they compete with new IBM computers by offering IBM's older computers, and they affect the ratio between the lease and purchase prices of given computers. Both effects are involved in what follows.

As discussed in the section on leasing in chapter 6, customers choose between purchase and lease on the basis of their needs, their attitudes toward risk, the cost of capital, and the prices and other costs involved in the various financial alternatives under consideration. When lease prices are low relative to purchase prices, the number of customers that lease will increase; when lease prices are high relative to purchase prices, the number of customers that purchase will increase if, and only if, customers have no alternative but to lease or purchase *from manufacturers*. That will generally not be the case in competitive markets. In such markets, when lease prices become temporarily high relative to purchase prices, it becomes profitable for third-party arbitrageurs to enter, acquire equipment by purchasing it from manufacturers and others, and then lease it to end users. In this process, the arbitrageurs act on the "spread" between lease prices and purchase prices. When lease prices become high relative to purchase prices, the arbitrageurs compete in offering equipment for lease, thereby bidding down lease prices and increasing the ratio between purchase prices and lease prices, the so-called multiplier.[8.11]

The phenomenon of bidding down lease prices and hence increasing purchase/lease "multipliers" is thus a symptom of competition. High lease prices relative to purchase prices attract entry and competition by arbitrageurs, who then bid down the lease prices. The result of this entry and competition is to alter the ratio between lease prices and purchase prices to the point at which only efficient arbitrageurs find it barely profitable to remain in business.

When leasing companies choose to engage in this arbitrage process, they accept the costs involved in putting money down on the date of purchase and receiving returns spread out over time, and they accept the risks of ownership of the equipment, including the risks of price changes, obsolescence, and the inability to place or keep equipment on lease. They have borne those risks when they have believed that lease prices charged by manufacturers were high *and would remain high long enough* to allow them to obtain a profit in their arbitrage activities.[66]

Such assumptions, of course, while leading a company to enter the market in order to engage in arbitrage, may turn out to be erroneous. When arbitrageurs underestimate the competition they will experience from other arbitrageurs, from equipment manufacturers, and from other suppliers, or when competition brings down lease prices (and thereby narrows the spread between lease and purchase prices) faster than arbitrageurs expect, they may very well incur losses. That is what happened to a number of computer leasing companies.

Leasing companies began to grow rapidly in the middle to late 1960s, purchasing large amounts of IBM's and other manufacturers' equipment and leasing it to end users in competition with IBM and others. Several factors combined to cause that growth, all of which made the arbitrageur's spread more attractive.[67]

The most important factor in the growth of leasing companies was the introduction by IBM of System/360, which leasing companies purchased in large numbers because they felt that the equipment's compatibility and modularity features, its flexible configurability, its equal facility for performing scientific and commercial applications, its widespread customer acceptance, and IBM's substantial investment in its

---

8.11. The "raw multiplier" is the ratio of purchase to lease price. The "effective multiplier" involves an adjustment to the raw multiplier to take account of maintenance charges and warranties.

software gave it an enhanced remarketability and a potential for long useful life.[68]

In part as a result of those beliefs, most leasing companies utilized ten- to twelve-year, straight-line depreciation for their System/360 equipment, depreciation that necessarily implied the assumption that the equipment being depreciated would remain more or less continuously on lease at high and relatively stable lease rates for up to fourteen years after its announcement. Leasing companies adopted those depreciation practices even though IBM and other computer equipment manufacturers utilized accelerated depreciation or substantially shorter depreciable lives (for example, four to six years); and by the late 1960s, IBM management and industry observers were publicly stating that new equipment would be introduced within the next few years that would reduce the value of System/360 equipment. When that equipment did begin to be introduced, with IBM's announcement of the first System/370 models in June 1970, leasing companies had an average of seven to seven and a half years of the then obsolescent System/360's carrying value on their books. Even at that time, several leasing companies regarded the newly announced System/370 equipment as merely an enhancement of System/360 and not a new generation; they decided, therefore, to skip System/370 and to wait until the next "generation" to restock their portfolios.[69]

Leasing companies were able to raise money relatively cheaply to finance their equipment acquisitions. During 1967 and 1968, when the bulk of leasing company purchases of System/360 occurred, interest rates were low, and the stock market was in its "go-go years" and particularly favored companies associated with data processing. Through a combination of relatively slow depreciation and other accounting liberties, leasing companies were able to increase their apparent earnings dramatically, which in turn caused their stock prices to soar to astronomical price-to-earnings ratios and enabled them to raise literally billions of dollars of both equity and debt capital, which they used to purchase additional computer equipment. In addition, the Investment Tax Credit had the benefit, for those leasing companies that could take advantage of it, of reducing the purchase price of new computer equipment by approximately 14 percent on a pre-tax basis.[70]

As a result, very soon after the announcement of System/360, leasing companies had made a major investment in it. Even before IBM announced the "3 × 3" price change, raising lease prices and decreasing purchase prices by 3 percent on September 29, 1966, leasing companies had purchased over $60 million of System/360 equipment.[71] Starting in 1969 and continuing into the 1970s, however, a number of events occurred that both reduced the spread on which leasing companies operated and showed that a number of the assumptions on which many such companies had based their rapid growth during the 1960s had been erroneous. As a result, several leasing companies incurred losses in the years after 1969.

In April 1969, the Investment Tax Credit was withdrawn and remained unavailable, with minor exceptions, until August 1971. Further, starting in 1969 and continuing through 1970, interest rates rose sharply, and the stock market fell. At the same time, the financial press soured on leasing companies, along with other so-called glamour companies, and a number of articles appeared that were harshly critical of the accounting methods used by leasing companies and of the way leasing companies did business generally. As a result, leasing company stock prices plummetted, and their access to other forms of capital was severely restricted. At the same time, the economy fell into recession, with the result that end users of computer equipment cut back on new acquisitions, thereby making remarketing of equipment more difficult for leasing companies and reducing the lease rates they could get for their equipment.[72]

Perhaps most important of all, by 1969 System/360 equipment was five years old, and in the interim, other manufacturers had introduced products with improved price/performance. In June 1970, IBM itself began introducing its new System/370 family of computers. Those new product announcements seriously affected the value of leasing companies' 360 equipment. However, because leasing companies had failed to foresee accurately the introduction of improved price/performance products, they continued to purchase System/360 equipment relatively late into the product's life—three to four years after announcement. Further, because leasing companies utilized slow, straight-line depreciation, they still had substantial amounts of System/360 carrying value undepreciated on their books at the time IBM announced System/370. As a result, many leasing companies in the early 1970s were faced with the unhappy prospect of having to keep their then obsolescent 360 equipment more or less continuously on lease without any significant lease rate erosion for the next seven to seven and a half years in order to continue to show a profit on it.[73]

The position in which leasing companies found themselves during the early 1970s was exacerbated by the fact that the initial leases for the great bulk of leasing company equipment began to expire and that many leasing companies were for the first time faced with the task of remarketing their equipment. This was a much more substantial undertaking than had been the initial placement of equipment (when, by and large, leasing companies had relied on the manufacturers to configure and market the equipment) and was a task for which many leasing companies were unprepared. The task of remarketing was made more difficult by the fact that leasing companies' 360 equipment was being offered in competition with newly announced, improved price/performance products. This caused many leasing companies to offer reduced prices for their 360 equipment in order to make them more attractive. In addition, the large growth in the number of leasing companies themselves and the emergence of peripheral equipment suppliers during the second half of the 1960s intensified competition.[74]

The result of these occurrences was just what one would expect in a competitive market. As lease rates dropped and other costs increased more rapidly than had been anticipated, thereby reducing the arbitrageur's spread on which leasing companies operated, the less efficient leasing companies suffered losses. Those losses were often manifested in "big bath accounting," by which companies took massive writedowns in an attempt to correct retroactively prior accounting abuses and bring the carrying values of their equipment down to more appropriate levels.[75]

After a period of retrenchment, those older leasing companies that had run their operations efficiently expanded their business, and many new leasing companies entered the market and grew. Those companies—old and new—acquired IBM System/370 equipment for leasing in unprecedented volumes. Leasing companies' purchases of 370 CPUs were significantly greater than leasing companies' purchases of 360 CPUs at comparable points in the product cycle. A similar statement applies to total purchases.[76]

Despite the fact that the history of leasing company activity is what most economists would expect of a competitive market, the government contended that certain actions by IBM during the period of the late 1960s and early 1970s were anticompetitive acts directed at leasing companies, "undermining" their profitability so that "very few of these firms were able to justify purchasing IBM 370 systems on a risk-lease basis." The IBM actions singled out by the government fall into two general categories: pricing actions by which IBM allegedly adjusted the multiplier (the ratio of purchase to lease price) or increased maintenance prices to make it unprofitable for leasing companies to purchase certain IBM products for lease to end users; and actions by which IBM allegedly "trapped" leasing companies that had purchased IBM products and were then allegedly forced to take capital losses when IBM did something unexpected. The latter contentions relate to IBM's announcement of the 370/158 and 168 in August 1972.[77]

Changes in the Multipliers

System/370   According to the government, IBM increased System/370 multipliers and maintenance prices over those for System/360 in an effort to "undermine the viability of leasing companies." The government charged that those actions made it uneconomical for leasing companies to purchase 370 equipment for lease to end users, thus " 'lock[ing]-out' leasing companies from continued growth."[78]

The facts are more complicated than this. Since the purchaser of a machine accepts the risk of obsolescence, we would expect to see multipliers falling over the life of a product. The appropriate comparisons, therefore, are between multipliers on generally comparable equipment at comparable points in the product cycle, and such comparisons of System/360 and System/370 multipliers do not yield any clear pattern one way or the other. Even the less appropriate comparison of multipliers at the time of the 370 announcement shows 370 "effective multipliers" only 3 to 10 percent higher than 360 "effective multipliers."[79]

Further, it was the combination of the factors listed earlier, not just such relatively minor price changes, that affected leasing company purchase patterns in the early 1970s. Not surprisingly, by the mid-1970s, when the outlook had brightened, leasing companies bought substantial amounts of System/370 equipment having multipliers similar to those about which the government complained. In particular, leasing companies purchased significantly more 370/158s and 168s (announced in August 1972) than any other IBM model, 360 or 370. The 158 and 168 CPUs had effective multipliers at least as high as—and generally higher than—the effective multipliers of the 370 models about which the government complained most vigorously—the 165 and, especially, the 155. In fact, leasing company purchases of the 155 were also heavy, despite McAdams' testimony that it had a multiplier "designed to . . . foreclose leasing companies as competitors."[80]

As this suggests, whatever the multipliers were on System/370, the effect that the government claimed flowed from those multipliers did not occur. Far from being precluded, leasing companies and others purchased System/370 in very high numbers—and in much greater numbers than they had purchased System/360. Total direct and indirect purchases by leasing companies of System/360 CPUs and memory between 1966 and 1978 were $1.3 billion.[8.12] Their total direct and indirect purchases of System/370 CPUs and memory between 1971 and 1978 were more than double that—$3.0 billion. Total purchases from IBM of System/360 CPUs and memory by all customers were $2.3 billion. Total purchases from IBM of System/370 CPUs and memory by all customers were more than triple that—$7.7 billion. Leasing companies offered the acquired System/370 equipment on a variety of terms.[81]

It is, therefore, clear that the government's claims about System/370 multipliers misconstrued the facts. They also misconstrued economic analysis.

The very act of arbitrageurs entering the market leads to a narrowing of the arbitrageur's "spread," the widening of which created the opportunity for their entry in the first place. The spread is the price at which arbitrageurs do business. As in any competitive situation, when that price rises above cost, entry and expansion of competitors occur, which in turn bids the price back down. One must expect that under competition such spreads will be narrowed. So it was with leasing companies. At first, the spread under which they did business widened: lease prices increased in relation to purchase prices, and the multiplier decreased. This attracted entry and expansion, which caused the spread to narrow: lease prices decreased in relation to purchase prices, and the multiplier increased.

In more detail, the competitive process worked as follows to narrow the spread. IBM's ability to set either purchase prices or lease prices for System/370 equipment was circumscribed by competition, part of which was provided by leasing companies. In planning for System/370, IBM had to take into account the fact that leasing-company-owned System/360 equipment at discounted prices would compete with IBM System/370 equipment. For example, estimates in March 1969 showed that leasing-company-owned System/360 equipment would be "a major competitive product" and, if offered at a price discount of only approximately 30 percent, would compete effectively against System/370

8.12. Leasing companies purchase directly from the manufacturer. They also purchase indirectly by taking title to a machine purchased by an end user. The latter method has been employed when the user began by leasing from the manufacturer and acquired credit toward the purchase price.

at the prices then planned for the new system. This leasing company competition, along with competition from other IBM competitors, put a ceiling on the lease prices that IBM could charge for its System/370 equipment.[82]

Similarly, competition from leasing companies and others put a ceiling on the purchase prices that IBM could charge for System/370. In the period before the initial System/370 announcement, IBM management debated over the equipment's purchase prices because they were concerned that the prices were too high, in part because of high maintenance costs. The principal concern was that high purchase prices and high maintenance charges would cost IBM sales of System/370 CPUs, with many of the losses being to leasing companies and other owners offering discounted System/360 CPUs for sale or lease. That concern continued through early 1970, and as announced in June 1970, the purchase prices on the 370/155 and 165, as well as on other equipment, were lowered substantially from the values given them in the planning assumptions.[83]

Finally, as of 1969, maintenance costs (which affect the effective multiplier) were expected to be much higher on 370 than on 360, for which, with the benefit of hindsight, it appeared that maintenance prices had probably been set much too low. IBM management regarded this as generating a particular exposure to competition, especially to competition from leasing-company-owned 360 equipment. As a result, substantial efforts were successfully made that greatly cut maintenance costs by announcement time, and maintenance charges were later effectively reduced still further, in part by extending warranty periods.[84]

The result of the purchase, lease, and maintenance price adjustments that IBM made on System/370 in response to competition from leasing companies and others was that both purchase and lease of System/370 was brisk, exceeding that for System/360 at comparable points in the products' lives. With both purchase and lease business active, both purchase prices and lease prices for System/370 *must* have been low enough to compete. Since purchases were heavy and all purchasers (not just leasing companies) acquired maintenance services separately, it cannot have been the case that IBM's purchase and maintenance prices were noncompetitively high. Thus the only way in which the "multiplier"—effective or raw—could have been anticompetitive would be for IBM's lease prices to have been too low. Such a claim is consistent with the government's constant mistaken belief that low prices are a symptom of monopoly rather than competition, but in this case, there was not even a claim (and, of course, no evidence) that IBM's lease prices were below cost and therefore predatory.[85]

Such a claim would have been very strange. Purchase customers are presumably not less risk-averse than IBM and do not have *lower* costs of capital. It follows that with purchase prices competitive and lease prices below cost, purchase customers would find it profitable to switch from purchasing to leasing—a move they could make with the stroke of a pen. The same thing would happen if IBM's lease prices were competitive and its purchase prices monopolistic. Yet bizarre as such claims are, the government made them for the latter case. As we saw in the section on leasing in chapter 6, it claimed that IBM earned monopoly profits on *purchased* machines but not on leased ones, (calling this impossible charge "apparently paradoxical").[86]

In fact, a logical extension of the government's "multiplier" argument is that it would have been anticompetitive for IBM to have *refrained* from making the "3 × 3" price change in September 1966. That, of course, is an illogical position, but one that must be taken in order to argue that System/360 and System/370 multipliers should be compared at the time of System/370's announcement (that is, after the "3 × 3" price change for System/360 but prior to a comparable point in time in the life of System/370) or indeed to argue that the later multipliers were anticompetitive at all.[8.13]

The August 2, 1972, Announcements
The 370/158 and 370/168   On August 2, 1972, IBM made several major product and programming announcements, including the System/370 Model 158 and 168 processors. The 370/158 and 168 processors incorporated significant technological and price/performance improvements over their immediate predecessors, the 370/155 and 165.

One of the major technological advances of the 158 and 168 was their use of advanced semiconductor memory, called Field Effect Transistor (or FET) memory. With the introduction of FET memory on the 158 and 168, IBM was able to achieve in its large processors the advantages of a single, integrated packaging technology for both logic and memory circuits, which resulted in economies in production and packaging. Furthermore, FET memory was faster, more compact, and lower

---

8.13. The government also made multiplier claims concerning two of IBM's later and marginal 360 products, the 360/25 and 360/85. These claims present no new issues, and we do not discuss them explicitly.

priced than the core memory that had been used with the 155 and the 165.[87]

The 158 and 168 processors were also the first IBM processors to be announced with a "virtual memory" or "virtual storage" capability, providing users (as discussed in chapter 3) with an apparent main memory capacity substantially greater than the actual main memory capacity of their systems. This was considered by IBM to be "[a] major redirection of IBM System/370 technology," which was expected to have "a revolutionary effect on computer users for years to come." Virtual storage (which was due in part to the technological fallout of the 360/67 time-sharing development discussed earlier) could be added to the 155 and 165 processors by the acquisition of Dynamic Address Translation (DAT) hardware for a purchase price of about $200,000.[88]

The government contended that IBM announced the 370/158 and 168 processors two years after the 370/155 and 165 in order to make obsolete those two processors, which had been heavily purchased by leasing companies.[89] Before coming to the main economic issues raised by this claim, there are some subsidiary points that require discussion.

First, there is a patent inconsistency between the government's argument about the 158 and 168 and its charges relating to System/370 "multipliers." If leasing companies were precluded by the System/370 multipliers from purchasing 155s and 165s, then they could not have been hurt by the alleged premature obsolescence of those machines.

Second, the claim that after the 158 and 168 announcement leasing companies were stuck with prematurely obsolete 155s and 165s is at odds with the facts of leasing companies' purchases of those machines. After 1972 leasing companies purchased directly and indirectly almost $115 million of 155 and 165 CPUs and memory—more than the amount of 155 and 165 CPUs and memory purchased by leasing companies during the period 1970 through 1972. Moreover, there is no evidence that any leasing company wrote down the carrying value of its 155s and 165s. It is strange conduct indeed for companies that supposedly had just been "trapped" with unmarketable products to purchase more of those unmarketable products and to purchase them in greater quantities than they had before. IBM's own profit projections for the 155 and 165 as of the announcement of the 158 and 168 indicated continuing profitability.[90]

Third, the claim that IBM's failure to inform customers of the 155 and 165 about its not yet ready 158 and 168 was anticompetitive is at odds with the government's other claims about premature announcement, already discussed. In this connection, it is interesting to note that the complaint in *U.S.* v. *IBM* with its premature announcement claims had already been filed when the 370/155 and 165 were announced—an event hardly conducive to the early announcement of information about still somewhat distant products.

The government's claims concerning the 158 and 168 are inconsistent in other respects as well. The claim that leasing companies that owned 155s or 165s suffered losses because of the announcement of the 158 and 168 is inconsistent with the other claim (discussed later) that the 370/158 and 370/168 processors had their prices *raised* above the prices for the 370/155 and 370/165, respectively, in order to "offset IBM's price reductions on the memory products sold separately." If such price increases had not been matched by performance increases (and, if they were so matched, they are not properly considered price increases at all), then leasing companies and other owners of 370/155s and 165s would have experienced a *gain* from the 370/158 and 168 announcement. (Such a gain can also be inferred from testimony of McAdams on the cost of the DAT box to upgrade the 155 and 165.)[91]

Even accepting the claim that the August 1972 announcement caused a loss to owners of 370/155s and 165s, however, the conclusion is the same. The loss was one experienced by *all* owners of 155s and 165s, not merely by leasing companies. Moreover, the risk of such a loss— caused by the appearance of new and better products that make previously purchased products obsolete—is precisely the kind of risk accepted by all purchasers of all products. They purchase rather than lease when they believe that the relative prices of purchasing and leasing make the advantage of purchasing sufficient to enable them to take that risk.

As with any undertaking involving risk, outcomes can vary. Events can occur in the future that either make the risk worth taking or cause the risk to mature and thereby result in loss. Thus, if purchasers of the 370/155 and 165 correctly anticipated what would happen to their products in terms of obsolescence, then they got exactly what they bargained for. *Even if they did not anticipate what would happen, however, they still got exactly what they bargained for.* The risk that the 155 and 165—or any product—would become obsolete more rapidly than expected was a risk inherent in the decision to purchase or lease and was a risk that any purchaser necessarily takes when deciding to purchase. When products become obsolete more slowly than purchasers anticipate on the average, purchasers receive a gain; when products become obsolete faster than purchasers anticipate on the average, purchasers suffer a loss.

In short, what happened was consistent with the way a competitive market works. IBM was forced by competition to introduce the 370/155 and 165 in mid-1970. Had it not done so, it would have lost business to competitors. IBM offered the 155 and 165 for both lease and purchase. On leased machines, IBM itself took the risk of technological obsolescence; on purchased machines, the purchaser took that risk. Leasing companies, in this regard, were no different from any other purchaser.[92]

Alleged Anticompetitive Behavior in Peripherals and Memory, 1968-1972

In the 1960s, IBM encountered severe competition in its System/360 peripheral and memory products even before those products were delivered. In memory, disk storage, and tape storage as well as other devices, the technological leads and price advantages IBM held came under mounting attack as competitive systems manufacturers matched or copied IBM's innovations. Beginning even before the initial 360 shipments were made, IBM, pressed by that competition, introduced in 1964 and 1965 several price reductions and product improvements.[93]

In the mid-1960s, in addition to competition in peripherals and memory from its systems competitors and leasing competitors, IBM also began encountering competition for the very same equipment from "plug-compatible" manufacturers (PCMs). These companies began marketing individual peripherals and memory products directly to IBM end users as alternatives to the products IBM was marketing for use with its 360 processors and other 360 equipment. By 1970, multivendor systems were very common. The growing peripheral and memory competition from systems manufacturers and PCMs posed important competitive challenges to IBM. Well over one-half of "systems" are made up of peripherals. Significant losses in peripherals business, as well as in memory, mean potential losses of more than one-half of a systems manufacturer's business. Moreover, the price/performance of peripherals and memory in large measure determines the price/performance competitiveness of the systems that use them; thus, success in systems placement depends on the attractiveness of peripherals.[94]

As a result, IBM continued after 1965 to improve the price/performance of its peripheral products. Those efforts continued throughout the 1960s and 1970s. The results of those efforts were remarkable price and performance improvements in peripherals and memory, including disk storage capacity improvements from about 26 million bytes per disk spindle on the 2314 (1965) to about 1.3 billion on the IBM 3380 (1980); reduction in the cost of disk storage to the point that $1 of disk storage rental in 1980 (unadjusted for inflation) brought storage of about 1.2 million bytes, compared with 38 thousand bytes in the 2314 days; reduction in the prices of memory to the point where one megabyte of memory cost $15,000 to purchase (1980), compared with purchase prices of about $230,000 on System/370 processors—and the newer memories took only a fraction of the space the older ones did.[95]

The Antitrust Divison focused on the years 1968–1972 and identified certain product and pricing actions taken by IBM, which it said were engaged in "for the purpose or with the effect of restraining or attempting to restrain competitors from entering, remaining, or expanding in one or more of the [PCM] markets or submarkets." These actions—added to the government's complaint after IBM's 1973 loss at the district court level in *Telex* v. *IBM* and not removed after that decision was reversed in January 1975—*all* involved lower prices or better products. That alone should make one suspect that competition is being confused with monopoly. That suspicion is reinforced when one realizes that IBM's EDP revenue in the years involved grew more slowly than that of its competitors and was essentially flat from 1968 to 1972 while competitors' revenues almost doubled. The PCMs in particular grew substantially both then and later.[96]

2319 and the Integrated File Adapter
IBM announced the 2319 disk storage facility on September 23, 1970, as "a low cost, modular, large capacity and high speed direct access facility" for use with the System/370 Model 145, which was announced the same day. The 370/135, announced in March 1971, also used the 2319. As announced, the 2319 disk storage facility contained three 2314-type disk spindles and device-related control circuitry and attached to a file adapter (which performed the remaining control function) integrated within the Model 145 central processor (as opposed to the standard 360/370 channel, the device to which the 2314 and other disk drives had attached). The monthly rental for the three-spindle 2319 was set at $1,000. The price of the optional Integrated File Adapter (IFA) was $550 per month. The government raised a series of allegations of anticompetitive conduct concerning this disk file (which was re-

numbered the 2319A three months later) and its Integrated File Adapter (IFA) and concerning the 2319B version of the disk drive announced in December 1970 for attachment to System/360 processors.[97]

The 2319A Attachment   According to the government, "[t]he 2319 disk drive was a revised grouping of 2314 subsystem disk drives; IBM removed one spindle from the 231[3] [IBM's configuration of four 2314 drives in one box], and replaced this spindle with a portion of the control function normally found in the 2314 controller. The remainder of the control function was transferred to the 370/145 central processing unit and was called an Integrated File Adapter (IFA)."[98] The alleged effect of these product introductions was stated by McAdams:

The first step of integrating the control unit and the channel took away the market opportunity of the plug compatible people for the marketing of the control unit.

The second step [of changing the interface] effectively foreclosed on the 370 systems the ability of the plug compatible people to attach their devices to that integrated file adapter.[99]

The 2319A/IFA was, however, an optional offering. If there had been no benefit to it, the market would have rejected it in favor of PCM offerings or IBM's other disk products. IBM continued to offer its 2314 disk devices, which attached to the System/370 channel. Moreover, plug-compatible suppliers that offered disk subsystems (that is, a disk drive or drives and controller) to attach to the 360/370 channel prior to the 2319A and IFA could continue to do so. The 2319A/IFA was an optional alternative approach to attaching disk products that IBM believed had performance and cost advantages. For customers agreeing that the 2319A/IFA option was superior, it was clearly in their interest for it to be offered. For customers preferring existing products, those products (IBM and PCM) continued to be available. The 2319A/IFA did not in any way change the 360/370 channel or in any way impair the ability of PCMs to attach their products to that channel. And it was to that channel that PCMs attached their disk subsystems both before and after the 2319A/IFA announcement.[100]

The 2319A/IFA combination in fact offered disk storage to customers at a considerably reduced cost compared to the 2314/channel combination. The reduced prices, however, were not below cost; rather, they were achieved through cost reductions due to the integration of control circuitry into the central processing unit through the IFA and the reuse of excess 2314 spindles, which had or were expected to come off rent.

The integration of the control function within the CPU was a product design decision on the part of IBM that contributed to cost reductions and improvements in the resulting price/performance of the IBM 370/145 and 135 computer systems. The evidence is overwhelming that both IBM and other market participants historically recognized that the integration of control circuitry into the CPU provided a means of reducing manufacturing costs by the elimination of unnecessary frames, covers, and power and cooling devices and by the sharing of existing circuitry resources. Such integration was widely used within IBM from the earliest days of the industry; indeed, the decision to package control electronics in separate boxes with System/360 was questioned on cost grounds within the company, and some 360 models had integrated controllers.[101]

Given the history of integrating controllers into the CPU to reduce cost and space and to increase reliability, it was quite natural that when IBM management was planning for System/370, integration of control functions would be considered as a matter of good engineering design. Moreover, integration of control functions especially made sense for IBM's System/370 because between the time of the 2314 control unit and the 2319, IBM developed MST (Monolithic Systems Technology) logic circuitry, a technology far more compact than the SLT logic used with System/360. Indeed, far from originating as an attack on PCM inroads, the work on what became the 2319A/IFA started before PCM shipments of 2314 type drives. It originated with the system manager for the System/370 Models 135 and 145 who initiated the development of integrated file adapters to provide a low-cost disk file to make the smaller "entry level" 135 and 145 system configurations more competitive. That work led to the 2319A/IFA, largely because the new Winchester disk drive (the 3340) was far from ready at the time of System/370 announcement, while the new high-speed Merlin (3330) was too costly for the low-end systems. The 2319A/IFA was seen as the optimal solution in terms of cost.[102]

The integration of control in the CPU was seen within IBM as a definite technological gain in terms of power usage, error correction, and other items, especially cost. These facts were also recognized by IBM's competition and others inside IBM. Indeed, many other systems manufacturers also integrated controllers within CPUs both before and after the 2319. IBM itself continued to do so in many later models.[103]

There was contrary testimony at the trial from Thomas Gardner of Memorex[104] on the engineering wisdom of separating device-dependent and device-independent circuitry, but the fact that an individual competitor disagreed with the engineering decision is not dispositive. IBM cannot be considered to have committed an anticompetitive act by designing its products differently from the way competitors might have designed those products. Ultimately, the marketplace will decide if there is benefit to a design choice. That is especially true when, as here, the product is an additional option. Moreover, even if the product were not an additional option, when there is evidence of a reasonable engineering basis for a product design and when the price of the new product is not below cost, one must not conclude that the design was anticompetitive. To second-guess a firm's engineering judgments is to risk that in doing so, one will constrain new product or process innovations. To require certainty of judgment and penalize choices that after the fact are "wrong" is to chill the competitive process. The fact that competitors are inconvenienced by a particular product design is irrelevant. The provision of new and better products, like the lowering of prices, often injures competitors in the sense that it deprives them of business, but that is what must happen under competition.

Here, however, we need not worry about the effect on competitors; PCMs were able to, and did, attach at the channel through their own control unit and were thus not foreclosed by the 2319A/IFA. (Indeed, there is ample evidence that PCMs could have attached to the IFA if they had chosen to do so.) Customers could choose between attaching a 2319A or attaching a 2314 made by IBM or by a PCM. If PCM companies had a disk subsystem that offered the performance of the 2319A/IFA at a lower price, customers could have and would have taken it. Hence, if it were true, as McAdams said, that the IFA "took away the market opportunity of the plug-compatible people for the marketing of the control unit," it was not because PCMs could not attach their disk subsystems to the IBM CPU but because the 2319A/IFA alternative was less expensive to customers. That is exactly what competition is supposed to produce—a better product at a lower price.[105]

2319A Pricing   Was that lower price nevertheless predatory? Certainly the price per spindle of a 2319A was far below that of a 2314. The government alleged both that this was predatory and that it constituted price discrimination because "a user who did not choose the 2319A/IFA configuration for the 370/145 paid $1,320.00 more for the functionally equivalent 2314/2312/2318 configuration."[106]

At the time of announcement, IBM projected that the 2319A would earn profits of $56 or $58 million. Moreover, the $1,000 monthly rental price of the 2319A was the price at which IBM believed it maximized its profits on disk files as well as optimizing additional sales of 370/145 and 370/135 systems. The program was expected to be profitable even if all 2319s had to be newly manufactured; in fact, only a relatively small number were.[107]

Aside from the cost reductions involved in the integration of the control function, IBM was able to offer the 2319 at a lower per spindle price than the 2314 and nevertheless obtain substantial profits because the 2319 reused "2314 family files that were coming back almost by the trainload" to IBM as the result of PCM replacement. This possibility had been contemplated with IBM as early as 1967. At the time the decision was made to produce 2319s, the 2314s were already built and the costs were sunk. The cost of building the 2314s that were sitting idly in warehouses could not be avoided no matter how the 2319 prices were set.[108]

The 2319 was thus substantially profitable because IBM was able to reduce its costs in putting it out. Certainly, the 2319 was priced to save business that competitors would otherwise have had. But such price cutting fails the test of being predatory. It was precisely what was to be expected under innovative competition.

Under competition, an innovation or new product development is followed by a period in which the returns to the innovator are reaped through the charging of prices high in relation to manufacturing costs. When imitators learn to make the same or similar or slightly improved product, their entry bids prices down from that level. In the real world, such bidding down of prices does not happen through the action of anonymous auctioneers. When competitors enter, the original, innovating firm is faced with a loss of business. Its products begin not to sell. If they are leased, they begin to come back. To avoid that loss of business, the firm must cut prices. One of the ways a firm continues to make profits by cutting prices is to cut its costs. This is what competition is supposed to do.

It makes no difference that the PCMs may not have earned the profits they expected or lost business or even suffered losses. Under competition, the imitators come in expecting to make profits. Those expectations are based on the spread between prices and manufacturing costs that occurs before imitation. Quick imitators may, in fact, be able to earn such profits. As prices come down, as they inevitably must, the margin between prices and costs is cut. Imitators getting in late or having higher manufacturing costs than others or than the original innovator may suffer losses. None of them will earn profits as high or do as much business as they would if the original innovator had not cut its prices. Unless those lower prices are below the then avoidable cost, they are precisely what competition is supposed to bring about.

The contention that the 2319A disk drive represented a predatory price cut reveals a misunderstanding of the competitive process in which prices are driven down after imitation begins. The contention treats a basic symptom of competition—entry driving down prices—as a symptom of competition's opposite.

The other issue concerning 2319 pricing is that of "price discrimination." Price discrimination occurs when the same product (which has the same cost) is offered to certain customers at one price and certain other customers at a different price. Was it price discrimination for IBM to offer the 2319A at a per spindle price well below that at which it offered the 2314?

Many firms in the EDP market choose to change product designations or reuse old products when reducing prices, an outstanding example being RCA's repackaging of its Spectra 70 series as the RCA series in 1970. In such cases, the customers typically return the old equipment and order the less expensive equipment—just as IBM's 2314 customers returned the 2314s and ordered 2319As. Customers would otherwise replace their obsolescent equipment with equipment from a competitive manufacturer. To call this price discrimination is nonsense, even apart from the fact that the 2319A/IFA was not essentially the same product with the same costs as the 2314/2312/2318 configuration.[109]

The fact that the 2319A/IFA was not price discrimination appears quite sharply when one considers the question of its availability. For price discrimination to exist, there must be distinct and separate classes of customers for the products in question and the inability of customers in one class to acquire the product offered to another class. When a product is available to all customers, there is no price discrimination, and the 2319A/IFA was made available to all who wanted it.

Another way of looking at the matter is to observe that price discrimination is destroyed by arbitrage. If arbitrage can take place, then arbitrageurs can acquire the item at a low price and resell to those customers that would otherwise be willing to pay the high price. In such circumstances, the price spread disappears. How could an arbitrageur possibly have altered affairs in the case of the 2319? If price discrimination had been involved, an arbitrageur would have found it profitable to acquire a 2319 and then re-lease it or resell it to those users unable to take advantage of the low prices. But in the case of the 2319, the users against which discrimination was supposed to have been practiced are precisely those who *chose* not to take advantage of the low prices and preferred to stay with their 2314s (in order, in some cases, to change disk drives only once when the newer 3340 or 3330 became available). Having not wished to take advantage of the opportunity to acquire the 2319s from IBM at IBM's low price, such users certainly would not be interested in acquiring 2319s from an arbitrageur acquiring them at IBM's low price and then offering them so as to make a profit. But a fundamental property of price discrimination is that arbitrage would be profitable if it could take place.

In any case, calling the pricing of the 2319A "price discrimination" does not get one very far. In ordinary circumstances, price discrimination provides evidence of some market power. All firms in real world markets have some market power; price discrimination is certainly not evidence of monopoly power. Does the 2319 reveal the existence of excessive market power? If it did, it would reveal excessive market power not only on the part of IBM but on the part of any manufacturer and lessor of computer equipment or, indeed, of any durable good, since *any* company has the ability to recondition old equipment and put it out under a new number at a lower price.

The 2319B   Having planned only to make the 2319 available for use with System/370 to be shipped in August 1971, IBM found that its existing System/360 customers continued to return 2314s in favor of lower priced PCM devices. Not surprisingly, it found it profitable to make the lower priced alternative available to meet competition in old as well as new systems and announced the 2319B in December 1970.[110]

The 2319B was announced at the same price as the 2319A, into which it was field upgradable; that price, because of the reuse program, was expected to be profit maximizing. Despite the government's allegation to the contrary, it is obvious that this was neither predatory nor price discrimination. Indeed, the inability to discriminate was shown by the rush of returns of 2314s for 2319s, which were available to all. Finally, PCMs could still attach to the IBM channel and could have attached to the 2319B disk drive control unit interface had they chosen to do so.[111]

The Impact of the 2319   Not only is it evident on its face that the 2319 (A and B) was not predatory, it is also true that it did not destroy competition. Indeed, it a mistake to believe that the 2319 was "aimed" only at a particular set of competitors, the PCMs. As we have seen, it was introduced largely because of the need for a low-priced disk drive to keep the price of the smaller 370 systems down. That effect was in fact felt by IBM's systems competitors. Univac introduced its own 8424 disk storage subsystem "as an answer to the IBM 2319," and RCA felt concern about its system price. The PCMs themselves continued to prosper after the 2319.[112]

Tape Drive Issues
The government also claimed as anticompetitive conduct two instances of IBM's introduction and pricing of tape drives. These claims were as ill-founded as those about disk drives just discussed and reflect the lack of understanding of competition that characterized all the practice claims of the Antitrust Division.

The 2420 Model 5   In January 1968, IBM announced a new, advanced tape drive, the 2420 Model 7 for use with System/360 Models 50, 65, 75, and 85. That drive offered higher speeds and greater throughput than any tape drive then available in the industry. However, because of its high data rate, the 2420 Model 7 could not be used with systems smaller than the 360 Model 50; IBM therefore set up a separate program to design a different tape drive that would extend at a lower cost the technological advances of the 2420 Model 7 to users of smaller IBM systems. The resulting drive, the 2420 Model 5, was announced in December 1968 for attachment to System/360 Models 30 through 91.[113]

The Model 5 offered a recording format compatible with that of the Model 7, but it had one-half the speed of the latter drive. It had a monthly rental of $580, compared with $1,050 for the Model 7. Despite the admitted fact that the Model 5 was priced above cost (indeed, it was expected to be quite profitable), the government claimed that its price was anticompetitive because it had a "much lower mark-up over cost than the 2420 Model 7."[114]

The different prices of the Model 5 and the Model 7 reflected the fact that they were different products having different product costs. The D30X program, which led to the Model 5, was a "separate and distinct" program from the D30R, which had resulted in the 2420 Model 7. Although the Model 5 embodied most of the advantages of design that the Model 7 had introduced, the Model 5 had "a number of differences in terms of the design of the machine," and the component parts mostly differed from those of the Model 7. The goal had been to "cost reduce the then existing 2420 [Model 7], to make [the Model 5] a more manufacturable machine."[115]

In this factual context, one is hard pressed to see any anticompetitive behavior in IBM's introduction of the Model 5 tape drive. The government argued that the Model 5 was "priced to achieve a much lower mark-up over cost." But pressures to reduce profits, even the profits from innovative designs, are pressures of competition. Responses to those pressures by reducing prices and profit margins—still at profitable levels—is the very essence of competitive behavior, not predation.

Should IBM have reduced the price of the Model 7 to bring estimated "mark-ups" of the two models to identical levels? There are several answers to that question.

First, in a multiproduct firm, one cannot expect that profit margins, particularly those being estimated in the midst of product lives, will be identical. There are too many variables in a business to expect that, and real world competition does not permit it.

Second, it may well be that IBM should have reduced prices on the Model 7. Perhaps it was seeking the rewards of innovation on that high-performance product or concluded that the capabilities of that product would be worth the price to customers. In any event, one would expect that if the price were too high, in a competitive market, IBM would lose business on the Model 7 and gain business on the lower priced Model 5. That is exactly what happened. In August 1969, the president of IBM's domestic marketing organization wrote to IBM President T. V. Learson: "The last time we met, we discussed prices on our 2420 Model 7 tape drive. I told you then and Group has since confirmed that the 2420-7 will not meet forecast, but the 2420-5, which we believe is competitively priced, is ahead of forecast."[116] In any event, IBM's failure (if it was one) to reduce the price of the Model 7 to make it more competitive cannot make the competitive, profitable price of the Model 5 anticompetitive.

Should IBM have charged a higher price for the Model 5 to raise its markup to equal the markup of the Model 7? That would be the antithesis of what one expects of a competitive market, and it would serve no purpose except to benefit high-cost competitors at the expense of customers.

The 3420   IBM's development of tape drives did not stop with the 2420 Models 7 and 5. Building on the development effort that had produced those drives, a new, more ambitious program emerged around 1967. That program eventually resulted in the 3420 Models 3, 5, and 7 ("Aspen"), announced in November 1970, and Models 4, 6, and 8 ("Birch"), announced in March 1973. The Birch drives had a recording density nearly four times that of the Aspen drives, whose development had been accelerated because of competition from PCMs and leasing companies as well as systems manufacturers that were catching up with IBM's earlier tape drives.[117]

The prices of the 3420 tape drives were below those of the older 2420s, on whose technology the 3420s were based. The government did not contend that the 3420s were priced below cost but claimed nevertheless that they were anticompetitive, stating that "[t]he 3420 was a warmed-over 2420, announced by IBM with the intent of re-stricting competition in the IBM plug-compatible tape drive market without reducing revenue received from its own installed 2420 tape drives," although how such revenue reduction was to be avoided was not made clear.[118]

In fact, even the earlier 3420 drives (Aspen) were significantly im-proved over the 2420s and offered a performance in excess of that offered by any other manufacturer at the time. Among the many im-provements were a digital interface between the drive and its controller, which achieved improved reliability; a radial method of attachment, which allowed a malfunctioning tape drive to be repaired without taking a whole "daisy chain" of drives off line; and considerably lower man-ufacturing costs than the 2420. As already mentioned, the later (Birch) drives had a vastly increased recording density among other advances. These improvements were recognized both inside and outside IBM.[119]

All of this aside, even if the 3420 were a "warmed-over" 2420, which it clearly was not, that would not be evidence that it was anticompetitive. It is a normal part of competition in this market and elsewhere for companies to introduce modified versions of existing products. The fact that the 3420 was offered at lower prices is not evidence that it is anticompetitive. That is what is supposed to happen under competition.

Price cutting is conduct beneficial to users—the intended beneficiaries of a competitive economic system—and part of fair competition. It is not predatory and anticompetitive so long as the price-cutting firm does not price below cost in a deliberate loss-taking venture to drive out competitors in order to earn monopoly profits some time in the future. In the case of the 3420, no below-cost pricing was alleged. Indeed, the 3420 was priced well above cost. The Aspen products were expected to earn more than $300 million profit. The Birch products were projected to earn profits of $85 million. Moreover, IBM's PCM competitors continued to market their products successfully after IBM's announcement of the 2420 Model 5, Aspen, and Birch products.[120]

In summary, IBM's tape drive actions challenged by the government represented precisely the sort of behavior that competition produces: the introduction of better products and the reduction of prices to lower but still remunerative levels to acquire or retain business that would otherwise go to competitors. Monopoly is the power to *refrain* from such actions without having competitors take business away. Only the upside-down belief that it is predatory to engage in competition and monopolistic to lower prices and introduce better products could lead to a different conclusion.

Fixed Term Plan

Prior to May 1971, IBM offered its peripheral products only for either outright purchase or for rent on leases cancellable upon thirty days' notice. Since May 1971, while continuing to offer its products on such terms, IBM has offered a variety of optional multiyear lease options, the first being the "Fixed Term Plan" (FTP). FTP offered customers one- or two-year leases on certain peripheral products. Customers choosing the one-year option received an 8 percent discount from the thirty-day lease rate; customers choosing the two-year option received a 16 percent discount from the thirty-day lease rate. Customers choosing either the one-year or the two-year version were given the option of cancelling their leases prematurely by paying a set fee. IBM had no option to cancel the leases prematurely. At the same time, purchase prices on most products covered by FTP were reduced by approximately 15 percent.[121]

Subsequent to FTP, IBM offered customers a variety of other multiyear lease options, including the Extended Term Plan (ETP), announced in March 1972, and the Term Lease Plan (TLP), announced in March 1973. ETP (like FTP) applied to a number of peripheral products. TLP applied primarily to CPUs and CPU memories. The ETP option was for a two-year lease at 15 percent less than a thirty-day lease. By 1980, IBM was offering multiyear leases for virtually all of its products.[122]

As discussed in chapter 6, the risks of technological obsolescence and of changing requirements among other factors make it optimal for many customers to lease rather than purchase computer equipment. These same factors lead many customers to prefer short-term leases to the greater commitment involved in multiyear leases. Such forces were most powerful in the early days of computers.

As time went on, however, more and more customers became sufficiently sophisticated about EDP equipment and sufficiently confident about their ability to evaluate and use such equipment that they were prepared to make multiyear commitments if they could obtain a lower lease rate by so doing. Since such a longer commitment reduced risk to the vendor and reduced the costs of remarketing and reinstalling the same equipment, it is hardly surprising that vendors began to offer and customers to accept multiyear leases.[123]

By 1971, practically every competitor of IBM was offering multiyear lease options. Vendors doing so included systems manufacturers, plug-compatible peripheral suppliers, and leasing companies. Indeed, a number of leasing companies started up with the specific intent of offering an alternative between purchase and thirty-day rental. IBM was virtually alone in not offering such options.[124]

Not surprisingly, by 1971, IBM found that it was losing business to competitors offering multiyear lease options. Customers were demanding such options, and such losses were projected to continue. Further, the recession of 1970–1971 caused business to reevaluate costs and in some cases reduce their stocks of leased EDP equipment. IBM experienced more equipment returns than did its competitors in part because its only lease terms permitted cancellation on thirty-days notice while the longer leases of its competitors did not. The advantage of letting customers bear more of the risks of changing requirements in return for a lower lease price was brought home to IBM.[125]

The need for a longer lease option was also brought home to IBM in the spring of 1971 by the federal government. The General Services Administration (GSA) had requested multiyear lease plans as early as 1968, but in April 1971, it took a firm position. On April 23, GSA sent a letter to more than 300 companies supplying EDP equipment (including IBM) asking for longer-term leases. A week later on April 30, the comptroller general of the United States reported to Congress concerning the acquisition of automatic data processing (ADP) equipment:

The rental of equipment under multiyear leases, as an alternative to short-term rentals, has become essential if the Government is to make maximum use of its limited funds for acquiring ADP equipment.

. . .

GSA should:

—By taking a more active role in contracting for ADP equipment, make sure that multiyear leases are used to the extent lawful and practicable.

—Require agencies to submit for GSA evaluation their decision to acquire ADP equipment under short-term rentals.

—Ensure that competition is obtained in acquiring ADP equipment under multiyear leases.

Federal departments and agencies should make sure that:

—Maximum practicable use is made of multiyear leases.

—Competition is obtained in acquiring ADP equipment under multiyear leases.

IBM announced its Fixed Term Plan twenty-eight days later.[126]

There is no suggestion in the trial record that IBM's prices under FTP (or ETP) were below fully allocated cost (let alone average variable cost or marginal cost). On the contrary, those prices were definitely profitable. Indeed, IBM had completed studies showing that a long-term lease plan in peripheral products would significantly reduce costs by reducing expenses associated with marketing, refurbishing and reinstalling of equipment, and related field engineering and remarketing. Savings were expected to exceed 17 percent, and this was the order of magnitude of the price reduction for two-year leases.[127]

IBM's May 1971 price reduction (which in many cases left its prices higher than those of its PCM competitors) led to a round of price cutting by systems manufacturers and leasing companies as well as PCMs, which continued to expand at IBM's expense.[128]

Despite all this (and without disagreeing with it) the Antitrust Division contended that FTP and ETP were "predatory" in that they involved "substantial price reductions" and that they represented a "lock-in" because there were "penalty charges for termination." The government also appeared to assert that FTP was somehow rendered anticompetitive by reason of the fact that in July 1971 IBM announced increases averaging less than 6 percent on certain products (particularly CPUs and CPU memories) not covered by FTP. Finally, government economic witness Lee Preston asserted that FTP constituted price discrimination because customers choosing FTP got a lower monthly rate for the same product than customers that did not.[129]

The Contention That FTP/ETP Was Predatory   All of the IBM products subject to FTP and ETP were in fact profitable (or more profitable) after those plans were instituted. Indeed, FTP was expected to increase IBM's profits on existing products to which it applied by $466 million. The government did not dispute these dispositive facts but focused on two others: first, that prior to May 1971 IBM had previously considered and rejected multiyear lease plans—in part because they were not sufficiently profitable; and second, that IBM estimated that in the first two years after FTP, it would receive less revenue for products covered by FTP than it would have received in the absence of FTP.[130]

The fact that IBM, at various times before offering FTP, considered longer-term lease plans and rejected them is wholly irrelevant. What matters is not how profitable a multiyear lease plan might have been at other times but whether it was expected to be profitable when it was adopted in May of 1971. We have already seen the factors that led to increased pressure on IBM for such a plan in the spring of 1971.

Turning to the other point, the government asserted that in the first eighteen months after FTP's announcement, revenues were expected to fall as a result of the discount offered. As a matter of arithmetic, that is clearly true (although it ignores the cost savings discussed earlier). As a matter of economics, it is wholly irrelevant. Particularly in a lease business, price reductions are likely to reduce revenue in the short run and *must* reduce the revenue received from any particular unit. IBM, however, did not have the alternative of renting the same quantity of equipment for the same length of time at higher prices. Competition did not permit it to do so. The whole point of adopting a long-term lease plan at lower prices was to market more equipment than would otherwise have been possible, either by inducing more customers to rent than would have done so at higher prices or by keeping the rented equipment out on lease for a longer period of time. The relevant comparison, therefore, is not between what was expected to happen under FTP and what would have happened if that same quantity of equipment had been out on rent for the same period of time at higher prices but rather between what was expected to happen under FTP and what would have happened if FTP had not been announced. The world had changed, and IBM was forced to change with it.

IBM expected FTP to be profitable on such terms. Its forecasts showed that over the program life of the products involved, it would gain more revenue from keeping the equipment out on rent than it would lose in the very short run (for example, eighteen months) by cutting prices.

Over the 1971–1975 period, the net revenue *gain* was projected as more than $700 million with gains in all areas of peripherals. This projected revenue increase was entirely the result of projected greater business; there was no assumption of any later price increase. Naturally, much of the increased revenue that IBM received would come from customers that would otherwise return the equipment and take the equipment of IBM's competitors, in particular that of plug-compatible manufacturers. This merely reflects the fact that under competition, a reduction in price keeps business from being lost to one's competitors. Such price reductions are what competition is supposed to accomplish.[131]

The Contention That FTP/ETP Was a "Lock-in"   The leases involved in the Fixed Term Plan did not have unreasonable or, indeed, very long terms. The maximum length was two years. Most companies in the market offered much longer-term leases.

Customers that accepted a Fixed Term Plan lease were less "locked-in" than customers that purchased. Customers taking leases for two years are unavailable to competitors only in the sense that there is no need for them to lease again, for they are already leasing. To persuade those customers to switch, competitors must offer them benefits that exceed the cost of breaking their existing leases. Similarly, customers that purchase might be said to be unavailable to competitors because they have already purchased. To get their business, a competitor must offer benefits that exceed the cost of disposing of their existing equipment. Customers on a two-year lease have, as it were, bought equipment for two years. Customers that purchase equipment have bought it forever. In both cases, they have no reason to buy again what they have already bought. Firms wishing to displace such equipment must offer users sufficient benefits to justify disposing of the equipment before the end of the time for which it was acquired.

The notion that customers were locked-in by FTP implies that customers were somehow forced to accept FTP. As already noted, this was not the case. IBM continued to offer its equipment on the same terms as before, continuing, in particular, to offer short-term leases. Customers could choose between those short-term leases and FTP (and purchasing, for that matter). They did not have to take FTP unless they wanted to do so. Customers purchase rather than take short-term leases if they believe that the relative prices involved in doing so justify accepting the risk that their requirements will change and that superior or lower-priced equipment will come along. Likewise, customers accept leases of one or two years rather than short-term leases when they believe that the relative prices involved in doing so justify accepting the risk that, during the period of the lease, their requirements will change or that superior or lower-priced equipment will come along.[132]

The government suggested that a "lock-in" was caused by the "termination charges" payable if a lease was broken. But such termination charges were merely one more option offered customers that wished to break their leases. Many of IBM's competitors offering multiyear leases imposed higher termination charges than did IBM or did not offer any premature termination option at all. This is entirely reasonable. Just as a customer who buys a machine does not have the option of returning the machine (a principal difference between buying and renting), a customer who "buys" a machine for two years does not have the option of returning it after thirty days (a principal difference between a thirty-day lease and a two-year lease).[133]

The erroneous notion that the Fixed Term Plan locked-in customers is curiously at variance with the equally erroneous view of the government that short-term leasing is a barrier to entry. What is involved in the spectrum from short-term leasing through longer-term leasing through purchase is the acquisition by a customer of more and more of the equipment in question. Equipment acquired by customers need not be acquired again. That is all that is reflected in the lock-in idea.

This might not be the case if IBM had refused to sell or offer short-term leases and offered its products *only* on extremely long lease terms (for example, ten to twenty years) with very high penalty clauses and restrictions as to how, and with what, those machines could be used. In such a case (like that of the leases in *U.S.* v. *United Shoe Machinery*), customers would be required to take more (and obligate themselves more to IBM) than they would have when buying the equipment. This was, however, not the case. No lease term offered by IBM could reasonably be described as making customers take more than they would if they were to purchase the machines. As it cannot possibly be anticompetitive to offer the machines for sale, it cannot be anticompetitive to offer them on terms involving a smaller commitment (at most only two years) on the part of the customer, especially when those terms are optional.[134]

In making the decision whether to sign up for FTP, customers accepted the risk that during the term of the lease, lower-priced equipment would come along. If the terms of FTP had not been sufficiently favorable to compensate for the acceptance of that risk, customers would not have taken it. In particular, it is not a tenable view (as McAdams suggested) that the Fixed Term Plan was anticompetitive because, by making it applicable to the new Merlin disk drive, the 3330, IBM ensured that customers would be locked in when plug-compatible manufacturers began to deliver their versions of the 3330. Aside from the fact that such a view supposes that 3330 deliveries to customers by IBM occurred all at once before deliveries of PCM equipment of similar type, such a view supposes customers to have been very shortsighted. By the date of announcement of the Fixed Term Plan (May 1971), plug-compatible manufacturers had already announced their intentions to deliver 3330-type drives. Customers could thus foresee the availability of such drives when they signed up for the Fixed Term Plan. If they had expected lower prices on such drives when available to be worth paying the higher short-term lease prices until they were available, then they would not have signed up for the Fixed Term Plan. If they nevertheless signed up for FTP, that only shows that taking FTP, with its lower prices and longer commitment, provided a greater benefit to customers than failing to sign up for FTP and later taking PCM drives.[135]

To sum up, the Fixed Term Plan was not forced on customers; other alternatives remained available. Further, customers were not enticed into FTP by a below-cost price. Rather, FTP represented an additional alternative, remunerative to IBM, that customers could take advantage of if they so chose. The expansion of customers' alternatives is a competitive, not an anticompetitive, act. It is the market that determines the worth of such additional options. If they are worthwhile, they succeed; if not, they fail and are abandoned.

It makes no difference that such an alternative was offered largely to induce customers to accept and retain IBM equipment instead of going to competitors. The offering of lower prices in order not to lose business inevitably takes some business that competitors would otherwise have gotten. Indeed, in a market characterized by innovative competition with its cycle of innovation and development followed by imitation and a lowering of prices, one expects to see prices come down when imitators come in. Competition compels the innovator to lower prices in such circumstances.

The Contention That FTP/ETP Was Price Discrimination   We need not linger over Preston's contention that FTP was a form of price discrimination because some customers did and some did not take advantage of it. Price discrimination involves offering the same product, costing the same amount, to different customers at different prices. Neither aspect applies here.[136]

Customers that took FTP as opposed to a short-term lease were acquiring the same physical product but not the same economic product. Acquiring the product under FTP included accepting the risk of obsolescence or of changes in requirements for the period of the lease. Acquiring the same physical product under short-term leases involved no such acceptance of risk. To compensate customers for accepting this risk, the price was lower, as were the costs to IBM.

Even apart from this, the Fixed Term Plan was available to all customers. Does it matter that only some customers found it profitable to take advantage of the Fixed Term Plan? Certainly not. In offering any product, some customers find it profitable to take it and others do not. IBM, like each of its competitors, found it necessary to offer lower prices for multiyear leases than for shorter leases to compensate customers for their greater commitment. As the government's expert witness Frederick Withington explained, "The longer the lease, the lower the monthly payment, I am sure, in every case."[137]

The Contention Regarding the CPU Price Increase   A few months after instituting the Fixed Term Plan, IBM raised the prices on some equipment not covered by the plan, in particular, on central processors. The price increase, announced in July 1971, went into effect for purchase prices on August 1 but was delayed in going into effect for lease prices because of the price freeze announced in August by the Nixon administration. It went into effect in early 1972 after the Price Commission approved the increase. Arthur D. Little's "Industry Comment" of September 1971 described the price increase as "an adjustment to inflationary trends in the economy."[138]

The government contended that the price increase was intended by IBM to "recoup, in effect, its revenue losses as a result of FTP." As it were, IBM was to shift profits from peripherals to CPUs, keeping *systems* prices constant. This contention stands out from nearly every other government contention in that it at least involves a price *increase* and, allegedly, one linked to an anticompetitive price decrease. As opposed to the contentions that merely complain of lower prices or better products, this one might, on its face, say something about monopoly.[139]

As we have already seen, over its life FTP was expected to *increase* both revenue and profits; there were no "losses" "to recoup." Moreover, the CPU price increase was more than justified on its own terms unrelated to peripheral products. Other manufacturers were also increasing their prices as a result of inflation at this time.[140]

It is a fundamental proposition of economic analysis that the prices that matter are not prices in money terms but prices in constant or "real" dollars; that is, prices relative to the prices of other goods, prices corrected for inflation. With the rate of inflation in 1970 and 1971, if IBM had left the money prices for its CPUs the same, this would have amounted to a price reduction in constant dollars substantially greater than was offset by the July 1971 price increase. There had been no adjustment for inflation of 370 CPU prices since their announcement in the summer of 1970 and no upward adjustment of 360 CPU prices for an even longer period of time.

Therefore, in the only sense relevant for economic analysis, the adjustment in CPU prices was not an increase. In real terms, CPU prices, like peripheral prices, *fell* during 1970–1971. If there had been no adjustment in the current dollar prices of CPUs, the price of CPUs in constant dollars would have fallen by the rate of inflation. As a result of the adjustment in the summer of 1971, real CPU prices fell by less than the rate of inflation—and less than the reduction in the prices of peripherals. But there is no reason why CPU and peripheral prices should move in lockstep.

Another way of seeing the superficiality of the claim that raising CPU prices without raising peripheral prices was somehow anticompetitive is to observe that IBM could have adjusted peripheral prices in two steps. It could first have lowered prices on those peripherals covered by the Fixed Term Plan to an extent even greater than it actually did. Then it could have adjusted all prices (CPUs and peripherals) upward to take account of inflation. Prices then would have ended up in the same position as actually occurred. Obviously, it made sense in making peripheral product price changes in May 1971 to take into account the effect of inflation and to combine that effect with the other factors considered. To have made a deeper price reduction in May 1971 followed by an adjustment for inflation in July 1971 on the same products would have involved two sets of price announcements for the same products. This would have been annoying and confusing to customers and would likely have caused even more complaints from competitors.

Even if prices had in fact been reduced on peripherals and raised on CPUs, this would not give rise to any inference of anticompetitive conduct. When products are not fully homogeneous, there is no reason to suppose that relative prices will always remain the same. Products have different costs, and demand for them varies in different ways. Under competition, one would not always expect to see constant relative prices of CPUs and peripherals. Rather, under some circumstances, one would expect to see changes in these relative prices. Such changes might take the form of raising some prices and lowering others; they might take the form of raising all prices by different amounts; or, as here, they might take the form of lowering all prices (when adjusted for inflation) by different amounts.

Which prices should we expect to see going down? In a world of innovative competition where imitators are producing one kind of product faster than another, we would expect to see prices being bid down relatively faster when imitators are coming in more quickly. The peripheral equipment under FTP, to a large extent, was equipment already being imitated or expected to be imitated easily by the plug-compatible manufacturers. The 370 CPUs, however, were only recently announced and just being delivered. We expect in that situation to find competition driving down prices in peripherals faster than in CPUs.

Similarly, we should expect to see competition driving down the prices of older CPUs relative to those of new ones, and this is just what happened in the CPU price adjustment. The older, System/360 machines had money prices raised the least (real prices decreased the most), and System/370 machines had money prices raised the most (real prices decreased the least), with System/3 (introduced in the late 1960s) in between. This was a natural outcome; leasing company competition was already marking down prices on the older CPUs.[141]

There was another reason for the apparent change in relative prices. In January 1972, Congress, as had been expected, reinstituted the Investment Tax Credit retroactive to mid-1971. The result was to provide benefits to many System/370 users that totally offset the effect of the CPU price increase. These benefits were not available on the older System/360 machines, which were not in new production, and the benefits were significantly less on peripherals (which fell into shorter useful life categories than CPUs) than on processors.[142]

In any event, there is no way in which the CPU price "increase" matched the FTP price reduction in terms of overall systems prices. Computer systems do not consist of CPUs and peripherals in fixed proportions. Depending on relative costs and customer needs, systems can be configured with more or fewer disk drives, more or fewer tape drives, and, indeed, more or fewer CPUs. Hence, the price changes of 1971 had a different effect on a system with high peripheral value relative to CPU value than they had on a system with a lower peripherals content. To put it differently, there is no one "systems price"; there are many different systems prices depending on the configurations of the systems involved. The price changes had different effects on different customers.

Further, it is not even true that the price changes offset each other on the average. Most customers choosing FTP (and all customers under ETP) had two-year leases—with discounts of 16 percent (for FTP) and 15 percent (for ETP) below the thirty-day rental rate. Peripherals average at least 50 percent and go up to 70 percent of a system's value. Thus, a 15 percent or 16 percent reduction on peripherals could hardly be matched by a 4 percent to 8 percent increase on CPUs. Even in money terms, systems prices decreased.

Both peripherals and CPU pricing reveal IBM as a company constrained by competition. With respect to CPUs, we see a company able to recover only a fraction of its increased costs resulting from inflation. With respect to peripherals, we see a company forced by customer demands and competitive offerings to add new lease options at reduced prices. If IBM could have avoided matching its competitors' lease terms and could have adjusted each of its product prices uniformly to match inflation, IBM (and its competitors) could have had a quieter life. But that would have been a less competitive market than the one that IBM faced—and a market in which consumers would have received fewer of the benefits that competition is designed to produce.

Integration of Disk Control Circuitry in System/370
Prior to IBM's introduction of its System/360, the interfaces by which peripheral subsystems attached to channels generally differed, leading to a proliferation of different peripherals for different CPUs. With its System/360 announcement, IBM stabilized that interface, permitting the same peripherals to be used across a wide range of IBM systems. Even after the System/360, however, the disk drive to controller interface remained "unique," necessitating a new control unit for each new disk drive. When IBM designed the interface for the 2319A, it moved some of these "device-dependent" components out of the controller and into the disk drive box, thereby gaining cost and performance improvements. This served as a precursor, pointing the way to a new method of attaching disk devices to controllers. The first products incorporating this "new attachment strategy" were announced in August 1972. Among other things, the device-independent control electronics were offered both as

stand-alone boxes and as devices housed inside the CPU ("Integrated Storage Controllers" or ISCs and "Integrated File Adapters" or IFAs).[143]

These product introductions permitted a number of improvements. First, because the controllers had only device-independent electronics, new controllers did not have to be developed and built (and paid for by customers) every time a new disk drive was developed, and several new disk drives were introduced in the next few years. Second, users gained flexibility, since different types of drives would attach to the same control unit at the same time. Disk drives could also be located further from the controller than before; more drives could attach to the same controller; and strings of devices could be switched from one control unit to another. Finally, integration of the control function into the CPU reduced costs and improved performance. These benefits were recognized both inside and outside IBM, and similar attachment strategies were later implemented by other disk manufacturers.[144]

The government contended that this change, particularly as embodied in the ISC, was an anticompetitive act—a substantial price reduction combined with a new attachment strategy designed to restrict the ability of PCMs to attach their 3330-type disk drives to the IBM System/370 models involved.[145]

We have already considered this sort of claim when discussing the 2319A and the IFA and need not treat it extensively. In the present case, there was not even a claim that the products involved were priced below cost, and indeed they were not. As for the new attachment strategy itself, aside from the benefits that accompanied it, it did not in fact foreclose PCMs. Indeed, the integration of disk control circuitry in System/370 offered the same potential benefits to PCMs as to IBM. Thus, to the extent PCMs were already marketing 3330-type subsystems, they could continue marketing those subsystems for attachment to the IBM channel, which was not changed by IBM's August 1972 announcement. Moreover, to the extent PCMs wanted to stabilize their disk drive to controller interfaces—thereby eliminating the need to develop new control units for each new disk drive they offered and making it possible to offer their customers the same advantages IBM offered—they were free to do that as well. At least Storage Technology, Memorex, CDC, and CalComp chose that path.[146]

It is hard to see in the government's contention anything other than a continued insistence that *any* change or price reduction that inconveniences a large firm's competitors is anticompetitive.

IBM System/370 Model 158 and 168 Processors

In 1972 IBM also announced what for five years were the two largest processors in its System/370 line: the Models 158 and 168. These machines offered significant performance improvements over the Model 155 and 165 processors announced with the initial System/370 announcements two years earlier, including increases in internal processing speeds of up to 30–40 percent. Two improvements were particularly important: the incorporation of "virtual memory"—making the main memory effectively available to the programmer far larger than the physical main memory itself—and the integration of memory inside the CPU. The government contended that this latter improvement and the resulting memory-CPU price structure were anticompetitive acts.[147]

Integration of Memory   The 158 and 168 processors were the first to be built by IBM using the advanced FET, or Field Effect Transistor, semiconductor memory technology. The FET memory was one-fortieth as large, five times more reliable, used one-seventh as much power, and cost only one-half as much to manufacture as the core memories used in the 155 and 165 processors. (Indeed, it kept on improving. By initial deliveries of the 158/168 processors in 1973, IBM was able to deliver FET memories one-eightieth as large as 155/165 memories.) These improvements permitted the 158 and 168 to be designed to house up to two and four megabytes of memory, respectively, within the processor itself, without the necessity of additional separate memory boxes. Customers could also choose to have lesser amounts, but a substantial amount of memory was included as a minimum. The minimum memory on the 158 was one-half megabyte, and that in the 168 was one megabyte.[148]

The government contended that such an integration of memory was anticompetitive conduct. It stated that "[t]he price reductions on the memories for the 370/158 and 370/168 coupled with the physical movement of the memory under the cover of the central processing units made it more difficult and expensive for plug compatible competitors to market their memory products. Moreover, the minimum amount of memory bundled with the CPU under a single price protected a substantial portion of the total memory market from these competitors."[149] This makes it sound as though integration of memory is an unusual event, occurring only for anticompetitive reasons. This is not the case.

CPUs will not operate without memory; indeed, the very definition of the term CPU generally is meant to include a minimum amount of memory. As a technical matter (in part because computers operate so quickly that the time spent in transmission of electrical impulses between cabinets is significant), integration of memory affords significant and well-recognized advantages in cost savings and improved performance. As a result, ever since Univac I, memory has been packaged separately only when its physical size makes integration impractical.[150]

Thus, it was the *non*integrated memories of the 155 and 165 and not the integrated memories of the 158 and 168 that were the exception (and even the 155 and 165 had small amounts of integrated memory). The earlier processors used obsolescent core technology in which each *half*-megabyte of memory required a stand-alone box to house about twenty cubic feet of memory. By contrast, a half-megabyte of FET memory, used in the 158 and 168 processors, took up about one-half cubic foot (and less by the time of delivery). This permitted IBM to return to what had always been considered best engineering practice.[151]

It is nevertheless true that the great technical desirability of integrating memory and CPU does not itself automatically imply that a single price must be charged for both, although this would involve a change in industry practice. Can it be said that in pricing the integrated memory together with the CPU or in including as much memory as it did, IBM was adopting a practice more restrictive than necessary?

In considering this question, it must be recognized at the outset that it is not at all clear that separate pricing of integrated memory in the 158 and 168 was technically feasible. Despite the fact that memory and processing are logically separate functions, it is not the case that they are necessarily performed by definable totally separate parts. Indeed, in the 158 and 168, at least, it appears impossible to say just what parts would constitute the separate memory that might have been separately priced.

This is, of course, dispositive, but put it aside and suppose that it were possible to solve that technical problem. Complex products are made up of many parts, but that does not imply that they are merely components or "bundles" of separate products that might therefore be separately priced. In general, we expect such a product to be sold as a single product either if customers desire to purchase the parts as a whole, with no substantial body of customers desiring to buy separately, or if there are substantial economies to producing and selling the product as a whole that would be lost if it were sold piecemeal. (Of course, such economies can make it cheaper for customers to purchase the whole rather than its parts, thus giving them a reason for preferring to do so.)

Both these properties are present in the integration of memory. Since CPUs will not function without memory, no customer desires to purchase a memoryless CPU. Indeed, as already remarked, the very definition of a CPU generally includes memory. Further, the cost and performance advantages of integration are substantial. To realize such advantages requires that processor and integrated memory be designed together. They must also be tested together to ensure that the processor (let alone the processor-memory combination) actually functions properly. Thus, provision of a memoryless CPU would require actual removal of the memory (supposing that to be feasible) and not merely failing to go on to include memory. Finally, the malfunction of an IBM processor with no IBM memory would make it difficult to allocate responsibility for failure and maintenance.

Putting these details aside, however, suppose that in fact IBM, in failing to separately price memory, supplied customers with something they did not want. As in the case of "bundling" of software and services, discussed in chapter 6, the existence of a substantial number of customers wishing to acquire less memory from IBM would have created an opportunity for IBM's competitors. Other systems manufacturers would have found it advantageous to provide less memory. Moreover, even if one believes that this effect was hampered by the costs of program conversion, those costs do not apply to conversion to IBM-program-compatible CPUs. After 1975, many vendors, following Amdahl, offered such products, and from at least then on, it cannot have been the case that IBM forced too much integrated memory on its customers. Any attempt to so do would have made it profitable for vendors of IBM-program-compatible CPUs to offer less memory or no memory at all with customers acquiring memory directly from PCMs. Yet IBM did not decrease the amount of memory integrated—even though many of its computers were on lease. Further, IBM-program-compatible CPU vendors also did not offer memoryless CPUs. Like IBM, they integrated the memory at a single price.

It must not be thought that this occurred because the PCM memory suppliers had been driven out. On the contrary, those suppliers, which had arisen in the late days of System/360 when memory was generally integrated, found that they not only survived but prospered, supplying add-on memories to customers, who generally required more, not less memory than was supplied by IBM as an integrated part of the CPU.[152]

Other Memory Pricing Allegations   The government did not focus on the memory pricing question in this way. Instead, it raised claims covering the entire structure of memory and CPU prices involved in the 158 and 168. It claimed that in announcing the 158/168 processors, IBM "reduced" the prices of the 158 and 168 processor memories and at the same time "raised" prices for the 158 and 168 CPUs over the prices for the predecessor 155 and 165 CPUs. In this way, IBM was said to have "balanced" prices between the memories and CPUs of the 158 and 168 and "shifted" profits from memories, which were subject to PCM competition, to the CPUs, which according to the government were in the "market" over which IBM had monopoly power. McAdams elaborated on these charges in the following manner:

The price of the central processing unit itself is substantially higher than the price of the central processing unit in the comparable pairs, the 168 versus the 165, the 158 versus the 155. . . .

. . .

. . . So it appears that there has been an increase in the price of the CPU, each of the later CPUs, at the same time that the separately priced memory has been very substantially reduced in its slope.

The implication from my point of view is that once again, IBM is price-balancing between products which were at the time subject to competition, that is, the addon memory itself, that is, the portion of the addon memory which was priced—only that portion was subject to competition, charging a low price for that, and the CPU itself, which was not subject to competition, charging a relatively higher price for that.[153]

To begin with, these allegations are somewhat misleading. IBM did not market "memory" as such; it marketed processors having greater or lesser amounts of memory. To say, for example, that the FET memory in the 168 was "priced" at $5,200 per month is not entirely accurate. That number is a derived price taken from the difference in rental prices among processor models and is called the memory "slope" within IBM.

There is no dispute, however, that the slope for IBM's new FET memories for the 158 and 168 processors was lower than the slope for the 155 and 165 memories. The number for a megabyte of 155 and 165 core memory was $12,000. The equivalent number for FET memory was about $5,200. Memory slopes had been falling markedly since the 1950s and continued to fall at accelerating rates in the 1970s as semiconductor technology was incorporated wholesale in computers. FET memory was far cheaper to produce than core memory—by about one-half. Hence, IBM was passing on to users lower costs in the form of lower prices. Indeed, that is all it was doing, for the FET memory was priced well above cost at the time it was announced.[154]

Despite these facts, McAdams found the $5,200 slope for the 158/ 168 memory too low, principally because of testimony from Burton Hochfeld (a former low-level IBM employee who left the company six months before the memory slope was established) that a memory slope below $6,000 per megabyte "would be so low that competitors would not be able to meet that price." This contention is factually incorrect (and contradicted by Hochfeld's own work within IBM). Within IBM it was correctly expected that memory costs would drop rapidly and that PCMs would be able to compete at slopes well below $6,000.[155]

What is more, it makes no difference whether IBM thought it was setting the memory slope below its *competitors'* costs. Competition does not subsidize the high-cost competitor, and IBM's memory slope was not below its *own* costs. In an attempt to avoid this, however, the government, as we have seen, contended that IBM somehow "balanced" its prices, raising 158 and 168 CPU prices to subsidize its "reduction" in FET memory prices. This is the only case other than that of the CPU price increase in which an alleged anticompetitive act is said to have involved profits from higher prices; as in that case, it is factually and analytically wrong.

As we have seen, the FET memory slope was "set," not "reduced" (and, if anything, the slope was "raised" over what the product and marketing groups within IBM were contending for); the slope was lower than slopes on earlier, different technology memories because the new FET memories were cheaper to produce; and the slope selected for FET memories was projected to be profitable. Hence, there is no situation here of CPU "profit" gains being used to subsidize memory losses. There were no memory losses to subsidize.

Turning to CPU pricing, it is certainly true that the absolute prices of the 158 and 168 processors were higher than those of the 155 and 165, respectively. Similarly, the 155 and 165—which contained little integrated memory in their cabinets and hence in their prices—were substantially higher priced than the 360 Model 50 and 65 processors, respectively. But prices standing alone do not tell us anything. As we have seen, computer equipment can only be measured by price for a given amount of performance. The 155 and 165 offered significant price/performance gains over their 360 predecessors; the 158 and 168 did the same compared to the 155 and 165. Hence, a customer wishing to perform a given set of tasks would find he had to spend less with a 158 or 168 processor than with a 155 or 165 and might, for example, if he had a 165, take a smaller model 168 or 158 (with appropriate amounts of cheaper memory) and perform his tasks more cheaply.[156]

Moreover, it is not correct to suggest (as McAdams did) that the 158 and 168 were "essentially the same" as the 155 and 165 processors, with the addition of virtual memory. The 158 and 168 were entirely new machines. More than 50 percent of the parts were different; the design programs, including the virtual memory development projects, were different; and the newer products offered significant performance improvements. If this were not the case, users would have flocked to the "cheaper" 155 and 165 machines and bypassed the so-called higher priced 158 and 168. In fact, the 158 and 168 processors were very popular. Indeed, the Department of Justice itself proposed to procure a 168.[157]

Of course, the claim that the 158 and 168 were "essentially the same" as the 155 and 165 but higher priced is in flat contradiction to the claim that the 158 and 168 made the 155 and 165 obsolete and thus damaged leasing companies that had been "trapped" into buying 155s and 165s. If the 158 and 168 were merely higher-priced versions of the 155 and 165 with the addition of the DAT box to the latter system to provide virtual memory, then leasing companies and other users of the 155 and 165 made a capital gain when the 158 and 168 were announced.[158]

One cannot escape the view that the Antitrust Division and its economic witnesses failed to understand how prices change and thrashed about to find some story in which changes are bad if they inconvenience competitors. In the present instance, one version of what happened involved lowered prices on the 158 and 168 CPUs facing one set of competitors (leasing companies), while an opposite version involving increased prices on the same CPUs was needed for the contention that low memory prices were predatorily aimed at another set of competitors (PCM memory suppliers). So both versions were asserted. This is protection of competitors rather than of competition.

In fact, neither story is of predatory behavior. In particular, the facts of the 158/168 and of their FET memory show no "balancing" of any kind. On the contrary, the prices were profitable for products offering greater price/performance and passing on to users advantages achieved by innovation and lower costs. That kind of pricing is what competition is supposed to bring about.

None of the actions complained of by the government as anticompetitive acts directed against PCMs in the period 1968–1972 were other than one would expect under competition. They were all profit-maximizing without being justified by monopoly profits. Moreover, they certainly failed to drive out or significantly restrain PCM competition. Efficient PCM companies, such as Storage Technology, grew and prospered. By June 1980, the government's own industry expert witness, Withington, testified that, in his view, IBM should consider "first and foremost" the plug-compatible product offerings of its competitors in pricing new processors and peripherals for its 4300 series.[159]

The Alleged Practices: Conclusion

None of the actions that the government contended were predatory were anything of the kind. Each of them was expected to be profitable—taking proper account of additional revenues and avoidable costs. None of them was followed by the rise in prices to a monopolistic level that is the *sine qua non* of predation. None of them came close to driving out competitors. On the contrary, IBM's actions were not only consistent with competition, they were generally compelled by it.

Monopoly profits are earned through high prices and inferior products. The notion that acts showing a pattern of lower prices and better products are the behavior of a monopolist is a confusion of the workings of competition with its opposite—monopoly. Only a confusion of high market share with monopoly power, of the competitive desire to gain business with the intent to monopolize, and of protection of competitors with protection of competition would require even a dominant firm to refrain from such actions.

Of course, it is possible that—considering long-run equilibrium positions only—society would be better off if a dominant firm did not reduce prices and introduce better products as competition increased. This *might*, under rather special circumstances, result in a long-run equilibrium with more firms and lower prices than if the dominant firm were allowed to compete. Yet the belief in such an outcome is at best speculative and one that loses sight of the importance of dynamic behavior. Moreover, the behavior on the part of the dominant firm that might bring it about cannot easily be codified as part of a pro-competitive policy. Such a policy encourages firms to react to competition by competing. If that reaction is fair in the sense that it meets the tests given at the beginning of this chapter, then competition is doing its job. It is a major mistake to confuse that with predation.

Chapter 9

Economics, Economists, and Antitrust Policy

As we saw in chapter 1, the *Alcoa* and *United Shoe Machinery* cases opened up tempting possibilities to those charged with enforcement of Section 2 of the Sherman Act. To prove a violation of Section 2, it was no longer necessary to prove that particular acts were illegal in themselves. Rather, it was only necessary to show that monopoly power had been attained—and attained deliberately through a course of conduct that could have been avoided. That possibility offered the opportunity to attack monopoly as a structural phenomenon—at least when the monopoly structure was the result of deliberate, if not themselves illegal, actions.

Two major pitfalls in the pursuit of that possibility also existed and continue to exist. The first pitfall was opened in part by Judge Hand's market share dictum in *Alcoa*. This was the possibility that attempts to prove monopoly power would simply become attempts to prove a high market share and that proper analysis of the constraints on power would degenerate into a semantic debate on market definition.

The second pitfall also derived in a way from the undue importance given to market share. If monopoly power was to be equated with high share and deliberate attainment of that power made an offense, then deliberately seeking business could become a matter for prosecution. This invited mistaking the ordinary intent to compete and the actions forced by competition for deliberate attempts to attain or to keep power, despite Hand's warning that "[t]he successful competitor, having been urged to compete, must not be turned upon when he wins."[1] It also kept open the possibility so attractive to lawyers that documents could be found reflecting the intent to gain business through specific acts that, in the context of the case, could be shown to be wrongful. Indeed, it widened that possibility, since the class of wrongful acts had been made potentially much larger than before.

Under these circumstances, intelligent enforcement of Section 2 requires a serious understanding and use of economic analysis. Without such analysis, Section 2 enforcement inevitably tumbles into the pitfalls described, and antitrust prosecution degenerates into verbal games. The following should be a required checklist for the Antitrust Division in bringing or continuing Section 2 cases (and most of the items apply with little change to other areas of antitrust enforcement).

1. Does the case depend crucially on the definition of the market? If that definition is altered, can the same facts be described in a way that leads to the same outcome? If the case really turns on market definition—and especially if small changes in definition are likely to lead to large changes in other arguments or conclusions—then there is something wrong. In such circumstances, market definition is obscuring the facts rather than organizing them, and the outcome is being affected by the way in which the analyst chooses to categorize the information.

2. Closely related to this question is the following. In reaching the proposed market definition (or in dealing with other aspects of the case), is one forced to explain away a substantial amount of what appears to be competition? Is one leaving out important constraints on the behavior of the firm in question? Does the proposed market definition really pay attention to the choices made by customers (demand substitutability)? To the alternatives open to competitors (supply substitutability)? It is certainly possible, as in *Cellophane*, that observed substitution only takes place because prices are at the monopoly level. Is this more than a theoretical possibility? If a great deal has to be explained away, one should take a hard look at the explanation, for it may be that the analysis is being forced to suit the needs of the market definition rather than vice versa.

3. The crucial question to be answered in a Section 2 case is whether the alleged monopolist has the power to raise prices to noncompetitive levels or to offer inferior products without losing customers. Hence attention should focus on what constrains a firm's power to do this. In considering the measurement of market share and its role in the case, one wants to know not merely whether the share of the firm in question is large but whether it would remain large if the firm attempted to exercise its supposed power. The direct answer to this question is obtained by examining whether existing competitors can readily expand and new ones can enter. If there is direct evidence that they can, this is dispositive. Reliance on market share measurement is only second best, if that.

4. To the extent that the case relies heavily on market share evidence, are the market share statistics *capable* of revealing anything about power? In part, this depends on a proper definition of the market. In part, as in the *IBM* case, it may depend on *how* market share is measured.

While measures of share of capacity have their uses, measures that depart very far from the simple case of looking at current revenues (or value added) for the firm in question divided by current revenues (or value added) for *all* firms competing with it should be viewed with suspicion if used as the primary measures of market share.

5. Since the crucial question of what happens if the firm attempts to exercise monopoly power depends so closely on whether other firms can enter and grow, the analysis of barriers to entry should play a central role. This is particularly so since correct analysis here can at least partially compensate for mistakes of overly narrow market definition. A proper analysis of entry barriers, however, must do more than recite the difficulties and expense that entrants must overcome. Such an analysis must examine whether there are long-lasting advantages that accrue to incumbents. In considering this question, it is important to remember that the necessity to compete with aggressive incumbents is not in itself an entry barrier. *An entry barrier must permit incumbent firms to restrict output or output quality and thus effectively raise prices and earn monopoly profits without attracting entry.* One cannot conclude that entry barriers exist because profits now being earned above current costs are not high enough to justify a potential entrant's incurring the costs of entry that are sunk costs to incumbents.

6. Direct evidence of monopoly profits in terms of the profit rate of the firm as a whole is almost certainly meaningless. Analyses based on accounting rates of return tell nothing and should not be undertaken. A case that depends on such analyses is questionable at best.

7. In considering both entry barriers and the acts by which the firm in question achieves or maintains its position, one must be careful not to confuse the acts expected under competition and the determination to win with anticompetitive acts undertaken to monopolize. To avoid such confusion, one must clearly delineate what one would expect to see under competition. Only acts that depart from such a competitive standard can be anticompetitive; these will be acts that are not profit maximizing except for the monopoly profits to be earned after competition is reduced or destroyed.

8. In considering whether an entire course of conduct is monopolization, it is wise to ask whether the acts involved can in fact lead to monopoly profits. If every act under criticism involves lower prices or better products, the case has most likely fallen into the trap of confusing share with monopoly and competitive efficiency, foresight, and industry with deliberate monopolizing behavior. Direct evidence of monopoly

profits may be impossible to get, but the case must show that such profits are likely. Such profits are not likely (and entry barriers do not exist) if to gain or to keep a large share, the firm must continually compete harder.

9. In all of this, one must not forget that competition constitutes a process whose functioning in real markets cannot adequately be understood by supposing that only long-run equilibrium matters. In the competitive process, there are profits and losses, winners and losers. Just as the successful competitor "must not be turned upon when he wins," so the unsuccessful firm is not to be succored by the Antitrust Division when it loses.

The Government's Case in *U.S.* v. *IBM*

The government's case in *U.S.* v. *IBM* failed badly on every one of these points. That failure can be regarded as stemming from two basic underlying errors.

First, the government and its economists approached market definition without concern for its purpose. They considered not the firms and products that constrained IBM by competing with it but those firms and products that met an arbitrary technical definition. Firms were included in the government's market *not* if they offered copies of IBM's products but only if they themselves were full-blown copies of the IBM corporation. Not surprisingly, the government's economists then found that only full-blown entry into such a market is possible and, ignoring the plain facts of competitive entry, concluded that entry was difficult.

The second underlying error that the government's economic analysis committed was to suppose that a dynamically changing competitive market whose basic feature is technological change can be analyzed in terms of theoretical long-run equilibrium. As a result, the Antitrust Division lawyers and witnesses constantly mistook the price and product change compelled by competition for the restrictive behavior of monopoly. Indeed, the whole of the government's case was a reiteration of complaints about *lower* prices and *better* products—the antithesis of what monopoly produces. The government saw only the effects that such lower prices and better products had on competing firms, which would find life easier in a less competitive market. It failed to see the gains that such competition brought to customers and thus failed to understand what competition is all about.

To arrive at a share that confirmed its conclusions, the government distorted the purpose of market share measurement. It chose a measure of market share that did not match its market—counting in IBM's obsolete machines and counting out competitive machines with the same or superior capabilities. It counted IBM's past successes in IBM's share forever and counted the successes of many of IBM's competitors as though they were IBM's. It counted the possibility of IBM's future success in IBM's present share, ignoring the very real possibility of IBM's future failure.

The government's economic analysis did not understand the nature of a barrier to entry. It looked at the costs of entering borne by incumbent and entrant alike and supposed erroneously that incumbents have an advantage because they have already borne such costs. At bottom, its claimed barriers amounted to no more than capital requirements, for which there is no evidence that incumbents and entrants have different costs—despite an attempt to inflate such requirements vastly by requiring full-blown entry in order to be counted in a full-blown market. The overwhelming record of entry was simply *defined* away.

The government economists failed to understand what economic profits are, whence they arise, or how to measure them. They confused the rewards that competition provides for innovation and efficiency and the incentive it gives for expansion with the ill-gotten gains that stem from a monopolist's ability to restrict output and refrain from product improvement. They moved from the fact that in long-run competitive equilibrium there are no *economic* profits to the erroneous conclusion that high *accounting* rates of return found in a market in constant disequilibrium must imply the lack of competition.[9.1]

Finally, the government's economic analysis, assuming IBM to have had monopoly power, but faced with the fact that IBM did not behave as a monopolist does—restricting output and output quality and raising prices—managed to distort IBM's competitive acts into "anticompetitive" ones. Nothing is more revealing about the government's case than its constant complaint of low rather than high prices as the symptom of monopoly.

Alan McAdams himself was plain enough in this regard. He would require a firm that has a large share because of its innovations to price

9.1. Indeed, to apply that conclusion to IBM, McAdams undertook a series of adjustments to the data that were guaranteed to produce the desired result and one of which was a pure algebraic artifact.

at either the short-run monopoly price without regard for competition or the long-run competitive equilibrium price (long-run marginal cost). Thus, he testified that a firm introducing a price reduction on an existing product but still holding the price "substantially above cost" was engaged in an anticompetitive act if it was "an action specifically designed to maintain its current customers and add new customers." For the Antitrust Division, there was no such thing as competitive adjustments. When prices fell over time due to competition, it interpreted that fall as predatory, citing statements of the rational and inevitable intent not to lose business as evidence of an attempt to drive out competitors.[2]

In fact, as this book has made clear, correct analysis shows the computer industry to be highly competitive and IBM to have been and to be under continual pressure to lower its prices and to improve its products.[9.2] Yet where competition exists, the government—folding, spindling, and mutilating the precepts of economic analysis along the way—saw monopoly. The protection of competition demands better service.

What Went Wrong?

The *IBM* case was a disaster. It began with a plainly erroneous view of the facts (the question whether IBM offered boxes separately). It moved forward with an economic theory that made progressively less sense as it developed and changed in the course of the case (with the government's "market," in particular, becoming increasingly narrow as more firms entered the industry). The result was a tremendous waste of time and resources.

How might the IBM disaster have been avoided? More important, how can such disasters be avoided in the future? What procedural safeguards seem appropriate for Section 2 (and other) antitrust cases to ensure the application of the criteria listed earlier in this chapter?

We do not believe that any fundamental change in the law is needed. The problem, we think, lies not in the law itself or in judicial interpretations of it, which in general have been consistent with *sound* economic analysis. On the other hand, while proper economic analysis is not at odds with the *Alcoa* decision, that decision, as we have seen,

9.2. Economists may speculate as to whether it is also true that the organization of the industry is in some sense optimal, but this is a somewhat different question. In view of the unparalleled history of progressive performance, however, it seems to us dangerous to hope to do better by tinkering with the structure of the industry.

created pitfalls that can only be avoided through well-understood, well-thought-through economic analysis. *Alcoa*, through Hand's dictum on market share and making deliberate attainment of monopoly power an offense, created the environment that produced the *IBM* case.

Thus, while no fundamental change in the law is required, it would be very desirable if lawyers and judges were always conscious of the pitfalls involved. To this end, it seems to us that much would be gained and little lost if evidence on "intent" ceased to be thought relevant. *Alcoa*, as we have seen, made it all too easy to mistake the natural competitive intent to gain business for a predatory intent to gain market share, which is easily but wrongly equated with monopoly power. The government in the *IBM* case introduced massive numbers of documents purporting to show such intent. That introduction alone accounted for a nonnegligible part of the length of the trial and of pretrial discovery. Yet such documents prove little or nothing in a situation in which acts are not wrongful in themselves. What matters is the acts themselves, their consequences, and whether they differ from acts expected under competition, not whether they were undertaken to gain business at the expense of competitors—an "intent" common to competitive and monopolistic acts alike. The concentration of the government on evidence of intent greatly lengthens the trial of a Section 2 case and serves mainly to obfuscate it.[3]

Removing the relevance of evidence of intent, however, would only go part way to avoiding disasters like *IBM*. What was plainly lacking in the Antitrust Division's pursuit of the *IBM* case was an adequate, powerful, internal review procedure designed to ensure that the case made sense in terms of economic analysis at the beginning and continued to make sense as it developed. For once the case had begun, it rolled on for twelve years controlled by those closest to it, with no one in the Division standing to gain if it were stopped and without (so far as we know) any extensive and systematic review by an assistant attorney general until Sanford Litvack appointed a task force for this purpose at the end of the Carter administration. Litvack went out of office before taking action and was followed by William F. Baxter, whose systematic review in the fall of 1981 ended in the dismissal of the case as "without merit."

Criticism of the organization and internal procedures of the Antitrust Division is not new. In 1971 Richard Posner (now a judge in the United States Court of Appeals for the Seventh Circuit) wrote,

The present organization of the Antitrust Division is highly decentralized. . . . In most periods the Division is dominated by the individual trial lawyers and supervision is minimal. They owe their authority . . . mostly to default. The traditions of supervision and hierarchy are very weak in the Division. . . .

. . . It would be only a slight exaggeration to say that, in the early 1960s, the only real coordination of antitrust policy took place in the Solicitor General's office, where coherent theories were formulated for the antitrust cases bound for the Supreme Court. The Court expressed its dismay at the liberties taken by the Solicitor General with the theories urged by the Division in the lower court [*United States* v. *Arnold, Schwinn & Co.*, 388 U.S. 365, 371-2 n.4, 374 n.5 (1967)], but the lack of theoretical coherence in the Division's positions made major surgery unavoidable.[4]

Posner's comments on the role of economists in such a setting are also illuminating.

With the occasional exception of the special economic assistant to the Chief of the Division ([a]. . . happy innovation of Donald Turner), the Division's economists today are handmaidens to the lawyers, and rather neglected ones at that. The indifference (and sometimes hostility) of lawyers toward economists in the antitrust enforcement agencies is an old story. The lawyers are in firm command and the better economists are not attracted.[5]

In the *IBM* case, economists (but not those of the Division's staff) played a much greater role than this would suggest, but economics itself functioned only as a "handmaiden" to the lawyers.[9.3] Indeed, with a structure such as that described by Posner, that is the only role that economics is likely to play. The Division's trial lawyers are not likely to search for or heed economists who take as their task a serious review of why the trial lawyers' case lacks economic coherence.

Yet such a review within the Antitrust Division is badly needed. In principle, it occurs as part of the function of the Economic Policy Office, but that function, probably inevitably, waxes and wanes with the importance attached to economics by different assistant attorneys general. While the importance has plainly grown under Baxter, it is also plain that, for whatever reason, the Economic Policy Office played no role in the 1970s in halting the IBM disaster through a serious review.

The Antitrust Division needs to regularize its procedure for the systematic review of the economic analysis involved in its cases. Independent of the trial lawyers, there should be a body whose job it is to

9.3. McAdams played so large a role, however, that the identities of master and servant often seemed to have become confused.

consider the economic theories of the Division's cases along the lines given earlier in this chapter. Such a body, possibly growing out of the Economic Policy Office, must include able economists. Moreover, that body needs to be taken very seriously, and the reviews it undertakes must not end when complaints are brought, for as in the *IBM* case, the theories underlying a particular case can change as the case approaches trial and during the trial itself. It must therefore be understood that such an Economic Review Board will occasionally call for the dismissal of cases that trial lawyers wish to pursue and that it will be normally expected that such dismissals will in fact occur.

A natural and complex question is whether dismissals so recommended should be reviewable (other than by the attorney general). Should the provisions of the Tunney Act[6] on antitrust settlements also apply to such dismissals so that once a case is brought, the presiding judge has the power and the obligation to hold public hearings and review any dismissal decision? In answering this question, we are aware of the danger of being unduly influenced by the experience of the *IBM* case; nevertheless, we believe that there are sound reasons for avoiding such a review. We find the reasons compelling despite the superficially appealing argument that a review procedure that applies to settlements should, a fortiori, apply to dismissals when the government does not even get part of what it sought in bringing a case.

When a settlement is overturned by a court, the parties, each of whom has compromised to reach that settlement, must go on with the litigation (if they do not negotiate another settlement). This they are presumably prepared to do if the settlement is ruled out. The case of a dismissal stemming from an Economic Review Board recommendation, however, would be quite different. In such a circumstance, the lawsuit would be dismissed because the Antitrust Division had decided that it did not make sense to pursue it. In that situation, it is hard to see how a judge could force the Division to pursue a case in which it no longer believed.

A second reason for not subjecting such dismissals to judicial review is also a practical one. In a Tunney Act proceeding, if the judge is to avoid an entire trial of the case, the natural thing to do is to ascertain that the settlement is consistent with the theory on which the complaint was brought. In fact, although the Tunney Act does not state the requirement in this form, judges have followed this procedure (at least once over an intervenor's protest) rather than attempting to ascertain directly whether the settlement will be procompetitive.[7] In so doing, the judge naturally relies on the Antitrust Division to have formulated a sensible theory.

When the Economic Review Board recommends dismissal of a case, however, it will do so for precisely the reason that the Division's theory does *not* make sense. Hence, the reviewing judge cannot sensibly ask whether dismissal is warranted in the light of the government's theory. Any review must involve a full evaluation of that theory itself. There is, of course, no reason in principle that such a review cannot take place. Further, there is no reason in principle that such a review need be as lengthy as a full trial. The issues to be examined are those of economic analysis, and at one level, a determination along the lines just given as to whether the government's theory makes sense may be possible without a full-dress trial of the entire matter. Unfortunately, things are seldom so simple, and as we hope this book has demonstrated, considerable knowledge of the facts may also be required. Hence it may be hard to keep such proceedings within bounds.

Judicial review of dismissal decisions stemming from Economic Review Board recommendations thus strikes us as impractical (although we would recommend that such decisions be in the form of written, publicly available opinions). Moreover, to require such judicial review would be to make dismissal through internal review harder and more costly. The present problem within the Antitrust Division is to get such internal dismissal reviews undertaken at all, not to curb their excessive use.

Epilogue: The Expert Witness Experience

We have had a good deal to say about the use and misuse of economics by the Antitrust Division and its economists. Similar considerations apply to the proper role of economists as consultants or expert witnesses in antitrust (or other) litigation on behalf of any party and to the relation of such activities to research.

Participation in a great antitrust case can be professionally rewarding to an economist. There is a sense of excitement in applying economic analysis to real, detailed situations and possibly helping to improve judicial understanding of economics. Moreover, there is, as in *U.S.* v. *IBM*, an unparalleled opportunity for research and reflection on the experience; we were immersed in the material of the IBM case and the computer industry in a way in which few economists studying any industry ever are (or perhaps want to be).

Such participation, however, as either research or, ultimately, expert witness activity itself, requires skillful handling of the tools of economics and an objectivity that is not always easy to keep. We do not mean to imply that there are often situations in which lawyers and economic witnesses make arguments they know to be wrong. That does not happen if lawyers and witnesses are smart. Good lawyers will realize that arguments known to them to be wrong will be unlikely to stand up on cross-examination. Intelligent economists will realize that their principal assets are their professional reputations, whose values exceed the rewards of acceding to a particular request.

The danger instead is subtler than this. It lies in the gradual but continual immersion in the case itself. Witnesses, working closely with the trial lawyers, may gradually take on their point of view; they may come to want to win and thus be drawn into acting as law partners rather than as independent experts. The danger lies not in being tempted to step across some well-defined line, but in remaining certain where the line is.

There are certain things that economists can do to protect themselves (and the lawyers) from this danger. First, they should insist that the initial investigation of the economics of the case be made independently and without restriction. Second, just as the Economic Review Board suggested above should keep the Antitrust Division from prosecuting cases lacking any seriously coherent economic theory, so the expert economic witness should find others to serve the same function. For example, it is wise for the witness to have an independent colleague or staff—independent of the witness as well as of the trial lawyers— one of whose functions is to say "No." Such assistants can be given a devil's advocate role and can sharpen the thinking of the witness. More important, by constantly forcing the analysis to stand up to relatively detached professional scrutiny, an independent observer or staff can preserve the witness from temptation.

Such self-imposed review procedures, however, cannot protect those who do not want to be protected. The trial lawyer who brings or defends a case without proper attention to its economic content will always be able to find an economist willing to act enthusiastically. If they do not institute proper review procedures, if neither of them understands the economics of competition and monopoly at more than a superficial level, or if they do not undertake a detailed study of the facts, the lawyer and the economist can persuade themselves of the justice and economic sense of their cause even when it will not stand up to rigorous analysis. Enmeshed in a web of their own confusion, they may strike out in any direction that seems promising.

Such a situation, of course, does the ultimate client a great disservice. Private clients, however, can switch law firms in their own interest. When, as in the prosecution of *U.S.* v. *IBM*, the ultimate client is the public itself, this is not possible, and it is therefore especially important to install institutional safeguards. Government antitrust cases are too important to be left to the trial staff of the Antitrust Division.

Complaint

UNITED STATES DISTRICT COURT

FOR THE SOUTHERN DISTRICT OF NEW YORK

UNITED STATES OF AMERICA,	)	
Plaintiff,	)	
v.	)	Civil Action No. 69 Civ. 200
	)	Filed: 1/17/69
INTERNATIONAL BUSINESS MACHINES	)	
CORPORATION,	)	
Defendant.	)	

COMPLAINT

The United States of America, by its attorneys, acting under the direction of the Attorney General of the United States, brings this action against the defendant named herein and complains and alleges as follows:

JURISDICTION AND VENUE

1. This complaint is filed and this action is instituted against the defendant under Section 4 of the Act of Congress of July 2, 1890, as amended (15 U.S.C. §4) commonly known as the Sherman Act, in order to prevent and restrain the continuing violation by the defendant, as hereinafter alleged, of Section 2 of the Sherman Act. (15 U.S.C. §2).

2. Defendant International Business Machines Corporation has offices, transacts business and is found within the Southern District of New York.

DEFENDANT

3. International Business Machines Corporation, hereinafter referred to as "IBM," is made a defendant herein. IBM was organized under the laws of the State of New York in 1911 and assumed its present name in 1924.

4. IBM is the largest manufacturer of information handling systems in the world. It develops, manufactures and markets electronic and punched card data processing machines and systems, as well as electric typewriters, dictation equipment, and related supply items. In 1967 IBM had total revenues of $5,345,291,000 with total assets of $5,598,670,000 and net income of $651,500,000.

5. IBM conducts its worldwide business through 11 divisions and three subsidiaries. The Service Bureau Corporation, a wholly-owned, but independently operated subsidiary, furnishes data processing services on a fee or contract basis to its customers in the United States. Science Research Associates, Inc., acquired by IBM in 1964 and now operated as a wholly-owned subsidiary, develops and markets instructional and guidance materials and a wide variety of intelligence, aptitude and achievement tests. IBM World Trade Corporation, another wholly-owned subsidiary, conducts all of IBM's business, except that of Science Research Associates, Inc., in over 100 countries outside the United States.

TRADE AND COMMERCE

6. As used herein, a computer is an electronic device which processes information as desired by activating electronic impulses in pre-defined sequences. Digital computers, which represent over 95% of all computer sales and leases, are machines which process information which is symbolized by numerals and processed in that form.

7. A computer system, sometimes referred to as an electronic data processing system, consists of a machine or a group of automatically intercommunicating machine units capable of entering, receiving, storing, classifying, computing and/or recording data, which system includes at least one central processing unit and one or more storage facilities, together with various input and output equipment.

8. Computer hardware includes all the physical components used in a computer system. Computer software includes the programming know-how and materials necessary to make the computer hardware

operative. Computer support includes all manpower and other assistance necessary to make and keep the computer hardware and software operative.

9. The general purpose digital computer is one which has general commercial application and is offered for sale or lease in standard model configurations. Special purpose digital computers are designed for particularized needs or purposes and are produced for use by a limited number of customers but not made generally available to all customers.

10. The computer industry is an extension or outgrowth of the electrical tabulating industry. Electrical tabulating machines are devices for recording on a unit basis, and automatically classifying, computing and printing alphabetic and numeric accounting and statistical information by controlled electrical means. IBM was originally organized as the Computer-Tabulating-Recording Co. and from 1911 to 1933 it owned a majority of the capital stock of, and controlled, the Tabulating Machine Company, a corporation organized in 1905 under the laws of the State of New Jersey. During this period IBM operated in the tabulating field through The Tabulating Machine Company, which was merged with IBM in 1933. The tabulating business continued to represent the major product line of IBM until the advent of the electronic computer in the 1950s.

11. In 1932 the United States filed a civil antitrust suit against IBM and Remington Rand, Inc. charging that they had unreasonably restrained and monopolized interstate trade and commerce in tabulating machines and tabulating cards by entering into agreements in which they agreed:

    (a)   to lease only and not sell tabulating machines;

    (b)   to adhere to minimum prices for the rental of tabulating machines as fixed by IBM, and

    (c)   to require customers to purchase their card requirements from the lessor or pay a higher price for the rental of machines.

The agreements between IBM and Remington Rand, Inc. were cancelled in 1934 prior to the trial of that suit, and the issues presented by the agreements were withdrawn from the case. The lease provision requiring the lessees to purchase cards from the lessor was adjudged to be illegal by this Court. (13 F. Supp. 11, affirmed 298 U.S. 131).

12. On January 21, 1952 the United States filed another civil antitrust suit against IBM charging that it had violated Sections 1 and 2 of the

Sherman Act by attempting to monopolize and monopolizing interstate trade and commerce in the tabulating industry. The complaint alleged that IBM owned more than 90% of all the tabulating machines in the United States and manufactured and sold about 90% of all tabulating cards sold in the United States. This suit was terminated by the entry of a consent judgment by this Court on January 25, 1956 (Civil Action 72-344).

13. Although a few experimental computers were assembled during the late 1940's, the general purpose digital computer did not have its beginning until the early 1950's. The first installations of general purpose digital computers were made by Remington Rand, Inc. beginning in 1951. IBM followed with its first general purpose digital computer being produced and delivered near the end of 1952.

14. Remington Rand, Inc., which was later merged with Sperry Corporation to form Sperry Rand Corporation, took the early lead in the development and sale of general purpose digital computers. However, IBM surpassed that company in the sales of such computers by the late 1950's. Both companies' early activities in the general purpose digital computer marketplace were regarded primarily as extensions of their earlier activities in the tabulating industry. The prior customers for the tabulating machinery presented an inherent source of potential users of general purpose digital computers.

15. The computer industry has been one of tremendous growth. By 1955 some 400 computers had been installed in the United States. By 1960 the number of installations approximated 6,000 and by the end of 1967 the number of computer installations exceeded 43,000. In terms of total revenues from the sale or lease of general purpose digital computers, the industry has seen an increase from approximately $600,000,000 in 1961 to in excess of $3,000,000,000 in 1967.

16. IBM's total revenues from the sale or lease of general purpose digital computers in the United States increased from $506,668,000 in 1961 to $2,311,353,000 in 1967. During this period of time IBM's share of total industry revenues of these products varied from approximately 69% to approximately 80%. In 1967 IBM's share of such revenues was approximately 74%. Its nearest competitor in 1967 had revenues of approximately $156,000,000 or 5% of the total.

17. Approximately 76% of the value of all general purpose digital computers shipped in the United States in 1967 were shipped by IBM while its two nearest competitors together accounted for about 8% of such shipments. At the end of the same year, approximately 67% of

the value of all installed general purpose digital computers in the United States was represented by machines that had been manufactured by IBM.

18. IBM manufactures general purpose digital computers at its plants located in Poughkeepsie and Endicott, New York, and manufactures parts, components and subassemblies at numerous other plants in the United States. Such computers and related products are shipped to customers located throughout the United States.

OFFENSES

19. Beginning in or about 1961 and continuing up to and including the date of the filing of this complaint, the defendant has attempted to monopolize and has monopolized the aforesaid interstate trade and commerce in general purpose digital computers in violation of Section 2 of the Sherman Act (15 U.S.C. 2). Said offenses are continuing and will continue unless the relief hereinafter prayed for is granted.

20. Pursuant to and in furtherance of the aforesaid attempt to monopolize and the monopolization, the defendant has pursued a manufacturing and marketing policy that has prevented competing manufacturers of general purpose digital computers from having an adequate opportunity effectively to compete for business in the general purpose digital computer market, and has done, among other acts, the following:

   (a) Maintained a pricing policy whereby it quotes a single price for hardware, software and related support and, thereunder, (i) discriminated among customers by providing certain customers with extensive software and related support in a manner that unreasonably inhibited the entry or growth of competitors; and (ii) limited the development and scope of activities of an independent software and computer support industry as a result of which the ability of its competitors to compete effectively was unreasonably impaired;

   (b) Used its accumulated software and related support to preclude its competitors from effectively competing for various customer accounts;

   (c) Restrained and attempted to restrain competitors from entering or remaining in the general purpose digital computer market by introducing selected computers, with unusually low profit expectations, in those segments of the market where competitors had or appeared likely to have unusual competitive success, and by announcing future production of new models for such markets when it knew that it was unlikely to be able to complete production within the announced time; and

(d)   Dominated the educational market for general purpose digital computers, which was of unusual importance to the growth of competitors both by reason of this market's substantiality and by reason of its ultimate impact on the purchasing decisions in the commercial market, by granting exceptional discriminatory allowances in favor of universities and other educational institutions.

EFFECTS

21. The aforesaid offenses have had, among other things, the following effects:

(a)   The defendant has monopolized and continues to monopolize the general purpose digital computer market in the United States;

(b)   Actual and potential competition in the manufacture and marketing of general purpose digital computers in the United States has been restrained; and

(c)   Competitors of IBM have been improperly deprived of the opportunity to earn competitive profits on their general purpose digital computers and actual and potential competitors have been discouraged from entering or continuing in the business of manufacturing and marketing general purpose digital computers.

PRAYER

WHEREFORE, the plaintiff prays:

1. That the Court adjudge and decree that the defendant has attempted to, and did monopolize interstate trade and commerce in the general purpose digital computer industry in violation of Section 2 of the Sherman Act.

2. That the defendant and all persons, firms, and corporations acting in its behalf or under its direction or control be permanently enjoined from engaging in, carrying out, or renewing any contracts, agreements, practices, or understandings, or claiming any rights thereunder, having the purpose or effect of continuing, reviving, or renewing the aforesaid

violation of the Sherman Act, or any contract, agreement, combination or conspiracy having like or similar purpose or effect.

3. That the defendant hereafter be required to price separately and to offer to sell or lease separately, and to sell or lease separately to any applicant upon such terms and conditions as the Court may direct (a) general purpose digital computers; (b) peripheral equipment; (c) computer software; and (d) other customer support which it manufactures or offers to its customers.

4. That the defendant hereinafter be required to refrain from the use of special allowances, buy-backs of computer time, or research grants, in the sale or lease of any and all general purpose digital computers, peripheral equipment, computer software and other customer support equipment or services which it manufacturers or offers to any of its customers, where the effect of such practices may be unreasonably to inhibit the entry or growth of competitors.

5. That the defendant hereinafter be required to refrain from entering into the production of computer hardware which is not likely to result in returns reasonably related to returns from other computer hardware products sold or leased, or which could be sold or leased, by the defendant.

6. That the defendant hereinafter be required to refrain from the announcement of the development or production of any planned computer hardware or software until such product has been subjected to its normal testing.

7. That the plaintiff have such relief by way of divorcement, divestiture and reorganization with respect to the business and properties of the defendant as the Court may consider necessary or appropriate to dissipate the effects of the defendant's unlawful activities as hereinbefore alleged in this complaint, and to restore competitive conditions to the general purpose digital computer industry.

8. That the plaintiff have such other and further relief as the nature of the case may require and the Court may deem proper in the premises.

9. That the plaintiff recover the costs of this suit.

RAMSEY CLARK
Attorney General

BURTON R. THORMAN

EDWIN M. ZIMMERMAN
Assistant Attorney General

JOSEPH H. WIDMAR

BADDIA J. RASHID

WILLIAM B. SLOWEY

LEWIS BERNSTEIN
Attorneys,
Department of Justice

HAROLD J. BRESSLER
Attorneys,
Department of Justice

Amended Complaint

UNITED STATES DISTRICT COURT

FOR THE SOUTHERN DISTRICT OF NEW YORK

UNITED STATES OF AMERICA,	)	
Plaintiff,	)	
v.	)	Civil Action
INTERNATIONAL BUSINESS MACHINE [*sic*]	)	No. 69 CIV 200
CORPORATION,	)	Filed: 1/17/69
Plaintiff.	)	

AMENDED COMPLAINT

The United States of America, by its attorneys, acting under the direction of the Attorney General of the United States, brings this action against the defendant named herein and complains and alleges as follows:

JURISDICTION AND VENUE

1. This complaint is filed and this action is instituted against the defendant under Section 4 of the Act of Congress of July 2, 1890, as

amended (15 U.S.C. §4) commonly known as the Sherman Act, in order to prevent and restrain the continuing violation by the defendant, as hereinafter alleged, of Section 2 of the Sherman Act (15 U.S.C. §2).

2. Defendant International Business Machines Corporation has offices, transacts business and is found within the Southern District of New York.

DEFENDANT

3. International Business Machines Corporation, hereinafter referred to as "IBM," is made a defendant herein. IBM was organized under the laws of the State of New York in 1911 and assumed its present name in 1924.

4. IBM is the largest manufacturer of information handling systems in the world. It develops, manufactures and markets electronic and punched card data processing machines and systems, as well as electric typewriters, dictation equipment, and related supply items. In 1967 IBM had total revenues of $5,345,291,000 with total assets of $5,598,670,000 and net income of $651,500,000.

5. IBM conducts its worldwide business through 11 divisions and three subsidiaries. The Service Bureau Corporation, wholly-owned by IBM at the time of the filing of the original complaint herein, was transferred to Control Data Corporation in January 1973 as part of the settlement of an antitrust action brought by that company against IBM. Science Research Associates, Inc., acquired by IBM in 1964 and now operated as a wholly-owned subsidiary, develops and markets instructional and guidance materials and a wide variety of intelligence, aptitude and achievement tests. IBM World Trade Corporation, another wholly-owned subsidiary, conducts all of IBM's business, except that of Science Research Associates, Inc., in over 100 countries outside the United States.

TRADE AND COMMERCE

6. As used herein, a computer is an electronic device which processes information as desired by activating electronic impulses in pre-defined sequences. Digital computers, which represent over 95% of all computer sales and leases, are machines which process information which is symbolized by numerals and processed in that form.

7. A computer system, sometimes referred to as an electronic data processing system, consists of a machine or a group of automatically intercommunicating machine units capable of entering, receiving, storing, classifying, computing and/or recording data, which system includes at least one central processing unit and one or more storage facilities, together with various input and output equipment.

8. Computer hardware includes all the physical components used in a computer system. Computer software includes the programming know-how and materials necessary to make the computer hardware operative. Computer support includes all manpower and other assistance necessary to make and keep the computer hardware and software operative.

9. The general purpose digital computer is one which has general commercial application and is offered for sale or lease in standard model configurations. Special purpose digital computers are designed for particularized needs or purposes and are produced for use by a limited number of customers but not made generally available to all customers.

10. The computer industry is an extension or outgrowth of the electrical tabulating industry. Electrical tabulating machines are devices for recording on a unit basis, and automatically classifying, computing and printing alphabetic and numeric accounting and statistical information by controlled electrical means. IBM was originally organized as the Computer-Tabulating-Recording Co. and from 1911 to 1933 it owned a majority of the capital stock of, and controlled, the Tabulating Machine Company, a corporation organized in 1905 under the laws of the State of New Jersey. During this period IBM operated in the tabulating field through The Tabulating Machine Company, which was merged with IBM in 1933. The tabulating business continued to represent the major product line of IBM until the advent of the electronic computer in the 1950s.

11. In 1932 the United States filed a civil antitrust suit against IBM and Remington Rand, Inc. charging that they had unreasonably restrained and monopolized interstate trade and commerce in tabulating machines and tabulating cards by entering into agreements in which they agreed:

  (a) to lease only and not sell tabulating machines;

  (b) to adhere to minimum prices for the rental of tabulating machines as fixed by IBM, and

(c)   to require customers to purchase their card requirements from the lessor or pay a higher price for the rental of machines.

The agreements between IBM and Remington Rand, Inc. were cancelled in 1934 prior to the trial of that suit, and the issues presented by the agreements were withdrawn from the case. The lease provision requiring the lessees to purchase cards from the lessor was adjudged to be illegal by this Court. (13 F. Supp. 11, affirmed 298 U.S. 131).

12. On January 21, 1952 the United States filed another civil antitrust suit against IBM charging that it had violated Sections 1 and 2 of the Sherman Act by attempting to monopolize and monopolizing interstate trade and commerce in the tabulating industry. The complaint alleged that IBM owned more than 90% of all the tabulating machines in the United States and manufactured and sold about 90% of all tabulating cards sold in the United States. This suit was terminated by the entry of a consent judgment by this Court on January 25, 1956 (Civil Action 72-344).

13. Although a few experimental computers were assembled during the late 1940s, the general purpose digital computer did not have its beginning until the early 1950's. The first installations of general purpose digital computers were made by Remington Rand, Inc. beginning in 1951. IBM followed with its first general purpose digital computer being produced and delivered near the end of 1952.

14. Remington Rand, Inc., which was later merged with Sperry Corporation to form Sperry Rand Corporation, took the early lead in the development and sale of general purpose digital computers. However, IBM surpassed that company in the sales of such computers by the late 1950's. Both companies' early activities in the general purpose digital computer marketplace were regarded primarily as extensions of their earlier activites in the tabulating industry. The prior customers for the tabulating machinery presented an inherent source of potential users of general purpose digital computers.

15. The computer industry has been one of tremendous growth. By 1955 some 400 computers had been installed in the United States. By 1960 the number of installations approximated 6,000 and by the end of 1967 the number of computer installations exceeded 43,000. In terms of total revenues from the sale or lease of general purpose digital computers, the industry has seen an increase from approximately $600,000,000 in 1961 to in excess of $3,000,000,000 in 1967.

16. IBM's total revenues from the sale or lease of general purpose digital computers in the United States increased from $506,668,000 in

1961 to $2,311,353,000 in 1967. During this period of time IBM's share of total industry revenues of these products varied from approximately 69% to approximately 80%. In 1967 IBM's share of such revenues was approximately 74%. Its nearest competitor in 1967 had revenues of approximately $156,000,000 or 5% of the total.

17. Approximately 76% of the value of all general purpose digital computers shipped in the United States in 1967 were shipped by IBM while its two nearest competitors together accounted for about 8% of such shipments. At the end of the same year, approximately 67% of the value of all installed general purpose digital computers in the United States was represented by machines that had been manufactured by IBM.

18. IBM manufactures general purpose digital computers at its plants located in Poughkeepsie and Endicott, New York, and manufactures parts, components and subassemblies at numerous other plants in the United States. Such computers and related products are shipped to customers located throughout the United States.

OFFENSES

19. Beginning in or about 1961 and continuing up to and including the date of the filing of this amended complaint, the defendant has attempted to monopolize and has monopolized the aforesaid interstate trade and commerce in general purpose digital computer systems, in violation of Section 2 of the Sherman Act (15 U.S.C. §2). Said offenses are continuing and will continue unless the relief hereinafter prayed for is granted.

20. Pursuant to and in furtherance of the aforesaid attempt to monopolize and the monopolization, the defendant has pursued a manufacturing and marketing policy that has prevented competing manufacturers of general purpose digital computer systems from having an adequate opportunity effectively to compete for business in the general purpose digital computer systems market, and has done, among other acts, the following:

> (a) Maintained pricing policies, including the quoting of a single price for hardware, software and related support, which (i) discriminated among customers by providing certain customers with extensive software and related support in a manner that unreasonably inhibited the entry or growth of competitors; and (ii) limited the

development and scope of activities of an independent software and computer support industry as a result of which the ability of its competitors to compete effectively was unreasonably impaired;

(b) Used its accumulated software and related support to preclude its competitors from effectively competing for various customer accounts;

(c) Restrained and attempted to restrain competitors from entering or remaining in the general purpose digital computer systems market by introducing selected computer products, with unusually low profit expectations, in those segments of the market where competitors had or appeared likely to have unusual competitive success, and by announcing future production of new models for such markets when it knew that it was unlikely to be able to complete production within the announced time;

(d) Dominated the educational market for general purpose digital computer systems, which was of unusual importance to the growth of competitors both by reason of this market's substantiality and by reason of its ultimate impact on the purchasing decisions in the commercial market, by granting exceptional discriminatory allowances in favor of universities and other educational institutions;

(e) Attempted to monopolize and has monopolized interstate trade and commerce in tape drives and their associated controllers, disk drives and their associated controllers, and add-on memory devices, for attachment to IBM's general purpose electronic digital computer systems for the purpose or with the effect of restraining or attempting to restrain its competitors from entering, remaining or expanding in the market for general purpose electronic digital computer systems or in the submarkets for said peripherals or any of them;

(f) Engaged in various pricing and marketing practices with regard to its peripheral equipment for the purpose or with the effect of restraining or attempting to restrain its competitors from entering, remaining or expanding in the market for general purpose electronic digital computer systems or in the submarkets for said peripheral equipment or any of them; and

(g) Maintained pricing and marketing policies which had the purpose or the effect of creating or maintaining a lease-oriented environment so as to raise the barriers to entry or expansion in the market for general purpose electronic digital computer systems and submarkets thereof, or any of them.

EFFECTS

21. The aforesaid offenses have had, among other things, the following effects:

(a) The defendant has monopolized and continues to monopolize the general purpose digital computer systems market in the United States;

(b) Actual and potential competition in the manufacture and marketing of general purpose digital computer systems, and in submarkets thereof, in the United States has been restrained; and

(c) Competitors of IBM have been improperly deprived of the opportunity to earn competitive profits on their general purpose digital computer systems and actual and potential competitors have been discouraged from entering or continuing in the business of manufacturing and marketing general purpose digital computer systems.

PRAYER

WHEREFORE, the plaintiff prays:

1. That the Court adjudge and decree that the defendant has attempted to, and did monopolize interstate trade and commerce in the general purpose digital computer systems market in violation of Section 2 of the Sherman Act.

2. That the defendant and all persons, firms, and corporations acting in its behalf or under its direction or control be permanently enjoined from engaging in, carrying out, or renewing any contracts, agreements, practices, or understandings, or claiming any rights thereunder, having the purpose or effect of continuing, reviving, or renewing the aforesaid violation of the Sherman Act, or any contract, agreement, combination or conspiracy having like or similar purpose or effect.

3. That the defendant hereafter be required to price separately and to offer to sell or lease separately, and to sell or lease separately to any applicant upon such terms and conditions as the Court may direct (a) general purpose digital computer systems; (b) peripheral equipment;

(c) computer software; and (d) other customer support which it manufactures or offers to its customers.

4. That the defendant hereafter be required to refrain from the use of special allowances, buy-backs of computer time, or research grants, in the sale or lease of any and all general purpose digital computers, peripheral equipment, computer software and other customer support equipment or services which it manufactures or offers to any of its customers, where the effect of such practices may be unreasonably to inhibit the entry or growth of competitors.

5. That the defendant hereafter be required to refrain from entering into the production of computer hardware which is not likely to result in returns reasonably related to returns from other computer hardware products sold or leased, or which could be sold or leased, by the defendant.

6. That the defendant hereafter be required to refrain from the announcement of the development or production of any planned computer hardware or software until such product has been subjected to its normal testing.

7. That the plaintiff have such relief by way of divorcement, divestiture and reorganization with respect to the business and properties of the defendant as the Court may consider necessary or appropriate to dissipate the effects of the defendant's unlawful activities as hereinbefore alleged in this complaint, and to restore competitive conditions to the general purpose electronic digital computer systems market.

8. That the plaintiff have such other and further relief as the nature of the case may require and the Court may deem proper in the premises.

9. That the plaintiff recover the costs of this suit.

RAMSEY CLARK
Attorney General

BURTON R. THORMAN

EDWIN M. ZIMMERMAN
Assistant Attorney General

JOSEPH H. WIDMAR

BADDIA J. RASHID

WILLIAM B. SLOWEY

LEWIS BERNSTEIN	HAROLD J. BRESSLER
Attorneys,	Attorneys,
Department of Justice	Department of Justice

[Note: Despite the fact that the same attorneys purported to sign the amended and original complaints this was not the case. Ramsey Clark, for example, ceased to be attorney general within hours of the filing of the original complaint and had been out of office for several years when his signature was placed on the amended version.]

Stipulation of Dismissal

UNITED STATES DISTRICT COURT

SOUTHERN DISTRICT OF NEW YORK

....

UNITED STATES OF AMERICA, :

Plaintiff,   :

- against -   :   69 Civ. 200

:   (D.N.E.)

INTERNATIONAL BUSINESS   :

MACHINES CORPORATION,   :   STIPULATION OF

Defendant.   :   DISMISSAL

WHEREAS, the Assistant Attorney General in charge of the Antitrust Division and his staff undertook a review of this case in June of 1981; and

WHEREAS, that review has included a study of the trial record and a series of meetings with counsel wherein each of the issues in the case was presented in writing and orally and discussed and analysed at length; and

WHEREAS, that review has now been completed; and

WHEREAS, plaintiff has concluded that the case is without merit and should be dismissed and has so informed the defendant

IT IS HEREBY STIPULATED AND AGREED that this case is dismissed without costs to either side.

January 8, 1982

INTERNATIONAL BUSINESS

MACHINES CORPORATION,

by

_____

Thomas D. Barr

CRAVATH, SWAINE & MOORE

One Chase Manhattan Plaza,

New York, N.Y. 10005

Attorneys for the Defendant

UNITED STATES OF AMERICA

by

_____

William F. Baxter

Assistant Attorney General,

Antitrust Division,

United States Department

of Justice,

Washington, D.C. 20530

Attorneys for the Plaintiff

Lists of Witnesses

Plaintiff's Direct Case

Witness	Identification at time of testimony	Record citations	Comments
Allen, David D.	Vice President, Management Information Systems, CBS; formerly with IBM	Tr. 1534–1619, 15988–15996	Deposition read into transcript
Andreini, Richard C.	Vice President, System Marketing, Intersil, formerly known as AMS	Tr. 46870–49046	
Andrus, William E., Jr.	Program Manager, Engineering and Information Processing Standards, National Bureau of Standards; formerly with IBM	PX 3924 (Tr. 30453–30468)	Deposition read into transcript
Armstrong, Robert W.	Vice President, Marketing, Amdahl; formerly with IBM	PX 3871 (Tr. 16775–16795, 27945–28056) DX 12435	Deposition read into transcript; certain of IBM's counter designations marked as DX
Ashbridge, G. Harry	Vice President, Business and Market Opportunities, Telex	PX 3981, PX 3981A (Tr. 34778–35009)	*Telex* trial testimony read into transcript
Aweida, Jesse I.	President and Chairman of the Board, STC	Tr. 49050–49975	
Beard, Arthur D.	President, Formation; formerly with RCA	Tr. 8446–8748, 8941–9148, 9850–10365	
Beitzel, George B.	General Manager, DP Group, IBM	Tr. 16680–16699	Deposition read into transcript
Binger, James H.	Chairman of the Executive Committee and member of the Board of Directors, Honeywell	Tr. 4487–4881	

Name	Position	Reference	Note
Bloch, Richard D.	Private consultant with Genesis Group, an investment and venture capital concern; formerly with GE and Honeywell	Tr. 7560–8037	
Brooks, Frederick P., Jr.	Professor of Computer Sciences, University of North Carolina; formerly with IBM	PX 3490 PX 3490A (Tr. 22649–22873)	Deposition read into transcript
Brown, Gordon R.	Senior Vice President, Marketing and Planning, Peripheral Products Company, a subsidiary of CDC	Tr. 50977–53394	
Brueck, Robert L.	President and member of the Board of Directors, MRI Systems	Tr. 21996–22298	
Bullen, Richard H.	Consultant; formerly with IBM	Tr. 20470–20492	Deposition read into transcript
Butters, Stephen J.	Institutional Funding Manager, Putnam Management	Tr. 43630–43862, 46369–46697	
Clapp, William M.	Loan Officer, Western Region, Corporate Banking Division, Crocker National Bank	PX 4563A (Tr. 54901–55023)	*Memorex* deposition testimony read into transcript
Cohen, Harvey	President and Chief Executive Officer, International Communications Sciences; formerly with SDS/XDS	Tr. 14425–14744	
Conrad, Anthony L.	President and Chief Executive Officer, RCA	Tr. 13819–14198	
Cooley, Henry E.	Director, Development Staff, Systems Product Division, IBM	PX 3938 (Tr. 31825–31946)	Deposition read into transcript
Currie, F. Rigdon	Director, Special Businesses, Xerox	Tr. 14894–15768	

Witness	Identification at time of testimony	Record citations	Comments
DeSio, Robert W.	Director, High Performance Systems, DP Division, IBM	PX 3819 PX 3881 (Tr. 24437–24933, 30170–30172)	Deposition read into transcript
Eckert, J. Presper	Vice President, UNIVAC Division, Sperry Rand; cofounder, Eckert-Mauchly Computer Co., later acquired by Sperry Rand	Tr. 710–1123	
Enfield, Jerry A.	President, The Computer Software Company	Tr. 19839–21129	
Fassig, Gerard J.	Program Administrator, IBM	PX 3939 (Tr. 31948–32297)	Deposition read into transcript
Faw, Hillary A.	Retired, Assistant Treasurer and Director, Business Practices, IBM (assisting IBM's legal staff)	PX 3549 PX 3873 PX 3873-A (Tr. 16488–16537, 22883–22929, 28278–28291)	Deposition read into transcript
Feigenbaum, Edward	Professor, Computer Science Department, Stanford University	PX 3879 (Tr. 29529–29583) DX 9108	Deposition read into transcript; certain of IBM's counter designations marked as DX
Femmer, Max E.	Corporate Resident Manager, Mountain States, IBM	PX 3941 (Tr. 32970–33003, 33279)	Deposition read into transcript
Fernbach, Sidney	Head of the Computation Department, Lawrence Livermore Laboratory	Tr. 370–709	

Figueroa, Howard G.	Vice President, Management Services, DP Division, IBM	PX 3859 (Tr. 2953–2962, 16094–16127, 27570–27679)	Deposition read into transcript
Folger, Jay D.	Senior Account Marketing Manager, DP Division, IBM	Tr. 1623–1775	Deposition read into transcript
Forese, James J.	Assistant General Manager, Finance, IBM Europe	Tr. 16656–16674 DX 13411	Deposition read into transcript; certain of IBM's counter designations marked as DX
Friedman, Gary B.	Vice Chairman and Executive Vice President, Itel	Tr. 50340–50963	
Gardner, Thomas E.	Member, Memorex Litigation Staff	Tr. 36731–37031, 37221–37497, 38045–38635, 38794–39159	
Gartner, Gideon I.	Oppenheimer & Co.; formerly with IBM	Tr. 3526–3556 DX 13412	Deposition read into transcript; certain of IBM's counter designations marked as DX
Gibson, John W.	President, Components Division, IBM	PX 3489 (Tr. 2280–2283, 2942–2952, 22574–22648)	Deposition read into transcript
Goetz, Martin A.	Senior Vice President and Director, Software Products Division, Applied Data Research	Tr. 17419–19060	
Guzy, D. James	Vice President, CDC; formerly with Memorex	Tr. 32312–32932, 33130–33677, 35936–36084	
Hangen, John J.	Senior Vice President, Corporate Affairs, NCR	Tr. 6230–6547, 10399–10956, 11324–11331	
Hewitt, James M.	Vice President, Product Marketing, IBM	Tr. 2247–2278	Deposition read into transcript

Witness	Identification at time of testimony	Record citations	Comments
Hindle, Winston R., Jr.	Vice President—Group Manager, Digital Equipment Corporation	Tr. 7312–7505	
Hochfeld, Burton M.	Security Analyst, F. Eberstadt and Company; formerly with IBM	PX 3980 (Tr. 34578–34777)	*Telex* trial testimony read into transcript
Horton, Thomas R.	Director, University Relations, IBM	PX 3874 (Tr. 25152, 25461–25483, 25534, 28548–28593)	Deposition read into transcript
Howe, Robert H.	Director, Marketing, Corporate Headquarters, IBM	Tr. 27668	Deposition read into transcript
Hume, Warren C.	Senior Vice President, IBM	PX 3942 (Tr. 1500–1530, 33006–33041)	Deposition read into transcript
Humphrey, Watts S.	Director, Endicott Laboratory, IBM	PX 3878 (Tr. 29194–29199)	Deposition read into transcript
Imershein, Richard E.	Manager, Commercial Analysis Programs, IBM	PX 3861 (Tr. 3516–3525, 27690–27697) DX 13413	Deposition read into transcript; certain of IBM's counter designations marked as DX
Ingersoll, John L.	Manager, Investor Relations, GE	Tr. 8039–8441	
Jackson, Robert S.	Real Estate Evaluator, World Trade, IBM	PX 3649 (Tr. 21364–21365, 23053–23232)	Deposition read into transcript
Jakes, Andrew M.	Vice President, Continental Illinois Bank	Tr. 43877–44153, 49976–50303	
James, Jack	President, Telex Computer Products	PX 3982 (Tr. 35009–35190)	*Telex* trial testimony read into transcript

Name	Position	Exhibit / Transcript	Notes
Jatras, Stephen J.	President, Telex	PX 3983 (Tr. 35191–35287)	*Telex* trial testimony read into transcript
Jones, Gilbert E.	Chairman of the Board, World Trade, IBM	Tr. 16580–16582	Deposition read into transcript
Jones, Reginald H.	Chairman of the Board and Chief Executive Officer, GE	Tr. 8751–8892	
King, Jack H.	Manager, Applications Services Department, Xerox	Tr. 14746–14891	
Kuykendall, Eugene L.	Manager, Market Analysis, IBM	Tr. 3563–3636, 15997–16005 DX 1504	Deposition read into transcript; certain of IBM's counter designations marked as DX
Lacey, John W.	Senior Vice President, Corporate Plans and Development, CDC	Tr. 6552–6872	
La Veau, Phillip J.	Manager, Commercial Analysis, DP Division, IBM	Tr. 3488–3508	Deposition read into transcript
Learson, T. Vincent	Retired, Chairman of the Board, IBM	Tr. 26922–26933, 28381 DX 13414	Deposition read into transcript; certain of IBM's counter designations marked as DX
Lee, Warren	Senior Investment Officer, Bank of America	PX 4264 (Tr. 41695–41775)	Deposition read into transcript
Macdonald, Ray W.	Chairman of the Board and Chief Executive Officer, Burroughs	PX 366 (Tr. 6881–6979, 7531–7558)	Deposition read into transcript
Mather, Winton E.	Marketing Manager, Oakland Public Sector, IBM	PX 3880 (Tr. 29586–29590)	Deposition read into transcript
Maurer, Joseph P.	Manager, Corporate Pricing, IBM	PX 3869 (Tr. 16030–16093)	Deposition read into transcript
McAdams, Alan K.	Associate Professor, Managerial Economics, Cornell University School of Business	Tr. 53311–54155, 58876–69595	Deposition read into transcript

Witness	Identification at time of testimony	Record citations	Comments
McCollister, Edwin S.	Director, Market Development, International Group, Burroughs; formerly RCA Vice President	Tr. 9159–9849, 10958–11617	
McDermott, James P.	Director, Business Evaluation, Corporate Headquarters, IBM	PX 3862 (Tr. 16611–16654, 27724)	Deposition read into transcript
McDonald, Robert E.	President and Chief Operating Officer, Sperry Rand	Tr. 2769–2929, 3733–4080, 4146–4319	
McManus, Frank L.	Manager, Market Research, Corporate Headquarters, IBM	PX 3863 (Tr. 16711, 27740–27746) DX 13415	Deposition read into transcript; certain of IBM's counter designations marked as DX
Metropolis, Nicholas C.	Life Scientist, Theoretical Division, Los Alamos Scientific Laboratory	Tr. 1124–1291	
Morse, Philip M.	Professor Emeritus, Massachusetts Institute of Technology, and member of the Board of Directors, CDC	Tr. 30957–30993	
Navas, John	Member, Memorex Litigation Staff	Tr. 39161–39272, 39432–40392, 41179–41687	
Norris, William C.	Chairman of the Board and Chief Executive Officer, Control Data (CDC)	Tr. 5596–6103	
Oelman, Robert S.	Chairman of the Executive Committee of the Board of Directors, NCR	Tr. 6115–6203	

Opel, John R.	Senior Vice President, IBM (currently IBM's President)	PX 3876 (Tr. 1430–1496, 20593–20600)	Deposition read into transcript
Page, Otis S.	Assistant to Vice President of Marketing, Memorex; formerly with IBM	PX 3943 (Tr. 3024–3039, 33046–33128)	*Telex* deposition testimony read into transcript
Palevsky, Max	Partner, Bart/Palevsky Productions, a motion picture production company; founder of Scientific Data Systems, later acquired by Xerox	Tr. 3119–3283	
Peirce, E. Read	General Auditor, Burroughs	PX 5048E (Tr. 59640–59656, 69537–69546) DX 8193 DX 14506	Deposition read into transcript; certain of IBM's counter designations marked as DX
Perlis, Alan J.	Professor of Computer Science, Yale University; formerly with Carnegie-Mellon	Tr. 1316–1373, 1810–2112	
Pfeiffer, Ralph A.	Corporate Vice President and President, DP Division, IBM	PX 3858 (Tr. 2964–2999, 16006–16021, 27536–27548) DX 13416	Deposition read into transcript; certain of IBM's counter designations marked as DX
Pier, Howard J.	Assistant for Management Systems, DP Division, IBM	Tr. 3042–3085	Deposition read into transcript
Preston, Lee E.	Professor of Economics, University of Maryland; formerly Professor of Economics, SUNY Buffalo	Tr. 71128–71653	

Witness	Identification at time of testimony	Record citations	Comments
Rathe, Gustave H., Jr.	Corporate Resident Manager, South Central States, IBM	PX 3870 (Tr. 27876–27890) DX 12436	Deposition read into transcript; certain of IBM's counter designations marked as DX
Rice, Alvin C.	Executive Vice President, Bank of America and Executive Officer of its World Banking Division	Tr. 45069–45473	
Rizzo, Paul J.	Vice President, Finance and Planning, IBM	PX 5045 (Tr. 59799–59800)	Deposition read into transcript
Robinson, Louis	Director, Standards and Systems Development Division, IBM	PX 3550 (Tr. 3000–3021, 22936–23049)	Deposition read into transcript
Rodgers, Francis G.	Vice President, Marketing, IBM	Tr. 16836–16952	
Rooney, Joseph W.	Executive Vice President, Data Services Group, Itel; formerly with IBM and RCA	Tr. 11684–12696	
Saalfeld, Richard L.	Personnel Director, European, Middle Eastern and African Division, Bank of America	Tr. 44330–44860, 62270–62403	Portion of cross-examination by deposition taken in London
Scherer, Frederick M.	Director, Bureau of Economics, Federal Trade Commission	Tr. 2294–2728	
Schmidt, Robert D.	Executive Vice President, CDC	Tr. 27199–27527	
Scott, Orland M.	Corporate Vice President and President, Field Engineering Division, IBM	Tr. 20496–20504	Deposition read into transcript
Shoemaker, Delbert L.	Chief, Standards Branch, Automated Data and Telecommunications Services, General Services Administration, U.S. Government	Tr. 30685–31172	

Smith, Paul C.	Manager, Financial Operations, RCA Computer Systems	Tr. 14240–14418	
Spangle, Clarence W.	Executive Vice President, Honeywell, and President, Honeywell Information Systems (HIS)	Tr. 4882–5594	
Spitters, Lawrence L.	Former Chairman of the Board, President, and Chief Executive Officer, Memorex	Tr. 42008–42110, 42282–42535, 42813–43186, 54157–54823, 55016–55487	
Strickland, Edward E.	Vice President, Senior Staff Officer, Corporate Growth, CDC	PX 5345 (Tr. 65147–65186)	Deposition read into transcript
Sturges, David M.	Assistant to Vice President of Finance, World Trade, IBM	Tr. 15926–15985, 44235–44238 DX 1592	Deposition read into transcript; certain of IBM's counter designations marked as DX
Teti, Louis J.	Manager of Market Requirements and Special Systems, General Systems Division, IBM	PX 4093 (Tr. 36254–36400)	*Memorex* and *Transamerica* deposition testimony read into transcript
Vaughan, James R.	General Manager, Engineering Services Marketing, CDC	Tr. 21129–21972	
Vilandre, Paul C.	Headquarters Operation, Itel; formerly with IBM	PX 3949 (Tr. 33693–33856)	*Telex* deposition testimony read into transcript
Watson, Thomas J., Jr.	Retired, Chairman of the Board, IBM	PX 3547 PX 3548 PX 3872 PX 3877 (Tr. 16592–16610, 28241–28249, 29043–29045) DX 13417	Deposition read into transcript; certain of IBM's counter designations marked as DX

Witness	Identification at time of testimony	Record citations	Comments
Weil, John W.	Vice President and Chief Technical Officer, Honeywell; formerly Director of Large Systems Research, GE	Tr. 6999–7310	
Weiss, Leonard W.	Professor of Economics, University of Wisconsin	Tr. 69614–71118	
Welke, Lawrence A.	President, International Computer Programs	Tr. 16977–17417, 19180–19650	
Whitcomb, Richard A.	Director, Product Planning, Itel; formerly with IBM	PX 3979 (Tr. 34182–34577)	*Telex* trial testimony read into transcript
Withington, Frederic G.	Senior member of professional staff, Arthur D. Little	Tr. 55493–58841	
Wright, V. Orville	President and Chief Operating Officer, MCI Communications; formerly with IBM, RCA, Xerox, and Amdahl	Tr. 12776–13808	
Wyngarden, H. Dale	District Manager, DP Division, IBM	Tr. 1779–1797, 2135–2198	Deposition read into transcript
Zeman, Morton I.	Corporate Director, Marketing, IBM	PX 3860 (Tr. 27632–27651) DX 13418	Deposition read into transcript; certain of IBM's counter designations marked as DX
Plaintiff's Rebuttal			
Kost, John C.	Director of Administration, IBM Data Processing Division	PX 7477 (85 pages)	Designations from *Transamerica* trial testimony
McAdams, Alan K.	See *Plaintiff's Direct Case*	PX 7409 (1073 pages)	Direct testimony by narrative statement; cross-examination by deposition

McGovern, Patrick J.	President and Chief Executive Officer, IDC	PX 7475 (521 pages)	Designations from *Transamerica* trial testimony
McKie, James W.	See *IBM's Direct Case*	PX 7476 (27 pages)	Designations from *Transamerica* trial testimony
McPherson, Kenneth A.	Senior Market Research Consultant, IDC	PX 7213 (2217 pages)	Direct testimony by narrative statement; cross-examination by deposition
Preston, Lee E.	See *Plaintiff's Direct Case*	PX 7411 (780 pages)	Direct testimony by narrative statement; cross-examination by deposition
Weiss, Leonard W.	See *Plaintiff's Direct Case*	PX 7410 (600 pages)	Direct testimony by narrative statement; cross-examination by deposition
Withington, Frederic G.	See *Plaintiff's Direct Case*	Tr. 112808–112951	

Plaintiff's Surrebuttal

McAdams, Alan K.	See *Plaintiff's Direct Case*	Tr. 114050–114227	Direct testimony both live and by narrative statement

IBM's Direct Case

Witness	Identification at time of testimony	Record citations	Comments
Ahearn, George R.	Manager, Systems Attachment, Los Gatos, IBM	DX 9009 (141 pages)	Designations from *Telex* trial testimony
Aikman, Walter M.	Vice President, Paine Webber	DX 7587 (15 pages)	Formerly on plaintiff's witness list
Akers, John F.	Vice President and Group Executive, DP Marketing Group, IBM	Tr. 96500–98125	
Anderson, William S.	President, NCR	DX 7635 (87 pages)	Formerly on plaintiff's witness list
Bangle, David	Manager, Memory Systems, Telex	DX 4731 (138 pages)	Designations from *Telex* deposition testimony
Barbour, Robert T.	Vice President and Regional Manager, CIT	DX 3895-A (97 pages)	Formerly on plaintiff's witness list
Baumol, William J.	Professor of Economics, Princeton University and New York University	DX 7643 (52 pages) DX 7643-A (9 pages) PX 6677 (48 pages)	
Benscoter, Don L.	Chairman of the Board and Chief Executive Officer, NRG	DX 5929 (106 pages)	Formerly on plaintiff's witness list
Bloch, Erich	Manager, East Fishkill Facility, and Vice President, Data Systems Division, IBM	Tr. 91438–93581	Portion of direct by narrative statement
Borch, Fred J.	Retired, Chairman of the Board and Chief Executive Officer, GE	DX 7259 (27 pages)	Formerly on plaintiff's witness list

Briloff, Abraham J.	Emanuel Saxe Distinguished Professor of Business and Professor, Accounting Department, Bernard M. Baruch College of City University of New York	Tr. 80631–81854	Portion of direct from *Memorex* trial testimony
Brown, H. Dean	Manager of Market Analysis, Zilog, a subsidiary of Exxon Enterprises	Tr. 82941–83904	Portion of direct by narrative statement
Buffett, Warren E.	Chairman, Berkshire-Hathaway; member of the Board of Directors of The Washington Post and various other companies	Tr. 100308–100737	
Calvin, Donald L.	Manager, Production Engineering, Telex	DX 4100 (36 pages)	Designations from *Telex* deposition testimony
Cary, Frank T.	Chairman of the Board, IBM	DX 8054 (Tr. 101323–101495) DX 8075 (Tr. 101497–101579) DX 8077 (Tr. 101581–101892) PX 3875 PX 6619 PX 6621 PX 6652 PX 6654 PX 6655 PX 6656 PX 6658	Designations from *Telex*, *Memorex* and *Transamerica* trial testimony and certain depositions. IBM had intended to call Cary as a live witness but withdrew him after plaintiff served trial subpoena calling for approximately five billion IBM documents for the purpose of preparing for his cross-examination.
Case, Richard P.	Group Director, Advanced Systems, IBM	Tr. 71997–74665, 77965–78684	
Cochlan, Paul T.	Director, Service, Sycor	DX 4101 (34 pages)	Designations from *Telex* deposition testimony

Witness	Identification at time of testimony	Record citations	Comments
Crago, Robert P.	Manager, Advanced Programs, Federal Systems Division, IBM; former Manager of SAGE Program, IBM	Tr. 85952–86269	Portion of direct by narrative statement
Custard, Raymond L.	Vice President, Divisional Management Systems, Westinghouse	DX 4112 (74 pages)	Designations from *Telex* trial testimony
Dallenbach, Robert B.	Director, Sales, Telex	DX 3117 (9 pages)	Designations from *Telex* deposition testimony
Daniel, Richard H.	Senior Vice President and Department Administrator, Security Pacific National Bank	DX 9100 (10 pages)	Formerly on plaintiff's witness list
Davidson, Sidney	Arthur Young Professor of Accounting and Director of Business Research, Graduate School of Business, University of Chicago; and Lecturer in Law, University of Chicago Law School	Tr. 98678–99085, 99127–99311	Portion of direct by narrative statement
Day, Rion G.	Manager, Communications Development, Telex	DX 4734 (67 pages)	Designations from *Telex* deposition testimony
Deacon, Amos R. P., Jr.	President, MDB Systems	DX 7641 (34 pages)	
DuBois, Russell C.	President and Chief Executive Officer, Varadyne Industries; formerly with Data Pathing	IBM's Offer of Proof; Order of 6/5/81	
Dubrowski, Raymond J.	Partner, Price Waterhouse & Co.	Tr. 84197–84587, 84827–84939	Portion of direct by narrative statement. Dubrowski presented an audited compilation of Census II depositions (DX 8224).
Dunlop, Robert B.	Vice President, Manufacturing, Corporate Staff, IBM	Tr. 93596–94791	

Name	Position	Exhibit/Tr.	Notes
Dunwell, Stephen W.	Retired, Engineer and Manager of STRETCH Program, IBM	Tr. 85507–85940	Portion of direct by narrative statement
DuVernay, David E.	Manager, Transportation Leasing and Financing Business, GE Credit	DX 5915 (10 pages)	Formerly on plaintiff's witness list
Egan, Richard J.	Senior Vice President, Manufacturing, Cambridge Memories	DX 9105-A (125 pages)	Formerly on plaintiff's witness list
Evans, Bob O.	Vice President, Engineering Programming and Technology, IBM; former President, Systems Development Division, Federal Systems Division and Systems Communication Division, IBM	Tr. 101031–101307	Portion of direct from *Transamerica* trial testimony
Evans, Thomas L., Jr.	Senior Associate Programmer, Raleigh, IBM	DX 4736 (16 pages)	Designations from *Telex* trial testimony
Findley, Gerald I.	Advisory Programmer, San Jose, IBM	DX 4737 (36 pages)	Designations from *Telex* trial testimony
Fisher, Franklin M.	Professor of Economics, Massachusetts Institute of Technology	DX 14971 (1527 pages) DX 14974 (1585 pages)	Direct testimony by narrative statement; cross-examination by deposition. DX 14971 is a Historical Narrative of the EDP industry prepared jointly by Professors Mancke, McKie, and Fisher.
Forrest, Henry S.	Senior Vice President, Government Relations, CDC	DX 13526-A (707 pages)	
Friend, Phillip A.	Consultant, Quantum Science	DX 7642 (37 pages)	Formerly on plaintiff's witness list
Gomory, Ralph E.	Director, Research, IBM	Tr. 98130–98670	

Witness	Identification at time of testimony	Record citations	Comments
Gruver, Howard L.	Vice President, Engineering Peripheral Equipment, Telex	DX 3099 (43 pages) DX 5155 (337 pages) DX 12687 (21 pages)	Designations from *Telex* deposition testimony
Hague, Merl T.	Manager, Advanced Requirements, World Trade, IBM	DX 4105 (51 pages)	Designations from *Telex* deposition testimony
Hambrecht, William R.	Partner, Hambrecht & Quist	DX 7918 (12 pages)	Formerly on plaintiff's witness list
Hansen, Robert H.	Advertising Specialist, CDC	DX 7636 (5 pages)	
Harris, Thomas I.	President, Optical Research Associates	IBM's Offer of Proof, Order of 6/5/81	
Hart, Donald E.	Head, Computer Science Department, General Motors Research Laboratories	Tr. 80117–80629 81856–81981	
Haughton, Kenneth E.	Manager, Advanced [Disk] File Development, IBM	Tr. 94794–95221	
Heavener, James R.	Manager, Profit Planning and Control, Telex	DX 14643 (8 pages)	Designations from *Telex* trial testimony
Heinzmann, Frank M., Jr.	Vice President, Computer Sciences, Eastern Airlines	DX 5154 (87 pages)	Designations from *Telex* trial testimony
Herzfeld, Valerius E.	Vice President, Business Planning and Development, Sperry Rand	DX 7630 (44 pages)	
Hill, David H.	Manager, Information Systems, General Motors	DX 4110 (79 pages)	Designations from *Telex* trial testimony
Holzer, Nathaniel L.	President and Chairman of the Board, Datawest	DX 7591 (75 pages)	
Hughes, Ernest S., Jr.	Retired, Manager, Technical Operations, Boca Raton, IBM	Tr. 33865–34114, 71888–71995	Direct and part of cross-examination taken in Miami, Florida due to illness; remainder of cross-examination taken by deposition

Hurd, Cuthbert C.	President, Cuthbert Hurd Associates; formerly with IBM	Tr. 86272–87472, 87634–88275	Portion of direct by narrative statement
Ice, Winston E.	Manager, Product Assurance, Telex	DX 4106 (32 pages)	Designations from *Telex* deposition testimony
Jacoby, Neil H.	Professor of Economics, Graduate School of Management, U.C.L.A.	DX 12701-A (153 pages)	
Jones, Desmond	Director, Program Development, Telex	DX 4735 (114 pages)	Designations from *Telex* deposition testimony
Jones, John L.	Vice President, Management Information Services, Southern Railway	Tr. 78685–80032	
Justice, Robert E.	Manager, Printer Systems, Telex	DX 4733 (148 pages)	Designations from *Telex* deposition testimony
Kaysen, Carl	Professor, School of Humanities and Social Science, Massachusetts Institute of Technology	DX 14975 (563 pages)	Direct testimony by narrative statement; cross-examination by deposition
Kevill, John F.	President, Disk Systems; formerly with Telex	DX 4742 (310 pages)	Designations from *Telex* deposition testimony
Knaplund, Paul W.	Vice President, Corporate Headquarters, IBM; former Group Executive, Development Group, IBM	Tr. 90456–91018	Portion of direct by narrative statement
Liptak, Thomas M.	President, General Technology Division, IBM	Tr. 84592–84824	Portion of direct by narrative statement
Mancke, Richard B.	Associate Professor of International Economic Relations, Fletcher School of Law and Diplomacy, Tufts University	DX 14971 (1527 pages) DX 14972 (1636 pages)	Direct testimony by narrative statement; cross-examination by deposition. DX 14971 is a Historical Narrative of the EDP industry prepared jointly by Professors Mancke, McKie, and Fisher.
Mascho, John G.	Former Controller, Telex	DX 4102 (51 pages)	Designations from *Telex* deposition testimony

Witness	Identification at time of testimony	Record citations	Comments
Mauchly, John W.	Cofounder, Eckert-Mauchly Computer Co., later acquired by Sperry Rand	DX 7584 (195 pages)	Formerly on plaintiff's witness list
McCarter, G. Berry	Director, Systems Development, DP Product Group Headquarters, IBM; former head of Product Test, IBM	Tr. 88357–88623	Portion of direct by narrative statement
McColough, C. Peter	Chairman of the Board and Chief Executive Officer, Xerox	PX 5029-A (8 pages) PX 5029-C (6 pages) DX 9103 (26 pages) Tr. 59360–59366, 66725–66728	Plaintiff also offered a small portion of McColough's deposition. Formerly on plaintiff's witness list.
McDowell, William W.	Retired, Resident Vice President, Endicott, IBM	DX 7594 (58 pages)	
McGrew, J. Douglass	Director of Operations, Computing and Telecommunications Services, Union Carbide	Tr. 76345–76521, 77118–80087	Part of McGrew's testimony was taken at Union Carbide's New York facilities
McKee, Donald E.	Member, Corporate Marketing Staff, Xerox	DX 7640 (163 pages) (not in evidence)	The Court reserved on IBM's offer of this deposition. Formerly on plaintiff's witness list.
McKenna, Bernard J.	Manager and Senior Loan Officer, Capital Equipment Financing and Leasing Department, Ford Motor Credit	DX 9099 (27 pages)	Formerly on plaintiff's witness list
McKie, James W.	Professor of Economics, The University of Texas at Austin	DX 14971 (1527 pages) DX 14973 (697 pages)	Direct testimony by narrative statement; cross-examination by deposition. DX 14971 is a Historical Narrative of the EDP industry prepared jointly by Professors Mancke, McKie, and Fisher.

Name	Title/Affiliation	Exhibit	Notes
McNamara, Thomas J.	Director, Data Systems, Honeywell	DX 7639 (102 pages) DX 7639-A (11 pages) PX 6678-A (66 pages)	Formerly on plaintiff's witness list
Meyer, Raymond F.	Senior Consultant, Network Consulting Group, Professional Services Division, CDC	DX 7638 (77 pages) PX 6679-A (48 pages)	Formerly on plaintiff's witness list
Miller, Arjay	Dean, Stanford Graduate School of Business	Tr. 84992–85308	Portion of direct by narrative statement
Morison, T. Lincoln, Jr.	Vice President, First National City Bank of Boston	DX 7589 (59 pages)	Formerly on plaintiff's witness list
Morris, John R.	General Manager, Product and Service Strategy Forecasting, CDC	DX 7637 (48 pages) DX 7637-A (10 pages) PX 6680-A (17 pages)	
Mueller, George E.	President and Chairman of the Board, System Development Corp.	IBM's Offer of Proof, Order of 6/5/81	
Nelson, James R.	Professor of Economics, Amherst College	DX 7644 (18 pages) DX 7644-A (16 pages) PX 6681 (67 pages)	
Nevitt, Peter K.	President, First Chicago Leasing	DX 7585 (17 pages)	Formerly on plaintiff's witness list
Northrop, C. Arthur	Controller, IBM	Tr. 82057–82739	
O'Neill, James J.	Vice President, Data Processing and Communication Services, American Airlines	Tr. 75677–77103	Portion of direct by narrative statement

Witness	Identification at time of testimony	Record citations	Comments
Peltzman, Samuel	Visiting Research Professor, Business Economics, University of Chicago	DX 7645 (38 pages) DX 7645-A (11 pages) PX 6682 (50 pages)	
Perkins, Gordon P.	President and Chairman of the Board, Monolithic Systems	DX 7590 (45 pages)	
Peterman, Neil R.	Independent Consultant and Engineer	Tr. 99340–100300	Portion of direct from *Memorex* trial testimony
Pfeiffer, Jane C.	Chairman of the Board, National Broadcasting Company, and member of the Board of Directors, RCA; former Vice President, IBM	Tr. 85312–85505	Portion of direct by narrative statement
Phillips, Almarin	Professor of Economics and Law, University of Pennsylvania	DX 7646 (62 pages) DX 7646-A (4 pages) PX 6683 (65 pages)	
Pickle, Robert J.	Director, Finance and Administration, Telex	DX 4108 (116 pages)	Designations from *Telex* deposition testimony
Ponton, Mark	Vice President, Marketing, N.Y. Banking Group, First National City Bank	DX 7631 (76 pages)	Formerly on plaintiff's witness list
Powers, Jonathan G.	Director, Financial Analysis, DP Group, IBM	Tr. 95247–96252	Designations from *Memorex* and *Transamerica* trial testimony
Prieto, Anthony	Engineer, Telex	DX 4103 (40 pages)	Designations from *Telex* deposition testimony
Quist, George	Partner, Hambrecht & Quist	DX 7919-A (18 pages)	Formerly on plaintiff's witness list
Rademacher, Hollis W.	Senior Vice President, Continental Illinois Bank	DX 9102 (212 pages)	Formerly on plaintiff's witness list

Name	Position	Exhibits	Notes
Repp, Dennis A.	Assistant Treasurer, Allstate Insurance	DX 7588 (11 pages)	Formerly on plaintiff's witness list
Ritter, James J.	President, Technology Equities	DX 5914 (77 pages)	Formerly on plaintiff's witness list
Robelen, Russell J.	Consultant	DX 7586 (19 pages)	Formerly on plaintiff's witness list
Rosovsky, Henry	Professor of Economics and Dean of the Faculty of Arts & Sciences, Harvard University	Tr. 100742–101003	
Sampson, Ralph	President, Computer Information Systems	DX 7592 (103 pages)	
Sapienza, Samuel R.	Dean, Wharton School, University of Pennsylvania	DX 9393 (235 pages)	
Sells, Raymond T.	Development Engineer, Telex	DX 4104 (87 pages)	Designations from *Telex* deposition testimony
Spain, Thomas A.	Corporate Director, Industry Relations, IBM	Tr. 88714–90284	Portion of direct by narrative statement
Stigler, George	Professor of Economics, University of Chicago	DX 7648 (30 pages) DX 7648-A (7 pages) PX 6684 (41 pages)	
Sullivan, Neal A.	Manager, Management Systems and DP, Rockwell Industries	DX 4111 (19 pages)	Designations from *Telex* trial testimony
Talvola, Michael A.	President, Systems Enhancement Associates	DX 9096 (50 pages)	
Terry, William E.	Vice President and General Manager, Data Products Group, Hewlett-Packard	DX 4113 (58 pages)	Designations from *Telex* trial testimony
Wade, Forrest L.	Engineer, San Jose, IBM	DX 4738 (20 pages)	Designations from *Telex* trial testimony
Walker, Brooks J.	Chairman of the Board, U.S. Leasing International	DX 3906 (67 pages)	Formerly on plaintiff's witness list

Witness	Identification at time of testimony	Record citations	Comments
Walkowicz, Thaddeus T.	Employee, National Aviation and the Rockefeller family	DX 5913 (12 pages)	Formerly on plaintiff's witness list
Welch, James F.	Senior Vice President, Chemical Bank	Tr. 74667–75661	A portion of Welch's direct testimony consisted of his *Telex* trial testimony; part of his testimony was taken at the Chemical Bank facilities
Williamson, James V.	Manager, Manufacturing Operations, Telex	DX 4107 (203 pages)	Designations from *Telex* deposition testimony
Wilmer, Richard K.	Senior Engineer, San Jose, IBM	DX 4739 (46 pages)	Designations from *Telex* trial testimony
Winger, Wayne D.	Manager, Storage Products Planning, Boulder Laboratory, IBM	DX 3098 (26 pages) DX 7619 (101 pages)	Designations from *Telex* trial testimony
Witschey, Walter R. T.	President, The Computer Company	IBM's Offer of Proof, Order of 6/5/81	
Woodward, Harper	Managing Partner, Venrock Associates	DX 7593 (21 pages)	Formerly on plaintiff's witness list
Yang, Harold S.	President, Enhancement Technology; formerly with IBM	DX 4741 (37 pages)	Designations from *Telex* trial testimony
IBM's Surrebuttal			
Fisher, Franklin M.	See *IBM's Direct Case*	DX 15010 (287 pages)	Direct testimony by narrative statement; cross-examination by deposition

IBM's Customer Witnesses

IBM originally intended to call seventy customer witnesses. Plaintiff agreed that if IBM would limit its live testimony to five customer witnesses, it would agree that the remaining sixty-five "would, if called to testify by IBM, testify substantially the same in substance and effect as the five user witnesses called. . ." (stipulation dated March 29, 1978, as amended by stipulation dated August 21, 1978). A list of the sixty-five witnesses whose testimony was so stipulated follows:

John P. Babecki (Nestlé Enterprises)

James F. Barcus, Jr. (Black and Decker Manufacturing)

Dr. Lawrence M. Blau (Hospital for Special Surgery)

Ralph T. Brannan (M. Lowenstein & Son)

Robert A. Bulen (Deere & Company)

James W. Cannon (SAFECO Insurance)

Lee W. Capps (Thermotics)

Dr. James L. Carmon (University System of Georgia)

W. Thomas Castleberry (Micor)

William K. Cool (B. F. Goodrich)

Dr. Pier P. Davoli (Alitalia)

Winson L. DeWitt (Brown & Williamson Tobacco)

Thomas H. Douglas (Southern Pacific Milling)

John C. Emery, Jr. (Emery Air Freight)

Rudolph R. Empric (PPG Industries)

Paul W. Finch (Valley National Bank of Arizona)

Robert F. Finley (Home Federal Savings and Loan Association of San Diego)

George L. Fischer (Seaboard Energy Systems)

Leland W. Fuchs (State of Illinois, Dept. of Transportation)

Norwick R. Goodspeed (People's Savings Bank)

Dr. James L. Grisell (Lafayette Clinic)

William A. Guy (Blue Cross of Southern California)

Don D. Hamachek (St. Francis Hospital Center)

John A. Heald (General Motors)

Frank M. Heinzmann, Jr. (Eastern Airlines)

Ralph D. Henderson (Bertea)

Alan M. Hill (Lawrence Paper)

Robert C. Houk (Lee Way Motor Freight)

John P. Jansky (Globe-Union)

Harold J. Jurgensmeyer (Knight-Ridder Newspapers)

Clarence M. Kelley (Department of Justice)

Roger S. King (Aluminum Company of America)

Grant M. Korth (Ore-Ida Foods)

J. Ralph Leatherman (Hughes Tool)

David C. Lowdon (Stone Container)

Dr. Patrick J. Martin (Xerox)

Charles A. Mays (H. J. Scheirich)

Donald L. McDowell (Vanderbilt University)

Thomas McMillan (National Westminster Bank)

James L. Meagher (S and T Industries)

Bill M. Meroney (Austin American-Statesman)

Kenneth Moosman (Management Systems)

Jack Moseley (United States Fidelity and Guaranty)

Dr. Thomas H. Mott, Jr. (Rutgers)

Angelo J. Musante (Los Angeles Times)

Edward J. Noha (CNA Insurance)

John L. Nold (Indiana University of Pennsylvania)

James W. Parsons (Chicago Bridge and Iron)

Larry P. Polansky (Office of the Court Administrator of Pennsylvania)

Thomas J. Prioreschi (Centennial Real Estate)

Dr. Arthur E. Rappoport (Youngstown Hospital Association)

Dr. Paul P. Reichertz (Mobil Oil)

Donald Schultz (Schultz Gas Service)

Herbert Seidensticker (Combustion Engineering)

Dr. Dick B. Simmons (Texas A & M University)

Lloyd R. Smith (Dow Chemical)

Wilton L. Smith (Firestone Tire & Rubber)

A. Ray Speer (Compac Services)

Per Svenonius (The Swedish Agency for Administrative Development Fack)

Terril D. Taft (Fred Ruepling Leather)

Robert E. Umbaugh (Southern California Edison)

Joe D. Weller (Capitol Federal Savings & Loan)

Paul O. Wierk (Northrop)

Floyd M. Wilkerson (Trans World Airlines)

Francis W. Winn (Computer Language Research)

Government Agency Witnesses

As part of its direct case, IBM offered 97 depositions of employees of government agencies. A tabular list of the deponents, their titles, and their agencies follows:

Deponent	Title	Affiliation
J. P. Abbadessa (DX 5404)	Assistant General Manager & Controller	Atomic Energy Commission
C. L. Allen (DX 5637)	Manager of Computer Operations, Computer Science Division, Union Carbide Corporation/ Nuclear Division	Atomic Energy Commission
T. B. Andrews, Jr. (DX 5418)	Associate Chief of the Analysis and Computation Division	NASA Langley Research Center
Dr. D. D. Aufenkamp (DX 5655)	Head, Computer Applications and Research Section of the Computer Research Division	National Science Foundation
A. E. Beutel (DX 5413)	Head, Computer Sciences Department	Naval Electronics Laboratory Center
J. E. Black (DX 7529)	Chief of the Electronics Branch, Data Collection Division	Army White Sands Missile Range
Col. J. H. Blakelock (DX 5406)	Director of the Computer Center, Aeronautical Systems Division	Air Force Systems Command
A. M. Blaso (DX 5647)	Acting Director, Logistics Data Management Division, Office of Standards and Quality Control	General Services Administration
A. G. Blue (DX 5644)	Assistant to the Director, Information Processing Techniques Office	Department of Defense Advanced Research Projects Agency
D. A. Bowers (DX 5414)	Head, Technical Liaison and Support Division	Navy ADPE Selection Office
R. J. Brachman (DX 7521)	Chief, Fire Direction and Diagnostic Systems Division	Army Frankford Arsenal
F. W. Brennan (DX 5648)	Deputy Director of the Operations Support Division	General Services Administration
L. G. Bright (DX 9072)	Director of Research Support	NASA Ames Research Center
R. S. Brodsky (DX 5638)	Assistant Director of the Division of Naval Reactors for Reactor Safety and Computation	Atomic Energy Commission

Deponent	Title	Affiliation
R. P. Brown (DX 5409)	General Engineer	Ballistics Missile Defense Program Office
Dr. R. H. Bruns (DX 5652)	Division Chief, Computer Systems Division	NASA Kennedy Space Center
P. J. Budd (DX 5425)	Chief of the Data Management Directorate	Veterans Administration
Dr. H. P. Carter (DX 5405)	Manager of the Computer Sciences Division, Union Carbide Corporation/ Nuclear Division	Atomic Energy Commission
R. S. Cook (DX 5649)	Director of the Management Information Systems Division	General Services Administration
D. A. Crone (DX 9071)	Deputy Director of the ADP Procurement Division	General Services Administration
J. J. Daunt (DX 9069)	Chief of Uniform Crime Reporting Section	Federal Bureau of Investigation
Dr. R. M. Davis (DX 5421)	Director of the Institute for Computer Sciences and Technology	National Bureau of Standards
G. E. Deakins (DX 7254)	Head, Test Data Division	Navy Pacific Missile Range
T. R. Dines (DX 9073)	Chief of the Computation Division	NASA Ames Research Center
R. Doane (DX 7519)	Deputy Commander for Command and Management Systems of the Electronic Systems Division	Air Force Systems Command
J. J. Donegan (DX 5419)	Chief of the Operations Support Computing Division	NASA Goddard Space Flight Center
A. B. Doty, Jr. (DX 5639)	Chief, Simulator and Human Factors Division	Wright-Patterson Air Force Base
R. F. Douglas (DX 3833)	Chief of the Data Processing and Control Branch in the Directorate of Range Operations	Air Force Eastern Test Range
Lt. Commander D. R. Dumke (DX 7255)	Contracts Division Officer of the Supply Department	Naval Air Station, Point Mugu
B. L. Farrar (DX 7523)	Chief, ADP Operations	Defense Communication Agency

Deponent	Title	Affiliation
Dr. D. W. Fife (DX 7537)	Supervisory Computer Systems Analyst and Chief of the Computer Science Section of the Institute for Computer Sciences and Technology	National Bureau of Standards
W. W. Francis (DX 5416)	Director, Information Systems Office	Department of State
H. Frazier (DX 5423)	Executive Assistant to the Director, Geophysical Fluid Dynamics Laboratory	National Oceanic and Atmospheric Administration
G. Friedman (DX 7539)	Assistant Bureau Director	Social Security Administration
Col. G. R. Fullerton (DX 5410)	Commander	Army Computer Systems Support & Evaluation Command
E. Gold (DX 6257)	Director of the ADP Procurement Division	General Services Administration
D. T. J. Green (DX 7526)	Head, Amphibious and Mine Warfare Analysis Division	Naval Weapons Laboratory
W. E. Hanna, Jr. (DX 5656)	Director of the Bureau of Data Processing	Social Security Administration
Col. W. W. Higgins (DX 9067)	Deputy Comptroller for Data Automation	Office of the Assistant Secretary of Defense
G. N. Hiniker (DX 5834)	Chief of the Leaseback Branch, Automated Data Management Services	General Services Administration
Dr. G. Hintze (DX 5642)	Director of Flight Simulation Laboratory	Army White Sands Missile Range
T. A. Holden (DX 5650)	Chief of the Excess Equipment Utilization Branch	General Services Administration
S. Jeffery (DX 9077)	Chief of the Systems and Software Division of the Institute for Computer Science and Technology	National Bureau of Standards
R. W. Johnson (DX 5646)	Chief of the Data Systems Division	United States Coast Guard
L. A. Koschmeder (DX 7533)	OAO Mission Operations Manager	NASA Goddard Space Flight Center
C. C. Kraft, Jr. (DX 7530)	Director of the Johnson Space Center	National Aeronautics and Space Administration
W. R. Lawrence (DX 5412)	Chief of Operations of the Surplus Property Utilization Program	Department of Health, Education and Welfare

Deponent	Title	Affiliation
R. E. Lealman, Jr. (DX 7258)	Chief of the Electrical Guidance and Control Systems Division, Launch Vehicle Operations	NASA Kennedy Space Center
R. H. Levine (DX 7524)	Associate Director, Defense Communications Engineering Center	Department of Defense Communications Agency
Capt. T. R. Luce (DX 6256)	Project Officer at the Directorate of Computer Technology	Air Force Space and Missile Systems Organization
E. J. Mahoney (DX 7528)	Deputy Director of the Division of Financial and General Management Studies	General Accounting Office
B. A. Markey (DX 5651)	Director of Centralized Mail List Services for Region 8	General Services Administration
V. W. Masson, Jr. (DX 13535)	Assistant Head of the Computation Department	Lawrence Livermore Laboratory
J. M. Mayer (DX 5640)	Chief of the Computer Engineering Branch, Navigation and Guidance Division, Avionics Directorate, Aeronautical Systems Division	Air Force Systems Command
Capt. H. F. McCue (DX 5411)	Chief, Automatic Data Processing Systems Center	Defense Intelligence Agency
J. R. Medlock (DX 5835)	Deputy Chief, Checkout Automation and Programming Office	NASA Kennedy Space Center
A. S. Melmed (DX 6258)	Head, Special Projects Section, Office of Computing Activity	National Science Foundation
P. J. Menardi (DX 5651)	Director of Administration for Region 8	General Services Administration
M. K. Morin (DX 7531)	Project Manager of the STAR Project Office	NASA Langley Research Center
Major G. G. Moss (DX 5833)	Chief, Requirements and Applications Division and Director, Teleprocessing	Air Force Communications Service
B. H. Mount, Jr. (DX 7518)	Manager of the Mathematics Section	AEC Bettis Atomic Power Laboratory
J. J. Normile (DX 5415)	Head, Special Projects Division	Navy Automatic Data Processing Equipment Selection Office
D. H. Onks (DX 9068)	Director for ADP Plans and Review, Directorate of Data Automation	Office, Assistant Secretary of Defense, Comptroller

Deponent	Title	Affiliation
R. L. Owen (DX 9074)	Chief of the Networks Engineering Division	NASA Goddard Space Flight Center
R. P. Parten (DX 7532)	Chief of the Spacecraft Software Division, Data Systems and Analysis Directorate	NASA Johnson Space Center
Dr. J. R. Pasta (DX 5424)	Director of the Division of Computer Research	National Science Foundation
J. J. Purcell (DX 7533)	Project Manager of the Orbiting Astronomical Observatory	National Aeronautics and Space Administration
T. N. Pyke, Jr. (DX 9078)	Acting Chief, Computer Networking Section, Computer Systems Engineering Division, Institute for Computer Sciences and Technology	National Bureau of Standards
W. B. Ramsay (DX 9079)	Chief of the Computer Services Division of the Institute of Computer Science and Technology	National Bureau of Standards
N. J. Ream (DX 9070)	Special Assistant to the Secretary of Navy	Navy ADPE Selection Office
R. L. Reeves (DX 5836)	Director, Slidell Computer Complex	NASA Marshall Space Flight Center
C. R. Renninger (DX 5422)	Staff Assistant to the Director of the Institute for Computer Sciences and Technology	National Bureau of Standards
Maj. Gen. J. B. Robbins (DX 5407)	Director & Commander, Directorate of Data Automation	Air Force Data Automation Agency
Dr. L. G. Roberts (DX 7525)	Director, Information Processing Techniques Office	DOD Advanced Research Projects Agency
Dr. M. E. Rose (DX 7538)	Chief of the Mathematics and Analysis Branch	Atomic Energy Commission
M. F. Row (DX 5645)	Chief of the Data Processing Section, Computer Processing Division	Federal Bureau of Investigation
Lt. Col. J. C. Ruth (DX 7520)	Director of the Digital Avionics Information Systems Program of the Avionics Laboratory	Air Force Systems Command
C. F. Ruths (DX 7522)	Deputy Commander	Army Computer Systems Support and Evaluation Command
N. B. Siegel (DX 5654)	Attorney	NASA

Deponent	Title	Affiliation
Dr. J. B. Slaughter (DX 7527)	Head, Information Systems Technology Department	Naval Electronics Laboratory Center
Dr. J. Smagorinsky (DX 5423)	Director of the Geophysical Fluid Dynamics Laboratory	National Oceanic and Atmospheric Administration
M. L. Springer (DX 5417)	Director, Management Information and Data Systems Division Office of Planning & Management	Environmental Protection Agency
J. C. Stokes, Jr. (DX 9075)	Chief, Ground Data Systems Division	NASA Johnson Space Center
H. D. Strong (DX 7534)	Manager, Automatic Data Processing Requirements Office	NASA Jet Propulsion Laboratory
C. N. Swearingen (DX 5653)	Chief, Computers Division, Astrionics Laboratory	NASA Marshall Space Flight Center
J. J. Tallman (DX 5641)	Chief, Computer Branch Electronics Engineering Division	Air Force Communications Service
E. F. Thomas (DX 5408)	Chief, Airborne Instrumentation Engineering and Test Division, Weather Instrumentation System Program Office	Air Force Electronic Systems Division
H. W. Thombs (DX 7256)	Head, Programming Systems Branch	Naval Weapons Laboratory
H. W. Tindall, Jr. (DX 7535)	Director, Data Systems and Analysis Directorate	NASA Johnson Space Center
W. O. Turney (DX 7253)	Chief of the Contracts Office	Army Ballistic Missile Defense Command
E. N. Videan (DX 5420)	Director of Data Systems	NASA Flight Research Center
J. H. Walker, Jr. (DX 7257)	Assistant Head, Technical Applications and Acting Head of the Computer Programming Division for the Warfare Analysis Department	Naval Weapons Laboratory
K. R. Webster (DX 5654)	Chief of the ADP Management Branch, Office of Tracking & Data Acquisition	National Aeronautics and Space Administration
F. S. Wojtalik (DX 9076A)	Chief of the Guidance and Control Division Astrionics Laboratory	NASA Marshall Space Flight Center

Deponent	Title	Affiliation
C. H. Woodling (DX 7536)	Chief of the Flight Simulation Division of the Data Systems and Analysis Directorate	NASA Johnson Space Center
S. G. Wynn (DX 5412)	Director of the Office of Surplus Property Utilization	Department of Health, Education and Welfare
M. B. Zimmerman (DX 5643)	Technical Advisor to the Assistant Vice Chief of Staff for Automation	Army Management Systems Directorate

Except where indicated, all references are to the trial record or briefs in *U.S. v. IBM*. The following abbreviations are used: DX for Defendant's Exhibit; JX for Joint Exhibit; PX for Plaintiff's Exhibit; Tr. for Trial Transcript; Dep. for Deposition. When exhibits are depositions or transcripts from other cases, this is indicated after the exhibit number. Four documents are defendant's exhibits, but they are referenced so often that we do so by name. The first is the Historical Narrative (DX 14971), which was jointly written by Franklin M. Fisher, Richard B. Mancke, and James W. McKie and forms part of the trial testimony. It is a detailed economic history of IBM and the industry as revealed in the voluminous record of the case. (A revised version is being published as Fisher, Mancke, and McKie, *IBM and the U.S. Data Processing Industry: An Economic History*, New York: Praeger, 1983). References to the Historical Narrative serve two purposes. First, they refer to a more detailed discussion of the facts than is desirable or possible to give in the present volume. Second, the Historical Narrative is not itself primary evidence or source material. References to it are in fact to the wealth of evidence cited in its referenced pages, thus avoiding an even larger proliferation of citations in the present volume than would otherwise be necessary.

The Mancke Testimony (DX 14972), the McKie Testimony (DX 14973), and (considerably less often) the Fisher Testimony (DX 14974) are also referenced by name and, to an extent, serve the same purposes as the Historical Narative. These three documents are the narrative statements forming the principal testimony (in addition to the Historical Narrative) of Mancke, McKie, and Fisher as economic witnesses for IBM. Unlike the Historical Narrative, the Fisher, McKie, and Mancke testimonies have not been published (although the present volume has its origin in the Fisher Testimony) but are available as part of the trial record, as are most of the other documents and transcript pages cited.

Chapter 1

1. *United States* v. *International Business Machines Corporation*, Docket number 69 Civ. (DNE) Southern District of New York.

2. See Lester C. Thurow, *New York Times*, October 19, 1980, Section 3, p. 2.

3. 26 Stat. 209 (1890) as amended, 15 U.S.C.A. paragraphs 1–7 (1977).

4. *United States* v. *Standard Oil of New Jersey, et al.*, 173 Fed. 177 (1909), 221 U.S. 1 (1911); *United States* v. *American Tobacco Company*, 221 U.S. 106 (1911).

5. *United States* v. *Aluminum Company of America, et al.*, 148 F. 2d 416 (1945); *United States* v. *United Shoe Machinery Corporation*, 110 F. Supp. 295 (1953), affirmed by the Supreme Court in 347 U.S. 521 (1954).

6. *United States* v. *United States Shoe Machinery Corporation*, 110 F. Supp. 295 (1953) at 341.

7. *United States* v. *Aluminum Company of America, et al.*, 148 F. 2d 416 (1945) at 424.

8. *United States* v. *United States Steel Corporation, et al.*, 251 U.S. 417 (1920) at 451.

9. *United States* v. *Aluminum Company of America, et al.*, 148 F. 2d 416 (1945) at 430.

10. *United States* v. *E. I. duPont de Nemours and Company*, 351 U.S. 377 (1956).

11. Historical Narrative, pp. 41–44.

12. Historical Narrative, pp. 141–147.

13. Historical Narrative, pp. 273, 279–290.

14. Historical Narrative, pp. 351–357, 379–381, 491, 495–498, 619–623.

15. Historical Narrative, pp. 290–96, 678–682.

16. Historical Narrative, pp. 300–301, 327–34, 750–796.

17. Historical Narrative, pp. 323–327.

18. Historical Narrative, pp. 1274–1286, 1338–1340.

19. Historical Narrative, pp. 750–796, 968–973, 975–980, 1043–1064.

20. Historical Narrative, pp. 488–618, 1125–1144.

21. See, for example, Houthakker Dep. Tr. 108–120.

22. Edwin M. Zimmerman, "Memorandum for the Attorney General," received by the attorney general's office on December 23, 1968; see especially pp. 30–31, 44.

23. Judge David Edelstein signed the order reopening discovery on April 25, 1978.

24. *Telex Corporation* v. *IBM*, 510 F. 2d 894 (10 Cir. 1975), 367 F. Supp. 258 (N.D. Okla 1973), *cert. dismissed*, 423 U.S. 802 (1975).

25. *Control Data Corporation* v. *International Business Machines Corporation*, 368 Civ. 312 (Minnesota).

26. *Greyhound Computer Corporation* v. *IBM Corp.*, 559 F. 2d 488 (9th Cir. 1977). Judge Craig's opinion appears in the record at p. 4056 of the transcript.

27. *California Computer Products, Inc.* v. *IBM Corp.*, 613 F. 2d 727 (9th Cir. 1979). Judge McNichols's opinion appears in the record at pp. 10076–11080 of the transcript.

28. *Memorex Corporation* v. *IBM Corp.*, 448 F. Supp. 228 (N.D. Cal. 1978), 458 F. Supp. 423 (N.D. Cal. 1978) and 636 F. 2d (9th Cir. 1980).

29. *Transamerica Computer Corporation* v. *IBM Corp.*, 481 F. Supp. 965 (N.D. Cal. 1979).

30. Charles Dickens, *Bleak House*, 1853 (New York and Toronto: Signet, 1964).

Chapter 2

1. Historical Narrative, pp. 923–943 and 1067–1068; Akers, Tr. 96932.

2. See *U.S.* v. *E.I. duPont de Nemours and Company*, 351 U.S. 377 (1956) at 391.

3. *U.S.* v. *Aluminum Company of America, et al.*, 148 F. 2d 416 (1945) at 430.

4. See, for example, *U.S.* v. *Aluminum Company of America, et al.*, 148 F. 2d 416 (1945) at 430 and *U.S.* v. *United Shoe Machinery Corporation*, 110 F. Supp. 295 (1953) at 297.

5. *U.S.* v. *Aluminum Company of America, et al.*, 148 F. 2d 416 (1945) at 424.

6. This is true on several levels. For a formal treatment as regards the stability of equilibrium, see Franklin M. Fisher, "Stability, Disequilibrium Awareness and the Perception of New Opportunities," *Econometrica*, vol. 49, no. 2 (March 1981), and especially *Disequilibrium Foundations of Equilibrium Economics* (Cambridge, U.K.: Cambridge University Press, 1983).

Chapter 3

1. *U.S.* v. *E. I. duPont de Nemours and Company*, 351 U.S. 377 (1956).

2. Richard A. Posner, *Antitrust Law: An Economic Perspective* (Chicago and London: University of Chicago Press, 1976), pp. 127–128; G. W. Stocking and W. F. Mueller, "The Cellophane Case and the New Competition," *American Economic Review* 45 (March 1955), pp. 29–63, and Carl Kaysen and Donald F. Turner, *Antitrust Policy* (Cambridge, Mass.: Harvard University Press, 1959), p. 102.

3. See, for example, DX 7409A: McAdams Rebuttal Narrative Testimony, pp. 145–149; DX 4710: Weiss Rebuttal Narrative Testimony, pp. 3–7; DX 4711: Preston Rebuttal Narrative Testimony, pp. 1–13.

4. See, for example, F. Lamond, "Minis and Micros—Stealing the Show?" *Datamation*, International Edition, February 1982.

5. Case, Tr. 72016–72019; JX 1, pp. 28–29.

6. Perlis, Tr. 1352, 1811–1814; Historical Narrative, pp. 1341–1521.

7. J. Jones, Tr. 78714; Withington, Tr. 56170–56171; Mancke Testimony, pp. 974–976.

8. Mancke Testimony, pp. 981–982.

9. Historical Narrative, pp. 85–89.

10. See Historical Narrative, pp. 149–153.

11. Historical Narrative, pp. 280–281, 1045–1051, 1522–1525; Mancke Testimony, pp. 964–969, 973–988.

12. Fernbach, Tr. 586–594; DX 1; DX 2; DX 3; DX 4; DX 5; Historical Narrative, pp. 100–101, 1318–1320; Mancke Testimony, pp. 978–985.

13. Historical Narrative, pp. 311–312, 471, 938, 1049–1051, 1318–1320; Mancke Testimony, pp. 417–419.

14. Mancke Testimony, pp. 185–89; A. M. Turing, "On Computable Numbers, With an Application to the Entscheidungs–problem," *Proceedings of the London Mathematical Society*, 1936, pp. 230–265.

15. Case, Tr. 73329; Evans, Tr. 101129; Mancke Testimony, pp. 158–168, 172–175, 183–189, 191–199, 271–287.

16. Historical Narrative, pp. 56–66, 851–865, 1226–1240; Mancke Testimony, pp. 498–505.

17. Norris, Tr. 6065–6066; Withington, Tr. 55521–22, 56772, 56868–70; Historical Narrative, pp. 759–796, 851–865, 1003–1025, 1188–1198, 1226–1240; Mancke Testimony, pp. 360–362, 367–370, 376–378, 385–395, 436–441, 452–456, 498–504, 528–536, 538–540, 543–545, 555–572, 656–661, 689–693.

18. Examples of the record evidence from which this list is derived include Binger, Tr. 4514, 4593–4594, 4933, 5180–5181; Briloff, Tr. 80765; Enfield, Tr. 20143–44; Fernbach, Tr. 539; Goetz, Tr. 17489–90; Hindle, Tr. 7401–7407, 7443–7445; Spain, Tr. 89602–04; Withington, Tr. 55848, 57006, 112931–32; DX 1968, p. 6; DX 2583; DX 2584; DX 2585; DX 2586; DX 2587; DX 2588; DX 2589; DX 2590; DX 2591; DX 2592–A; DX 2594–A; DX 2882; DX 2883; DX 2891; DX 2930; DX 2954; DX 3379; DX 3704, p. 2; DX 3941; DX 4756–A, p. 39; DX 4904; DX 4905; DX 4906; DX 4909; DX 6213; DX 6297; DX 9099, pp. 9, 16, 31; DX 11236; DX 11336; DX 11820; DX 12437; DX 12438; DX 12641; DX 12675; DX 12829; DX 13249; DX 13396; DX 13895; DX 13945; DX 14083; DX 14330. See also evidence cited in Historical Narrative, pp. 1037, 1041.

19. Akers, Tr. 96675–76; Binger, Tr. 4646; Currie, Tr. 15460–61, 15554; Knaplund, Tr. 90495–96; McDonald, Tr. 3922–23; Norris, Tr. 6038.

20. Akers, Tr. 96666–67; J. Jones, Tr. 78714; O'Neill, Tr. 76243; Withington, Tr. 56170–71, 58268–76; Wright, Tr. 13539–41, 13556–57.

21. Akers, Tr. 96666–68; Hansen, Tr. 10413–14; McCollister, Tr. 11357; Rooney, Tr. 12410; Withington, Tr. 56190–93; Wright, Tr. 13540–41, 13556–57; Mancke Testimony, pp. 438–441.

22. Historical Narrative, pp. 759–796, 1003–1025, 1188–1198; Mancke Testimony, pp. 436–441, 657–659.

23. Plaintiff's Pretrial Brief, pp. 2–3, 49, 73; Plaintiff's Opening Statement, Tr. 5, 50.

24. Plaintiff's Pretrial Brief, pp. 49, 73; Plaintiff's Opening Statement, Tr. 54–55.

25. Plaintiff's Pretrial Brief, pp. 50–51, 58, 61–62, 65; Plaintiff's Opening Statement, Tr. 50–51; McAdams, Tr. 53604–5, 63760–61, 63888–89, 64307–8; PX 5452; PX 5455A, pp. 13–15. See paragraph 9 of the original and amended complaints given in the appendix.

26. Plaintiff's Pretrial Brief, pp. 73–75, 327; Plaintiff's Economic Analysis, pp. 65–66; Plaintiff's Statement of Triable Issues, Market Definition, paragraph 9.

27. Plaintiff's Statement of Triable Issues, paragraph 4.

28. Plaintiff's Complaint as amended, pp. 9–10; Statement of Triable Issues, p. 2; see also McAdams, Tr. 66542–46.

29. PX 5455-A, pp. 1–2, 4, 7, 10, 13; DX 2973, pp. 4–5.

30. Withington, Tr. 112937–41.

31. McAdams, Tr. 63526–27, 63540, 63556, 63565–74, 63595; see also Plaintiff's Admissions, Set IV, paragraph 15.3(a)(4).

32. Withington, Tr. 56190, 56192–93; Historical Narrative, pp. 817–826, 946–949.

33. Withington, Tr. 57659–60; Historical Narrative, pp. 389–400, 1304–1308, 1313–1316; Mancke Testimony, pp. 457–463.

34. Historical Narrative, pp. 185, 201, 205, 208, 239, 243–249, 1180–1183.

35. Withington, Tr. 56386–87, 112932, 112937–44; Historical Narrative, pp. 1188–1198.

36. Dunlop, Tr. 93851, 93853, 93873–74, 94166, 94170–72, 94221; Norris Tr. 6018–6019; Withington, Tr. 56233–34; DX 9299; DX 9300; DX 9301; DX 9302; DX 9303; DX 9304; Historical Narrative, pp. 944–952; Mancke Testimony, pp. 477–451, 617–626.

37. Historical Narrative, pp. 885–906, 975–980, 1003–1025, 1053–1058; Mancke Testimony, pp. 442–449.

38. Mancke Testimony, pp, 603–608.

39. Peterman, Tr. 99344, 99444–45, 99725–56; DX 4333, p. 1; DX 4572; DX 5067; DX 8015; DX 8016; DX 8017; DX 8018; DX 8019; DX 8020; DX 8021; DX 8022; DX 8023; DX 8024; DX 8025; DX 8026; DX 8027. Paragraphs 138 and 140 of the Classified NSA Stipulation (DX 3420A) are also relevant to this point.

40. Mancke Testimony, pp. 614–617.

41. Mancke Testimony, pp. 617–626.

42. Mancke Testimony, pp. 170–342.

43. PX 320, p. 13; Mancke Testimony, pp. 183–185, 273–274.

44. Withington, Tr. 55521–22, 56868–69, 56917–18, 56942–46, 56986, 57001, 58655–56, 58809–11, 112863–65, 112882–83; Mancke Testimony, pp. 155–169.

45. McAdams, Tr. 53608.

46. Mancke Testimony, pp. 187–198, 200–208, 225–342.

47. Mancke Testimony, pp. 167–168, 205–206.

48. McAdams, Tr. 58897, 58908.

49. Beard, Tr. 8958–8959, 8990, 9072, 10342–43; Cohen, Tr. 14667–71, 14684–86; Norris, Tr. 5874, 6006; Palevsky, Tr. 3137, 3243–3245, 3254–3256; DX 53; DX 54; DX 978.

50. Withington, Tr. 55734–35.

51. Compare DX 2953, pp. 2–3, and McAdams, Tr. 63552, with Withington, Tr. 112931–32.

52. Eckert, Tr. 875; Spangle, Tr. 4916. Numerous other examples of varying definitions are collected in Mancke Testimony, pp. 355–359.

53. R. Bloch, Tr. 7767; Hindle, Tr. 7457; Mancke Testimony, pp. 360–362.

54. Fernbach, Tr. 672–673; Hindle, Tr. 7415–7417; Mancke Testimony, pp. 376–395.

55. Mancke Testimony, pp. 401–410. See generally Mancke Testimony, pp. 353–410; McKie Testimony, pp. 109–120.

56. Withington, Tr. 56154, 58593, 112910–11; Mancke Testimony, pp. 406–410.

57. DX 165, p. 15.

58. Hindle, Tr. 7315–7316; Peterman, Tr. 100119–20; Mancke Testimony, pp. 454–457.

59. McAdams, Tr. 63873, 64259–60; Historical Narrative, pp. 717, 732–733.

60. McAdams, Tr. 61033, 63798–99, 63820, 69064–67; Withington, Tr. 55524–25; PX 5452, pp. 5–6; see also PX 7409A: McAdams Rebuttal Narrative Testimony, pp. 57–108.

61. Mancke Testimony, pp. 411–431.

62. Withington, Tr. 58167–69, 112827–28, 112910–12, 112931–32, 112941.

63. McAdams, Tr. 53597–611, 63869–75, 63878–79, 64264–68, 64325–26.

64. McAdams, Tr. 53521, 53523 (emphasis added).

65. Withington, Tr. 112916, 112932.

66. Withington, Tr. 112827–28, 112910–12, 112931–32, 112941; Mancke Testimony, pp. 402, 409–410.

67. Plaintiff's Economic Analysis, p. 65; PX 2388, pp. 99, 117; PX 2567, p. 110; PX 3058, p. 3; PX 3064; PX 4315A, p. 16; DX 876; DX 2241; DX 11336; DX 11460; DX 11643; Historical Narrative, pp. 827–830; Mancke Testimony, pp. 528–536.

68. Historical Narrative, pp. 975–979.

69. Withington, Tr. 57002–05, 57027–28, 58630–31; Historical Narrative, pp. 828–830, 918–922.

70. Withington, Tr. 57002–05; PX 2685, p. 57; Historical Narrative, pp. 1027–1030.

71. Plaintiff's Economic Analysis, pp. 65–66.

72. See also Mancke Testimony, pp. 538–540.

73. Plaintiff's Admissions, Set IV, paragraphs 15.1–15.2; Mancke Testimony, pp. 555–557.

74. Historical Narrative, pp. 840–841; Mancke Testimony, p. 566.

75. Norris, Tr. 5698, 5818–5821, 5829–5830.

76. Currie, Tr. 15349, 15606, 15611–12, 15614; see also Rooney, Tr. 12039–40; Mancke Testimony, pp. 557–566.

77. Withington, Tr. 55816–17, 56986, 56992–93; see also Mancke Testimony, pp. 566–570.

78. R. Jones, Tr. 8848; Macdonald, Tr. 6900; PX 2388, p. 117; PX 2437, p. 102; see also Mancke Testimony, pp. 571–572.

79. McAdams, Tr. 60982; Preston, Tr. 71191–92, 71195; Weiss, Tr. 69687–88, 70449–50.

80. See Darius W. Gaskins, Jr., "Alcoa Revisited: The Welfare Implications of a Second–Hand Market," *Journal of Economic Theory* 7 (March 1974), pp. 254–271; and Franklin M. Fisher, "Alcoa Revisited: Comment," *Journal of Economic Theory* 9 (November 1974), pp. 357–359.

81. Withington, Tr. 112938, 112943–44; Historical Narrative, pp. 1194, 1266–1273; Mancke Testimony, pp. 642–647.

82. Mancke Testimony, pp. 631–647.

83. Historical Narrative, pp. 1266–1271.

84. Binger, Tr. 4568; Hindle, Tr. 7387; see also Andreini, Tr. 47618; McCollister, Tr. 11524–25; DX 4242, pp. 5–6.

85. E. Bloch, Tr. 91475–78; Dunlop, Tr. 93636–37, 93647–51, 93839–40; DX 1404A, p. 8 (App. A to JX 38); DX 9157A.

86. Akers, Tr. 96582–83; PX 6467; Mancke Testimony, pp. 898–899.

87. Historical Narrative, pp. 1188–1191.

88. Historical Narrative, pp. 1029–1030, 1036–1037.

89. Plaintiff's Opening Statement, Tr. 48.

90. Historical Narrative, pp. 1289–1291, 1317–1319, 1321–1325.

91. Historical Narrative, pp. 1073–1087, 1098–1103, 1107–1114, 1145–1187, 1321–1337.

92. Historical Narrative, pp. 1003–1026, 1104–1106, 1121–1124, 1188–1240.

93. Historical Narrative, pp. 1138–1139, 1241–1249.

94. Historical Narrative, pp. 1026–1030, 1037–1042, 1417–1418.

95. J. Jones, Tr. 79321.

96. Historical Narrative, pp. 926–952, 1338–1521; McKie Testimony, pp. 71–75, 85–87, 114–116, 148–149.

97. Historical Narrative, pp. 1359–1360, 1412–1428, 1451–1459.

98. Plaintiff's Statement of Triable Issues, pp. 3–4; Plaintiff's Pretrial Brief, p. 88.

Chapter 4

1. Edward S. Mason, "The New Competition," chapter 17 in Edward S. Mason, *Economic Concentration and the Monopoly Problem* (Cambridge, Mass.: Harvard University Press, 1957), pp. 379–380, emphasis in the original.

2. McKie Testimony, p. 287.

3. See McKie Testimony, pp. 221–223, 284–285.

4. See, for example, John W. Verity, "IBM Wins Again," *Datamation*, February 1982, pp. 46–48. This position was also adopted by Gerald Brock, *The U.S. Computer Industry: A Study of Market Power* (Cambridge, Mass.: Ballinger, 1975).

5. DX 3812; DX 8224, Field B.

6. Dubrowski, Tr. 84237–38, 84321–23, 84329; DX 3814; DX 8224, Field C.

7. DX 9042: Jerbasi, Tr. (Telex) 2891–2892; DX 9059–9065.

8. DX 13657, p. 5; DX 13658, p. 4; DX 13659, p. 4; DX 13660, p. 3.

9. DX 13945, pp. 7, 9.

10. Withington, Tr. 112930–31; DX 12690, p. 29.

11. See Mancke Testimony, pp. 696–704; McKie Testimony, pp. 184–205.

12. J. Jones, Tr. 78990; DX 3726.

13. Withington, Tr. 56556–57. See also DX 12690, pp. 35–36.

14. Currie, Tr. 15752–53.

15. Plaintiff's Economic Analysis, pp. 42, 46.

16. PX 5455A; see Mancke Testimony, p. 896.

17. See Preston, Tr. 71211.

18. See Preston, Tr. 71212; Withington, Tr. 57645–47.

19. Akers, Tr. 96932; Mancke Testimony, pp. 883–890.

20. Withington, Tr. 55625, 57184–85, 57189–90.

21. Withington, Tr. 57173–76, 58083; DX 2612B.

22. Weiss, Tr. 69712–13, 70455.

23. Weiss understood this. See Weiss, Tr. 69714–15.

24. Withington, Tr. 55692.

25. Preston, Tr. 71531–35.

26. Preston, Tr. 71376; Withington, Tr. 55692.

27. Withington, Tr. 56412.

28. Withington, Tr. 56520–21.

Chapter 5

1. Such lower R&D costs were testified to by several witnesses (Cary, Tr. 101333–39, 101629–31; Haughton, Tr. 95170; Spitters, Tr. 55286–87; also Navas, Tr. 41395–96).

2. McCollister, Tr. 9697.

3. Hangen, Tr. 10423–24.

4. R. Jones, Tr. 8861, 8865, 8867.

5. Hindle, Tr. 7447–7448; DX 517, p. 2.

6. R. Bloch, Tr. 7761–7762.

7. See also Currie, Tr. 15340 (Xerox); DX 426, pp. 7–8 (Burroughs); DX 467A, p. 10, DX 14088, p. 4, and DX 7635: Anderson dep., Tr. 103–106 (NCR).

8. Further examples are given in Mancke Testimony, pp. 935–944, 955–959.

9. DX 5423: Smagorinsky dep., Tr. 119–120.

10. Hart, Tr. 80227.

11. DX 7642: Friend dep., Tr. 32–33.

12. PX 4830, p. 29.

13. DX 12690, pp. 35–36.

14. J. Jones, Tr. 78990, 78996; DX 3726.

15. Withington, Tr. 56560.

16. Withington, Tr. 56557.

17. DX 1404A (App. A to JX 38).

18. DX 1406.

19. DX 4806.

20. PX 1077, pp. 1–2.

21. PX 1630, p. 2.

22. See, for example, Historical Narrative, pp. 376–384, 750–780, 797–865, 981–1042, 1065–1273.

23. Plaintiff's Pretrial Brief, pp. 240–241.

24. These and many other comparisons can be found in Mancke Testimony, pp. 963–988.

25. See e.g., Beard, Tr. 8493–8494, 10081–82 (RCA); Hangen, Tr. 6350–6351, 10861–62 (NCR); McDonald, Tr. 2883–2884 (Sperry Rand); Norris, Tr. 5653 (CDC); Mancke Testimony, pp. 848–851.

26. Preston, Tr. 71244–48, 71280; Weiss, Tr. 69757–58.

27. See, for example, Beard, Tr. 10092–93; McDonald, Tr. 4188–4190; Norris, Tr. 6039–6040.

28. See Lacey, Tr. 6800–6801; McDonald, Tr. 4207–4208, 4212, 4290; Norris, Tr. 6039.

29. For a nontechnical exposition, see F. M. Fisher, "Multiple Regression in Legal Proceedings," *Columbia Law Review* 80 (May 1980), pp. 702–736. More technical expositions can be found in any standard econometrics text.

30. The so-called "hedonic regression" method was originated by Andrew Court in the 1930s (who applied it to automobiles) and has been developed and applied (generally to automobiles and other consumer durables) by Zvi Griliches and his followers. See, for example, P. Cagan, "Measuring Quality Changes and the Purchasing Power of Money: An Exploratory Study of Automobiles"; P. Dhrymes, "Price and Quality Changes in Consumer Capital Goods: An Empirical Study", and Z. Griliches, "Hedonic Price Indexes for Automobiles: An Economic Analysis of Quality Change" in *Price Indexes and Quality Change*, Z. Griliches, ed. (Cambridge, Mass.: Harvard University Press, 1971).

31. See F. M. Fisher, Z. Griliches, and C. Kaysen, "The Costs of Automobile Model Changes Since 1949," *Journal of Political Economy* 70 (October 1962), pp. 433–451 for an example of such use of regressions also used elsewhere to estimate consumer valuations.

32. Historical Narrative, pp. 281, 285–286, 335–336; Mancke Testimony, pp. 1028–1031, 1069–1071.

33. Historical Narrative, pp. 320–321, 323–324, 327.

34. Akers, Tr. 96675–76; Knaplund, Tr. 90495–98.

35. DX 1404A (App. A to JX 38); DX 2973.

36. Historical Narrative, pp. 412–414.

37. McAdams, Tr. 63900–1; DX 2973.

38. Historical Narrative, pp. 376–384.

39. Data for both IBM and its competitors were taken from the GSA price lists or from *Auerbach Computer Technology Reports: Standard EDP.* Data were for all technically permissible combinations of CPU, memory, console, and power supply. Where the price of the console and power supply was not included in the price of the CPU-memory combination, the price of the least expensive power supply and console that could be legitimately configured with the CPU-memory combination was used, since, where such prices are not separately stated, it is generally evident that the least expensive versions are used, with more expensive versions being optional features. Lease prices were used with separately stated maintenance charges for Univac in 1968 added on. IBM engineers reviewed the configurations and the data and supplied occasional missing information.

40. The results for the other regressions and the corresponding price/performance comparisons can be found in DX 14943. There are also two addition times given in separate issues of *Auerbach* for the 360/75, but the difference between them is very small. The results reported use the later estimate; use of the earlier estimate barely affects the third significant digit in the results.

41. In the case of the CPU-memory transfer rate, the BUS variable understates the transfer rate of the CDC 6600. See *Auerbach Standard EDP Reports* (10/68), pp. 264:011.100, 264:051.100.

42. The price cuts were calculated from prices from the GSA price lists for fiscal 1965 (as of mid-1965) and fiscal 1966 (as of mid-1966). See also Historical Narrative, pp. 379–380.

43. DX 1525.

44. See Historical Narrative, pp. 379–381.

45. Beard, Tr. 10103–05; McCollister, Tr. 9646, 9724–9725, 9729.

46. Mancke Testimony, pp. 913–918.

47. Knaplund, Tr. 90475–76, 90489, 90503–05; PX 1099A, p. 1.

48. Withington, Tr. 56591–92; PX 4829, p. 16.

Chapter 6

1. DX 8224.

2. See Historical Narrative, pp. 1069, 1073, 1081, 1088, 1098, 1104, 1107, 1115, 1149–1150, 1160–1161, 1166–1167, 1172, 1175, 1180, 1186–1187, 1189–1191, 1200, 1208 and sources cited therein; see also record evidence cited in Mancke Testimony, pp. 705–740; McKie Testimony, pp. 242–183.

3. Historical Narrative, pp. 923–926, 1067–1068; Mancke Testimony, pp. 696–699; McKie Testimony, pp. 238–283.

4. DX 7528: Mahoney dep., Tr. 158; DX 12690, p. 17; DX 12291, p. 9; DX 14491, p. 14.

5. See evidence cited in Historical Narrative, pp. 750–796.

6. See, for example, J. Jones, Tr. 79325; DX 467A, pp. 7–8, 10.

7. Withington, Tr. 56637–38, 112946.

8. See, for example, Historical Narrative, pp. 1118–1191 (Amdahl); 1022–1025 (AMS); pp. 671–90 (CDC); 1228–1231 (Cincom); 1149–1159 (Data General); 1184–1187 (Datapoint); 989–992 (DEC); 819–821 (Greyhound); 1098–1103 (Hewlett-Packard); 1200–1203 (Intel); 767–775, 1016–1021 (Memorex); 1203–08 (National Semiconductor); 1195–1198 (Paradyne); 691–712 (SDS); 1011–1015, 1121–1122 (STC); 762–765, 1003–1011 (Telex); 1175–1179 (Wang).

9. See generally, evidence cited in Historical Narrative, pp. 750, 797, 823, 1226–1240.

10. See, for example, Historical Narrative, pp. 1188 (Amdahl); 775 (ISS); 241 (CDC); 691–692 (SDS); 1011–12 (STC).

11. See evidence collected in the Historical Narrative, pp. 1338–1520.

12. See, for example, evidence cited in the Historical Narrative, pp. 17–20 (ERA/U.S. Government); 203–205 (GE/Bank of America), 213 (Electrodata/Allstate Insurance); 764 (Telex/DuPont).

13. Withington, Tr. 56144–56, 56161–62, 56164, 58167–68, 58257–58, 58593, 112931–32. The history and growth of these firms is described in the Historical Narrative, pp. 981–985, 989–995, 1000–1002, 1098–1103, 1107–1114, 1145–1159, 1184–1187, 1258–1267 and the Mancke Testimony, pp. 696–750.

14. Withington, Tr. 112912, 112932, 112941.

15. McAdams, Tr. 53560–61; Weiss, Tr. 69720–25, 69728–29; see also Preston, Tr. 71241–43.

16. See Joe S. Bain, *Barriers to New Competition* (Cambridge, Mass.: Harvard University Press, 1956), pp. 53–113. But see George J. Stigler, *The Organization of Industry* (Homewood, Ill.: Richard D. Irwin, Inc., 1968), pp. 67–70; William J. Baumol, John C. Panzar, and Robert D. Willig, *Contestable Markets and the Theory of Industrial Structure* (New York: Harcourt Brace Jovanovich, 1982).

17. DX 12308, p. 31; DX 12310, p. 5; DX 13886, p. 1; Historical Narrative, p. 1149.

18. DX 14219, pp. 36–37; Historical Narrative, p. 1160.

19. DX 12395, p. 31; Historical Narrative, p. 1180.

20. DX 12395, p. 23.

21. See evidence cited in Historical Narrative, pp. 750, 797, 823, 1126–1140.

22. McAdams, Tr. 53560–61; Preston, Tr. 71240–44; Weiss, Tr. 69722–25, 69730.

23. R. Bloch, Tr. 7636–7637, 8024–8025.

24. Rooney, Tr. 12380–83; see also Rooney, Tr. 11854.

25. McCollister, Tr. 11157–58.

26. Cohen, Tr. 14464–65, 14470–71; Currie, Tr. 15082, 15095, 15301.

27. Plaintiff's Pretrial Brief, p. 157.

28. See McAdams, Tr. 53523–24, 53560–61, 53585–87; Weiss, Tr. 69737–38.

29. Weiss and Scherer noted this. See Weiss, Tr. 70543; Scherer, Tr. 2336.

30. McAdams, Tr. 53585–87; Weiss, Tr. 69736–39, 70520–33, 70535–36, 70543–44; Withington, Tr. 55962–66. See Historical Narrative, pp. 543–546, 606–618 for the facts regarding the losses of GE and RCA.

31. Withington, Tr. 55735–37, 55961–62, 55996–97, 57096, 57124–27. Other estimates offered by the government to show the capital required for entry into the production of

computer systems ranged from $10 million to $50 million to enter "a very limited market area" (PX 4912); $150 million to $500 million for full-line entry (PX 4913); $500 million to $2 billion "to develop and produce a family of general purpose systems" (PX 4912). It is worth noting that S. P. Bowers, author of PX 4913, thought the estimate in PX 4912 was "much too high."

32. McAdams, Tr. 63760–61, 64264; Withington, Tr. 57131–32, 112931–32, 112941; PX 5455A; PX 5456.

33. The record is replete with examples of single product firms successfully expanding their product lines; many such firms are discussed at pp. 718–735 of the Mancke Testimony.

34. Beard, Tr. 8998–9001, 9023–9024, 10301–02; Binger, Tr. 4848; MacDonald, Tr. 6898–6899; McCollister, Tr. 9623, 11361–62; Norris, Tr. 6097–6098; Oelman, Tr. 6145–6147; Palevsky, Tr. 3197–3205; Withington, Tr. 58365–66.

35. Goetz, Tr. 17421; Hindle, Tr. 7350–7351; PX 384, p. 1.

36. Andreini, Tr. 47143–45, 48130–34; Guzy, Tr. 32385–86; Navas, Tr. 41249–52; Mancke Testimony, pp. 795–797.

37. CDC: Norris, Tr. 5804–5806; DX 284, p. 7. See also DX 296 and Historical Narrative, pp. 250, 686–687. Honeywell: Binger, Tr. 4547–4548; Spangle, Tr. 5076–5077, 5080–5081, 5099. Telex: James, Tr. 35050, 35053–54. DEC: Historical Narrative, p. 716.

38. Briloff, Tr. 80705–06, 80720–28, 80980–82; Buffett, Tr. 100346–63; Welke, Tr. 17401–03; DX 9100: Daniel Dep., Tr. 12–14; DX 9106: Rice Dep. Tr 15–21.

39. Plaintiff's Pretrial Brief, pp. 41–42; Plaintiff's Economic Analysis, pp. 33–35; McAdams, Tr. 59787–92.

40. Beard, Tr. 10078–80, 10221; Bloch, Tr. 7675–7676; Hangen, Tr. 6359; McCollister, Tr. 11090; Norris, Tr. 6049–6050; Wright, Tr. 13485–86; JX 3, p. 2; Mancke Testimony, pp. 799–806.

41. Historical Narrative, pp. 872–876.

42. Historical Narrative, pp. 797–798, 826–830.

43. Plaintiff's Pretrial Brief, p. 335.

44. Historical Narrative, pp. 828–830.

45. Plaintiff's Pretrial Brief, p. 158; see also Plaintiff's Opening Statement, Tr. 84–85.

46. See, for example, R. Bloch, Tr. 7873; Enfield, Tr. 19989–93, 20748–49, 20974–75; Hart, Tr. 81933–41; J. Jones, Tr. 79008–10; McCollister, Tr. 11068–69; Withington, Tr. 57006; Mancke Testimony, pp. 829–831.

47. Rooney, Tr. 11824, 12073–75, 12085–94, 12116, 12125–26; Withington, Tr. 112917; Historical Narrative, pp. 304–309, 495–497, 552–553, 619–621, 1188–1194, 1205–1206.

48. King, Tr. 14766–69; Historical Narrative, p. 1138; Mancke Testimony, pp. 840. The NSA Stipulation, DX 3420A (classified), paragraph 259 is of interest here.

49. Hart, Tr. 80193; Withington, Tr. 57677–83; DX 3753, p. 8; Mancke Testimony, pp. 843. Withington also testified that only 10 percent of the users of what he classified as "general purpose" systems in 1971–1977 converted from the computer system of one manufacturer to another, but during this time most users changed their systems in "modular" fashion, thereby avoiding a total system change (Withington, Tr. 56192–94, 57680–83). Moreover, all the users converting within manufacturers were available to other manufacturers for conversion at similar costs.

50. Historical Narrative, pp. 308–309, 619–623.

51. Historical Narrative, pp. 551–553, 1188–1198, 1203–1208.

52. Withington, Tr. 55994–55995; Mancke Testimony, p. 832.

53. Bundling and its history are discussed in detail in the Historical Narrative, pp. 56–68, 451–472, 851–865.

54. Plaintiff's Pretrial Brief, pp. 194, 201; Plaintiff's Economic Analysis, p. 28; McAdams, Tr. 54099; Preston, Tr. 71377–71379.

55. Plaintiff's Pretrial Brief, pp. 220–221.

56. Plaintiff's Pretrial Brief, p. 231; PX 3390.

57. R. Bloch, Tr. 7753–7754; McCollister, Tr. 11041–11043; Norris, Tr. 6058; Welke, Tr. 17380–81, 17343–46; PX 1096, p. 1.

58. Beard, Tr. 10090, 10094, 10098; R. Bloch, Tr. 7577, 7603–7604, 7751–7755; Goetz, Tr. 17500–01; J. Jones, Tr. 78796–97, 78808–09, 78815–17; McCollister, Tr. 11041–43; Norris, Tr. 6066; Spangle, Tr. 5092; Weil, Tr. 7225; Welke, Tr. 19225–28, 19230; DX 1096, pp. 1–2; DX 4088: Schelling dep., Tr. 14–15; DX 8182: Bramson dep., Tr 12–13; Historical Narrative, pp. 451–452.

59. Beard, Tr. 8497; McCollister, Tr. 9649–9653.

60. DX 1172, pp. 1–2; see also Withington, Tr. 56592; DX 4815.

61. PX 4833, p. 9; see also Welke, Tr. 19617–19618.

62. MacDonald, Tr. 6926–6930 (Burroughs); Spangle, Tr. 5086–5089, DX 13712 (Honeywell); DX 65, p. 2, DX 69, pp. 3, 5, DX 98, p. 12 (Univac); DX 366, p. 3, DX 367, p. 19, DX 370, pp. 5, 19 (NCR); Historical Narrative, pp. 467–470.

63. McCollister, Tr. 11047–56, 11061–62, 11369–70; Welke, Tr. 17345, 17371–72, 19225–29, 19336; Withington, Tr. 56782–83.

64. Enfield, Tr. 19908; Welke, Tr. 17007–11, 17069–70, 17372–73.

65. Akers, Tr. 96555–56 (IBM); McCollister, Tr. 9648–9649, 11370–72 (RCA); DX 426, p. 12, DX 427, p. 4 (Burroughs); DX 402, p. 10 (NCR); DX 1096, p. 1.

66. Akers, Tr. 96555–57; Enfield, Tr. 19878–79, 19886–88; Welke, Tr. 17017; DX 4793.

67. Enfield, Tr. 11911–12.

68. See Enfield, Tr. 19862, 20249–50; Welke, Tr. 17373–75.

69. See R. Pfeiffer, Tr. 16019–22; DX 4793.

70. Enfield, Tr. 20740–41, 21073–74; Goetz, Tr. 17476–77; Perlis, Tr. 1347, 1921–1922; 1996–1997; Welke, Tr. 19206–07, 19223, 19592; PX 4829, pp. 27, 29; Historical Narrative, pp. 856–857.

71. DX 9110, pp. 1–2, emphasis added; Historical Narrative, pp. 851–856.

72. Goetz, Tr. 17497; Welke, Tr. 17078–83, 17156–58, 17162–64, 17383–87, 17392–96, 19195, 19216–17, 19349–50, 19354; Withington, Tr. 56790–91; PX 4833, p. 28; DX 1049, p. 5; Historical Narrative, pp. 854–855, 858–859.

73. Welke, Tr. 17166, 17180–81.

74. Currie, Tr. 15387–88; MacDonald, Tr. 6901–6902; Spangle, Tr. 5092–5094; Welke, Tr. 17074, 17389–91.

75. On this point, cf. R. Bloch, Tr. 7605.

76. Historical Narrative, pp. 247–249, 693–696, 717.

77. Historical Narrative, pp. 467–470.

78. Beard, Tr. 8526–8528, 9938, 9944–9947; Enfield, Tr. 19911–12. C. Kaysen, *United States v. United Shoe Machinery Corporation* (Cambridge: Harvard University Press, 1956), especially pp. 141–145.

79. Plaintiff's Opening Statement, Tr. 81–82; Plaintiff's Economic Analysis, pp. 29–30.

80. McCollister, Tr. 11476–77; Norris, Tr. 6069–6070; Vaughan, Tr. 21732–35; Withington, Tr. 55898; Mancke Testimony, pp. 822–823.

81. Vaughan, Tr. 21258–59, 21549–50; Mancke Testimony, pp. 823–825.

82. Vaughan, Tr. 21426–28, 21437–39, 21743–52, 21762–63; DX 60, p. 31; DX 12405, p. 13; Mancke Testimony, pp. 826–828.

83. Withington, Tr. 55990; see also Vaughan, Tr. 21769.

84. Vaughan, Tr. 21183–84, 21456–57.

Chapter 7

Parts of this chapter have appeared as Franklin M. Fisher and John J. McGowan, "On the Misuse of Accounting Rates-of-Return to Infer Monopoly Profits," *American Economic Review* 73 (March 1983).

1. Comprehensive reviews of this literature are given in Leonard Weiss, "The Concentration-Profits Relationship and Antitrust," pp. 184–217 in Harvey J. Goldschmid, H. Michael Mann, and J. Fred Weston, eds., *Industrial Concentration: The New Learning* (Boston: Little, Brown, 1974) and in Frederick M. Scherer, *Industrial Market Structure and Economic Performance* (Chicago: Rand McNally, 1980), pp. 267–295.

2. See, for example, the various industry studies, including that for the computer industry by Alan K. McAdams, in Walter Adams, ed., *The Structure of American Industry* (New York: Macmillan, 1982). See also the discussion in Philip Areeda and Donald F. Turner, *Antitrust Law* (Boston: Little, Brown, 1978), vol. II, pp. 331–341.

3. An excellent summary is given in Ezra Solomon, "Alternative Rate of Return Concepts and Their Implications for Utility Regulation," *Bell Journal of Economics and Management Science* 1 (Spring 1970), pp. 65–81, and the particular problem with which we shall be principally concerned are analyzed in Thomas Stauffer, "The Measurement of Corporate Rates of Return: A Generalized Formulation," *Bell Journal of Economics and Management Science* 2 (Autumn 1971), pp. 434–469. Stauffer attempted to overcome that problem in his testimony on behalf of the Federal Trade Commission in the Ready-to-Eat Cereals Litigation (*re Kellogg, et al.*, FTC Docket 8883). See also J. Leslie Livingstone and Gerald L. Salamon, "Relationship Between the Accounting and the Internal Rate of Return Measures: A Synthesis and Analysis," in J. Leslie Livingstone and Thomas J. Burns, eds., *Income Theory and Rate of Return*, College of Administrative Science, The Ohio State University, 1971.

4. See, for example, F. Modigliani and M. Miller, "The Cost of Capital, Corporation Finance, and the Theory of Investment," *The American Economic Review* 48 (June 1958), pp. 261–297.

5. See McAdams, Tr. 53569, 53576–77; Weiss, Tr. 69865–68.

6. PX 7409A: McAdams Rebuttal Narrative Testimony, pp. 237–240, 267–270, and PX 7409A: McAdams dep., Tr. 115–116, 129–131 and 537–542.

7. McAdams, Tr. 59198–200, 59280–81; Preston, Tr. 71260; Weiss, Tr. 69825.

8. PX 7409A: McAdams dep., Tr. 473–477 contains an excellent statement of McAdams's "iterative process," which he also described elsewhere in his testimony. For testimony about the "confirmatory" rate of evidence about profits, see Weiss, Tr. 70893–94; PX

7409A: McAdams Rebuttal Narrative Testimony, pp. 227–228; PX 7410: Weiss Rebuttal Narrative Testimony, p. 12; PX 7410: Weiss dep., Tr. 407–408, PX 7411: Preston dep., Tr. 647–651.

9. Preston, Tr. 71413, 71631–32; Weiss, Tr. 69867–69, 69876–77, 69891–93, 70588–90, 70645–46; PX 4917; PX 4919–25; PX 5459–66; PX 5470–76; PX 5527; PX 5549; PX 5637–5644.

10. DX 14454; Mancke Testimony, pp. 1020–1022.

11. McAdams, Tr. 59132, 59156.

12. McAdams, Tr. 59156.

13. McAdams, Tr. 59126–27.

14. Akers, Tr. 97131–32, 97992–93; McAdams, Tr. 53584–90, 54117–20, 59786–92; DX 8074, pp. 7, 34; Historical Narrative, pp. 372–373.

15. McAdams, Tr. 59145; PX 4920; PX 4921; PX 4924–4925; PX 5461–5462; PX 5465–5466; PX 5471–5472; PX 5475–5476; PX 5639–5640; PX 5643–5644.

16. PX 7410: Weiss dep., Tr. 192–293; see also Tr. 14–15, 71–84, 290–324.

17. PX 7409A: McAdams Rebuttal Narrative Testimony, p. 231.

Chapter 8

1. For a treatment of predation in the context of innovation, see J. A. Ordover and R. D. Willig, "An Economic Definition of Predation—Pricing and Product Innovation" *Yale Law Journal* 91 (1981), p. 8.

2. There has been extensive debate in the literature over whether the proper test is "average variable cost," "short run marginal cost," "long run marginal cost," or some combination of these, given the circumstances. P. Areeda and D. Turner, "Predatory Pricing and Related Practices Under Section 2 of the Sherman Act," *Harvard Law Review* 88 (1975), p. 697; R. Posner, *Antitrust Law: An Economic Perspective* (Chicago and London: University of Chicago Press, 1976), pp. 184–196; F. M. Scherer, "Predatory Pricing and the Sherman Act: A Comment," *Harvard Law Review* 89 (1976), p. 868; P. Areeda and D. Turner, "Scherer on Predatory Pricing: A Reply," *Harvard Law Review* 89 (1976), p. 891; O. Williamson, "Predatory Pricing: A Strategic and Welfare Analysis," *Yale Law Journal* 87 (1977) p. 284; Note, "Antitrust Law—The Vertical Price Squeeze as Predatory Pricing Under Section 2 of the Sherman Act," *N.C.L. Review* 56 (1978), p. 735; P. Areeda and D. Turner, *Antitrust Law* (Boston: Little, Brown, 1978), vol. III, paragraphs 711–715; P. Areeda and D. Turner, "Williamson on Predatory Pricing," *Yale Law Journal* 87 (1978), p. 1337; P. L. Joskow and A.K. Klevorick, "A Framework for Analyzing Predatory Pricing," *Yale Law Journal* 89 (1979), p. 213. For the present analysis we need not address this issue because the results would be the same whatever cost standard is employed.

3. See Historical Narrative, pp. 401–402.

4. See Historical Narrative, pp. 402–407.

5. Knaplund, Tr. 90519–21; JX 10 paragraphs 1, 7, 8; Historical Narrative, pp. 406–408.

6. McCarter, Tr. 88413; JX 10, paragraphs 30, 33, 35, App. A; DX 3162; DX 3167; DX 3224; DX 3266; Historical Narrative, pp. 409–411.

7. Knaplund, Tr. 91016; DX 1185, p. 4; Historical Narrative, p. 411.

8. Plaintiff's Pretrial Brief, p. 242.

9. Davidson, Tr. 98856–57; Knaplund, Tr. 90524–25, 90529, 90779–80; Norris, Tr. 5963, 5969–5973, 5976–5978; PX 367, pp. 5–6; PX 3071C, p. R-014; DX 298; DX

8224, p. 5. CDC had financial problems in part due to possible misrepresentation by customers as to IBM's offerings.

10. Brooks, Tr. 22718; Faw, Tr. 22929–30; Knaplund, Tr. 90526–27, 90530–31; PX 3071C, pp. R-011, R-014.

11. Knaplund, Tr. 90526–28; Powers, Tr. 95313–14.

12. Knaplund, Tr. 90523–24, 90529–30; JX 10, paragraph 3; PX 1469; DX 3171; DX 5423, Smagorinsky, dep., Tr. 94; DX 7692, p. 3; DX 13526, Forest dep., Tr. 106–107; Historical Narrative, pp. 405–406.

13. Davidson, Tr. 99804–08, 99869–70, 98780–813; Faw, Tr. 22898; Knaplund, Tr. 90527–29; PX 3071C, p. R-014; DX 9041; DX 9431; DX 9438; DX 9439; DX 9440; DX 9441; DX 9442.

14. See Historical Narrative, pp. 409–410.

15. McAdams, Tr. 61519–20.

16. Davidson, Tr. 98808, 99275–86; Knaplund, Tr. 90530–31.

17. See Davidson, Tr. 99275–87.

18. Knaplund, Tr. 90539; Historical Narrative, pp. 412–413.

19. PX 2567, p. 93; Historical Narrative, pp. 414–416.

20. Plaintiff's Pretrial Brief, pp. 254, 257; Plaintiff's Economic Analysis, p. 62.

21. Palevsky, Tr. 3195; DX 45, p. 2; Historical Narrative, pp. 693–712.

22. Knaplund, Tr. 90542; McAdams, Tr. 53651–54; PX 1541, p. 6; PX 3071C, p. 20; DX 1154; DX 9037, pp. 1–3.

23. Historical Narrative, pp. 417–419.

24. PX 1194A, pp. 1–3.

25. PX 2811, pp. R-2–3, emphasis in original.

26. PX 2964A, pp. 5–6, R-28–29.

27. Hart, Tr. 80278–79; Wright, Tr. 12799, 12802–07, 12938; Historical Narrative, pp. 424–428.

28. Hart. Tr. 80293; Wright, Tr. 1825–1826, 12905–08, 12936–37; Historical Narrative, pp. 428–431.

29. Wright, Tr. 12881–82; PX 1427; PX 6209; Historical Narrative, pp. 431–432.

30. PX 2227A, p. 6; Historical Narrative, pp. 432–433, 435.

31. Case, Tr. 73403, 73612–13, 73578–79; Hart, Tr. 80318–19, 81900–01; PX 3473; Historical Narrative, pp. 435–436.

32. See Perlis, Tr. 1963–1969, 2054; Wright, Tr. 13287–92; DX 894.

33. Plaintiff's Pretrial Brief, p. 254; See also McAdams, Tr. 54109–13.

34. R. Jones, Tr. 8867–8868. Historical Narrative, pp. 488–512.

35. Knaplund, Tr. 90538–39, 90915–17, 91012–13; McAdams, Tr. 53654–55; DX 3397A; DX 9082, p. 2.

36. PX 2988, p. R-003; DX 1144; Historical Narrative, pp. 435–436.

37. Cary, Tr. 101808–09.

38. Akers, Tr. 96537–40; Ashbridge, Tr. 34905–07; Historical Narrative, pp. 360–362.

39. McAdams, Tr. 53648. Cf. DX 7647: Scherer Dep., Tr. 154.

40. On the development and announcement of System/360 see, generally, Historical Narrative, pp. 269–367.

41. DX 1404A (App. A to JX 38), expecially pp. 57, 74–91; DX 4773, p. 3; Historical Narrative, pp. 271–277; see also DX 8886, p. 43.

42. Evans, Tr. 101128; Knaplund, Tr. 90471; Historical Narrative, pp. 279–345; Mancke Testimony, p. 1035.

43. PX 1900, p. 9; Historical Narrative, pp. 344–345.

44. DX 1406. See also Historical Narrative, pp. 346–349.

45. Historical Narrative, pp. 351–354.

46. Brooks, Tr. 22782–84; Knaplund, Tr. 90477, 90485–88; DX 1172; DX 2983; DX 4815; Historical Narrative, p. 358.

47. Knaplund, Tr. 90475–77; JX 38, paragraphs 22, 23; Historical Narrative, p. 362.

48. McCarter, Tr. 88362–65, 88368–71, 88405; PX 2126; DX 8994.

49. McCarter, Tr. 88370–71, 88385–87; Historical Narrative, pp. 146–147.

50. McCollister, Tr. 9635–9638; Norris, Tr. 5848; Spangle, Tr. 4997–4998; Weil, Tr. 7009, 7063–7064, 7181–7182; JX 38, paragraph 18; DX 1172, p. 1; Historical Narrative, pp. 358–362.

51. Brooks, Tr. 22787–88; DX 1172, pp. 1–4.

52. Knaplund, Tr. 90552–53; DX 4740: Evans, Tr. (Telex) 3934; DX 9038; Historical Narrative, pp. 279–340, 367–371; Mancke Testimony, pp. 1043–1045.

53. Enfield, Tr. 20294–97; Perlis, Tr. 1347–1348; Historical Narrative, pp. 364–366.

54. PX 307, pp. 2–3; Historical Narrative, pp. 312–314, 366–367, 372.

55. PX 1630, pp. 1–2.

56. See Cary, Tr. 101780–81; Evans, Tr. 101118–19.

57. Plaintiff's Statement of Triable Issues, pp. 13–14.

58. JX 10, paragraphs 4, 5, 8, 12, 13; PX 1034; PX 1045.

59. E. Bloch, Tr. 91920, 91498; Knaplund, Tr. 90520–21, 90530; JX 10, paragraph 1; PX 1150; DX 3420A (classified), paragraphs 387–415, especially paragraphs 403, 411–415.

60. McCarter, Tr. 88409; JX 10, paragraphs 5, 8, 16, 17, 21; DX 1142; DX 3420A (classified), paragraphs 387–415, especially paragraphs 403, 411–415.

61. E. Bloch, Tr. 91940–43; Case, Tr. 22640–41; Gibson, Tr. 73594–95; JX 10, paragraphs 30, 33.

62. Wright, Tr. 12823, 12881–84, 13335–36, 13359.

63. Wright, Tr. 12842, 12879, 13360, 13364–65; PX 1826; DX 898, p. 2; Historical Narrative, pp. 432–433.

64. Weil, Tr. 7232–7234; Wright, Tr. 13375–76, 13673–74; Historical Narrative, pp. 364–366, 433–435, 503–512, 568–570.

65. PX 2126, especially pp. 27, 34–37.

66. JX 3, paragraph 18–19; PX 4436, pp. 2–3; PX 4437, p. 1.

67. Historical Narrative, pp. 807–814.

68. Historical Narrative, p. 808.

69. Spain, Tr. 88767–68; PX 3485, p. 16; PX 4834, p. 43; DX 10495, p. 3; Historical Narrative, pp. 803–804, 1030–1031, 1035–1036.

70. Buffett, Tr. 100359–63; Welke, Tr. 17401–02; Historical Narrative, pp. 800–801, 810–813.

71. Spain, Tr. 88729; PX 4260, pp. 3, 23; PX 4322, p. 11; Historical Narrative, pp. 806, 810.

72. Briloff, Tr. 81081–82; PX 4371, p. 4; Historical Narrative, pp. 814–816.

73. Briloff, Tr. 80724; Davidson, Tr. 98766–67; Historical Narrative, pp. 817, 1031–1032.

74. Spain, Tr. 88754; PX 3105, p. 8; DX 1911; Historical Narrative, pp. 817, 1035.

75. Historical Narrative, p. 1033.

76. JX 4, paragraph 38; DX 9416A, pp. 3, 5.

77. Plaintiff's Pretrial Brief, p. 327; Plaintiff's Economic Analysis, p. 73.

78. Plaintiff's Pretrial Brief, p. 328; McAdams, Tr. 53673, 53708–09.

79. The comparisons are collected in Fisher Testimony, pp. 768–771. Comparison of "raw multipliers" yields similar results.

780 McAdams, Tr. 53673; DX 9416A; Fisher Testimony, pp. 774–777.

81. Rice, Tr. 45082–83, 45248, 45260–61; DX 9416A; DX 9417; Historical Narrative, pp. 809–810, 821–823, 825, 975–976, 1042.

82. PX 2388, p. 117; DX 14201, pp. 1–2; Historical Narrative, pp. 829, 918–920.

83. DX 14479; Historical Narrative, pp. 829, 920–921.

84. PX 2399, p. 4; PX 4608, p. R-001; DX 14201, pp. 2–3; Historical Narrative, pp. 829, 920–921.

85. DX 9416A; DX 9417.

86. Plaintiff's Pretrial Brief, pp. 127–128.

87. Historical Narrative, pp. 1045–1048.

88. DX 1640; Historical Narrative, pp. 1047, 1049–1050.

89. Plaintiff's Economic Analysis, pp. 72–73; McAdams, Tr. 53811–14.

90. PX 3989, pp. 7, 9; DX 9416A.

91. Plaintiff's Pretrial Brief, p. 312; Andreini, Tr. 47062; McAdams, Tr. 53851–52; PX 4352; PX 4530; PX 4531, p. 3.

92. Cary, Tr. 101394–95; PX 3256C, pp. 1–2; PX 4324; PX 4421, p. 2; DX 4740; Evans, Tr. (Telex) 3961–3962; Historical Narrative, pp. 916–917.

93. Historical Narrative, pp. 385–395, 750–796, 878–882.

94. Plaintiff's Pretrial Brief, p. 35; Historical Narrative, pp. 320, 750–753, 757, 759–762, 1340; Mancke Testimony, pp. 432–463.

95. Historical Narrative, pp. 878–906, 965–980, 1043–1066, 1286–1337, 1523–1524.

96. Plaintiff's Statement of Triable Issues, pp. 16–18; Fisher Testimony, pp. 977–1012.

97. JX 38, pp. 988–993; PX 4527, pp. 1–3; PX 4528.

98. Plaintiff's Pretrial Brief, p. 298; see Plaintiff's Statement of Triable Issues, pp. 16–17.

99. Plaintiff's Economic Analysis, pp. 77–78; McAdams, Tr. 53768.

100. Gardner, Tr. 36895–96; PX 4527, pp. 2, 4; DX 4242, p. 8; DX 4342, p. 2; DX 4756B, pp. 102, 109; see also PX 4142.

101. Hurd, Tr. 86412–13; PX 2209, pp. 1, 15, 17; DX 1656; DX 1657; DX 1658; DX 1659; DX 4753.

102. E. Bloch, Tr. 91501–02; Haughton, Tr. 94912–15, 95021–22; Rooney, Tr. 12101–03; PX 2635A, p. 2; PX 3930, pp. R-1, 3–4, 9, 10, 12; PX 4138, pp. 2–3; PX 4139; PX 4149; DX 1453; DX 1454, pp. 1–3; DX 1456; DX 4740: Evans, Tr. (Telex) 4010–4011; Historical Narrative, pp. 903–906.

103. Case, Tr. 73959–63; Cooley, Tr. 31927–28; Gardner, Tr. 38956–59, 39110–11 (but see Tr. 36852); Hangen, Tr. 10480–82, 10574–75; Haughton, Tr. 95020–22; Page, Tr. 33096; Peterman, Tr. 99380–84; Rooney, Tr. 11684, 11688, 11929–30, 12103, 12258–59; Teti, Tr. 36381; Withington, Tr. 58806; PX 3257A; PX 3359A, p. R-002; PX 4215, p. 11; PX 4537; PX 4541; PX 4542; PX 4968; DX 4103: Prieto dep., Tr. 39–40; DX 4731: Bangle dep., Tr. 65–66, 152–154, 279–282; DX 4735: D. Jones dep., Tr. 18; DX 4740: Evans, Tr. (Telex) 3920, 3977–3979, 4023–4024; DX 4742: Kevill dep., Tr. 523–524, 705–706; DX 4753; DX 4754; DX 7630: Herzfeld dep., Tr. 21–22; DX 9395; DX 14027, p. 10; DX 14055, p. 3.

104. Gardner, Tr. 36852.

105. Peterman, Tr. 99431–32; DX 8024; Mancke Testimony, pp. 603–609.

106. Plaintiff's Pretrial Brief, pp. 298–299; see also Plaintiff's Economic Analysis, p. 77; McAdams, Tr. 53774–78.

107. Powers, Tr. 95325–52, 95356–62 95515, 95994; Fassig, Tr. 36454–59; PX 3137; PX 3850, p. 25; DX 1693; DX 9373, p. 2; DX 9374; DX 9375; DX 9386.

108. Haughton, Tr. 95021–24; Powers, Tr. 95351–57; Whitcomb, Tr. 34505–07; PX 3663, p. 5; DX 1452; DX 1457, p. 1; DX 4740: Evans, Tr. (Telex) 4011, 4023–4025.

109. Cohen, Tr. 14667–68; McCollister, Tr. 9816–9820; Navas, Tr. 39532–33, 41448; PX 4468, p. 8; DX 1485; DX 1853; DX 4735: D. Jones, dep., Tr. 3, 104–05, 107; Historical Narrative, pp. 583–591.

110. JX 38, pp. 988–993; PX 3147; PX 3965; PX 4149; PX 4151; PX 4160.

111. Plaintiff's Pretrial Brief, pp. 299–300; Plaintiff's Statement of Triable Issues, pp. 16–17; Dunlop, Tr. 93812–13; Hochfeld, Tr. 34643–44; McAdams, Tr. 64737–64, 66415; Peterman, Tr. 99431–33; Powers, Tr. 95363–72, 95389–90, 95996–97, 96247–48; Whitcomb, Tr. 34505; DX 4740: Evans, Tr. (Telex) 4024–4025; DX 8024; DX 9374, p. 5; DX 9377.

112. Plaintiff's Pretrial Brief, pp. 297, 300; Ashbridge, Tr. 34832; Hochfeld, Tr. 34733–34; James, Tr. 35078; McAdams, Tr. 68577; Powers, Tr. 95406; Rooney, Tr. 11929–30; Whitcomb, Tr. 34321–22; DX 4740: Evans, Tr. (Telex) 4115; DX 7630: Herzfeld dep., Tr. 22–25; DX 7632, p. 4; DX 7897.

113. Aweida, Tr. 49051, 49080, 49091–93; Whitcomb, Tr. 34203; JX 38, pp. 840–841, 932; PX 2333, p. 3; PX 3096A, p. 3; PX 3237A, pp. 7–9, 11–12, 14–17; PX 6644, p. 2; DX 5155: Gruver, dep., Tr. 31, 42; DX 7751, pp. 3–6; DX 7752, p. 1; Historical Narrative, pp. 390–393, 885–890.

114. Plaintiff's Pretrial Brief, p. 303; Plaintiff's Statement of Triable Issues, pp. 16–17; JX 38, pp. 840–841, 932–933; PX 2435A, p. 14; PX 2583, p. 31.

115. Aweida, Tr. 49093–94; JX 38, p. 932; PX 2213A, p. 17; PX 2435A, pp. 19–20; DX 1769, p. 1, DX 4740: Evans, Tr. (Telex) 4142–4143; DX 5155: Gruver, dep., Tr. 38, 40; DX 7698; DX 7710, pp. 2, 9;

116. PX 2480, p. 1; PX 3826C, p. 1; PX 5564; PX 6405, p. 3; see also Plaintiff's Pretrial Brief, pp. 303; Historical Narrative, pp. 886–889.

117. Aweida, Tr. 49617–22; Cooley, Tr. 31942; JX 38, pp. 981–983, 1104–05; PX 4033, pp. 20, 28–29, 32–33; PX 5360; DX 2158; DX 3087, pp. 1, 2, 5, 7, 9; DX 3116, pp.

A, 1, 2, 3, 6, 12, 13, 28; DX 4740: Evans, Tr. (Telex) 4122–4124; Historical Narrative, pp. 891–895.

118. Plaintiff's Pretrial Brief, p. 303; Plaintiff's Statement of Triable Issues, pp. 16–17.

119. Aweida, Tr. 49400; Beard, Tr. 9054; G. Brown, Tr. 51629–30, 51676–77; Case, Tr. 73735–36; Cooley, Tr. 31826, 31940–41; JX 38, pp. 840, 932, 981, 982, 985, 1104–1105; PX 3784B, p. 36; PX 3962, pp. 3, 8; PX 4708A, p. 12; DX 145, pp. 4–8; DX 2110, p. 4; DX 2137; DX 2182, p. 10; DX 2404; DX 2969A, p. 3; DX 3094; DX 3117: Dallenbach dep., Tr. 3, 223; DX 3119, pp. 1–2, 4–5; DX 3538; DX 4201, pp. 1, 6; DX 4226, p. 12; DX 4253, pp. 2, 5–7, 9, 17–22; DX 4267; DX 4268; DX 4421, pp. 1–2; DX 4735: D. Jones, dep., Tr. 139–142; DX 4740: Evans, Tr. (Telex) 4122–4123, 4129–4131, 4135–4143; DX 5155: Gruver dep., Tr. 56, 59–60, 65–68, 70–72, 77, 79, 87–94, 366–368; DX 7619: Winger, Tr. (Telex) 5681, 5698, 5700–5716; Historical Narrative, pp. 890–898, 971–972, 1054–1055.

120. Powers, Tr. 95394; PX 4216, pp. 72–74; DX 7781; DX 13475.

121. PX 4145; PX 4592, p. 2.

122. PX 4529; DX 9405, pp. 860, 865, 1037, 1049, 1054, 1058; DX 12248; DX 14480; DX 14481.

123. Spangle, Tr. 5060; Spitters, Tr. 54423–24; PX 4288, p. 43; PX 4832, p. 10; DX 4112: Custard, Tr. (Telex) 3054–3055.

124. Ashbridge, Tr. 34910–11 (Telex); Aweida, Tr. 49504; G. Brown, Tr. 52600 (CDC Peripherals); G. Brown, Tr. 52613 (Honeywell); Friedman, Tr. 50372–73 (Itel); Hangen, Tr. 6371–6372 (NCR); Macdonald, Tr. 6983 (Burroughs); McDonald, Tr. 3924–3925 (Univac); Norris, Tr. 5862–5863 (CDC); Palevsky, Tr. 3207 (SDS); Rooney, Tr. 12364 (RCA); Spitters, Tr. 54433; Withington, Tr. 55630–33, 55899, 56631; PX 3458, p. 3; PX 4832, p. 10; DX 295; DX 4243, p. 1; DX 4355, p. 1.

125. Cary, Tr. 101364–65, 101373, 101470–71, 101673; Powers, Tr. 95417–20, 95446, 95787–88; Rooney, Tr. 11859; PX 4205, p. 2; PX 4552, pp. 4–5; PX 4834, p. 12; PX 4836, pp. 1, 7; DX 977.

126. Cary, Tr. 101672–73; DX 4349, pp. 12, 27; DX 4355, pp. 7, 8, 27; DX 4381, p. 1.

127. Cary, Tr. 101376–77, 101379, 101678, 101692; Powers, Tr. 95416, 95428–74; PX 3277, pp. 39–40; PX 4122, pp. 1–4; DX 9380; DX 9382; DX 9383; DX 12176.

128. Ashbridge, Tr. 34994–95; Aweida, Tr. 49522; Cohen, Tr. 14426–27, 14645, 14654–56; Conrad, Tr. 13823, 13937–38; Friedman, Tr. 50341, 50443–44; Powers, Tr. 95482; Rooney, Tr. 11861; Saalfield, Tr. 62323–24; PX 3698, pp. 2, 3; PX 4472, p. 14; PX 4476, p. 9; PX 4836, pp. 28–29; DX 977; DX 1545, pp. 1–2; DX 1910; DX 1911; DX 4323, p. 3; DX 4559, p. 1; DX 13426.

129. Plaintiff's Pretrial Brief, pp. 304, 306, 309, 310; Preston, Tr. 71610–11.

130. Powers, Tr. 95474; DX 9381, p. 3; DX 9383, pp. 2, 4.

131. DX 9380, p. 8.

132. See DX 4110: Hill, Tr. (Telex) 3485; DX 4112: Custard, Tr. (Telex) 3053–3054; DX 5154: Heinzmann, Tr. (Telex) 3366–3367.

133. Friedman, Tr. 50572; Spangle, Tr. 5530; PX 4288, p. 43; DX 2223, p. 16; DX 4242, p. 1; DX 4578, p. 4; DX 5139, p. 1.

134. *U.S.* v. *United Shoe Machinery Corporation*, 110 F. Supp. 295 (1953), affirmed by the Supreme Court in 347 U.S. 921 (1954). See C. Kaysen, *U.S.* v. *United Shoe Machinery* (Cambridge, Mass.: Harvard University Press, 1956).

135. McAdams, Tr. 53815–16; DX 1269, p. 8; DX 4756C, pp. 69, 156.

136. Preston, Tr. 71610–11.

137. Withington, Tr. 56631.

138. PX 3303; PX 4845, pp. 1, 4; DX 1671.

139. Plaintiff's Pretrial Brief, p. 309.

140. Cary, Tr. 101700; PX 4752, pp. 8, 53, 55; PX 4845, p. 4; DX 412B, p. 2; DX 685; DX 4107: Williamson dep., Tr. 445–446.

141. Cary, Tr. 101694.

142. DX 14137.

143. Case, Tr. 74033–34, 74120–25; Haughton, Tr. 95017–23; JX 38, pp. 28, 549, 694–695, 813, 971, 988, 1072–1074; PX 3182, p. 3; PX 3204, p. 4; PX 3363, p. 2; PX 3687; PX 4171, p. 27; PX 4173, pp. 1, 5, 8; PX 4530; PX 4531; PX 4533; DX 3651B; Historical Narrative, pp. 332–335.

144. Ashbridge, Tr. 34845–46; G. Brown, Tr. 52421–23; Case, Tr. 74034–36, 74053–54, 74059, 74075–77; Gardner, Tr. 38423–24, 38996, 39028–29; Haughton, Tr. 95023–25, 95030–31, 95039; McAdams, Tr. 65959–60; Navas, Tr. 41601; Peterman, Tr. 99381–84, 99388; 99430; Powers, Tr. 95548; JX 38, pp. 1072–1074; PX 3205, p. 7; PX 3784B, p. 46; PX 4167, pp. 4–5; PX 4174, p. 4; PX 4184, p. 209; PX 4530; PX 4536; PX 4538; PX 4539; PX 4540; DX 1435; DX 1437, pp. 1–3; DX 1482B, p. 9; DX 1490, p. 1; DX 1498, p. 2; DX 1655; DX 3651B; DX 4222, p. 25; DX 4385, pp. 1, 7–8; DX 9362A; DX 12223; DX 12224.

145. Plaintiff's Pretrial Brief, pp. 301–302; Plaintiff's Statement of Triable Issues, pp. 16–17.

146. G. Brown, Tr. 51350–54, 52650–59, 52663–64; McAdams, Tr. 65869–70, 65946, 65969–76; Powers, Tr. 95544–48; PX 3320A; PX 4337, pp. 3–4; DX 1663; DX 2647; DX 9389; DX 13137.

147. PX 3293B, p. 3; PX 4530, p. 1; PX 4531, p. 1; DX 4740: Evans, Tr. (Telex) 4028–4029; Historical Narrative, pp. 1045–1051. See also DX 4345, p. 2; DX 4561, p. 2; DX 4364, p. 2; DX 4445, p. 20.

148. E. Bloch, Tr. 91547; DX 4740: Evans, Tr. (Telex) 3967–68, 3974; DX 9153; DX 9163, p. 20.

149. Plaintiff's Pretrial Brief, p. 312; see also Tr. 70812.

150. Andreini, Tr. 46966–67, 46977, 48714–15, 48774–75, 48779; Beard, Tr. 10126–27; E. Bloch, Tr. 91549–50; G. Brown, Tr. 51902, 52025–28, 52030–32; Case, Tr. 73924–25, 73928–32; Currie, Tr. 15542–43; Eckert, Tr. 882; Fernbach, Tr. 461; Hughes, Tr. 71900; Hurd, Tr. 86613–14, 86617–18; McCollister, Tr. 11187–88; McDonald, Tr. 4051; Rooney, Tr. 12329–31; Schmidt, Tr. 27305; Shoemaker, Tr. 31082; Welch, Tr. 74705; DX 1783, pp. 7, 15, 23; DX 4100: Calvin dep., Tr. 4–6, 178–179; DX 4103: Prieto dep., Tr. 233–234; DX 4107: Williamson dep., Tr. 4, 9–10, 472, 474–475; DX 4113: Terry, Tr. (Telex), 3191, 3296–3297; DX 4731: Bangle dep., Tr. 64–66, 152–154, 159–160, 279, 282; DX 4735: D. Jones dep., Tr. 3, 15; DX 4740: Evans, Tr. (Telex) 3975–3977, 3980; DX 4753; DX 5424: Pasta dep., Tr. 92–93; DX 7590: Perkins dep., Tr. 11–12, 27–34; DX 7630: Herzfeld dep., Tr. 10–20; DX 7639: McNamara dep., Tr. 30; DX 9105A: Egan dep., Tr. 10, 13, 17, 22, 38–39, 100, 114–115; DX 9109A, p. 3.

151. E. Bloch, Tr. 91543, 91547; Rooney, Tr. 12508–10; PX 3175; PX 3293B, p. 4; PX 4505, pp. 2, 4; DX 1667; DX 4740: Evans, Tr. (Telex), 3968, 3982–3984; DX 9153; DX 9163, p. 20.

152. DX 411, pp. 4–5, 9–10; DX 1976, p. 12; Historical Narrative, p. 1313; Fisher Testimony, pp. 978–979, 986–1004, 1009–10; McKie Testimony, p. 179.

153. Plaintiff's Pretrial Brief, p. 312; McAdams, Tr. 53851–52.

154. E. Bloch, Tr. 91551; PX 3187A, pp. R-2, R-3; PX 3293B, p. 3; PX 3385, p. 2; PX 4530; PX 4531; PX 9405, pp. 1048–1049; DX 911, p. 55; DX 1896; DX 4104: Sells dep., Tr. 415–425; DX 9109A, p. 4.

155. McAdams, Tr. 53847, 53996; PX 3187A, pp. R-2, R-3; PX 3980: Hochfeld, Tr. (Telex), 1537; PX 4530; PX 4531; PX 5346A: McAdams "Annotations," p. 35; DX 1667, p. 3; DX 1669; DX 1670; DX 3236; DX 4238, pp. 4, 12, 15; DX 4740: Evans, Tr. (Telex) 3920, 4002–4003.

156. JX 38, p. 82; PX 3385, p. 2; PX 4505, pp. 2–5; PX 4530, p. 2; PX 4531, p. 3; Historical Narrative, pp. 963–965.

157. DX 4430; DX 4740: Evans, Tr. (Telex) 4027; DX 7630: Herzfeld dep., Tr. 10–20; DX 9109A; Historical Narrative, pp. 1342, 1345–1346, 1352–1353, 1376, 1379, 1382, 1386, 1402, 1410, 1445.

158. Plaintiff's Economic Analysis, pp. 72–73; McAdams, Tr. 53811–14.

159. Withington, Tr. 112937, 112940. On the growth of PCMs, see Fisher Testimony, pp. 977–1012.

Chapter 9

1. *U.S.* v. *Aluminum Corporation of America*, 148 F. 2d 416 (1945) at 430.

2. McAdams, Tr. 65237–40, 65250.

3. Cf. Judge Charles Wyzanski's related remarks in *United States* v. *Grinnell Corporation* 236 F. Supp. 244 (1964) at 247–248.

4. Richard Posner, "A Program for the Antitrust Division," *University of Chicago Law Review* 38 (Spring 1971), p. 533.

5. *Ibid.*, p. 532.

6. Antitrust Procedures and Penalty Act, 15 U.S.C., paragraphs 16(b)–(h).

7. *United States* v. *National Broadcasting Company*, Motion to Intervene by Columbia Broadcasting Company, Civ. No. 74–3601–RFK (C.D. Cal.).

Index

An index of IBM equipment follows.

Accounting profits
 and depreciation, 226–228
 vs. economic profits, 220, 223
 and monopoly profits, 219–220
 and opportunity costs, 224
 and rents, 224–226
Accounting rate of return
 analysis, after-tax, 267–269
 analysis for firm as average, before-tax,
  261–266
 analysis for individual investments, before-tax, 258–261
 conceptual problem in, 238–240,
  250–253, 257
 vs. economic rate of return, 234,
  239–241, 242–253, 260–261, 269
 examples of, after tax, 243t, 245t, 248t,
  250t, 251t
 government misunderstanding of, 345
 in government testimony, 254–257
 and growth rate, 263–266
 IBM vs. other firms, comparison, 255
 measurement problems for, 234–238
 and monopoly profits, 253
 propositions on, 240–242
 U.S. average of, 242n
Add-on memory, 10. *See also* Memory
 from PCMs, 335–336
 as submarket, 13, 61–62, 68
 and System/370, 309, 333–336
 and 360/90 allegations, 280
ADP (Automatic Data Processing Corporation). *See* Automatic Data Processing Corporation
ADP Fund, as government self-leasing
 device, 193
AEC (Atomic Energy Commission), utilization alternatives of, 86
Akers, John, 59, 207, 382
Alanthus, 56t, 94
Alcoa case. *See United States* v. *Aluminum Company of America*
Amdahl, 56t

compatible CPUs by, 66
and compatible software, 201
IBM compatibility of, 198
as IBM competitor, 92–94
and installed-base measure, 124
memory provided by, 335
and software, 211
success of, 11
in System/360 competition, 10
American Airlines, EDP selection by, 95
American Telephone and Telegraph. *See*
 AT&T
American Tobacco case. *See United
 States* v. *American Tobacco Company*
Ampex, 56t
 as IBM competitor, 93
 as part-of-system vendor, 54
 in System/360 competition, 10
AMS, marketing by, 189
Anticompetitive behavior
 alleged attacks on leasing companies,
  303–310
 alleged in peripherals and memory,
  310–321, 331–340
 conditions of, 271–272
 CPU price increase as possible, 323,
  328–331
 FTP/ETP as possible, 321–331
 vs. IBM profit-seeking, 339, 343 (*see
  also* Competition)
 multiplier change as possible, 304–307
 planned obsolescence, 308–310
 predatory pricing, 273–276 (*see also*
  Predatory pricing)
 premature announcement, 289–299 (*see
  also* Premature announcement)
 price discrimination, 213–214, 316–317,
  323, 327–328
Antitrust Division, U.S. Department of
 Justice. *See also United States* v. *IBM*
 criticism of, 347–350
 economics misuse by, 1, 350
 on IBM behavior, 120
 price misunderstanding by, 338
Antitrust law, soundness of, 1, 346–347

Index of IBM Equipment